E

MW00906997

Cabreza has written a wonderfully engaging memoir. She expertly weaves together moments of heart-pounding adventure and moments of quiet, profound reflection. The result is a compelling story of a life lived with admirable gusto and deep thoughtfulness. I enjoyed every minute of it.

- Daniel James Brown,
Author of *The Boys in the Boat and Facing the Mountain*

Reading this book will bring you into experiences leaving you breathless! Joan, the ultimate, before-her-time-risk-taker, brings us a show-and-tell personal travelogue. We are brought to the precipice of her relationships, oceans, cultures, cuisines, dangers, ecological findings, and her search to find God. The story is powerful and I know God will use it to encourage and inspire many people who read it, both believers and seekers.

- Dr. Gary Gulbranson.
Pastor Emeritus, Westminster Chapel, Bellevue, WA

Breaking free from her early Midwest childhood to satisfy her yearning for adventure and pursue her scientific interests, Joan's numerous jaw-dropping escapades, near encounters with death, and miraculous encounters with God take us on decades of adventure difficult to put down. Her captivating writing style, sense of humor, passion, knowledge, zest for life and quest for faith make this a must-read for anyone who loves life, loves to learn, or just needs a good break from their own lives. While not a "religious book," it is a beautiful testimony to God working behind the scenes of our lives to draw us to Him and "fill the hole" we all have to know Him.

- Candace Brown Doud,
Former Bible Study Fellowship Teaching Leader, and Author

SEARCHING

A Memoir

Searching

A Biologist's Journey

JOAN H. CABREZA

XULON PRESS

Xulon Press
2301 Lucien Way #415
Maitland, FL 32751
407.339.4217
www.xulonpress.com

Paperback ISBN-13: 978-1-66286-286-1
Ebook ISBN-13: 978-1-66286-287-8

Table of Contents

Introduction and Acknowledgments

MY GRANDDAUGHTER, JENNA, ONCE ASKED ME WHAT it was like growing up in the 'old days.' Later, she said, "It sounds fun." It was, although certainly different than today's world. The post-war world of the 1950s had an ambiance of excitement and hope; we had won WWII and the future seemed bright and unlimited. Times were simpler, less hectic, and people shared a sense of community that appears lost today. I hope this story provides a feel for that world of yesterday.

The biological world is very different today too. Ecosystems are disappearing. Many of the pristine rainforests, coral reefs, and expansive prairies I worked in have altered or vanished and can never be experienced in the same way again. It saddens me how much of the natural world I was privileged to experience in the 1950s-1970s has vanished, *just within my lifetime.* I hope readers will find the ecosystems of my life's journey also of interest.

The lives of my Gen Y grandkids are so different from those of my Traditionalist Generation that sometimes we seem like two separate species. Personally, I think we had more fun back then. Today's safety-conscious world curtails and regulates the ability to do many of the risky, even outright dangerous, things I did when younger. My son David said, "Mom, you could have been dead so many times." He was right.

This is a story of travels, adventures, and relationships, but as I wrote about some dangerous experiences and unusual rescues, only then did I begin to see a spiritual thread quietly running in the background behind the scenes. Then I realized this is as much a story of God's faithfulness as it is of my adventures. It is not a religious book, *per se,* but I hope it will encourage readers to search for God's fingerprints in their own lives.

I thank Candace Doud for the genesis of this book. She once said, "God gave each of us our own experiences for a reason." My experiences were so unusual, I began pondering why He gave me those that He did. That spurred me to put pen to paper, and I thank all those from Westminster Chapel who encouraged me to write my stories. My convoluted spiritual searching spanned several decades and countries. Many readers will identify with parts of it.

I'm indebted to my patient husband, Carlos, who absorbed my share of our voluminous yardwork for the past two years so I could write. My son David encouraged me to write my story and provided many valuable suggestions as he waded through the drafts; his critical editorial eye found flaws and helped me focus. I thank Pramila Paomanabhan for her insightful comments; her questions helped me round out and unify the story. I also thank my friend Martha Lentz, a geologist-turned-artist, for her creative maps and illustrations. She's proof life begins, not ends, at retirement.

The Jerry Jenkins Writers Group and Pacific Northwest Writers Association provided invaluable training on various topics, and helped convert my writing into a more conversational style than the scientific material I am accustomed to writing. My developmental editor, Vanessa Garrett, provided helpful suggestions on format and flow. Rachelle Braido, Joan Kopczynski, Sue Block, Cathy Duchamp, Candace Sullivan, and other members of the Pacific Northwest Writers all provided valuable critique and insights. Ellis Felker, Val Mangion, Barbara Kappock, Geri Almand, and others were cheerleaders, inspiring me to write and share my stories.

I've attempted to be as accurate as possible. My old diaries provided interesting details I had long forgotten, and the stories are as accurate as I can recall them. Although words in the dialogs may differ slightly from the original, their meaning is intact. Most of Guam's village names have since changed, and I have changed the names of most people, a few places, and some identifying details to protect identities.

REFLECTIONS

(2021)

"Life can only be understood backward,
but it must be lived forward."

– Soren Kierkegaard

- *One* -
Looking Back

Redmond, WA 2021

O N A BRIGHT FALL SEATTLE AFTERNOON, AS I RELAX at home in a deck chair on the stone patio, Mike's Hard Lemonade in hand, a four-foot male great blue heron stands patiently fishing along the shore of our pond. Observing him, I realize we're a lot alike. Herons are notoriously skittish; a few years earlier, even a shadow of a movement *inside* the house, two hundred feet from the pond's edge, startled him into frantic flight, and he disappeared into the nearby watershed. Over time, the heron has changed, relaxed, and learned to trust us. He can be himself here. Like the heron, I'm finally comfortable at home in my world.

Now, often as though in greeting, the heron announces his arrival with a loud, harsh, and grating squawk as he makes an awkward landing on his favorite branch in a hemlock tree near the pond.

I respond, "Hi there. I see you," and he turns his head in acknowledgment. From his perch high in the hemlock, he scans the water for any movement signaling a potential meal.

For several years he's been almost a daily visitor, stalking fish and giant bullfrog tadpoles. As a biologist and environmental scientist, I appreciate him for that; bullfrogs are invasive on the West Coast and eat anything that fits into their giant mouths, including, hard as it is to visualize, even baby ducklings. The heron's assistance in reducing the bullfrog population helps balance the pond ecology.

Now, middle-aged in heron-years, he seems more secure. His head swivels to keep a watchful eye on my husband and me when we're outside, but he tolerates our presence and no longer bolts when he sees us. I pass within ten feet of him as I go out to feed my chickens, and I talk to him as I approach so he knows I'm not trying to sneak up on him. When the chickens hear my voice, they rush from the coop, clucking in anticipation of food, and the heron turns to watch the chickens' reactions.

Sometimes he stands on our dock sunbathing, opening his wide six-foot wingspan toward the sun, drying his feathers after fishing. He feels comfortable and at peace in our pond and his world. The heron appears content to stand fishing day after day, but I wonder, *Deep down inside, does he yearn for something more?*

I did. The conservative, small-town Midwest 1950s monoculture of my childhood never resonated with me, and the gender expectations and cultural restraints on women were suffocating. I had no desire to follow the herd on the well-trodden path to high school, then (if lucky) to college, then to marriage, with the ultimate goal of being a perfect housewife and mother.

I desperately yearned for a life of adventure, but that seemed reserved for boys. Most girls collected storybook dolls. I collected bugs and loved exploring the outdoors. Even from second grade I wanted to become a scientist, but except for my sixth-grade teacher, no one encouraged or took me seriously because women were expected to be secretaries, nurses, or teachers, if they worked at all. Not science teachers, though; in the 1950s, science was still considered a man's profession.

Does the heron yearn for adventure too? He's more adventurous than the other herons. Although several herons live nearby, he's the only one to risk leaving the protection of the watershed to visit our pond. I assume he has experienced his share of adventure: perhaps eagles trying to snatch his babies, storms blowing down his nest, or boys with BB guns, shooting at anything that moves. At some point, he's possibly weathered them all.

As I contemplated the heron's life from my deck chair, my own diverse adventures flipped like a slide show through my mind. My long chain of experiences stemmed from a single conversation with a professor in 1963 and a spontaneous decision to jump into an undefined and ambiguous program in the steamy jungles of Central America. It redirected my life and led to almost two decades of biological work in Asia, the Philippines, and Guam.

In 1967, when I announced I was emigrating to Asia to get married, my parents couldn't understand it. We won WWII; America was the greatest country on earth. Why would I want to leave? Their world was centered in Glen Ellyn, a Chicago suburb, almost 100 percent WASP (White, Anglo-Saxon Protestant.) My fiancée was Asian, which seemed difficult for them to fathom, but I had been all over Costa Rica and Asia for three years, and our worlds were now so different. People in my world were mobile and comfortable in many different cultures. My parents were neither very mobile nor comfortable with other cultures. Their inability to appreciate, much less understand, my lifestyle choice presented personal challenges for all of us.

My years away provided exhilarating experiences in jungles and on coral reefs, from an erupting volcano to a super typhoon. Along the way, I encountered fascinating creatures from dragonflies and spiders to venomous snakes, poison toads, and an enormous tiger shark. Several experiences also had supernatural or spiritual components. Along the convoluted way, I eventually rediscovered my country and found myself, my life's passion, and my faith.

My experiences changed me, but they also changed my parents. They began to see beyond their narrow cultural bubble. As they grew to accept my choices and appreciate my lifestyle and cultural differences, their mentality began shifting from small-town America into the global Family of Man.

Last year the heron appeared on our pond with a female. They sat in the tree and fished in the pond. It was as if he tried to show her, "It's OK here," but she seldom returns. Perhaps, like my parents, she's still more comfortable in her own pond.

I marvel at how much of what influences me today has roots in my earliest days. Today when I'm harvesting our organic garden, I often flash on Mom standing in our 1945 WWII Victory Garden, sending me to follow our sprawling cucumber vines into the field to pick the cucumbers, because she hated garter snakes and garden spiders. But I liked them. My love of gardening and passion for the environment began in the early days and have book-ended my life.

Steve Jobs, founder of Apple and Pixar, told the 2005 graduating Stanford class: "[Life happens] as a series of seemingly disconnected dots. You can't connect the dots looking forward; you can only connect them looking backward. You have to trust your gut that the dots will somehow connect in the future… Believing the dots will connect gives you the confidence to follow your heart even when it leads you off the well-worn path, and that will make all the difference."[1]

That proved true for me. Following my heart, trusting my gut, and persevering despite opposition and the unknown made all the difference. After almost two decades abroad, I returned to the States as a different person and found my niche in the Pacific Northwest. Sometimes it takes decades for pieces of life to fall into place. It's been a wild ride, but to truly appreciate it, it helps to understand growing up in the 1950s in small Midwestern towns like Glen Ellyn, Illinois…

- *Two* -

Post-War Life

<u>Glen Ellyn, IL 1946 -1953</u>

DAD WAS STILL ADVENTUROUS AND FUN IN THE EARLY days after WWII. When I was three, he taught me to make snowmen and play games. One sunny spring day several months after he returned from the War, as we walked up Bryant Avenue toward Grandmother's house, we passed a rickety treehouse in a big maple tree.

"It's still here!" he exclaimed with surprise, pride, and nostalgia. "This was my treehouse as a boy." I couldn't imagine him playing up there as a boy. I doubt he ever imagined that eighteen years later, he would bring a small daughter up inside there, either.

"Let's climb up. I don't think people will mind, do you?"

I struggled to climb the steps nailed on the tree, proud I could do it myself. In the treehouse, Dad pointed to some distant tall buildings. "See that? That's Chicago." Although thirty miles away, without today's smog or urban sprawl, Chicago's tall buildings were clearly visible across the prairie. Around them, suburbs scattered like small islands within large swaths of seemingly limitless open land because the U.S. population was a scant 140 million. It was a different world.

When I was born in 1943, America had been at war for almost eighteen months. During WWII, practically every family became a military family; over sixteen million Americans were mobilized. In mom's family, everyone who could serve had enlisted. The Army drafted Uncle Phil at eighteen, and sent him to Cherbourg, France, to fight in the Battle of the Bulge and then into Germany. Aunt Connie's husband John volunteered for a so-called suicide mission to dismantle German underwater obstacles on Omaha Beach in advance of Allied landing craft. John and most of his unit died on D-Day in June 1944.

After John's death, Aunt Connie joined the Red Cross in Saipan. Later she married my Uncle Quentin, who served in Guam. In 1944, when the war effort shifted into high gear, the government began calling up men with children and drafted Dad. Since he was an artist, they placed him in Naval Intelligence and sent him to Pearl Harbor to make three-dimensional rubber invasion maps.

When the War ended, servicemen began straggling home based on their time in service. Glen Ellyn's small population of 9,500 lost over 100 men. Many others lost limbs or survived horrendous experiences against unimaginable odds. Yet men were expected to return from the battlefield one day and somehow revert effortlessly back to being fathers, farmers, or storekeepers the next, as though they had never left.

But they were no longer the same men. War imprinted on the men, and the impacts rippled through their lives for years. We called it shell shock in WWI and battle fatigue in WWII. Today it's called PTSD, and although recognized, little counseling or assistance existed to help men cope with the horrors they had experienced. That was possibly one reason so many vets later became alcoholics, and men in our family did not escape.

When Dad returned from war, he brought large rubber invasion maps he had made of Iwo Jima and an unnamed island. He also brought a pastel landscape he had drawn on Oahu's windward side. It's dated 1945, so the war must have either been winding down or ended, and he had some free time on his hands.

The picture depicts the massive stone cliffs of Hawaii's Pali Pass with a coconut-filled valley below. In contrast to the flat Midwest, Hawaii's swaying palm trees, ocean, and tall, vertical cliffs seemed magical. Every time I looked at his drawing, I felt a sense of familiarity and yearning; it was almost a sense of deja vu. Perhaps it was a premonition. Two decades later, I would discover my career had surprising parallels with both dad's wartime map-making and his picture.

Dad was quite a talented artist, but the Hawaii landscape was the only thing I ever knew him to draw for fun. I wondered if he even enjoyed art or whether my grandmother and grandfather had propelled him into art school because they were both artists themselves. Once, seeing me staring at the picture, Dad pointed out that the coconuts were perched on top of the palm trees, instead of hanging below the fronds, like typical palms.

"Your grandmother could never keep her hands off other people's work," he remarked with annoyance. She'd never seen a coconut tree, but that hadn't hindered her. Feeling the painting needed 'improvement,' she added coconuts and a tiny Hawaiian hut. Since pastels are impossible to erase, the coconuts and hut remain to this day, a testament to grandmother's ability to have her way in almost everything. Today the picture, coconuts and all, hangs in my entryway.

Glen Ellyn was one of the older Chicago suburbs, a small upper-middle-class suburb with above-average annual income, infrequent crime and graffiti, and an excellent school system. Glenbard High School, one of the better schools in the Chicago area, resembled an ivy-covered castle and sat regally atop a hill overlooking Lake Ellyn, so picturesque it was used in the 1986 teen movie, *Lucas*.

Old money in the vicinity included the Mortons of Morton salt; the McCormicks, publishers of the Chicago Tribune; and early settlers, the Churchills. They established their legacies with parks: the nearby 1700-acre Morton Arboretum, 500-acre Cantigny Park, and 255-acre Churchill Forest Preserve. Other public amenities included a park system that provided swimming and tennis lessons, a golf course, and an excellent library. Kids had a wide variety of opportunities.

The older, established area of Glen Ellyn boasted elegant houses with large columned porches and broad stairways, set back from the elm-lined streets on spacious manicured grounds, radiating self-assurance and afflu-ence. That wasn't our neighborhood.

In the wet, muddy spring of 1947, Dad and Mom bought their first house for $12,000 in a new development of ten tiny brick starter homes carved out of the Illinois prairie on the outskirts of Glen Ellyn. The new subdivision mirrored thousands of other cheap post-war housing devel-opments springing up all over the country to accommodate the millions of returning vets and the 76.4 million baby boomers that followed. Vets bought every house, and our street swarmed with over two dozen young children, all nearly the same age.

Our new subdivision appeared invisible to the Glen Ellyn adminis-tration. The street sprouted potholes like mushrooms, and was patched and re-patched with poor quality asphalt so often the surface resembled a patchwork quilt. Snowplows often missed our road in winter, and months could elapse before someone arrived to replace burned-out streetlights.

Our house's few redeeming features included a large front picture window, a decent-sized backyard, and several feet of prairie topsoil, so rich that people seeded lawns into the rototilled ground without soil amendments.

The clean air smelled of warm earth and sunshine in the summer, and the songs of meadowlarks and red-wing blackbirds drifted through the air. But in the winter, indoors, the house stank of stale cigarette smoke, and the freezing prairie winds whistled through the poorly caulked single-pane windows, competing with the noisy rattle of the furnace.

The rooms were cramped, the closets microscopic, storage space non-ex-istent. Ugly black linoleum prompted Mom to remark, "The builder must have found a fire sale on cheap linoleum," and they bought a small gray carpet to cover most of the living room. Still, mom appreciated the utility room off the kitchen, where her first automatic washer replaced the old washboard and wringer washing machine.

My parents had grown up in nicer Glen Ellyn houses, and this starter home was a step-down for them. All I had ever known was a small attic apartment on Bryant during the War, so this seemed spacious to me. Even as we moved in, my parents said, "It's OK for now, but I doubt we'll live here long." However, when I was five, my sister Lynn arrived, closely followed by the twins, Steve and Phil, and we remained there for twelve years.

Dad was handy. He built a small wooden overhang above the front door, "To give the house front a small spark of personality and to differentiate it from the other houses on the block," he said. When the family expanded to include the twins, he carved another bedroom from the already tiny living room. The six of us lived almost on top of each other. I shared a room with Lynn, our wooden bunk beds freeing up only enough space to shoehorn in a small shared dresser and bookcase.

Dad built additional overhead cabinets in the kitchen and bought two benches to flank a small table, providing an eating nook. Although it required contortions to slip into the benches, the six of us ate dinner together in the nook for a short time. Then everything changed.

"It's kind of tight in there; I'll eat later to give you all more space," Dad said.

I protested. Dad worked all day, and dinner was the only chance we had to see him, but he wouldn't be dissuaded. Instead, while we all ate, he relaxed with a martini or three before his dinner. If Mom wanted any chance to talk with him, she had to postpone her dinner to join him, so we lost dinner time with her, too. That left the four of us. Lynn and the twins were close in age, but much older, I had nothing in common with them. I gobbled down my food and disappeared outside or into my room to read. After that, we never all ate dinner together except on holidays.

I often asked Mom, "Why don't you eat now anyhow? Aren't you hungry?"

"I'll wait until your father is ready to eat," she said, although she often hadn't had lunch. Over time, her wait became longer and longer.

Dad and Mom were an attractive couple. With flawless English complexion and hazel eyes, Mom could be stunning. Only five-foot four, she loved three-inch spike heels, and always wore makeup, a hat, heels, and sometimes gloves, just to go downtown. Despite four small children, she changed for dinner every night before Dad came home. A perfect Fifties housewife, Mom looked to Dad for her opinion on almost everything. She smoked his brand of cigarettes, voted Republican as he did, and consulted him on everything. "Do you think I should wear the black dress or the red?" or "What would you like for dinner?" She would ask almost as if she had no opinions, but I knew she did, and occasionally she forcefully asserted them.

With his easy grin, mustache, black wavy hair, and standing slightly over six feet, people often compared him to Clark Gable. He was the main martini mixer and the life of the party. Our neighbors, the Carps and the Wallaces made frequent appearances at our door, drinks in hand, and martini time became a social hour. As it lengthened, their dinners became later. Many of their friends and neighbors were heavy drinkers, and over time, many became alcoholics. Our neighborhood wasn't unique; today, many in my generation admit to having an alcoholic parent.

Around age twelve, I asked for a sip of dad's martini. He gave me one.

"Yuk! That tastes terrible! How can you drink that?"

"You learn to like it," he said.

"That's dumb. Why do you have to learn to like something? Why don't you drink something you like from the start?"

"It's a social thing," he said.

It seemed to be one of those 'fit in with society' things. People gave dad's boss's wife, a recovering alcoholic, a lot of grief when she began drinking 7-Up at parties. Even though 7-Up was much cheaper than gin, Dad was annoyed at having to buy it when she came over. "It's a nuisance," he said. "Why can't she just go along with everyone else?" Conforming seemed very important to him. *That's crazy. Why should anyone force themselves to do something just to conform?* The drinkers seemed to take her sobriety as a rebuke to their drinking, but she stuck to her guns.

Most adults also smoked. In the mornings, we awoke to overflowing ashtrays and houses reeking of smoke. Everyone marinated in second-hand smoke, but nobody connected this to the many bouts of tonsillitis or ear infections their kids suffered every winter. Kids never questioned the heavy drinking and smoking lifestyle because we knew nothing else, and the movies glamorized it.

Little exercise mitigated this unhealthy lifestyle because Glen Ellyn worried about appearances, dignity, and being proper. Only kids exercised. Adults didn't exercise or jog. It was considered undignified; they needed to act their age. One Saturday in 1952, a man came running past our front window wearing funny, short shorts and gym shoes. The martini crowd in our living room broke into gales of astonished laughter and wisecracks. Instead of saying, "Maybe we should be out there exercising too," Mr. Carp said, "Let's invite him in—he looks like he needs a drink!" We had just seen our first jogger.

Glen Ellyn held traditional values. Elementary schools began each day with the pledge of allegiance and the Lord's Prayer, and celebrated Christmas with nativity pageants every December. The town celebrated national holidays with elaborate parades and July 4th fireworks. On Halloween, school children painted all the windows in the downtown business district with appropriate scary scenes.

Every family on the block attended a church. Although a knowledgeable bible believer, Dad didn't like organized religion, and he stopped attending early on, but he hauled us kids to the Congregational Church Sunday School every week. Church felt like another school, and I greatly resented losing part of my precious weekend to it. It also meant I had to wear a dress, which thrilled my grandmother. She looked to me to satisfy her desire for the daughter she never had, but I didn't fit her expectations. She tried to curl my hair with her curling iron, which I resisted. She bought me fancy dresses and coats. I hated them.

Every year she asked, "What do you want for Christmas?"

Every year I said, "A book." And every year I got another dress.

Eventually, Grandmother gave up and I got a book: *Pilgrim's Progress*. But who gives an eleven-year-old a Christian allegory written in the 1680s? I started reading and got as far as the part about the 'Slough of Despond' before I bogged down in despondency myself. Understanding neither allegories nor Christianity, I never finished it.

Most people in Glen Ellyn had few, if any acquaintances, let alone friends, from other ethnic groups. The community provided little chance to know anyone unlike themselves. Even in 1960, it was still 99.5 percent White and only 3.9 percent foreign-born. We never saw Blacks or Latinos. Few first-generation Europeans, or even foreign accents, existed in our small town. No one mentioned Jews, and many people even considered the small minority of Catholics a bit suspect. The only Asian I ever saw owned the Chinese chop suey place, and he probably didn't live there. Many people were bigots and didn't even recognize it.

During and after the War, millions of refugees flooded into the States and they didn't all look like us. Most went to the big cities, and few ended up in Glen Ellyn. Once with a bit of pensive frown, Mom referred to someone as "dark-skinned and foreign-looking." From her tone, I gathered she equated that with inferiority or lower class. It surprised me because she never spoke like that. But then, Glen Ellyn didn't have many people like that.

"What's wrong with looking different?"

"Nothing, of course. Why would you think that?"

"Because you sounded like there was." She was surprised.

Mom's comment was probably more classist than racist. Before the Great Depression, her father had co-owned the Kewanee bank, and they had been part of the monied upper class. When his partner embezzled bank money and the bank crashed, Grandfather spent most of his own money repaying customers who had lost their deposits. Their money was now gone, but some of the elitist attitudes remained. They often seemed to feel a slight superiority over others unlike themselves.

If Mom and Dad had known that some of the "dark-skinned foreign-looking" people were future family members and that my family would be spread over three continents, they would have been speechless.

EARLY DAYS IN THE POST-WAR MIDWEST

(1948–1963)

"Be yourself; everyone else is taken."

– Oscar Wilde

- *Three* -

Freedom and Frustration

Glen Ellyn, IL 1953-1956

I WAS A TOMBOY, AND I GENERALLY GOT INTO TROUBLE when I played with my neighbor, Bobby, because we were both adventuresome and game for anything. WWII's lingering influence impacted our play, and we often fought wars with handmade slingshots, practiced throwing knives, and shot his BB guns at cans in the swamp. Bobby taught me the names of different airplanes and ships and the Army, Navy, and Marine songs. We became blood brothers, cutting our fingers and pressing them together to mingle our blood.

Bobby's cute innocent face, winning smile, and carefree attitude camouflaged a lack of conscience. He stole things he didn't need or want, apparently just for the thrill of getting away with something. He had been eyeing a pocket knife display in the College Avenue Store, and once there, he jammed ten knives into his pockets.

"Go ahead! You take something too."

"I don't want anything."

"C'mon. We're here. He's not watching."

Perhaps he wanted to share the blame if he got caught or convinced himself stealing was OK if we both did it. I finally stole a five-cent Chunky candy bar. The next time the store owner saw us coming, he scowled and blocked us at the door.

While we left on vacation, Bobby broke into our house. I collected rocks, and my collection contained a small box of mineral specimens. One labeled "gold" contained a microscopic speck of shiny yellow. When we returned from vacation, I immediately noticed someone had pried it from the box.

"Mom, someone was in here and stole my rock."

"Don't be silly; no one came in. You probably just lost it."

"No, it was glued in. I know who took it, and I'm going to get it back." I marched over to Bobby's house and pounded on the front door. No one was home. Frustrated, I climbed up a big boxelder tree next to Bobby's bedroom and, without a second thought, broke in through the window. My small gold rock sat on his dresser. I took it back and stole a wicked-looking hunting knife while I was at it. He had begun talking about cutting up animals, which scared me. I reasoned if he had no knives, that would stop him, so I brought them home and stashed them deep inside my closet.

Later, I confronted him. "You broke in and took my gold rock."

"Oh yeah, I did it." He didn't try to deny it, feel ashamed, apologize, or offer to return it. *Does he even realize he no longer has it?* He didn't even seem to know why he had taken it. The one speck of gold was worthless. He just saw a chance to get in the house and prowl around, wanting to take something, anything. He grabbed the rock because he thought it might have value. Fortunately, he missed dad's shotguns.

When I asked how he got in, he shrugged and said, "The back door was open."

We had gone away on a two-week vacation without locking the doors. "Oh. I guess we just forgot," Mom said. In the Fifties, people didn't worry much about locking their doors when they went out.

When I got older, I earned twenty-five cents an hour babysitting the Wallace kids next door. Mom was a great cook and always interested in trying something new, so when I returned, she asked, "What did she leave you for dinner?"

"Chili con carne." A meat, potatoes, and vegetable family, we had never had that.

Dad was derisive. "How does she expect to keep a husband when she cooks like that?"

"What's wrong with chili?"

"Men want a good dinner when they come home."

That didn't sit well with me. Dad clearly thought a woman's priority should be to get a husband and then exist to make his life comfortable.

"It was good. I liked it. If my husband doesn't like what I make, he can jolly well cook his own." The conversation degenerated rapidly from there.

Women seemed to have little time or autonomous life of their own. Most men believed their contribution to the family was sufficient if they brought home a paycheck; from what I could see, few assisted around the house or helped with the children. With four small kids, I was surprised Mom even had time to make dinner. I longed to be a boy. They had more fun and wouldn't have to worry about making perfect dinners.

I doubted slaving over a stove making dinner was initially high in mom's priorities, either. She was exceptionally bright and had desperately wanted to attend college, but the Great Depression forced her to work as a secretary before marriage. Now she concentrated on being a good wife and dealing with the demands of four young children, three under the age of two.

Childhood was fun and carefree, but the adult lifestyle seemed stifling, particularly for women. Gender inequality was the norm. Men expected to get their way and presumed the women would somehow fall in step with it. And most did.

Wives stayed home to care for the house, their husbands, and family. For the few that worked, gender bias against women was blatant in almost all professions except secretarial, nursing, and lower grade teaching. In the 1940s, many states even had laws preventing married women from working because they took jobs away from men. Most states abolished those laws during the war, but the assumption that men should receive better pay than women because they were the breadwinners, continued for decades. Few women could challenge and rise beyond the limited opportunities and constraints the male power structure imposed.

Mom sometimes mentioned things she wished she had done. "I always wanted to visit England," she said, wistfulness tinging her voice. And she often said, "I wanted so badly to attend college, but I had to work because it was the depression." She spoke as if thirty-five was too old for her dreams to be attained. *That's sad. I don't want to have a life of unfulfilled dreams like that.*

Mom and Dad, eclectic readers, subscribed to numerous magazines. I devoured *National Geographic, Life, Readers Digest, Guideposts*, and anything with adventure stories, and longed for my own exciting and dangerous adventures.

Then one month, *Life* magazine featured an inspirational explorer. He had grand, heroic adventures climbing glaciers, tramping through jungles, taking African safaris, and trekking mountain wilderness trails. He did them because, when a boy, he listed all the exciting things he wanted to do when he grew up. Then, as an adult, he methodically set about doing them.

I want to do all that too, I thought. He became my role model, and at twelve, I started a goal list. My initial list of thirty items included visiting Hawaii and a rainforest, winning a trophy and setting a sports record, learning to scuba dive and ride a unicycle, owning a pet skunk, and finding a human skull. They weren't everyday childhood goals in Glen Ellyn, but they were theoretically possible.

Mom and Dad thought the list interesting, smiled patronizingly, and missed the point. It wasn't a passive wish list; it was a goal list, and required action. I began looking for ways to progress toward my goals.

As I grew older, I expanded the list to include things like teaching someone to read, becoming fluent in a foreign language, and reading through the Great Books. Today, I still add new goals and check off completions, and I've completed over 160 of the 200 items on the list. The initial short list of goals helped me dream about my future, and provided seven decades of inspiration and focus, broadening and enriching my life more than I could ever have imagined.

In status-conscious Glen Ellyn, no adults ever wore jeans except farmers. And Mrs. Morphy. Mrs. Morphy was born in Colorado, and refreshingly different from other adults on the block.

"Call me Katy," she said.

When Mom heard that, she frowned slightly and said, "It's disrespectful for you to call her that." I knew Mom looked askance at Katy's jeans too, but Katy was everyone's favorite mom, and she was the only adult who took us swimming and encouraged us to stretch ourselves with new activities.

The Morphys were active, practical people and they built a garage, stone patio, vegetable garden, and a compost pile. Not heavily into martinis, they brewed dandelion wine, and they smoked Raleigh's because the packs had coupons redeemable for merchandise.

Getting free stuff sounded good. I asked Dad, "Why don't you smoke Raleigh's too?"

"Camels are more manly," he said. Somehow this seemed important to him, but it made no sense to me. *Did that make Mom manly if she smoked them too?*

I loved exploring the outdoors with Katy's daughter, Jenny, and Brenda from up the street. Jenny, serious and calm-natured, was on the swim team and also took ballet. Although she was two years younger than I and a year younger than Brenda, she sometimes seemed the most mature.

Brenda, small but adventuresome, turned everything into an aggressive competition, which often landed us both in trouble. We were kindred spirits. We dressed in our daily uniform of jeans, flannel shirts, and blue boy's jackets, and we looked almost alike, except for her dark ponytail and my long blond braids.

We spent every available minute outside. A swamp, fields, and woods surrounded our tiny island of houses. The swamp's cattails attracted nesting redwing blackbirds, wild canaries, and cardinals, and scattered willow thickets, cottonwoods, and open-water areas supported frogs, salamanders, and snails. Water striders sped across the water through the pond weeds.

The soft cooing of mourning doves and the twitter of robins awoke us early in summer dawn, and the high, whistling calls of redwing blackbirds pulled us outside to explore the swamp. There we built forts and had cat-tail fights. We brought home countless tadpoles in mason jars, fed them lettuce pieces and watched them develop legs and become miniature frogs.

Around dusk, fleets of mosquitoes emerged from the swamp. Every week all summer, a spray truck cruised down the street right around din-nertime, bathing the entire area in a billowing white cloud of DDT. The terrible-smelling cloud hung in the air, particles drifting into houses and onto dinner plates. Some kids even followed the truck, playing in the cloud. Few questioned its safety, although Mom said, "It might not be good for you to breathe that stuff." It took several decades before people understood the hefty health and environmental price DDT exacted.

Our favorite play area, a mile-long swath of open field at the end of the street, extended from College Avenue in downtown Wheaton to almost downtown Glen Ellyn. It blazed with native wildflowers in summer, and swarms of buzzing bees and clouds of butterflies covered them so thickly that the flowers almost pulsated. Rainbows of bluebonnets, pink wild roses, white Queen Anne's lace, purple coneflowers, and yellow daisies carpeted the field. Swallowtails, monarchs, cabbage, and sulfur butterflies flitted from flower to flower, and songs of meadowlarks, wild canaries, cardinals, and orioles echoed through the tall grasses. After the rain, a moist earthy scent mingled with the perfume of wildflowers. Some odd round depres-sions we called "whirlpools" dotted the field. In retrospect, they were pos-sibly old buffalo wallows.

We used Golden Nature Guides to learn the names of the local birds, plants, reptiles, and insects, what they ate, and where they lived. Insects were still so numerous everywhere that after even a couple of hours in the car, the windshield was so plastered with insects that it needed washing.

Brenda and I became obsessive butterfly collectors. We made nets and spent days in the field amassing impressive collections that we framed in glass Riker mounts. Monarch butterflies migrated from Mexico for the milkweeds. I brought home their fat, velvety soft, striped caterpillars and watched with wonder as they each made a beautiful hanging jade chrysalis, the top ringed with gold dots.

Within two weeks, a butterfly struggled to emerge from its chrysalis, tiny wings wrapped around its fat body like a shroud. Then the body shrank as the wings gradually filled with fluid and unfurled. I learned the hard way that helping it emerge crippled it. Without exerting effort to emerge, the wings never expanded, remaining on the butterfly as they had been in the chrysalis, shriveled, folded, and useless.

Once we discovered Seattle's Ye Olde Curiosity Shop sold tropical butterflies, we saved all our money to order amazing things: Madagascar's rainbow-tailed *Urania ripheus*, "the world's most beautiful moth," the giant atlas moth, and *Morpho*, the iconic iridescent neon-blue butterfly. My collection expanded until Riker mounts filled the entire bedroom wall.

The human world felt superficial and confining, but I always felt at ease in the field. I sensed an almost spiritual connection with the universe there. I never lost that love of nature, and eventually, that time in the field would shape my future.

The Hamiltons, the oldest couple on the block, had neither children nor a sense of humor. They mixed little with the other neighbors and didn't welcome children. They seemed uptight, easily annoyed, and compulsive about their perfectly manicured yard, so we delighted in harassing them. We would never have defaced anything with graffiti, but somehow wet cement didn't count. We carved our initials into any fresh cement we could find. When the Hamiltons poured a new concrete driveway, it just begged for decoration.

"Hey, Hamiltons have a new driveway," Brenda suggested.

"Yeah! Let's go see if the cement is dry yet."

It was still wet. The temptation was too great to ignore, and Brenda and I each claimed one side of the driveway. Brenda was happily writing her name in giant letters all over Hamilton's wet cement and then realized

I had made only a small "JH" on my side. Unknown to me, she decided to rectify this lopsided situation by writing my name on her side of the driveway in giant letters, not once but several times. She added Jenny's initials for good measure.

That night Old Mrs. Hamilton called, ice dripping from her words. "Would you carve your name on your mother's new table?"

I was mystified. "We don't have a new table," I said, wondering why she thought we did. Then she asked to talk to Mom. I finally realized she referred to her driveway, but it seemed like a big fuss for only two small initials.

"Well…. I might have added your name a couple of times," Brenda admitted when I told her about the call. We casually strolled over to view our artwork the next day but, unfortunately, Mr. Hamilton had covered it with new cement.

Everybody knows everyone else's business in small towns. It was even easier for us because all houses on the block shared a party line, manually connected by a live telephone operator. Everyone's phone rang when anyone received a call, but the operator used a different ring for each home. One long and two short rings meant our house. With this system, anybody could listen in on anyone's calls if they wanted to.

Old Mrs. Hamilton, usually a silent listener, obviously had time on her hands. Whenever we were on the phone, we heard a click as she picked up, so we deliberately said things to annoy her. Once, just to let her know I was on to her, I couldn't help saying, "Hi, Mrs. Hamilton!" and she rewarded me with the immediate click of a phone returned to its cradle.

Her listening pleasure was sadly short-lived because our neighborhood soon received a separate telephone exchange, and each house received a separate telephone line and a seven-digit phone number. Soon, area codes were established, and we could even call long-distance without a live operator.

When spring days lengthened, turning winter snow into slushy patches, we burst from our confining houses with soaring spirits and excitedly raced to soggy pockets in the field to look for new pussy willows, the first sign of spring. In June, we picked sweet wild strawberries, onions, and violets that carpeted the woods and searched for scattered clumps of asparagus. Old Mr. Hamilton and a hermit also competed for the asparagus.

The hermit, Glen Ellyn's equivalent of a mountain man, lived deep in the field, in an unpainted two-room wooden shack with a tar-paper roof. A small sagging front porch held a single decrepit wooden rocking chair. His shack projected an aura of intrigue and mystery. We speculated about two glass gallon jugs containing yellow liquid hanging on the porch wall flanking his front door.

"It's hydrochloric acid," someone said.

We peered down into a mysterious open metal shaft nearby.

"Maybe it's a bottomless pit," someone else said.

"Yeah! I bet he dumps bodies down there," someone else said. More practical, Dad suggested it was the hermit's well, and warned us about falling in.

Some grownups labeled him as "not quite right," but most believed him harmless. He seemed an interesting character, and we might have tried getting to know him but, like the Hamiltons, he didn't like kids much. Whenever we approached his shack, he came running out in old denim overalls, pulling up his suspenders, his long shaggy gray beard and wild hair flying in the wind, eyes flashing angrily under his bushy eyebrows. He chased us, waving his arms like a windmill. Once, he even picked up one of the gallon jugs as if to throw it. That cinched it; it was acid.

"You dang kids git outta here!" He shouted. Rebuffed, we tormented and spied on him.

The hermit had lived alone for decades without power or running water. Some adults speculated the few old, gnarled, and moss-covered apple trees growing near his shack were a legacy from the famous Johnny Appleseed. The hermit's "hydrochloric acid" was probably homemade cider from his trees, but the uncertainty effectively kept us off his porch.

Eventually, some well-meaning busybody reported him to the authorities. Probably the Hamiltons since they lived closest to him. The city evicted him and condemned his house. The minute he left, of course, we went in to explore.

The only thing left behind was an old hand-crank Victrola Phonograph with dozens of old records. I brought some home. Mom wanted to throw them out but, curious, Dad said, "Go soak the filth off of them and let's see what they are." When we played them on our scratchy record player, Dad recognized them as old songs from the 1920s. Somehow, we didn't consider this theft, but it became a moot point because the city bulldozed the hermit's house the following day.

A few months later, I saw him, still in his faded overalls, slumped in a rocking chair on the front porch of a house downtown, his eyes vacant, staring blankly out at the street without recognition. I felt a pang of sympathy. When the bulldozer tore apart his house, it also tore apart his life, and moving seemed to have sucked the remaining spark out of him. He was the last of the hermits, extirpated by do-gooder busybodies.

Even without electricity or running water, his primitive life in the field looked more enjoyable to me than the sanitized, regimented urban life in town. *I could live as he did.* And within a decade, I would have a chance to do that.

Holidays were significant events in Glen Ellyn. We held annual parades on Memorial Day, July 4th, and Glenbard High School Homecoming. We eagerly awaited Memorial Day because it marked the unofficial transition from spring to summer, signaling the imminent end of the school year and the opening of the town swimming pool.

Summer vacation lasted until after Labor Day. Three months of magnificent leisure and unstructured freedom stretched ahead, each day a blank slate, without the distractions and tyranny of computers, cell phones, or social media. We rarely watched TV; its five black and white channels showed little but boxing and wrestling matches.

I remember the summers as blue-skyed, golden sunny days. We entertained ourselves, and led unregulated, unsupervised, outdoor lives. After breakfast, we grabbed a sandwich and an apple and took off on day-long hikes or bike rides, often gone until dinner. We explored neighboring towns, the Forest Preserve, and the Arboretum, biking for miles and miles. It was safe. No one worried about us.

In the mornings, more out of curiosity than concern, Mom asked, "Where are you off to today?"

Usually, I didn't know, which elicited a generic response. "OK, just come home for dinner at the six o'clock whistle."

During WWII, fearing the war might reach the U.S. mainland, Glen Ellyn installed an ear-blasting air raid siren downtown. After the war, they still tested it every evening, but re-named it the 'six o'clock whistle.' We heard its rising and falling wail all over Glen Ellyn, so moms used it as a dinner call because we had no excuse for not hearing it, even over a mile away. No one considered its impact on the vets who had seen action in Europe and probably flinched and looked for an air-raid shelter every time it blew.

Seldom bored, we explored woods and fields, collecting insects, bird nests, animal bones, and other treasures. Spring rains sometimes exposed Indian arrowheads in freshly-plowed farm fields. The woods held owl pellets, regurgitated gray furballs with tiny bones inside that told us what the owls had eaten. My friend Byron gave me a treasured cow skull, turning Brenda green with jealousy because, competitive to the end, she couldn't beat that. I collected so many animal bones my sixth-grade friends nicknamed me Bony Joan.

Although it seemed a remote possibility in Glen Ellyn, I thought, *Sometime I'm going to find a human skull.* My collection of rocks, shells, and butterflies expanded into fossils, skulls, arrowheads, turtle shells, antlers, snake and fox skins. They overflowed our wall and bedroom bookcase. Poor Lynn probably felt she lived in a museum but, five years younger than I, she never protested.

We picked buckets of blackberries and wildflowers and spent hours looking for small pieces of crinoid and coral fossils on new, graveled roads. We placed pennies on the railroad track for passing trains to crush into distorted oblongs, and in fall, we put pumpkins on the track. When trains hit pumpkins, they exploded in magnificent orange showers of seeds and pulp, and elicited furious shouting, loud, angry whistle blasts, and fist-waving from the train engineers.

We lay on the lawn looking for animal shapes in the clouds, searched for four-leaf clovers, put on plays in Jenny's garage for ten cents admission, and went from house to house, begging popsicles from each mom in turn. When Midwest thunderstorms rolled in, our marathon monopoly games stretched for two or three days. We climbed trees, carving initials into our favorites. At night we lay in the yard, making wishes on shooting stars.

We pedaled to Sunset Park on humid summer afternoons and joined a seething mass of kids crammed into the small 25-yard public swimming pool. Some days it was standing room only, but we could talk Katy into taking us to the less-crowded Family Hour swim from 5:00-7:00 p.m. Many people worried about the swimming pool because of polio, but hot and humid Chicago summers without pool passes seemed a death sentence worse than polio, and most families bought passes anyway. We expected a vaccine to come out soon.

Katy encouraged me to join Jenny on the swim team. The water confidence it developed helped me get my first real job and probably saved my life on several future occasions.

Soon sounds of grinding bulldozers and rattling dump trucks began interrupting summer days, and new construction began filling vacant lots. After construction workers quit for the day, we explored the new houses, scrounging leftover wood scraps and loose nails. The workers planned to burn the scraps anyway, and it saved them from construction clean-up. We used the larger pieces to build forts in the field, the swamp, and Brenda's backyard.

We used the smaller scraps to make bonfires on a newly-bulldozed street through the field beside the Morphys. The relentless construction produced enough scrap wood to make huge bonfires almost every night for an entire summer. We couldn't foresee all the changes this construction portended.

We spent Saturday afternoons at the Glen Theater, watching a double feature on a giant screen. It charged 11 cents for kids and 14 cents for adults. A black and white Disney cartoon or two and a grainy ten-minute news segment on the WWII European occupation and reconstruction always preceded the Glen's black and white movies. The solemn, deep narrative voice can still be heard today on old clips of WWII footage, and hearing it transports me right back to the Glen Theater.

In 1954, when science fiction became popular, we excitedly awaited the black and white versions of *Creature from the Black Lagoon*, *Them*, and *Invasion of the Body Snatchers*. One day they showed only a single movie, *The High and the Mighty*, but it was in color! The theater jumped its price to 25 cents for kids and 50 cents for adults. Outraged, I had to ask for an increase in allowance.

After that, the Glen discontinued double features, black and white movies, war reconstruction news and cartoons in favor of a single, color movie, but it continuously replayed so we could sit through a favorite film a second or even a third time, free. We sat through three consecutive runs of *20,000 Leagues Under the Sea* just to watch the giant squid scene.

The town went all-out for July 4th. In contrast to the solemn Memorial Day parade, this parade marched joyfully and noisily through downtown, ending at Lake Ellyn, where the town sponsored a day of free hot dogs, pie-eating contests, three-legged races, sack races, and candy hunts. It culminated after dark with impressive fireworks over Lake Ellyn.

In the late afternoon, our family always went to a big outdoor potluck in West Chicago, a rural suburb west of Glen Ellyn, where dad's hunting buddy, Blaine, owned an old farmhouse on five acres. Each of the ten families attending the picnic chipped in ten dollars to buy an impressive array of assorted fireworks. Unregulated fireworks sales allowed anyone to purchase anything from huge colorful skyrockets, starbursts, and pinwheels to Roman candles, cherry bombs, and sparklers.

After a big potluck dinner fueled by hunting stories and pitchers of martinis, once it became dark, everyone dragged their folding lawn chairs onto the back lawn to watch the fireworks. The dads ignited them with flares, and we watched them running around in front, backlit in the smoky red glow, having as much fun as the kids. We had front row seats; skyrockets exploded right overhead. Apparently, no one considered liability or the possibility of something going seriously wrong, like setting Blaine's field on fire.

Usually, all went well but one year, just as the show began, one of the dads somehow dropped his lighted flare into the large fireworks box. The flare ignited the entire stash of fireworks at once, sending Roman candles and skyrockets whistling and whizzing alarmingly low overhead and sideways, in every direction.

It took a second to comprehend what was happening before shrieks and cries of "Duck!" and "Run!" sent everyone diving for cover. We experienced the entire half-hour show as a spectacular firework display in about a minute. Someone quickly stamped out a small grass fire. By pure luck, nobody was injured, but incidents like this eventually led to fireworks regulation. No one ever admitted to dropping the flare.

Blaine stopped the shows a few years later because so many onlookers began parking along the roadside to watch that they created traffic and other problems. But the crowd attested to the quality of the displays.

Our favorite after-dark pastime, ringing doorbells, always promised excitement. One night I suggested, "Hey, wanna ring some doorbells?"

Brenda was game. "Yeah! Let's do the Cliffe's. He always gets so mad." Mr. Cliffe took himself very seriously. I don't recall ever seeing him laugh. His furrowed eyebrows and narrowed eyes generally mirrored exasperation about something, and I thought his thin face and pointed nose resembled a weasel.

Although he had children, he didn't like anyone playing in his yard, something unusual on a street where everyone's fenceless yards were connected and considered common play territory. He was humorless, which elevated him right up with the Hamiltons on our hit list, and made him a frequent target. We rang his doorbell and ran off, leaving him scowling on the empty doorstep, peering out into the dark.

A slow learner, he fell for the doorbell trick night after night. Eventually, he upped the ante and began waiting for us behind the door. When we rang the bell, he immediately yanked it open catching us off-guard only a few feet from the door. For us, it was a game, but he became irate. Once, he actually burst outside and chased us, the only time we ever saw an adult run. We were faster but, having almost been caught, we needed a new approach. The next night we were at it again.

I had a great plan. "We could hide in the front bushes; he'll never try to go in there!"

"OK. You take this side; I'll take the other."

We rang the bell and ducked into the thickly overgrown junipers flanking his front door, silently watching from our hideouts as he yanked open the door and peered angrily into the night. We waited until he closed the door, and it felt safe to come out. His response was so satisfying that we rang his doorbell multiple times, night after night.

Finally, he had enough. Instead of opening the front door, he tiptoed out the back door, crept around the house, and hid in the shadows. We rang the bell twice, watching the door with expectation from our hiding place in the evergreens, but he never came to open it. We figured he'd finally learned to ignore us like the Hamiltons had, which took all the fun out of it.

When it felt safe to leave the bushes, we emerged. To my terror, I felt a firm hand clamp down on my shoulder, and another grabbed my collar. Brenda fled.

"You think this is funny, do you? Well, we'll see what your parents have to say about this." His grip firmly on my collar, he marched me across the street to our house and stabbed angrily at the front bell.

I'm in for it now, I thought, so I lied. "I'm supposed to go in the back door because my shoes are muddy." It left him alone at the front door, complaining to my parents. I snuck quietly in the back door and listened from the kitchen while Mr. Cliff ranted indignantly about "young hooligans" ringing his doorbell.

Mom looked upset, but Dad listened sympathetically and said, "Don't worry, Rad, I'll take care of it." But once he left, Dad laughed, called Mr. Cliff a 'pantywaist,' and looked more amused than angry.

I appeared in the living room. "I knew you were back there," Dad said. "I hope you've been having a good time."

"Yep, we have," I said. Dad remembered how it was to be a kid. As a boy on Halloween in the 1930s, before the "treat" part of "trick-or-treat" went mainstream, Dad used to tip over outhouses, something much more serious than our pranks, especially when someone happened to be sitting in one at the time.

Swarms of flashing lightning bugs lit up the magical, warm summer nights. We often played flashlight tag after dinner until being called inside. The game involved eight or ten kids of various ages and ranged over several blocks. A combination of tag and hide-and-seek, the idea was to hide in the dark until the "it" caught you or tagged you with a flashlight beam. Then you joined in the hunt until you found everyone else. The heart-pounding excitement even surpassed harassing the hermit.

Our neighbor Ward worked at the University of Illinois Lab. One year, he was doing bioluminescence research. "I'll pay you a penny for each lightning bug you catch,' he said. This seemed more productive than flashlight tag. Another year we caught nightcrawlers for him. That was harder.

"Turn on the lawn sprinkler for a few minutes first," Dad said. "They'll think it's raining." It tricked the worms, drawing them out of their holes. They stretched out, almost a foot long, luxuriating in the wet grass. Worms have a keen vibration sense, so we had to sneak up very quietly and grab quickly. Part of their body always remained anchored in the hole, so if they sensed us coming, they could contract with lightning speed, slipping through our fingers, and zipping down their hole. Ward paid five cents a worm, but it was much more challenging than catching lightning bugs.

Sometimes we camped outside overnight in the Morphys' 6-man canvas tent, a war souvenir. Its heavy wood poles were more challenging to set up than dad's Navy pup tent, but it was roomier. We set up tents in our backyard or the field behind Morphys, brought food stashes, and told ghost stories by flashlight. Then we terrorized the neighborhood, spying in windows, scaring people, and raiding Hamilton's extensive garden.

Our parents allowed us to camp anywhere but the hermit's field because the Aurora & Elgin and the Chicago & Northwestern railroad tracks ran behind it. In those days, Hoboes often hopped the freights and rode the rails, sometimes jumping off when the train stopped at College Avenue station. Dad knew something about hoboes because at sixteen he ran away from home and hopped a freight car out West for the summer. Perhaps feeling Dad needed to break away a bit from Grandmother's controlling influence, Grandfather even slipped him fifty dollars, a lot of money in 1931. I admired Dad for his youthful sense of adventure.

Brenda and I badgered our parents for horseback lessons at Ledbetter Farms on St. Charles Road. Many horses needed to be prodded or kicked even to break into a slow trot, but we loved it and swore when we grew up, we'd own horses. We enjoyed cantering the most, but the class mostly walked and seldom broke a trot. We had only occasional short canters around the small corral.

Each year Ledbetters held a horse show in their large outdoor arena. We coveted the colorful, showy ribbons, but few horses had any pep, so the ribbon you won depended more on your horse than your riding skill.

"Let's enter the pair class," Brenda suggested. Pairs of riders would demonstrate various gaits while riding in unison around the track. We were excited, because we drew younger, lively, and well-matched horses in the lottery.

"I think we have a good chance at the blue ribbons this time," I said.

The event began well. We moved together perfectly in the walk and the trot, but I could feel my horse beginning to tremble with excitement. Next came the cantering. Both horses sensed a chance to run, something they were seldom allowed to do. Without warning, they took off. They skipped the canter demonstration altogether and went straight to a gallop, careening with abandon around the track, each trying to outrace the other. We made an effort to rein them in, but the horses were determined.

Brenda and I had always wanted to gallop but, like the horses, we were rarely allowed to canter, let alone gallop. All thoughts of trying to stay together evaporated. We grinned at each other, stopped trying to hold them back, let the horses have their heads, and sat back to enjoy the ride as they careened madly around the track. We spectacularly wrecked the pair class, we lost the blue ribbons, and the Ledbetters, watching from the bleachers, looked terrified. We came in last, but we had our best ride ever.

We never had much money, but we were the only family on the block that took an annual two-week vacation. We always went to Lake Michigan, and one year we planned to return via the Charlevoix ferry. It was a perfect place to test the Lake Michigan currents.

Dad refrained from drinking until after work but, on vacation, he could begin drinking around noon. For two weeks, as he enthusiastically worked his way through his vodka bottles, I rescued them from the trash. Then I carefully worded notes in red ink with my new silver fountain pen, inserted them into the vodka bottles, and tightly sealed the lids. I prepared seven bottles.

The warm sunny weather lured dozens of ferry passengers outside to the stern to enjoy the breeze. Midway across Lake Michigan, I hauled my bottles out on deck.

"What are you doing with all those?" Dad was embarrassed to see how many I had.

"I'm doing current experiments. I want to see where they go."

"Put those away. This looks bad. What will people think?"

"I don't care what they think. Why do you? You don't even know them." Despite my protests, he confiscated three bottles and pitched them in the trash. If Dad worried about what strangers might think, obviously, on some level he recognized he drank too much, but he seemed unable to admit it or deal with his problem.

It took time to write those notes, and if he felt embarrassed, I thought he shouldn't be drinking so much. For the first time, I realized how angry his drinking made me. I marched purposefully to the rail and pitched the four remaining bottles overboard with grand ceremony, one at a time, to the interest and amusement of the crowd on the stern.

The following summer, two envelopes, each with a red 2-cent first-class stamp, arrived within weeks of each other. I was elated; the bottles had found their way out of Lake Michigan to Lake Superior. My currents hypothesis was proven!

Like most people in Glen Ellyn, my parents lived in comfortable, narrow, monocultural bubbles, preoccupied with superficial things like appearance, cars, and status. There seemed to be 'proper' ways of doing almost everything, and most people were sufficiently concerned about what others thought to conform.

My parents never objected to my expanding nature collection, but I felt they were humoring me, waiting for me to grow out of this 'stage' and become a Proper Young Lady. *They're just worried I'll embarrass them*, I thought. *Well, too bad.*

WWII's Rosie the Riveter made women in the workplace more acceptable, but the ultimate goal for girls was still marriage. The subtle pressure started in high school. From parents to school guidance counselors, everyone steered many bright young women away from science and engineering courses into softer subjects like literature or elementary teaching. It was assumed they wouldn't have demanding careers.

Modern women were encouraged to attend college mainly to become well-rounded and be an asset to their husbands' careers. Once they earned their degrees, women were expected to marry, settle down, and become happy homemakers.

As I grew older, those attitudes, which I had previously found unfair and frustrating, became increasingly demoralizing and suffocating.

"Joanie broke the mold," Mom said almost proudly in my early years but, as I grew older, being outside the mold became less acceptable. At twelve, she intensified her efforts to pry me from my tomboy ways and shoehorn me into something more socially appropriate. I felt her actions were self-serving, and they irritated me the older I got. We fought constantly over jeans.

Serious pressure began mounting at home and at school to make me become "more of a lady." With jeans and flannel shirts still my preferred uniform, I was on a collision course with my parents, grandparents, and the school.

My sixth-grade teacher, Mrs. Johnson, even sent notes to the principal and to Mom, saying I needed to stop wearing jeans to school, but her mistake was sending the note home with me. I'm sure Mom would have welcomed it, but somehow the note never made it home.

My parents seemed to live worried about some unwritten rules dictated by society, whoever *they* were, and society's expectations were beginning to zero in on me. I declared, "I'm wearing jeans my whole life, like Katy."

More laid-back than Mom, Dad smiled indulgently, sure I would come to my senses eventually. "No, you won't. You'll see. You'll need to fit into society."

"No. I won't. I don't give a rip about society. I'm going to live as I want." Society put a definite crimp in adult lives, and I wanted no part of it. My parents thought I would outgrow my rebellion, but I was dead serious. I didn't care about breaking society's rules because the rules didn't make sense to me, and I wasn't willing to become a human sacrifice on the altar of society's expectations.

I preferred exploring the outdoors to wearing dresses or looking pretty, and I had no intention of being told what I should do or wear. I didn't know how to accomplish the goals on my list, but I knew most things would require jeans, and I chafed at dress restrictions. The life I was born into wasn't fitting well.

Glen Ellyn had beautiful autumns. When fall announced itself with slanting afternoon sun and shorter, cooler days, the oaks, maples, sumacs, and chokecherries dropped a glowing palette of red, orange, yellow, and purple leaves over the yards. Without air pollution regulations, people raked their leaves to the curb and burned them, filling the crisp air with a sweet, woodsy smell. School kids earned money raking leaves, painted windows in the downtown business district with appropriate scary scenes, and planned for Halloween.

"Trick or Drink," the Carps sang out, appearing at our house, martinis in hand. Halloween was still a children's holiday; the adults hadn't hijacked it yet.

Halloween's main objective, of course, was the giant candy haul, and I expected to fill half a large grocery bag. We could count on several dozen large-sized candy bars, plus an assortment of everything from gum, suckers, and loose candy, to boxes of dots, chocolate-covered raisins, and even an occasional cookie, taffy apple, or popcorn ball. We didn't worry about candy safety back then.

I carefully painted the bones on my skeleton costume with luminescent paint to glow in the dark, hoping it would be the scariest costume on the street. Who knows how long Brenda, Jenny, and I might have continued to trick-or-treat but for an encounter with Old Mrs. Hamilton. At 9:00 p.m., we arrived at Hamilton's house, pounded loudly on the door, and shouted "Trick or treat!" in unison.

Mrs. Hamilton cracked the door warily, and peered out at us. She was curt. "You're too late; we're all out of candy." Then looking again, she recognized us. "Aren't you all a bit old to still be trick-or-treating?" Probably. We protested, but it sounded hollow, even to me.

Then she became uncharacteristically friendly. She opened the door wider.

"Well, let's see what you've got." We proudly opened our bags to show off our haul. She pawed through my candy, taking just a little too long, as she held up various pieces, examining each with interest.

"My, you've got a lot here!" Then to my horror, she reached into my bag and extracted a Nestle's Crunch bar, my favorite. We all stood there in shock, too surprised to protest, as she went into each bag, removing a choice piece.

"Thank you!" she said, retreating into the house. She gave us a sly, triumphant smile as she closed the door. We stared at each other in dismay, trying to process what had just happened. She had finally turned the tables on us. This time we got tricked, and she got treats. That was our last year trick-or-treating.

In winter, everyone looked forward to ice skating on Lake Ellyn. Hotel Glen Ellyn created the artificial lake in 1889 but, when the hotel burned down, the land became a public park with the lake as its focal point. Once ice reached the required thickness, the city cleared any snow on the ice with a snowplow, and allowed skating.

In 1937, the town added a wooden boathouse, which became a lively winter gathering place. Inside, skaters laced up ice skates on the long wooden benches, bought hot chocolate and snacks, and warmed themselves beside an occasional oversized log fire blazing in the vast cobblestone fireplace. Ice skating was popular, and hundreds of children and adults skated every weekend.

In the mid-Fifties, Lake Ellyn must have been nearly three fourths of a mile in perimeter, and it even had a small treed island a few yards offshore of the boathouse. Brenda and I liked to test our physical limits, and there are things you can only learn about yourself when you are challenged.

"I bet you can't skate around the lake 30 times."

"I bet you can't!" It took all day, but we felt satisfied to know we could do it.

Unfortunately, Lake Ellyn became a victim of progress. Around 1955, the high school filled eleven acres to add a football field, cinder track, and a stand of bleachers. Somehow the island disappeared too.

In the Seventies or Eighties, the city began using salt to de-ice the winter roads, and since most of the town eventually drains into the lake, no doubt much of the salt ended up there. Whether because of salt, climate change, or a combination of the two, skating seems now an unpredictable shadow of its former glory.

I grew to hate the word 'progress'. As Europe struggled to rise from the ashes of war, America emerged intact and found itself a superpower. Peace ushered in an incredible period of prosperity and a massive development boom. The environmental impacts of growth, unmitigated by environmental protection, were enormous. Fueled by post-war euphoria, European immigration, the baby boom, and an economic surge, natural areas were logged, bulldozed, and filled at an alarming rate. Then they were lost altogether as new housing developments invaded and displaced farmland and forests without mitigation or consideration for their natural functions.

New cities and suburbs exploded almost overnight across the country, merging the previously isolated suburbs into miles of interstate urban sprawl.

Progress abounded in Glen Ellyn too. We watched, distraught, powerless to stop the bulldozers, as our fields, woods, and swamps disappeared under houses, playgrounds, ballfields, and asphalt. New houses filled every empty lot and began nibbling away at the edges of the field. The number of homes on our street doubled, and Glen Ellyn's population eventually tripled to 27,000.

Dad's treehouse was gone, but I doubt we could have seen Chicago clearly from Glen Ellyn anyhow; pollution was turning the air ozone-brown.

The city filled the five-acre swamp to accommodate more houses without even a nod to its natural drainage function. Today, people would prize its open space and protect it as a Class 1 wetland. Within a few decades, the United States would destroy over fifty percent of its wetlands.

What remained of the magical field became open space in a manicured park, complete with ball fields and an asphalt path.

"Look at what's happening," we complained to our parents. "They're wrecking the swamp! And they built a house on our blackberry patch!"

But Dad just said, "It's the price of progress."

From my point of view, this wasn't progress; it was a nightmare. Most adults acted as if air, land, and water were infinite resources, but the way everything was headed, I envisioned the entire earth paved over, the forests all logged, the rivers all dammed, oceans polluted, the animals gone, the land full of trash, and the smog-filled air unbreathable. Watching it happen, but being powerless to stop it, felt frightening and suffocating. I decided to fight for the wild places when I grew up, if any remained by then.

Between the cultural roles of women and the total disregard for the environment, this country was truly messed up. I was determined to get out.

- *Four* -

Seeking the Unknown

<u>Glen Ellyn, IL 1953-1956</u>

A LL OF US WERE CURIOUS ABOUT THE SPIRITUAL world, so when Bobby's older sister Kate obtained a crystal ball and suggested we hold a séance to see if we could contact 'somebody out there,' I was game. As the oldest and owner of the ball, Kate volunteered to act as a medium.

"It'll be cool. The spirits will make knocking noises and levitate a table to show they're present and willing to answer questions."

Watching a table levitate sounded intriguing, so we decided to hold a seance at Bobby's.

Everyone understood the concept of good and evil, and if asked, of course we would have preferred contacting something friendly. Still, we gave little thought to what might happen if we encountered something ominous. We were more interested in seeing if we could get a response from anything.

After dinner, four of us sat in Kate's small, musty bedroom in near darkness, hunched around a tablecloth-covered card table, staring into an opaque crystal ball. Kate switched on the ball, and it began emitting a soft glow. It looked authentic compared to the wicked witch's ball in the Wizard of Oz. She presented questions to it in a low, serious voice. I stared at the ball with concentration, willing it to start swirling pictures like the witch's ball, but it just sat there, blank and glowing slightly.

"Can you see anything, Kate?"

"Maybe…I think something's moving in there," Kate said, her voice tinged with hopefulness. Then, "No, I don't think so…or maybe, but it's not very clear." That was an understatement.

She asked the ball questions, and we heard no audible response, but soon the table began rocking up and down, followed by a couple of muffled, hollow knocks.

"They are here," Kate intoned in a solemn voice, but the spirits either had no voices or poor communication skills and after an hour, hearing nothing more, we gave up. I suspected Kate had lifted the table from underneath with her knees, although she denied it. We decided the ball must be defective. It was our last séance.

A few months later, having given up on the ball, Brenda and I turned to the Ouija board I received for Christmas. It promised more specific responses than knocks or a rocking table. We sat on my bedroom floor, hunched over, resting our four hands lightly on the planchette, and asked the Ouija a question. After a slight pause, the planchette began gliding across a board filled with letters A to Z and stopped on a letter. Then it moved to another, then another, and spelled out answers.

Some sessions were more productive than others. The planchette seemed to move on its own, sometimes slowly, sometimes quickly. Often it moved aimlessly around the board, spelling out gibberish. When it moved rapidly, it surprised both of us.

"Are you pushing it?" Brenda asked with excitement.

"No, I'm not. Are you sure *you* aren't pushing it?"

"No. I swear! I'm not doing anything!" If we were both truthful, and somehow it moved on its own, it indicated someone was 'out there'. Still, neither of us completely trusted the other's denials. The Ouija's answers to our questions weren't very informative, but it kept us sufficiently intrigued to play with it off and on for a few months. It seemed harmless enough; we had no idea how dangerous this could be or who/what might be on the other end of the planchette.

One day Brenda said, "Let's ask Ouija for the initials of our future husbands." If we intended to test the board's validity, the question was useless because it would be years before we could verify the answers.

We asked about my husband. The planchette moved to C, onto B, and returned to C again. C-B-C...*three initials?* I only expected two. "That's weird. Why are there three initials? It can't make up its mind. Let's see if it does better with you."

The results for Brenda's husband were even stranger. The planchette moved to A, then to B, wandered around the board a while, settled back on B again, and moved to D. Brenda frowned. "A-B-B-D. Four letters? Who has four initials?"

"The planchette isn't working right today; it never went past the D. Something's wrong."

"Forget this. It's not working. Let's go play in the field."

We went out to find something more interesting, but I recorded it in my diary, then forgot about it for over 60 years. In 2015, reading my old journal, the entry astounded me. I had married Carlos Cabreza, but he always used his middle initial B, signing everything CBC. Brenda eventually married Andy Barnett but later divorced and married Ben Davis, thus the four letters. Divorce was almost unheard of in the Fifties, so the possibility of two husbands never entered our minds, but the predictions were spot-on.

The probability of those seven letters happening in the correct sequence is simply the product of the seven individual probabilities multiplied together. The probability of the correct letter is one in twenty-six, so the chance of all seven initials in the correct sequence is 26 to the seventh power, over eight billion to one. The accuracy was phenomenal.

We encountered something on the other end of the planchette that day, and since it knew the future, whatever we met wasn't bound by the same laws of time and physics as we are. Fortunately, we didn't realize Ouija's potential for accuracy at the time, or we would have played with it more.

I learned only years later that Ouija is more than just an interesting toy; many consider it a dangerous portal into the occult. Randall Baer says it well: "*This game is no game at all; it is really a matter of playing with occult fire. This is a potent technique for demonic spirits to entice the curious, ensnare the dabbler, and possess the habitual user"*[2]

A board came back into my life 20 years later on Guam, but by then, having had more personal occult experiences in the Philippines and understanding its occultic connection, I broke it into pieces, and stuffed it in the trash.

A couple of years after the crystal ball and Ouija board, my search for someone or something 'out there' had a breakthrough. One week in junior high, our regular Sunday school teacher was absent, and we had a substitute. He started a class discussion with a question. "How many of you believe there is a God?" Most hands went up.

"Why do you believe that?" People's answers became pretty vague.

"The universe couldn't just happen; somebody had to make it."

"I don't know...I just feel He's there."

"I look up into the sky, see all the stars, and I just know He exists."

The teacher nodded, unsurprised. "The Bible tells us the beauty and complexity of nature are proof of a designer, so men have no excuse for denying He exists."

Then he said something very significant. "If you believe there is a God, shouldn't you decide whether you want to be on His side or not?"

Hmm. I'd never given it a thought. I assumed I *was* on His side. After all, who wants to be on the 'bad guy's' side? I accepted God's existence and figured He was floating out there somewhere, but I wasn't getting any messages from Him, and I didn't expect to. Although I credited Him with creation, I didn't think of Him as interactive.

The teacher continued. "Belief He exists is important, but that's not enough. You can't be a fence-sitter. Either you're with Him, or you're not. You need to make a conscious decision, one way or the other."

Then class ended. There was no pressure, no more discussion, and we never saw the teacher again. Nor did I ever hear anyone else say anything so simple but profound and vital, and he had planted a seed.

I went home, ate lunch, and tried to read, but the thought kept nagging me. *You need to make a conscious decision about which side you're on.* Despite years of Sunday school, I had little information on either side. Being outdoors cleared my head, so I decided to go to my thinking place to mull this over.

My thinking place was an old chokecherry tree in the field, carved with my slowly fading initials. Despite the cool, cloudy fall day and the promise of rain, I climbed up about eight feet and sat down on a broad branch to consider the matter. Something deep inside told me this decision could be critical. I figured I should give it some deliberate thought, so I thought about it for about 30 seconds and then made what I believe was the most crucial decision of my life. I said, "God, I want to be on your side." That was all, nothing more, but the nagging stopped, and I felt at peace. The branch began feeling uncomfortable, and a few sprinkles began falling, so I climbed down and ran home.

Soon, however, I began sensing a nudge to return Bobby's knife that I stole the day I broke into his house to reclaim my gold rock. Digging around in the bottom of my closet, I discovered I had stashed away more of his knives than I remembered. I had five or six large knives, including a sinister-looking switchblade and several long, sharp-bladed hunting knives. I knew stealing was wrong, but I took them when he began talking about cutting up animals. Yet, whenever I took one away, somehow, he always managed to acquire another. When I returned them, Bobby was astonished but not angry. "Gee, thanks. I thought I just lost them."

Soon, he moved away, and it was the last I saw or heard of Bobby.

I wandered through a bewildering variety of beliefs and isms for the next fifteen years. Many had nuggets of truth, but none fully resonated with me. God is patient but not pushy, and He kept his hooks in me, until eventually, we connected in an amazing way. Over the years, I also encountered people from that Sunday School class and discovered most had become Christians too. I wouldn't be surprised if it were all because of that one man.

- *Five* -

Witless and Fearless

Glen Ellyn, IL 1957-1961

MOM AND DAD HAD BOTH ATTENDED GLENBARD and were popular in high school. Dad often told me, "High school will be the best years of your life." A typical angst-ridden freshman, science geek, and bookworm, I thought, *I sure hope not. If these years are the best years of my life, I'm doomed.*

I lived for the summers. The summer I turned 16, I obtained my Red Cross Senior Life Saving badge, my driver's license, and my first real job. Thanks to my Driver Ed teacher and swim team coach, Mr. Lazier, I became a lifeguard at Glen Ayre, a private swim club struggling to open near a new community north of Glen Ellyn. Sitting high on the lifeguard tower, keeping order over a pool of screaming, cannon-balling kids was daunting to an introvert like me, but the need to be outside, around water in the summer, overrode that.

We had finally moved to a larger house across town. Glen Ayre sat on the opposite side of Glen Ellyn, several miles outside the city limits. Like most families, we owned only one car, and Dad drove it to work.

"How do you plan to get to work?" Mom asked.

With typical teenage lack of foresight, I had given it little thought. "No big deal, I'll just ride my bike," I said, with naivete, stupidity, or both. It satisfied both Mom and Dad.

Glen Ayre sat on a poorly lit rural stretch of North Avenue, one of the area's busiest highways. My three-speed bike had only a tiny front bike light and a small rear reflector, yet my parents seemed unconcerned that I planned to bike alone for several miles on a busy highway, late at night, in the dark.

My shifts alternated each week between 9:00-6:00 p.m. and 12:00-9:00 p.m. It was still light when I finished the early shift, but closing the pool on the late shift would mean biking home in the dark. The first week I worked the late shift.

Without bike lanes, I rode on the bumpy gravel shoulder. The first day, riding to work took about forty-five minutes, no sweat, but riding home at night was traumatizing. Blaring truck horns and numerous close shaves punctuated my bike ride home. Huge semis roared past on the highway blowing dust and grit in my face, often so close the bike wobbled, once nearly blowing me over. After the first day, I realized riding my bike home from work at night was too dangerous.

Fortunately, one of the other lifeguards had gotten his first car. Seeing me ride in on my bike, Dan offered to drive me to work every day. He also drove two girls from the snack bar who hadn't given proper thought to transportation either. With typical teenage optimism, we all just assumed it would somehow work out.

Dan hadn't promised us rides home, but most Glen Ayre members had teenagers. The pool quickly became a hangout, and even when our shifts ended at six, most people hung around until the nine o'clock closing. Spontaneous parties and group dates formed nightly, and the lifeguards, considered VIPs, were always in demand. That pretty much guaranteed a date after work, and someone with a car would always offer a ride home. I never had to bike to work again the entire five summers I worked there. Although overworked and underpaid, I had fun and a fantastic tan. I received the pitiful sum of a dollar an hour. It was just the price of a travelogue.

My friend Nancy and I had become obsessed with foreign places, and were attending a series of travelogues. When the Lake Ellyn boathouse sponsored a documentary, *The East is Red*, about Mao Zedong and China's cultural revolution, we went. Vestiges of Senator McCarthy's 1950s communist witch-hunt still lingered. Two black-suited FBI agents met us at the door, scowling at everyone with disapproval. "If you want to watch this, you have to sign in first, and we're starting a file on everyone who attends."

A few people left. It didn't dissuade us, but they were intimidating. *Didn't these guys have anything better to do? Why didn't they go chase after some real Communists?*

Most travelogues fascinated us. The slides and movies of Peru, India, and Tibet opened up a whole new world of mountains and oceans, cultures, and lifestyles. Except for WWII vets, no one I knew had ever been outside the States; most hadn't even traveled far enough to see mountains or oceans. The travelogues urged me to explore exotic places, but I hadn't a clue how to accomplish that. Nevertheless, I began adding destinations to my goal list.

Glen Ayre's principal legacy to me was scuba diving. Scuba hit the public eye as a recreational sport in 1958. Thanks to Sea Hunt, where Lloyd Bridges fearlessly battled giant squids, ferocious sharks, moray eels, and other dangerous sea creatures on TV at 7:00 p.m. once a week, public excitement and curiosity about diving were growing. In 1961, scuba was essentially unregulated and still a novelty. People were cavalier about safety, and equipment was primitive; even Lloyd Bridges still used a double-hosed regulator and swam without a buddy.

One of Glen Ayre's members volunteered free scuba lessons at the pool. Alan had passed a YMCA diving course, but he wasn't a certified instructor. A dozen of us signed up. Most people just wanted to experience the novelty of breathing underwater. Once they tried it, sitting in relative safety on the bottom of the pool, their interest evaporated.

Alan gave two lectures and two short pool sessions with everyone sharing his single tank. With less than 10 minutes of underwater time, he pronounced us ready for an open-water certification test. Lance, one of the other lifeguards, and I were the only ones persistent enough to take the test. Lance, a big, handsome, take-charge kind of guy with a great tan and self-assured grin, was senior class president and a football player at his high school. He exuded self-confidence. Perhaps we were both over-confident.

On a gloomy grey Saturday, with the smell of rain in the air, Lance and I met Alan for our first open-water dive, that also doubled as a certification dive. We stood in wetsuits under the leaden sky, on the side of a small black pond in the middle of nowhere, staring uncomfortably down at the inky water.

Why did Alan choose such a terrible place? The pond's spongy ground and shrubby vegetation identified it as a peat bog. It looked decidedly uninviting, even ominous. The water contained so many organic solids that little light penetrated; even a white Secchi disk would be invisible a foot below the surface. It was no place to dive, let alone make a first open-water dive.

"First, we'll do a twenty-foot solo free-dive without a tank," Alan announced.

The water was so dark we couldn't see our hands before our masks. We had no lights, although they wouldn't have helped much anyway, given the volume of solids in the water. I liked seeing my surroundings, especially in unknown territory. Monsters from Sea Hunt swam unbidden into my head. With my imagination in overdrive, I visualized many dangerous things lurking below in the dark water. Rationally knowing nothing could live down there didn't help dispel the uneasiness.

Even without monsters, actual risks abounded. I gazed at the water, thoughts churning through my head. *Does he have any idea how deep this is? The bottom will be thick, soft muck; what if we plow into it and get stuck there? What if there are waterlogged tree branches or old cars down there, and we get tangled up in something? If we need help, can Alan even find us down there? How will we even know which way is up?* We had no idea of the pond's depth or what to expect in the way of entrapments lurking below. Worse yet, I had serious doubts whether Alan had any idea either.

Neither Lance nor I had ever made a free dive deeper than the bottom of the swimming pool, in perhaps ten or twelve feet of clear water. We should have refused on safety grounds, but with trepidation, hearts pounding, we mindlessly followed orders. Alan pointed to me. "You first."

Focus, I told myself. *You can do this. Let's get this over with.* Taking a couple of deep breaths, I descended into the inky blackness, swimming as deep and fast as I could, heart pounding, hands out in front in case of obstacles. I returned to the surface, gasping for air. I had no idea how deep I descended, but Alan couldn't have known either; he was floating around the surface on an inner tube.

"I guess you went deep enough. I followed you down until I saw your fins disappear." *Yeah, right. You couldn't have seen my black fins and wetsuit in this water. I bet you just watched from the surface.* Lance, feigning macho confidence that I knew he didn't feel, followed suit. I noticed Alan didn't submerge.

I doubt Alan knew anything about the place or had ever seen the pond before, let alone gone in the water. *Who would choose somewhere with zero visibility?* Perhaps it was the only deep, water body within a reasonable distance from Glen Ellyn. It wouldn't surprise me if we were the first, and likely last, people to ever enter this water. No sane person would swim or dive there, let alone bring two students on their first open water dive. It was ridiculous and foolhardy, but we weren't quitters.

"The scuba part of the test won't work well here," Alan admitted, pulling himself out of the pond. That was an understatement. "Let's go somewhere else next week for that." We breathed sighs of relief.

The following Saturday, under gathering storm clouds promising rain, we stood on the shore of an abandoned gravel pit, again staring down into uninviting murky water. It was only a slight improvement over the bog. With a let's-get-it-over-with feeling, we suited up in our rental gear and waded in.

"Buddy system. Hold hands and stay together," Alan said. Unlike today, where instructors accompany their class for several dives and monitor them closely, Alan didn't even enter the water. The silty, mud-bottomed pond, only about 25 feet deep, lacked vegetation; it was probably too dark for photosynthesis. The lack of sunlight and suspended clay particles in the gray, turbid water reduced visibility to about eight feet. We moved along the bottom, every kick of our fins stirring up billowing clouds of fine silt behind us. It remained suspended in the water, obscuring whatever visibility might remain on return. The dive highlight was a few silt-covered stones mired in the clay bottom. We stayed down perhaps ten minutes. I was seriously beginning to wonder what the big deal about diving was.

"Probably long enough," Alan noted when we surfaced. With no more experience than this, he said "Congratulations," pronounced us passed, and produced hand-drawn certificates saying we had "Passed to YMCA Standards." *Really?* Even I knew this was inadequate, but I checked off #9, Learn to Scuba Dive, from my goal list.

Diving wasn't a cheap sport. Tanks, backpacks, regulators, wetsuits, booties, buoyancy compensators, dive knives, weight belts, weights, masks, depth and pressure gauges, snorkels, and fins all added up. Undaunted, I bought a wetsuit, a tank, and the newest model single-hose regulator, a vast improvement over Lloyd Bridges' cumbersome double-hoses. At least I had enough brains to buy a depth gauge.

Except for wreck diving in the Great Lakes, the Midwest isn't known for great diving. Lance and I made several unmemorable shallow dives in local lakes, but then we heard about Racine Park in Wisconsin. The former limestone quarry was now a 40-acre spring-fed lake with fishing, swimming, and scuba opportunities. We had to try it. Mom looked uneasy about my going, but she didn't say no.

On a warm, bright sunny day, we took a day off work, loaded up our gear, and headed to Wisconsin in Lance's convertible, top down. At Racine, the bright sun smiled at us from a cloudless azure sky and sparkled on the amethyst water. The sound of *Moon River* floated to us over the water from a distant radio, and people began to fire up outdoor grills. Enthusiastic swimmers, fishermen, and sunbathers filled the park, enjoying the warm August weather. It looked so promising after our previous experiences.

The tank filler accepted our made-up certificates with only a cursory glance and one quick question. "I never saw certificates like these. Have you guys been diving before?" We assured him we had, and without further inquiry, he filled our tanks. I don't know what type of certificates he expected, because certification was neither required nor widely recognized. Today's universally recognized NAUI diver certification program had just begun, and PADI certification still lay six years in the future.

We suited up, clumsily duck-walked in our fins to the quarry's edge, spit and rinsed our masks to keep them from fogging, clamped our hands to our masks, and jumped in. The water was clear and beautiful. Shafts of sunlight danced down through the water, illuminating *Elodia* and other aquatic vegetation on the vertical, pale limestone walls. Sun glinted off tiny air bubbles shining on the bright green leaves, and we even saw a few minnow-sized fish. Seeing living things was exciting! We found it beautiful compared to the horrible bog and muddy pond experiences. We swam along the layered, vertical limestone wall, gradually descending to perhaps 50 feet, our deepest dive so far.

Lance, much larger than I, used air faster than I did, but we stayed down until he ran out of air and then surfaced, exhilarated. We followed the smell of grilling hot dogs to the snack stand and sat in our wetsuit bottoms having lunch, overlooking the quarry. As we discussed the dive, a guy stopped by our table.

Noting our wetsuits, he asked, "Did you guys find the 110-foot hole?"

"Hole? That sounds interesting! No one mentioned that. Where is it?"

New divers often view depths as records to be achieved, and to us, 110 feet seemed a magic number worth attaining. It was also the height of an eleven-story building. Lance and I exchanged excited glances, not even needing to discuss it. "Let's do it," we said together. On impulse, we decided to make a second, unplanned dive, breaking a cardinal rule of diving: never go deeper on the second dive than the first. Sticking to this rule lessens the possibility of getting the bends. There are a few exceptions today, based on time and depth ratios, but we didn't meet those either; this dive wasn't just a bit deeper; it was over twice the depth of our first dive.

The tank-filler frowned when we brought our tanks for refilling. "A second dive, so soon?" And he didn't look happy when Lance asked him about the 110-foot hole, but he waved vaguely toward a spot in the quarry.

Our training certainly wasn't comprehensive. Alan had given us a cursory, almost dismissive, theoretical discussion of the dive tables, saying, "I doubt you'll ever need to use dive tables. There aren't any deep places to dive around here anyhow." Except, apparently, Racine. We didn't even own copies of the dive tables, but we knew about the bends, or decompression sickness and nitrogen narcosis.

Bends aren't a concern when free-diving but, on scuba, a regulator increases the air pressure you breathe to match the increase in water pressure as you descend. The body uses the oxygen in the compressed air, but not the nitrogen, and nitrogen begins to build up in the tissues. The deeper the depth, the more pressurized the air, and the more nitrogen dissolves into the tissues.

Ascending, as the water pressure decreases, the tissues begin releasing nitrogen into the bloodstream, somewhat like opening a carbonated beverage under pressure. The body will exhale nitrogen, but ascending too fast causes nitrogen bubbles to form in the blood. These can cause embolisms or other problems almost anywhere in the body, and can be fatal. The depth, length of the dive, and ascent speed all factor into the risk of bends.

The dive tables state how long a person can safely remain at various depths. Exceeding these times requires a diver to decompress, or stop at specific depths for definite time periods during ascent, to allow nitrogen to escape the bloodstream.

"If we don't stay down too long, we can probably wing it without the dive tables," Lance said. Although without the dive tables we couldn't know how long was too long.

"Yeah, I think so. We won't stay there. Let's just touch down and then come up."

We geared up for our second dive, jumped in, swam to the bottom at 60 feet, and struck out in the approximate direction of the hole. Somehow, I assumed we would go along the bottom at about 60 feet and find the hole.

Quarries, of course, aren't dug that way. We followed the silty bottom for some time as I watched my depth gauge slowly increase from 60 to 70 feet. The beautiful water of the first dive was gone. At this depth, the water had absorbed most of the longer light wavelengths, and as we descended, the reds, oranges, and yellows gradually disappeared until everything appeared dull greyish-green. The bottom water became siltier and darker, uncomfortably resembling our certification dive. We continued to 80, 90, and 100 feet. *I didn't think we'd be down so deep so long before reaching the hole.* I began feeling nervous.

Then, at about 100 feet, the dark edge of a drop-off appeared through the silt-filled gloom. We had located the hole. Lance popped over the edge and sank into the dark hole, his fins stirring up a cloud of silt. He looked up, beckoning me to join him.

I slowly sank to the silty bottom, stirring up more silt. Lance grinned behind his mask, gleefully pointing to his depth gauge. One hundred ten feet. We swam around a bit, but there appeared little to see in the dim gloom except a couple of boulders and piles of silt.

Visibility was barely ten feet, and only the hiss of our inhalations and gurgling bubbles broke the weighty silence. The water felt pressingly heavy. I knew it was purely psychological, although breathing did seem more difficult. I had more than met my 100-foot goal. I felt uneasy; I had seen enough. We had already been at between 60 and 100 feet for longer than expected, although we couldn't be sure how long without dive watches.

A warning light began flashing in my brain. *We need to ascend.* I was acutely conscious of the passing time, but now Lance appeared to be in no hurry; all plans of a short dive seemed to have flown from his mind. Although the silty gloom promised nothing of interest, now he wanted to explore the hole. *Has he forgotten we had already been at depth for quite a while, swimming toward the hole?* In retrospect, perhaps this was a sign of narcosis.

Nitrogen narcosis, more common than the bends, can also occur at depth. It skews your sense of time and impairs judgment, reasoning, and coordination. Most divers experience it at some point, but often they aren't aware when it's happening. In the right circumstances, being 'narked' can cause fatal accidents.

I took a breath and then suddenly got almost no air at all. I sucked harder but couldn't get anything. My tank seemed empty.

What's going on? I can last longer on a tank than Lance, and he's not having air problems. I swam to him, giving him the "out of air" sign, a slash across my neck with my hand. His blank look told me either he didn't recognize the sign or wasn't inclined to buddy-breathe and share his air.

Although I understood the concept, I realized Alan hadn't taught us to buddy-breathe. *I can't stay here any longer; 110 feet is not a good depth to be airless!* The only way to get more air was to ascend. I remembered enough to know I couldn't leave Lance there, so I grabbed my protesting buddy and dragged him rapidly to the surface.

Ascending, as water pressure decreases, the compressed air in the lungs expands. To avoid lung damage, we knew to never to hold our breath under-water, exhale as we ascended, and ascend no faster than our bubbles, about sixty feet per minute. But, when the only air you have is in your lungs, it's counter-intuitive to ascend slowly and exhale, and I hadn't started up with the luxury of a full breath. An ascent that should have taken about two minutes probably took a minute. The air in my lungs was expanding so I didn't feel the need to breathe, and fortunately, half-way up, it burst from my mouth in a tremendous and unexpected explosion of bubbles. Otherwise, it would have damaged my lungs.

As we hit the surface, surprised and annoyed, Lance yanked out his regulator. "What's the *matter* with you?"

"Didn't you understand my sign? I'm out of air!" I gasped, taking a deep breath.

He frowned. "How can you be out of air?" I didn't know either. Back on land, we checked my pressure gauge. It registered empty, while Lance still had a third of a tank. I suspect the tank filler, skeptical about our second dive, deliberately underfilled my tank to force an early surfacing. I was very thankful he did; Lance had seemed ready to explore the entire hole.

We didn't realize the magnitude of our mistakes then but, looking back now, with the benefit of years of diving experience, I'm horrified. I can see at least nine glaring issues: little dive training or experience; no dive plan; no dive tables; insufficient time between dives; second dive much deeper than the first; no dive watches; no buddy breathing training; holding my breath; and ascending too rapidly. We broke practically every diving rule in the book. If the fill man hadn't underfilled the tank, we would have remained at depth longer and could easily have been in trouble, and I doubt any decompression chamber existed near the quarry.

After the long drive from Racine, we stopped at Lance's house, and his mom offered us a late dinner. I called home to let Mom know I would be late. She answered on the first ring, sounding almost frantic. "You come home right this instant!"

"Mom. Calm down. I'm OK. I'm having dinner at Lance's. I just called to let you know I'll be later than I thought. Relax. I'll be home in an hour or so."

Mom wasn't getting any support from Dad; he appeared even unaware I was diving.

Dad increasingly disengaged from the family and began spending most of his free time on the screen porch, a cigarette in one hand and a martini in another. Mom had once followed dad's lead on almost every decision, from his brand of cigarettes to his politics. Now, as his alcoholism progressed, she quietly began asserting herself. She took over the family finances, and shielding us, she became the glue holding the family together.

Once home, I fell asleep exhausted. I awoke the following morning to find my arm strangely heavy. It felt dead; I couldn't move it. As I visualized air bubbles in my veins, my first panicked thought was, *I have the bends!* I slapped and pinched my arm, willing it to regain feeling and movement. After what seemed an eternity, it regained feeling. Relieved, I realized I'd just slept on it wrong. My arm was asleep.

This experience impressed me with the need to take a comprehensive diving course and learn the dive tables so that I wouldn't repeat such a risky dive. But now summer was over, and I looked forward to college, my first step to escape.

- *Six* -

Prelude to Escape

Beloit, WI 1961-1963

BELOIT, A SMALL PRIVATE LIBERAL ARTS COLLEGE, HAD a reputation for good science. Its red-brick, ivy-covered buildings, and pretty wooded campus bordered the picturesque Rock River in Wisconsin. It was enthusiastically promoting its new Beloit Plan, which included an off-campus experience. It would pilot in 1964, but that was three years off; neither my parents nor I gave it a thought.

I can now see how God used Dr. Carl Welty, the biology department chairman, as His unwitting instrument in orchestrating my path. My first semester, as I trudged up the stairs of the old science building on the way to my job in the microbiology lab, the creaky wooden steps alerted Dr. Welty to my approach. As I passed his paper-stuffed corner office, he called out, beckoning me in with a broad smile that lit up his whole face.

"Are you planning to declare a biology major?" I was surprised he asked so early because most people declared majors at the end of their sophomore year, but I said yes. Then he became not only my department chair but also my major advisor, mentor, and friend.

A thin, wiry, energetic man with thinning gray hair, his bright eyes with round metal-rimmed glasses somehow reminded me of an owl, perhaps appropriate, as he taught ornithology. He was on the edge of retirement and just finishing the last draft of his life's work, *The Life of Birds*. It would become the definitive textbook on ornithology, earning him a place among the great ecologists. But that year his lectures were snoozers; he simply read from his draft manuscript because everything he wanted to say was already there.

His fun and informative birding trips in the gray pre-dawn light sometimes ended up at his house, where his wife Susan served us a big breakfast. The Weltys attended traditional Quaker meditation meetings, and for some reason, they invited me to attend. *Why not? It might be interesting.* I knew nothing about the Quakers, so I went once or twice, but silent meditation meetings weren't helpful to anyone wanting to explore either the Quakers' beliefs or their own. However, my brief interest started a close rapport with them.

The second semester, as I passed his office again, he called out and motioned me to a chair. He was just in a mood to talk. He also taught my ecology class, and he had assigned us a term paper on the ecosystem of our choice. "What's the topic of your paper?" He asked with interest.

Surprised, I said, "coral reefs." It was a strange choice for a Midwestern biologist since I had never seen a reef, but it held out the promise of an ultimate scuba experience.

A wide smile creased his thin face. Leaning back in his chair, arms behind his head, he launched into an in-depth discussion of reefs. Then he said with enthusiasm, "A girl who graduated last year is studying marine biology right now, in Hawaii. She received a graduate scholarship at a new government institute called the East-West Center. You might eventually be interested in that."

Mom and Dad had talked about college from the time I entered elementary school, but their concept of higher education topped out at four years; the words "graduate school" were neither in their vocabulary nor their budget. I knew a graduate degree was the wave of the future for science majors, but it certainly wasn't on my radar as a freshman, let alone at a school that far away.

When Uncle Phil moved to California six years earlier, the family was distraught; they felt they would never see him again. Hawaii was 5,000 miles away, over twice as far as California, and few Midwesterners had ever been there. At that point, I would probably never have seriously contemplated it. Welty's mention of the Center was a random comment. I never heard the name mentioned again, or even gave it a thought for almost four years.

The unspoken but deliberate goal of most girls attending college in the Sixties was an Mrs. degree, and the noose around the girls was tightening. The first steps toward this goal were often receiving a fraternity lavalier, or pendant, and then a fraternity pin. They symbolized commitment, and were often considered steps toward engagement.

When someone became lavaliered, pinned, engaged, or married, the dorm held an after-hours ceremony to announce these milestones. Everyone stood in a circle, singing the saccharine chorus, "*I give to you, and you give to me, true love, true love…*" as they passed a lit candle around the circle. The number of times it circled indicated the event's magnitude; one circling meant a lavalier, two a pinning, three an engagement. The undisclosed celebrant announced herself by blowing out the candle on the appropriate circling as it passed by. This elicited a chorus of excited screams and ecstatic congratulations. Marriage was the direction most girls focused on, but I couldn't envision it. It felt much too limiting and too soon to narrow my options.

I was athletic in a world where women's sports, if they existed at all, were unnoticed, unfunded, and poorly attended. Few women competed in anything, but Beloit had a makeshift women's swim team. After a two-year hiatus, I began competitive swimming again. We held only one swim meet, and Liz and I, both from the Glen Ellyn swim team, set three conference records, but that didn't merit even a line in the college paper; covering every play of the weekly football game in mind-numbing detail was apparently more important. Yet no one complained or called it discrimination.

I had hoped for a broad exposure to various points of view, people, and experiences in college, but Beloit still drew most of its students from the

Midwest and was culturally and ethnically very similar to Glen Ellyn. I had been impatient to leave Glen Ellyn, but Beloit was pretty much like still living there. For the first two years, I enjoyed the freedom of campus life, but I went home for summer breaks depressed. *Is this all there is?*

By my junior year, Theta sorority gatherings, dances, and frat parties were getting old. I began to disengage, feeling as though I were watching from afar as someone else went through the motions of my daily activities. I felt as if caught in a whirlpool, desperately struggling to avoid getting pulled under. Worse, thanks to advanced placement in biology, I had moved into upper-class courses my freshman year, so my senior year, I had taken everything, and had no more biology courses to look forward to.

Glen Ayre was always a fun-filled summer break, but this summer would be my last because next year, after graduation, I would need something more than a summer job. *But what? Where?* Nothing attracted me. The future was rapidly closing in and I had no idea what I would do, but my desire to escape the Midwest status quo was almost pathological.

"I don't much care where [I go]," said Alice in Wonderland, "as long as I get *somewhere*."[3] That's how I felt. I hungered for undefined adventure, and desperately wanted a wormhole to a different life, but had no idea how to change my circumstances.

After Christmas, I returned gloomily to the academic grind, unaware that events were already in motion to upend my life. In January, a note from Dr. Welty called me into his office. Without preamble, he asked, "Do you know Spanish?"

"I've had six years. I guess I'm fairly decent at reading, at least. Why?"

"Good. I thought you might be interested in this program." He waved me toward a chair, and proceeded to tell me about a program under the new Beloit Plan, about to begin in June. It would diversify the campus and encourage an off-campus internship or experience. One program was in Costa Rica.

"It sounds interesting! But it's not a language program, is it?"

"No, I don't think so. The National Science Foundation funds it. I don't know much about it or what's involved, but I thought you might be interested. It's a pilot program but, if things work out, they'll offer it every year." He professed to know little of the program's activities, goals or objectives.

"I'm sorry I can't give you more information, but I just happen to have the application form here, if you'd like it." There was no explanatory brochure, and the application provided no program detail or information of any kind. Still, I seized the opportunity like a drowning person grasping a life ring.

I never saw a single announcement or advertisement for the program, nor was I ever provided anything in writing. *Why hasn't anyone I talked to ever heard of it?* Over time, I concluded Welty had only a single application, and I was the only student he told. The lack of basic information seemed almost purposeful and mysterious, but I chalked up the lack of detail to it being a pilot program.

Students from all ten conference schools competed, so I assumed the competition would be stiff. As a biology major with six years of Spanish, I felt cautiously optimistic, but my grades, although good, weren't outstanding. I told Mom and Dad I had applied for the program. Mom, surprised but non-committal, looked to Dad for her opinion. Dad listened, but had few questions and showed little excitement or encouragement.

Two months later, I was excited to learn I was one of ten students selected for the program. The acceptance letter provided no additional information, and did nothing to dispel the program's vagueness. Still, I would receive 30 credits, and as a pilot, the program paid all the airfare, expenses, and tuition for my senior year, something my parents should appreciate. Lynn and the twins would soon all be in college at once, and Grandfather would soon require a nursing home; I'm sure Dad was wondering how to pay for everything.

When I called to tell them I was accepted, I thought they would be excited, but Mom was relatively quiet. Dad just said with complacency, "I knew you would." No excitement or congratulations. I felt a familiar irritation rising. Once again, his comment seemed to imply that anything I accomplished was expected, and somehow due to the fact that I was his child, rather than by my own efforts.

He had a few questions about the program, but I still had no answers, except that Dr. Welty indicated it involved the jungle. The previous month Dad hadn't allowed me to canoe the Boundary Waters area the upcoming summer, and rather than argue, he hung up the phone on me, so I was unsure what he would say about this. *Don't say no,* I thought. *Because I'm going, regardless.* He didn't, but he must have researched Costa Rica a bit because he began mumbling about fer-de-lance snakes and jaguars, and took out a life insurance policy on me.

Although I didn't realize it, I had just made one of those genuinely life-altering decisions that present themselves only a few times in a lifetime, where the choice either cements the status quo or changes the rest of your life. I jumped at the unknown path without worrying about the details, and left Beloit in June without a backward glance. My escape was underway.

Costa Rica: Into the Jungle

(1964–1965)

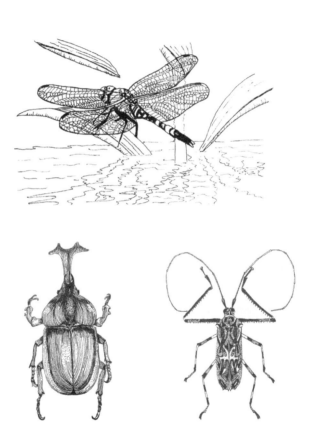

Rhinoceros Beetle   Harlequin Beetle

".... follow your heart even when it leads you off the well-worn path, and that will make all the difference."

– Steve Jobs

Costa Rica

- *Seven* -

Opening My World

San José, Costa Rica 1964-1965

THE COSTA RICAN PROGRAM MATERIALS PROVIDED no description of what we would do, or even what clothes to bring, except they appeared to be jungle-related: "Bring heavy leather boots, bug spray, poncho, and malaria pills, and get tetanus, cholera, typhoid, and yellow fever shots." I took my first plane ride to Miami, feeling I had grown wings and escaped, unaware that at the end of the year my life would be entirely re-focused.

Six of us met in Miami, and four others drove to Costa Rica from Texas in a VW van. After 4 ½ slow hours on an ancient Laksa Airlines prop plane, we arrived in San José the following day. Dr. Hunter, the program director, avoided customs, whisked us through the airport, and drove us to the Pension Francesa, a French boarding house in downtown San José.

Mom had been reading news on Costa Rica, and she had mentioned an erupting volcano. I hadn't expected to experience it so soon, but my first impression of San José was the volcanic ash, or *ceniza*, from Irazú volcano. It lay everywhere. Irazú was the southernmost of ten Costa Rican volcanoes and the highest mountain in the *Cordillera Central*. It produced no molten lava, but the explosion of superheated rocks created dense clouds of the gray, powdery ceniza. It erupted daily, and ashfall was now in the second year.

Ceniza accumulated so rapidly that eventually, people gave up trying to clean the streets. The wind blew it into drifts, accumulating in gutters and corners. It found its way into every crack and crevice, clogging up water systems, damaging car engines and anything mechanical. Afternoon rains converted it into muddy rivers that flowed down streets, clogging sewers, storm drains, ditches, and canals.

The Pension Francesa felt comfortable but not luxurious. An open-air courtyard in the center framed by archways, contained a tiled fountain and beautiful tropical plants, but what had once been a green oasis had become drab and dreary. The courtyard attracted volcanic ash like a magnet, and the Señora had lost the battle with ash long ago. Once-beautiful Cannas, palms, and fig plants now struggled for breath, their large leaves grey and drooping under the weight of the ash.

I shared a small, windowless but comfortable room with my new roommate, Liz. Like most anthropology majors, she wore no makeup, had a simple hairdo, and dressed simply in a plain tan dress and sandals. She seemed down-to-earth, unpretentious, and easy-going. *We'll get along well,* I thought.

Our room contained a shower and two single beds with kapok mattresses, still new enough to be relatively lump-free, although after the first few days our legs had large itching red welts the size of dimes. Someone said they were flea bites.

An unlimited supply of giant spiny-legged cockroaches lived inside the shower drain. We kept them in check by covering the drain with a plate except when using the shower. A small coil in the shower generated lukewarm water, but when volcanic ash clogged up the water system, we could be without running water altogether for several days. At first, I found the ash a fascinating novelty, but it rapidly became a major annoyance.

After lunch, Hunter drove us to an old two-story wooden building in downtown San José. A sign on the small green door identified itself as the Office of Tropical Science Research, aka the Tropical Science Center. We shared the office with the Organization for Tropical Studies (OTS). They were working on an Army project involving ants, birds, and other species, and I wondered why the Army cared about ants. Their researchers were older, often away in the jungle, and interacted little with us, but eventually I would join them in many of their camps.

The office didn't seem prepared for us. It lacked furniture, and was empty except for a huge heap of books in the middle of the floor. Supposedly this was the nucleus of an office library, but it looked more like everyone had simply emptied their private libraries of any unwanted books.

The other students felt as in the dark as I about the program, but the scientists and researchers provided no introductory or organizational meeting. Without office furniture or direction, we milled around in the empty office, making idle conversation, until Hunter said, "Go out and familiarize yourselves with San José." Liz, Tom, Jim, and I set out for our first third-world experience.

The program had provided no information on what to wear, so I brought very few clothes. I naively thought I could wear Bermuda shorts, my normal Beloit wear, but they discouraged us from wearing shorts on the street. Pants were acceptable, but my heavy jeans would be uncomfortable in the steamy heat, and my one skirt and dress wouldn't go very far.

Worse, neither downtown San José nor the pension had laundromats. The Señora said, "The pension can send laundry out to the women washing on rocks in the river, but it takes a week to return."

There's no way I have enough clothes for two weeks. Sending a week's laundry out to the river would leave me with nothing. Liz and Tom were similarly limited, so we headed to *Mercado Central* to go shopping.

Most third-world cities have a particular smell. As we entered the central market, we encountered a sour smell of rotting vegetables, garbage, chicken manure, unwashed people, and dried fish, incongruously mixed with enticing aromas of grilling meat, frying onions, and peppers. Sluggish gray wash water flowed in gutters along the aisles.

The noisy maze of small covered shops sold everything imaginable. Merchandise was heaped on tables, hanging from ceilings and walls, and crammed into every conceivable crevice. A fly-filled food section held slabs of unrefrigerated meat, chicken, fish, and heaps of odd things like pig ears, pig snouts, and entrails.

Jim eyed the unrefrigerated meat and pig snouts. "You don't suppose our pension buys its food here?" Of course, it did.

Tables piled with cellophane packets of spices, and pyramids of bright red tomatoes, shiny purple eggplants, golden mangoes, yellow bananas and pineapples, green guavas, brown coconuts, strange green spiny fruits and leafy vegetables, provided a rainbow of color in the otherwise drab market. Small cages held sad-looking, silent chickens and parrots. Other sections sold cheap aluminum cookware, garish colored shoes, handicrafts, and clothes.

Foreigners were rare in the market. As we walked the aisles, a non-stop barrage of irritating comments, a cacophony of hisses and catcalls swirled around us as hawk-eyed owners in every stall vied to engage us in conversation.

"Que Macha!" "How are you?" "What your name?" "Where you from?"

We weren't sure how to take these comments. *Are these derogatory, complimentary, or just a way to draw us into their store?* Other comments were more blatant. Leering glances and salacious comments assailed Liz and me from all sides as we pushed down the narrow aisles through the crowd. *Would they dare say these things to local girls?* I doubted it. We pushed on, resisting the temptation to answer. Even a glance or a slight hesitation in front of a stall increased their persistence. Most comments stopped altogether once we learned to stride purposefully through the aisles avoiding eye contact, and without slowing to look at the merchandise.

The market's crowded aisles, filled with pushing, jostling bodies, were a pickpocket's dream. We pushed and fought our way through the narrow passageways, gripping our wallets tightly, hunting for the clothes section. One look at the flimsy skirts and blouses in the women's section, and Liz and I headed to the men's section to bargain for cotton field pants and shirts. The pension charged $75 for room and board, leaving us $45 a month for discretionary expenses. We settled on a reasonable price of nine colones per item, about $1.50 each. Everyone also bought machetes, which came in handy almost immediately.

We began settling in. After a week, the pension's laundry returned from the river, everyone's clothes jumbled together in a big pile. Many things returned almost unrecognizable after being pounded to death, bleached, and dried on the rocks. I felt glad I had sent nothing out. After that, everyone hand-washed their clothes.

Office furniture arrived, and we received advisors. I was surprised to find I was the only biologist in this first group of ten students. Dr. Les Holdridge, a principal organizer of the Tropical Science Center and one of the world's foremost tropical ecologists, claimed me as his student. Fifty-seven, tall and lean with thinning grayish hair and a trimmed gray mustache, he looked much like a thinner, grayer version of Dad. He was energetic and brilliant, yet low-key, soft-spoken, and modest about his Life Zone model, that was now gaining international attention.

Holdridge's complex Life Zone model appeared to be the central basis for the program's National Science Foundation grant funding. The model was interesting, but I couldn't quite visualize its predictive applications. Biology projects, at least, were expected to tie into it, and I received the impression my work would help validate and ground-truth the model. It was nearly my last night in Costa Rica before I learned the real purpose of my work.

The program expected each of us to conduct a research project, but being unfamiliar with the culture and environment made proposing ideas for projects difficult. Time dragged. Long, half-hour coffee breaks morning and afternoon, plus a three-hour lunch, from 11:00 to 2:00, seemed excessive. *Is the staff unsure what to do with us, or are they just giving us time to adjust?* Later I realized the office simply ran on "Tico time" (Costa Rican time), and the day's schedule included a three-hour midday siesta.

Every day around lunchtime, from the office window, we watched a dark ash cloud billow from Irazú's 11,260-foot crater for over an hour. The wind carried the ash 33 miles into San José, and an hour or two after the eruption, the sky darkened, a heavy ash cloud blotted out the sun, and ash began softly drifting down like tiny gray snowflakes. It landed on our clothes and hair; the acidity made our scalps itch. Whenever ashfall began, a rainbow of umbrellas sprouted up on the sidewalks like mushrooms. Sometimes ash fell so thick and fast it restricted visibility to perhaps 100 feet and made breathing uncomfortable.

Our group of ten was a diverse bunch. Clint, an economics major, wore brown jeans with a large Texas belt buckle, utilitarian cowboy boots, and a big cowboy hat his dad made him bring "to represent Texas," although he seldom wore it. He was more student than cowboy, level-headed, thoughtful, generous, and projected quiet confidence and competence beyond his years. He was the kind of guy people counted on in a crisis. We hit it off and began dating.

Clint parked his green VW van on the street. Its Texas plates made it an irresistible target, and within a week, someone broke in and stole the expensive toolbox. He replaced the broken window, but within a few days someone smashed it again and stole a few minor items left in the back seat. Clint replaced the window a second time, and then decided it would be cheaper to leave the van empty and unlocked, hoping no one knew how to hotwire a car. Still, a few days later, someone entered again and, frustrated they found nothing to steal, grabbed the only remaining thing portable: a five-cent beaded trinket hanging from the mirror. Even a cursory glance through the windows showed nothing left to take, but people continued to enter almost daily, leaving ashy footprints all over the seats.

Liz began dating Tom, another anthropologist. His messy hair, round placid face, and Harry-Potter glasses belied a sometimes-volatile personality, but he had a heart for the local people and related well with them. I later discovered he could also roll with the punches in almost any situation. Clint, Liz, and Tom were the people I would interact with most during the year.

Tom roomed with Wayne, another anthropologist. His dark unruly hair, attractive angular face, and serious and thoughtful demeanor made him seem older than the others. He never dated because he had a girl back home, but we often played chess. His room had a small hole in the floorboards. We paid little attention to it, although we noticed it slowly enlarging over time. Sometimes we heard gnawing sounds, but no one seemed concerned about it.

One afternoon, as Liz and I relaxed in the common area, the room erupted with loud shouts and banging sounds, punctuated with shrill, high-pitched squeals. Wayne's door opened and shut quickly, and Clint emerged holding an enormous bloody black rat the size of a small rabbit, wrapped in a newspaper. Curious, Liz and I went over and knocked on the door. "Come in and shut the door fast," Wayne said.

When the hole reached about an inch in diameter, three giant black rats had suddenly erupted into the room without warning. Surprised to find people, they began wildly running and jumping around the room in a frenzy. Clint and Wayne were going after them with their new machetes. Two were still jumping around the room, squealing frantically. I had never heard rats squeal before; it was shrill and unpleasant. Liz and I immediately hopped onto Wayne's bed.

"There goes one! He's under the bed!"

"Get him, get him! Now he's under the chair!"

"Watch out…here he comes!" Slamming of machetes on the wood floor. "Missed him!" More machete whacking. More squeals.

"You flush him out, and I'll whack him!"

"Try to box him in the corner!"

This activity continued for some time until they cornered the second rat under Tom's bed. Wayne edged it out with a machete. It ran out, its shrill squeals echoing through the pension. Clint hacked it to death with his machete, almost destroying Tom's duffle bag in the process. Sensing his impending fate, the third rat somehow zipped past Wayne and smoothly slipped his fat body back through the small hole. Wayne upended a wastebasket over the hole to prevent reentry.

"Wow, that was a real bloodfest!" he announced, flushed with the satisfaction of a proud hunter. Whether "bloodfest" was a real word or not, it certainly fit. The floor, walls, beds, and Tom's duffle bag were all covered with evidence of the battle.

The Señora heard the commotion, appeared, calmly viewed the carnage, and said something about giant rats and small holes. She picked up the second rat by the tail, wrapped it up in a newspaper, and carried it away, acting as if this were an everyday occurrence.

Because rats have flexible cylindrical bodies and their clavicles are positioned differently from other mammals, they can squeeze through holes much smaller than they are. If their head can fit, the body can follow. A one-inch opening is generally considered large enough to be an invitation, so Wayne and Tom's golf-ball-sized hole placed a sizeable welcome sign under the pension. The cockroach colony in our shower now seemed a minor inconvenience.

In September, Wayne met a family wanting women boarders, and referred them to Liz and me. We believed we could learn more Spanish living with a family, so we moved to a large house not far from the office. The family wore black mourning clothes. The husband had recently died, and they were taking in boarders to make ends meet. The recently widowed mother, Doña Sofia, a pretty middle-aged woman, lived with her aging dragon of a mother, Doña Isabella; Amaya, a precocious girl of 16-going-on-25; and several younger siblings.

The family also employed a rather sullen older maid, who snooped in our belongings and slowly lowered the level in Liz's carefully hidden bottle of rum. She also did laundry, but Doña Sofia said, "Keep a tally of what you give her because anything nice quickly disappears." Perhaps they put up with her because most maids stole things. She supplemented her salary by having quickie sex behind a palm tree on the front lawn at night, a fact that if acknowledged, the Señoras would be forced to deal with, so they pretended not to notice.

The large, modern house had spacious, tall-ceilinged rooms and a broad curving staircase. More importantly, it had hot water and lacked fleas. Doña Sofia pointed out with pride that the bathroom fixtures were American Standard, imported from the States. They admired anything from the States, saying the best of everything came from there. Everyone in the friendly family played chess, and the kids were trying to learn some English. Our sizeable, airy room contained windows and a mirror, and we were immersed in Spanish, so it seemed ideal. And for most of the year, it was.

I was the only biologist in this first group, and most of our group would not be working in the jungle, but Dr. Holdridge wanted to give everyone a brief exposure before we began our projects. His cabin, unimaginatively called *La Selva*, or "The Jungle," was in Sarapiqui, near Puerto Viejo. I looked forward excitedly to this trip because, somehow, I knew I would spend most of the year in jungles.

- *Eight* -
La Selva

<u>Sarapiqui 1964</u>

N EAR PUERTO VIEJO, A DARK TANNIC-ACID-LADEN
river sliced through the dense jungle, its swift, down-cutting current
carrying silt, leaves, and tangled bits of jungle debris. We motored upriver
in low dugout canoes through the thick, shaded jungle to Holdridge's
weathered wood cabin. It sat in a small clearing well above the river and
back from the bank, elevated on posts. Several feet of unvegetated, eroded
riverbank indicated the river level swelled almost to the top of the bank
during the rainy season.

Inside the cabin, a dozen jungle hammocks encased in filmy white
mosquito nets hung suspended from the ceiling like giant cocoons. The
simple cabin lacked water or electricity and used kerosene lanterns and
channeled water from the roof into a barrel for drinking. *This is like the
hermit's house, although it's larger and better constructed. I hope I'll have a
chance to spend time here.*

Outside, a colony of giant greyish spiders hung on the ceiling below
the cabin. Their elongated, inch-long rectangular bodies and thin legs gave
them a somewhat sinister look. I saw no webs, but perhaps they needed
none, because with surprising agility, they sprinted aggressively after anything within reach. *Now I definitely appreciate the mosquito nets.*

The swift, dark river below the cabin was the perfect place to cool off
after the steamy jungle humidity. Everyone went swimming, but Holdridge

cautioned us to stay close to shore to avoid being swept downstream by the swift current.

Then the professors relaxed, watching us make dinner. Some oversight might have been helpful; someone placed our large chunk of frozen meat outside on a tree stump to thaw, and despite the noise of thirteen of us moving around the cabin, within minutes, a sizeable passing carnivore walked off with an easy dinner. Whether a large jaguar, panther, or puma, it was stealthy and unafraid.

After our meatless meal, we sat outside on log stumps in the small clearing, relaxing and enjoying the absence of civilization. As dusk fell, the jungle came alive with grunts, clicks, croaks, humming, and an occasional wild cry. A chorus of insects, frogs, and other animals serenaded us in stereo. Stars twinkled on in the clear, jet-black sky. Without interference from city lights, it looked like a giant hand had flung a shaker of diamonds across a velvet sheet. The astonishing number of stars elicited amazement from a few city types who, to my surprise, had never seen a completely dark night sky.

As we sat enjoying the relaxed, peaceful atmosphere and jungle ambiance, Clint's roommate Mike, who seemed uneasy with silence, picked up the guitar that accompanied him everywhere and began strumming and singing folk songs. I enjoyed them in the pension, but here it was annoying. *Just for once, can't we dispense with the noise of civilization?* It completely changed the ambiance, silenced the animals and the conversation, and turned the jungle experience into just another campout.

His playing ended abruptly when Antonio, a shy, handsome Costa Rican university student, jumped up from his stump with a painful cry and doubled over, moaning in agony. *A snake*, I thought at first. Searching around his stump with the lantern, Dr. Tosi found the culprit: a giant black ant, over an inch long, with formidable, oversized jaws. This introduced us to *Paraponera clavata*, the giant "bullet ant" famous for having the world's most painful insect sting. It's so-named because victims compare the sting to the pain of a gunshot. After biting the victim, then it adds insult to injury by twisting its abdomen around and simultaneously stinging it. The pain can last for 24 hours, and severe reactions may even require hospitalization.

Paraponera's enormous size distinguishes it from other Central American ants; it's second only to the giant Amazonian ants, which reach an incredible 1.6 inches. Paraponera tends to be a solitary forager but, leaving nothing to chance, while the professors looked for something to help Antonio, the rest of us jumped up to check around our stumps for ants. The ant killed the mood. We retired to enclose ourselves in the hammock cocoons for the night. We didn't see Antonio the rest of the trip.

At 5:30 a.m., I awakened to an avian concert in full voice. The first awake, I stood at the railing on the small front porch overlooking the river, absorbing a magical scene that etched itself in my memory. The morning breeze still held vestiges of scent from night-blooming flowers, and large flocks of noisy birds filled the sky, swooping and darting, circling back and forth across the river in the cool, misty pre-dawn glow, calling joyously to each other. Dozens of green, red, yellow, and blue *Amazona* parrots flew up and down the river, screeching loudly back and forth. A vast flock of colorful toucans wheeled and circled above the cabin, their oversized yellow and black beaks looking so top-heavy that their flight seemed miraculous. The entire jungle was singing, participating in a riotous celebration of life. A line from an old Sunday School hymn floated to mind: *"All nature sings, and round me rings, the music of the spheres."*[4]

As the first rays of orange tropical sun cleared the horizon, melting away a lingering mist and illuminating the towering tops of the 200-foot Ceiba (kapok) trees on the opposite side of the river, the sky exploded into molten gold. The gigantic Ceibas, with their massive buttress roots, conveyed such a prehistoric feeling I half expected to see a group of pterodactyls come flying over the trees. *This is how Eden must have looked.* It's hard to find God in the city bustle of a concrete jungle, but He feels very close in the raw wilderness. Perhaps that's why I felt so at home in the Glen Ellyn field.

By 5:45, everyone was awake. One at a time, yawning people in rumpled clothes emerged from their net cocoons, toothbrushes and towels in hand, and trudged to the outhouse to prepare for the day. *They missed the best show of the day.*

The jungle began only steps behind the cabin. A small opening in the wall of lush vegetation marked a narrow trail. A few steps down the trail transported us into a multiple-layered world of dense vegetation filled with tangled, twining vines, large, epiphytic-laden trees, and broad-leaved plants. Trees dripped with mosses, lichens, and bromeliads of every variety, flourishing in the high humidity.

In retrospect, La Selva was probably both jungle and rainforest. Costa Rica has both types of forest, and often the two are found close together. In rainforests, the thick canopy blocks most natural light, and most of the life lives in the treetops. In contrast, jungles have more vegetative undergrowth.

The vegetation was fascinating. Twenty-foot tree-fern trunks resembled palm trees but supported heavy, six-foot fern fronds. Thick, two-inch diameter woody vines climbed high into the trees, vying for their share of light. A strangler fig, looking like an alien species from a sci-fi movie, surrounded its host tree with heavy vine-like branches that constricted its growth and shaded the host's canopy with its foliage. It also competed with the tree's root system and would eventually kill the host plant. Once the host rotted away, the fig branches remained upright, forming a tall, cylindrical lattice-work basket.

The biodiversity overwhelmed me. Exotic plants of all kinds grew in dense profusion, everything oversized. I recognized some species grown in Chicago as houseplants, but here they seemed on steroids. Chicago's four-inch philodendron leaves grew a foot long, and poinsettias reached ten to fifteen feet high. Dense, layered vegetation of every size and type, permitted only filtered sunlight to penetrate down to the trail. Things decayed so quickly in this dim and humid environment that little decaying matter littered the ground. A somewhat damp, earthy smell permeated everything.

During the day, except for an occasional bird call, chattering monkey, or buzzing insect, the jungle remained surprisingly silent.

The trunks of the majestic Ceiba trees, *Ceiba pentandra,* are awesome when seen up close. The straight gray trunks reach 10 or more feet in diameter and 230 feet in height. Most of their branches grow near the top of the tree, and often trunks rise 100 feet before the first branches appear. Ceibas project high above the other trees, looking like vast leafy jungle umbrellas. Massive buttress roots attach high up on the trunk and extend out from the tree in all directions, supporting the tree.

Once thinking I heard a torrential rainstorm pelting the treetops, I looked up to see a cloudless sky, and realized perhaps there's an additional reason this is often called a "rain forest." It's not only the amount of actual rain; it's the sound. Stagnant water from the previous night's rain dripped down through thousands of treetops, vines, and branches, slowly rolling, dripping from layer to leafy layer, toward the ground. Multiplied by thousands of drops, it sounded like a torrential rainstorm.

Holdridge experimented growing local crops in small patches around the jungle. He grew guava, banana, papaya, lemon, cacao, and coconut trees, and small plots of pineapple, pejibaye, chayote, yuca, and ipecac.

"Scrounge for lunch," he said.

I grabbed a guava from an overgrown guava tree, and ate half of it. *This is softer than I expected. I wonder if it's overripe?* I looked closely at the remaining half. I knew it had many tiny seeds, but these seemed to be moving. I peered closer. Appalled, I realized that what I first thought to be small black seeds were actually the black eyes of small, white grubs. The remaining halves of dozens of them, writhing in death throes, stared accusingly at me. That did it. Discarding the guava, I looked for some bananas. I haven't cared for guavas since.

I found the small cacao tree the most interesting of all the crops because large ovoid ribbed pods grow directly off the tree trunk and lower branches. The young green, red or purplish pods turn orange or yellow when ripe, and pods in all stages of ripeness grow on the tree at once, making it quite colorful. Each pod contains 20-40 large black seeds, the raw material for chocolate.

The attraction of this fruit wasn't the bitter seeds but the slimy whitish pulp surrounding them. Although not visually appealing, the first taste hooked me. The strong taste was very unusual. It had no comparison. I could only describe it as "sharply tropical, neither sweet nor sour." *I could eat a lot of this,* I thought.

Noting my enthusiasm, Holdridge cautioned me. "You want to take it easy with those; they're mildly addictive." I could understand that. The pulp tasted better than chocolate.

The next day, taking machetes and sack lunches in our day packs, we set on a day-hike to learn survival skills. We learned to find stored water inside the hollow bejuco, a large woody climbing vine. We learned which plants were edible, which to avoid, and how to climb, harvest, and open coconuts. If desperate enough, we could also eat termites.

The numerous giant termite mounds were hard to miss. They jutted skyward like tall, red-clay stalagmites. Dr. Tosi poked at a mound with a stick, and seething masses of brown winged termites boiled out. I felt itchy just watching them. *At least my mouthful of guava grubs was soft; a mouthful of fat bodies with fluttering wings and scratchy feet would be unbearable.* Everyone opted to pass on termites except Tom. Seeming to enjoy an audience, he popped a live wiggling termite in his mouth, chewed a bit, and pronounced it good. I wasn't that hungry.

We surprised a large gray, black, and brownish *colmenero*, or giant anteater, *Myrmecophaga sp.*, having lunch amid a group of ten-foot mounds. His sharp four-inch claws were ripping into one of the massive termite mounds. The very odd and elongated, cone-like snout, long tongue, and sticky saliva allowed him to rapidly lick up the frenzied escapees. He could consume up to 35,000 live termites or ants a day. *How does it feel to have a stomach full of biting ants or live wiggling termites? And how long does it take before they succumb to gastric juices? He must have a stomach of steel.*

The whole animal looked strange. With a disproportionately large, bushy tail and long-haired legs, he shuffled along, looking somewhat like a moving haystack. His weird cone-shaped head was so odd I wanted to laugh in disbelief; he looked like a cartoon character.

Hearing our approach, the anteater turned to face us, reared up on his hind legs, and using his muscular tail to balance, spread his arms out as if in welcome. *I assume this is a warning posture, to make himself look large and ferocious.* He didn't need to worry. Giant anteaters are already sizeable; they reach eight feet from the tip of the snout to the tip of the tail. Although their claws are impressive, anteaters aren't particularly aggressive, so the scare posture didn't work.

Half an hour later, we heard grunting and barking noises and rounded a bend in the trail to face a herd of white-lipped peccaries, or javelinas, rooting in the soil for roots or grubs. Their sharp straight tusks make them the most dangerous of the peccaries, so we stopped and began backing off, but seeing our superior numbers, they turned and stampeded off into the undergrowth.

Costa Rica has thousands of ant species. I found the leafcutter ants the most interesting. Long processions of thousands marched single-file across the ground, each ant holding a large swaying piece of leaf several times larger than itself and up to thirty times its weight. They carried the leaf pieces vertically over their backs, and from a distance, they appeared like an armada of tiny green sailboats moving silently along the forest floor. So many ants walked the same winding path, they had worn a thin shallow trail into the dirt.

They don't eat the leaves; they carry the leaf pieces back to their ant-hill, storing them in underground chambers and using them as a mulch to farm fungus, the ant's primary food. Like other social insects, leafcutters have specialized functions; some stand guard, some cut leaves, and others inject the leaves with a secretion that digests the leaves and helps grow the edible fungus.

We learned to avoid a thin tree with thousands of fat black conical thorns encircling the trunk. The thorns caught our attention, but thousands of almost invisible tiny stinging fire ants swarm on these trees, and brushing carelessly against the tree invites a swarm of ants up your sleeves and down your shirt, their bites more painful than the thorns. I made a mental note to remember that tree.

Army ants made my skin crawl. I assumed they were a single species, but actually there are about 200 species of army ants, all predatory and nomadic. Unlike other ants, they have no permanent nests. They have with oversized jaws, and forage in large, shiny and aggressive seething masses, overpowering anything in their path by their sheer numbers. A slow death, being eaten alive by thousands of painful bites, seems particularly horrible; I pitied any animal that stumbled into their midst.

After our fascinating, although simple, jungle introduction, returning to the office was a let-down. This trip might be the anthropology students' only jungle exposure, but I expected to spend extensive time in the jungle. I boarded the dugout returning downriver to civilization, anxious to finalize my project and begin a more immersive and in-depth experience. I mentally checked #10, Experience a Tropical Rainforest, off my goal list.

On this sanitized trip, except for *Paraponera*, the peccaries, and our dinner-eater, we'd encountered nothing overly hazardous. But once I began spending time alone in the jungle, everyone warned me about various large and small dangers, and I would soon meet many of them. Holdridge was doing some unspecified jungle research, and we would spend much of the next ten months in diverse jungles and life zones all around the country.

- Nine -

Girl with a Net

Jungles 1964-1965

B ACK IN THE OFFICE, WE FINALIZED OUR PROJECT PRO-posals. Mine would connect with Holdridge's Life Zone model, the work making him famous in ecological circles. The model classified the earth into regions, or life zones, based on the mean annual temperature, relative humidity, and evapotranspiration, and also factored in altitude zones from alpine to lowland and latitudes from polar to tropical. Costa Rica contains eleven life zones, with names like Tropical Wet, Premontane Rain, Tropical Dry, and Low Montane Wet, and I would visit them all.

Holdridge deftly manipulated me toward dragonflies while making it appear to be my choice. I would collect and identify as many dragonfly species as possible from each life zone and obtain behavioral, environmental, and life zone information for each species. On the surface, it appeared to be a simple collection project. I didn't understand exactly how it connected to the life zone model; it felt like I lacked a piece of information.

Holdridge's contacts at the University and National Museum referred me to Dr. Thomas Donnelley, an entomologist at Rice University, who agreed to assist me with the taxonomy, a tedious process based mainly on wing venation patterns. I agreed to send a set of specimens to him for verification and another to Dr. Oliver Flint at the Smithsonian Institution. It surprised me the Smithsonian was interested. Dr. Tosi gave me his old tennis racket frame to make a net, and I set up a killing jar.

Perhaps because the American group had no other biologists, two Costa Rican university students joined us in the office. They also had collection projects. Elena, a tall and striking girl, collected tree ferns. She was feminine and seemed to tire easily, and I couldn't envision her having the mindset or stamina to carry around a heavy plant press through the jungle alone. Antonio caught geckos. Now recovered from his ant bite, he could lie motionless behind a log in the forest for hours, patiently holding a string, enticing geckos to enter his trap.

Summers roaming the 1950s Glen Ellyn fields catching bugs and butterflies made me comfortable with both my project and working alone in the jungle, but the Costa Rican jungle bore little resemblance to the sunny Glen Ellyn field. The jungle was a dark, steamy, humid, and complex ecosystem of dense vegetation, mud, rivers, impenetrable swamps, and streams. Almost everything in it seemed hostile. People continually warned me about everything from the impressive numbers of poisonous snakes, fifteen-foot crocodiles, and six-foot caiman, to jaguars, panthers, and pumas. Even bull sharks came up rivers at high tide. There were small things too: scorpions and spiders, army ants, ticks, leeches, hairy chiggers, biting flies, stinging insects, and swarming gnats. Mosquitoes transmitted various diseases, including malaria, dengue, yellow, and zika fevers. Plants were poisonous and carnivorous or filled with thorns and spines. Millipedes squirted poison, and even pretty, tiny frogs were poisonous.

With so many big things I could choose to worry about, except for taking malaria pills, I gave minimal thought to the parasites, insect-borne, and water-borne diseases. I worried more about getting lost. *Perhaps Dad was right to be concerned, but I still think his buying life insurance was a bit excessive.*

I worked alone, with only my machete for company, so Holdridge warned me about animals he had barely mentioned when the group visited La Selva. He was most concerned about venomous snakes. Twenty-three of Costa Rica's 162 known snakes were venomous, and at least 55 snake species called La Selva home.

"Keep a lookout on the ground, but watch overhanging branches because many snakes are arboreal," he said. He seemed particularly concerned about bushmasters, *terciopelos* or fer-de-lance, and cobras.

The Central American bushmaster, *Lachesis stenophrys*, the world's largest pit viper and the longest venomous snake in the Western hemisphere, reaches over twelve feet in length. Pit vipers have a heat-detecting pit between each eye and nostril. This bushmaster is particularly frightening because it can sense its victims by heat and is known to stalk people through the jungle. It tends to strike several times in succession, and even a juvenile's bite has a 75 percent mortality rate. I never saw one but, once, I heard something rustling behind me in the undergrowth, that seemed to be following my movements. With thoughts of bushmasters, I sped up.

People warned me most about the fer-de-lance, or terciopelo, *Bothrops asper*, another pit viper, considered to be the most dangerous Central American snake. *Terciopelo* means "velvet" in Spanish, and the pretty dark patches and cream-colored crisscross lines look almost velvety, but its sizeable triangular head and large eyes with vertical slit pupils, look alien and menacing. Its wicked-looking, nearly inch-long fangs, inject a rapidly acting, highly-toxic venom that includes anti-coagulants and digestive enzymes, so bite victims have little time to find help. It's aggressive and edgy, and where other snakes might feel threatened and run, the terciopelo often attacks.

I've never been particularly afraid of snakes, but the aggression of bushmasters and terciopelos was disturbing. I had to wait for a trip to Osa to actually meet the cobra.

We students traveled almost continually around Costa Rica, using Land Rovers, buses, trains, and *avionetas*, or light aircraft. Often several of us traveled together to share lodging and transportation. We never knew where we would stay or how long, so we learned to expect the unexpected, and to always threw a change of clothes into a bag before going anywhere.

We splurged on first-class tickets for longer train rides, because the cracked leather seats felt more comfortable than the hard wooden second-class seats. Train windows were always open, and the trains limped and creaked slowly along at 20 mph, stopping at every two-house "village" along the track. Trains never announced stops, and most places lacked signs, so we were continually having to ask ask people where we were.

At every stop, hordes of vendors jumped on, and rapidly swarmed the length of the train, selling everything from drinks, candy, fried bananas, French fries, and single cigarettes to sticks of gum, and handicrafts of every description. At the next stop, they all abruptly hopped off and caught the next train returning in the opposite direction, while a new group of vendors boarded the train to continue forward to an additional stop. The only way to avoid their annoying, non-stop solicitations was to pretend to sleep. I tried to avoid their eyes, but even glancing out the window invited a swarm of people to rush over and thrust their wares up to the open window, waving them pleadingly in my face.

I often accompanied Holdridge to obscure jungle locations to catch dragonflies while he disappeared to collect data he never shared much about. I stayed at any available lodging, from logging camps on the Osa and Nicoya peninsulas to various OTS jungle camps and La Selva. Sometimes I found a comfortable spot at Tres Rios coffee or Dole banana plantations, or less frequently, at private homes. On other occasions when things went sideways, I spent numerous stints in dingy flea-infested hostels, several nights in an abandoned schoolhouse, and even a night in a brothel.

I always enjoyed my time at La Selva, exploring the humid jungle and swimming in the river. After dinner, Holdridge and I played chess by lanternlight until bedtime. He played far better than I, and used established chess strategies I vaguely recognized, but my advantage was in having no standard system. It made my moves unpredictable and unexpected, so often we ended up tied.

When the office shut down for *Semana Santa*, or Holy Week, he invited me to join his wife, Clara, and youngest son, Greg, at La Selva for the holiday. Clara was a good cook, and it would be an opportunity for some relaxation, good food, company, and extended catching. I spent the days in the jungle looking for dragonflies and trying not to bushwhack too far off the narrow trails, because it would be so easy to get lost. It was also a chance to see Clint, who had been living at Hunter's farm for weeks, fattening pigs on jungle roots.

After a couple of days, Holdridge asked, "Have you found the swamp yet?"

I hadn't, so getting directions, I grabbed my machete, net, and killing jar and headed down a narrow trail I'd never noticed. Off to one side, a glimmer of sunlight through the dense vegetation promised fewer trees, indicating a swamp. I veered off the path. Tall reeds and grasses began replacing the trees, but it was dry season, and fortunately the swamp had little ponded water.

Holdridge talked a lot about snakes, but hadn't mentioned spiders. I plowed through the tall stiff grass, and almost at once, spied a new dragonfly larger than most, zipping over the tall grasses. Its remarkable speed and large territory made catching it a challenge. As it sped past, forgetting any other animals, I mindlessly barreled through the reeds and grasses, net in the air, oblivious to my surroundings, trying to keep up with it.

Just when I thought it would escape, it stopped abruptly, landing atop a tall grass stem. Finally, I had my chance. What a beauty! Its widely spaced eyes identified it as *Gomphidae,* a new family for me. I'd already sent 150 dragonflies to the Smithsonian, but this one would excite Dr. Flint.

Dragonflies' large compound eyes are marvelous. They see colors beyond human capabilities, including ultraviolet light, and each eye has several thousand facets, allowing them to sense movement from all angles at once. They were difficult to approach, because a dragonfly could watch me even when I was behind it; I needed to sneak up on this one carefully. As I looked around, gauging the best angle of approach, I realized a giant black tarantula hung motionless, perhaps a foot below it, on the same grass stalk. The dragonfly appeared unaware of its peril; apparently, it didn't worry about non-moving objects. I stared at the dragonfly, willing it to stay put while I evaluated how to catch it without including the spider in the net.

Tarantulas, the world's largest spiders, always look sinister because their slow and deliberate movements make them appear to be stalking something. Although only mildly venomous, they have fangs and bite. I suspected they could move quickly if they wanted to.

Spiders had never been my favorite animal. I still cringed, remembering sixth grade, when one of my long braids fell into my terrarium, and a giant garden spider seized the opportunity to stage an escape. It ran up the braid and onto my head with such speed and agility I didn't even notice it. It wasn't until I felt it roaming through my hair that I knew where it had gone. Although I collected them, that killed any desire I might have had for a more intimate acquaintance.

As I looked around for the best angle to approach the dragonfly, I realized that in my rush I had charged right into the middle of a tarantula clutter. That was unexpected. I'd never seen more than one tarantula at once. *I thought tarantulas were solitary, but at least here, they look gregarious.* I counted at least eight velvety, palm-sized spiders, and couldn't help marveling at their range of colors, from black, brown, tan, and even rust, to multi-color. They were spaced fairly evenly in an eight-foot diameter circle. And I was smack in the middle.

All were at attention and on full alert after my blundering entrance. Most tarantulas have eight eyes, and I could feel all sixty-four shiny black eyes swiveling, following my every movement.

Each spider hung motionless about chest height on its private grass stem, where, until I came along, it waited for an unsuspecting meal to come within reach. I felt a twinge of regret. The spider on the stem with "my" dragonfly probably felt elated at the prospect of a meal. Now I was about to dash his hopes.

Then a thought distracted me. *Surely, all the spiders in the swamp aren't only right here? Maybe I crashed through many of them, during my mad dash through the grass?* This thought diverted my attention from the dragonfly, and I stopped to check and ensure none clung to me. The body parts I could see looked spider-free.

Then another thought. *Some spiders can jump fifty times their body length. Do tarantulas jump?* Not much, I assumed, but my priority shifted from catching the dragonfly to exiting the circle.

The tarantulas sat spaced at about two-foot intervals, almost as if they maintained territories. I wondered how I had even entered the group without knocking some from the grass. *Or maybe I did, and now they're on the ground?* I checked the trampled grass but saw none.

They were hanging too close together for me to exit the group without brushing a spider stalk. *Somehow, I'll have to move a spider.* All I had was a net, and I didn't want to catch one. I tried using the net to push aside a spider stalk, but it didn't create enough passage space. I needed two hands. After several tries, I moved one spider-laden grass stalk to the side with my net and gingerly reached out to the adjacent spider stem. With my hand only a few inches above him on the stalk, I silently messaged the spider: *I am harmless; stay put and ignore my hand*, as I moved his stalk and squeezed out sideways between the two without dislodging either spider.

Once outside the group, I turned to look back for an alternate route to my dragonfly. All spiders except one still hung motionless. On the far side of the circle, my dragonfly and his spider were both missing. He must have pounced on it when my exit distracted the dragonfly. With regret, I realized I had missed the drama. He either jumped the short distance or produced a quick burst of speed. Either way, he was fast. If I couldn't have it, I hoped the spider enjoyed his lunch.

We often saw cattle and horses in the countryside, their bodies covered in raised circular bumps holding subcutaneous parasitic larvae called torsolo worms. Someone told us they had to be removed by winding them around a stick, but it sounded bizarre, and I couldn't visualize how that would work.

Although torsolos can be painful, they're generally considered harmless but, whatever they were, I certainly wasn't interested in hosting one. One morning, I awoke with a red dime-sized bump on my forehead. It grew larger and more tender by the day. Everyone watched with fascination as the lump grew taller, redder, and more prominent. When it approached the size of a split ping-pong ball, several of us became convinced I had a torsolo. The thought of a maggot living in my forehead required action.

I didn't understand how the stick worked, so I decided to slit open the bump with a razor blade and force it out. Liz, Mike, and Clint all crowded around to watch. Staring at the mirror, I carefully slit through the skin and watched as a flat light-colored ribbon-like thing slowly emerged. *A flatworm? Somehow, I expected a nematode.* I figured it would be long and thin if you were supposed to wind it around a stick. Then the 'worm' broke apart. It turned out to be a massive accumulation of very thick pus. I had a giant infection. Later I heard there was a common infection often mistaken for a torsolo, and that's what I had.

We all felt slightly disappointed.

Perhaps some misinformed person had confused torsolos with guinea worms, which are about the thickness of an angel hair pasta and up to a meter in length. Doctors remove Guinea worms by winding them around a stick, somewhat similar to reeling in a fish, but supposedly they aren't present in Costa Rica. Today I wonder if perhaps torsolos were actually botflies. The stick remains a mystery to me.

Meanwhile in the States, my friend Brenda and my cousin Gaile were taking entomology classes. Both wrote asking me to send them specimens, so I began collecting other insects. An American girl with a net sparked curiosity, and no matter where I went, I attracted a crowd of curious people asking questions. I often acquired an instant army of helpers who scurried around finding exciting things to show me, telling me where to look, and bringing me jars of amazing things I would never find on my own.

One brought some dead, two-inch, white cave cockroaches. Flat and round, they looked like miniature frisbees. In fact, they 'flew' well; I once caught two idiots tossing one around in the office. Another brought me a colorful, striped, armor-plated millipede, half an inch wide and four inches long. Millipedes are arthropods, not insects, and this species had the bonus of being poisonous. When threatened, it would curl into a ball and secrete a liquid containing hydrogen cyanide and benzaldehyde.

A gas station owner took me to see an oversized, multicolored Harlequin beetle, *Acrocinus longimanus*, easily the most striking insect I've ever seen.

It's beautiful, but not one of nature's best-designed bugs. The three-inch-long, inch-wide body has an elaborate black, red, and tan design, and two four-inch, stick-like legs longer than the body itself, extend stiffly out in front like robotic arms. Fortunately, it's a sap eater, so it doesn't need to move quickly. The front legs are so large and unwieldy that even lifting them to walk must require significant effort. I just picked it up, afraid my net might break it.

A rural school teacher gave me the carapace a colossal rhinoceros, beetle, *Megasoma elephas*, the size of a tangerine and a massive curved horn used for fighting. These beetles can weigh up to an ounce, and if you include the horn, measure up to five inches in length. The carapace is thick and tough, and its weight limits it to short ungainly flights. I've heard hitting one while driving can crack the windshield. Unfortunately, today they are scarce due to habitat loss and collectors (guilty as charged.)

Señor Martinez, an Alajuela dairy farmer and excited closet biologist, invited Antonio, Elena, and me to his farm. He helped Elena cut tree ferns, showed Antonio how to catch rodents, and insisted he could show me where to find dragonflies. I wanted to look near standing water in his open pasture, but he said he knew a better location and took me into the deep jungle. I tried not to show my frustration, but I expected fewer dragonflies there.

Just when I sensed we were wasting our time, I glimpsed a group of four beautiful navy, powder blue, and white butterflies flying in synchronized formation. Moving closer, I realized they weren't butterflies, but four gigantic striped wings, attached to a long, disproportionate five-inch blue body, thinner than the diameter of a pipe cleaner. The long dangling body drooped when it flew and appeared so delicate and fragile, I feared it would break in two.

Both dragonflies and damselflies, a close dragonfly relative, typically flutter their wings rapidly, almost like hummingbirds. The eight-inch wingspan of this insect made rapid fluttering difficult, and often it appeared to almost flap its wings, more like a bird. It flew only a few short yards at a time before alighting again, seemingly exhausted by the effort.

Señor Martinez became so excited he grabbed the net right out of my hand, leaving me standing net-less in frustration as he charged after it through the jungle. It looked so fragile I feared he would damage it, but he managed to catch it intact and brought it back proudly, like a hunter who had bagged a prize lion.

When sitting, dragonflies hold their wings out horizontally, while damselflies, their close relatives, typically fold their wings vertically above their bodies. This insect landed with horizontal wings. Entranced by the size, it was ten minutes before I realized it wasn't a dragonfly, but *Megaloprepus caerulatus,* a member of the world's largest damselfly species. I didn't see a single dragonfly on his farm, but *Megaloprepus* made up for not spending time in his pasture.

The biggest problem came from the smallest of creatures. The Organization for Tropical Studies (OTS) was camping in a remote premontane rainforest in Tapantí, near Panama, and I drove out with two new second-semester students, Dennis and Steve, to join them for a few days. Our group lacked equipment for overnight in-jungle trips, but OTS was well supplied with extra canvas tents, mosquito nets, and comfortable cots. The mixed group of older men and post-docs seemed very serious about their work but said little about their projects, and often disappeared into the jungle for long stretches.

Dr. Paul Slud, a renowned bird expert, was classifying bird species. I stopped to watch him string fine, almost invisible, mesh nets across the main flight pathways. He had chosen the location well, and the net began capturing a constant stream of birds almost immediately. When a bird flew through and became entangled, he carefully extricated, weighed, measured, took photos and notes, and released it. I thought it might be a good dragonfly location too, so I soon took my net and disappeared.

OTS didn't bring meat, so everyone was pleased when one of the hunters shot a tepezcuintle because it meant meat for dinner. Tepezcuintle, *Cuniculus paca,* is a large spotted rat-like rodent looking somewhat like a giant guinea pig. It can reach 26 pounds, and we had a big one for dinner that night. It tasted, as many things do, more or less like chicken. Later I kicked myself. *I should have asked for the skull.*

Dinner came. OTS opened up comfortable canvas folding chairs and sat in front of their tents to eat. Without chairs, the three of us sat on a large mossy log, discussing the day and enjoying a hot meal of rice, tepezcuintle stew, chayote, and beans. We relaxed in the advancing dusk, enjoying the campfire and the beginning of the nightly jungle chorus, when Dennis broke the mood. "Something's making me really itchy," he said, and began scratching frantically.

Almost on cue, all three of us began itching. The more we scratched, the more unbearable the itching became. My stomach and back felt on fire, a stinging torment as if we'd fallen on an anthill. Army ants came to mind. We looked for the source but saw no ants, mosquitoes, or flies. At that point, we should have had the brains to move off the log.

Sitting comfortably bite-free on their canvas chairs, OTS watched our frantic scratching with amusement but offered no assistance. *I bet they're thinking "greenhorns."* We might have expected something to be living in the log but, given the number of insects on the ground, the log seemed to be a more comfortable alternative. Initially, I thought lugging camp chairs into the jungle was ridiculous, but it had paid off.

Dennis pulled up his shirt and checked his stomach with a flashlight. Dozens of rapidly swelling red bumps encircled his waist. Close examination showed a small red dot in the center of each bump. Chiggers! They feed on skin, injecting digestive enzymes into the skin to break down the cells, and then they burrow in, leaving a small hole.

Thousands of almost microscopic bright red larval mites infested the log. They obviously thought us very attractive, and a silent army of them had discovered us with surprising rapidity. I could imagine them saying, "Wow! Three big buffet tables came right to our log." Everyone's itching seemed synchronized, so they had probably arrived *en masse* but, surprisingly, no one had felt either their climbing or their initial bites.

Desperate to stop the intense itching, we ran to search our bags, and smeared ourselves with everything from suntan lotion and lip balm to alcohol, but nothing worked. In desperation, thinking a paste might block the hole and cut off the chiggers' oxygen supply, I grabbed my tube of Maclean's toothpaste and smeared it on the bites. To my surprise, the itching stopped almost immediately. We slathered it on each other, using up most of the tube. We smelled like a perfume shop, but once we wore rings of toothpaste around our waists, the itching stopped, so we had a bragging contest to see who had the most bites. I found over 600 chiggers in a solid ring around my waist, the majority concentrated underneath the elastic waistband of my underwear. And I wasn't the winner.

I didn't care for Maclean's; it reminded me of Vick's VapoRub every time I brushed my teeth. But the local *farmacia* sold nothing else. The chiggers didn't seem to like it any better than I did, so I thought Maclean's would have great success marketed as an itch-reducing medication. I even wrote Maclean's a letter for fun, extolling its capabilities. They never responded.

After returning to San José, I stocked up on toothpaste because I was preparing to go into Costa Rica's deepest jungle, and wanted to be ready for more chiggers. However, I would discover Osa had many larger critters to worry about.

- *Ten* -

Disappearing Jungle

<u>Osa Peninsula 1965</u>

HOLDRIDGE AND I EXCHANGED UNEASY GLANCES IN the back seat of an avioneta as we plummeted into another air pocket. "I've never seen it this rough," he said, his words clipped and face strained. In 1965, a trip to the Osa Peninsula by jeep took seventeen uncomfortable hours over bumpy, dusty roads along the southern coast near Panama. In contrast, an avioneta took less than an hour, so we took the plane. Usually, the ride was uneventful, but today the turbulence thrust and lofted us violently upward one moment and plunged us down into air pockets the next. I tightened my seatbelt as we slid sideways, wind buffeting us like a kite in a windstorm.

Our pilot Max, white-knuckled at the wheel, eyes glued to the windshield, yelled over his shoulder, "Our elevation is dropping two-hundred feet one moment and bouncing upward one-hundred feet the next." He appeared unflappable but, perhaps hoping for the winds to die back, on the spur of the moment, he said, "Let's stop at my house for coffee," and landed on a field beside his house for an unscheduled break. We recovered with coffee and biscuits, waiting until the wind abated. Then we reboarded the avioneta and continued to our destination, a logging camp carved out of dense virgin Tropical Wet rainforest in the roadless wilderness of the Osa Peninsula.

This maze of dense and untamed rainforest, swamps, and rivers held the wettest, wildest jungle I worked in. Costa Rica has some of the most extraordinary biodiversity in the world, with over 500,000 wildlife species, and Osa is one of the particularly rich areas. Many of its species, from large cats like the jaguar, puma, and panther, to bull sharks and sea snakes, were hostile. It had the country's largest concentration of venomous snakes and crocodiles.

Holdridge bunked with the loggers in the primitive company barracks at the logging camp. "There's no more room in the barracks, but I'm leaving for a few days. You can stay at my house," the field boss said. *I bet the real reason isn't lack of space, but that the camp doesn't accommodate women.*

I had the house to myself for several days, except for the 13-year-old daughter and her giant red macaw. It surprised me the boss would leave his teenage daughter alone in a logging camp full of men, but then I realized perhaps Holdridge had timed our trip on purpose, so I had a place to stay, and she had company.

Logging was obviously big business. Despite being in the middle of nowhere, the unremarkable white tropical-style house had the only bathtub I ever saw in Costa Rica, a Stateside spring mattress, and even the latest avocado-colored refrigerator. The quiet house felt creepy at night, and I found it hard to sleep because I heard someone walking outside the house every night. I felt uneasy until the last night, when I realized the camp boss probably felt he had to provide us guards. What a nuisance for him.

After dinner, we had a special treat: a movie. Many workers had never seen a movie before, and excitement ran high. They didn't know the title but assured me it would be fantastic and begged me to stay up; I couldn't miss it. I tried to decline but, not wanting to deflate their excitement, I relented, found a stump, and sat down to watch, naively hoping I hadn't already seen it.

Excitement mounted. Conversation buzzed as someone brought out a portable projector with a large film reel, hung a sheet up on a tree for a screen, and started the projector. I needn't have worried about having seen the movie; it was a 45-minute black and white film on good logging practices. I should have known. I dozed off halfway through, but everyone else clapped loudly at the end and discussed it with excitement.

During the day, the unrelenting churning and grinding of bulldozers, loaders, and trucks, the high-pitched whine of chainsaws, and the rattle of chains and shouting voices filled the camp, a jarring contrast to the jungle tranquility. I wasn't allowed around the active logging, so I went to the newly logged areas, where new clearings attracted dragonflies.

Once, wanting to experience this diverse primeval ecosystem, I wandered off in the opposite direction from the logging, bushwhacked a small opening in the thick wall of vegetation, and struggled inside. Perhaps six feet in, dense vegetation already obscured the camp. *It would be so simple to get turned around within a few feet.* Carefully noting my entrance point, I edged in another ten feet. Untouched, natural complexity and diversity abounded. *There must be hundreds of species here still undiscovered by modern science and National Geographic. Could I be the first person ever to set foot in this spot?* Probably not, but it seemed easy to imagine.

The vegetation absorbed sound like a sponge, almost muting the sounds of churning bulldozers and whining saws. *If lost in here, how loud would a person need to scream to get rescued, assuming anyone was even listening?*

The jungle hummed and pulsed with life. *It's almost as if God's heartbeat throbs inside His creation.* It was always easier to sense Him away from civilization. Wanting to savor the moment, I remained motionless as life continued around me, oblivious to my presence. I watched and listened, letting myself become one with it. A poison dart frog, bright red with blue legs, stalked a bug; an animal cry echoed in the treetops; a bird hopped branch to branch; a parade of leaf cutter ants marched single file, carrying large leaf pieces to a nearby anthill; a few butterflies flitted through the vegetation, and flying insects buzzed from leaf to leaf.

Every time I'm here they're opening a new area. When will they stop? Will they continue until they log everything? What prevents them from logging the entire rainforest? All to enrich a few people, while the world loses a priceless and vital ecosystem.

Jungles and rainforests are the terrestrial equivalents of coral reefs in diversity; there must have been dozens of species within a few feet. Destroying this irreplaceable virgin habitat to benefit a few people harvesting logs, clearing for farmland, or making charcoal, was an unimaginable tragedy, hard to contemplate.

Eventually, I picked my way back to the entry point and exited into the clearing. The dense jungle supported such a diversity of life, but I saw few dragonflies. *They seem to like more open areas. Perhaps I'll have more luck on the new road.*

As I strolled along a new road the bulldozer had crudely slashed through the jungle only hours before, my eyes focused more on the air than the road. I didn't see the snake. Or rather, I didn't recognize it. I was vaguely aware of a thin, five-foot blackish branch on the road but I either stepped on it or kicked it without changing stride.

A loud hiss made me jump back. In a split second, the 'branch' coiled itself together, reared up an angry flat head two feet from my leg, and flared out a bright scarlet cobra hood. Locking its eyes on mine, it bared two impressive fangs and began weaving its flat head back and forth and side to side, following my movements. This snake was furious. I understood. *I would be furious too, if something big stepped on me as I was peacefully sunbathing on the road.*

The red warning coloration was so startling and unexpected that adrenalin and flight reflexes took over. I irrationally sprinted a few yards down the road, heart pounding.

One of the nearby loggers looked up. "Que pasa?"

"Pisé una cobra."

Unfortunately, instead of asking, "Were you bitten?" he grabbed a machete, ran up the road, and hacked it to pieces. I should have realized he would kill it, and not told him, but he was also protecting the loggers moving around the area. Sadly, once humans begin to interact with the jungle, it never remains the same for long. The road had been open only a few hours, and we had already killed something.

The cobra may have been relatively rare; I wish I had saved it to show Holdridge. I've researched it a bit since, and the closest I've seen to it is a picture on Google Images. Among all the images of red snakes is a thin long blackish snake with a faint red glow visible beneath the scales, called a red spitting cobra, *Naja pallida*. It looked like that, but *Naja*, native to Africa, is unlikely to be found in Costa Rica. Perhaps it was a related species.

Spitting cobras eject a stream of venom from holes in their fangs and aim for their victim's eyes. They have good aim, and neurotoxins in the venom can cause temporary or even permanent blindness. My cobra's head-weaving motion struck me as odd. *Was it a spitting cobra? Was he trying to locate my eyes? Gauge the striking distance?* I'll never know.

The following day, I saw a wide snakeskin, perhaps ten feet long, nailed to a board, drying. They had killed a 40-pound boa constrictor in camp. I felt sad. "Why did you kill it? It lived here first."

"It was either the snake or the cook," they said. I bought the skin for Dr. Welty, who mounted it with a plaque on the Beloit science building wall.

Holdridge disappeared until dinner each day. I was curious about what he did, but he shared only vaguely about his activity, although he appeared pleased with whatever data he collected.

Three weeks later, I returned to a different part of Osa for five days with Barbara and Sean, two new travel companions. The small strip of wooden buildings passing for a seaside town included a small run-down board building with a hand-lettered board sign, "Hotel." We rented all three rooms. The beautiful river delta, pristine white sand beaches, swamps, and scattered mangroves contrasted with the heavy inland jungle and supported very different and aggressive wildlife.

Osa was asphalt-melting hot; some days exceeded 110°, shimmering heat waves filled the air, and humidity hovered close to 100 percent. The sun reflected in a blinding sheet off the water, bleaching the landscape under its glare. Sweat poured down our faces despite the slight breeze off the ocean, stinging our eyes and drenching our clothes. Humidity enfolded us like a heated blanket, sapping our strength and energy. I could feel myself dehydrating.

Eight miles away, loggers were opening up another new area, and graders, tractors, trucks, and chain saws were busy tearing up the environment. The field boss loaned me a bike, and in the early mornings, the bike and I hitched a ride with one of the logging trucks to the staging area. Then I spent the day slowly biking back into town, stopping to catch wherever an area looked promising.

The place crawled with venomous snakes. I remembered the red-hooded cobra from my last visit, and appreciated my heavy leather jungle boots, despite the heat. Osa had almost all of Costa Rica's twenty-three venomous snake species, including the bushmaster, terciopelo, and the venomous yellow-bellied sea snake, *Hydrophis platurus*, an aquatic member of the cobra family.

I encountered my first sea snake at Osa as I waded knee-deep along the shoreline. I almost stepped on it. *What an abnormally long eel.* I bent down for a closer look. Then I saw the snake head and vertically flattened oar-like tail that made it an efficient swimmer. Oops. A snake. It eyed me, but it was unaggressive, and slowly swam off. Later, I discovered that they hang out on the bottom and some species can remain underwater for several hours. They have been known to swim as deep as 300 feet.

Sharks and barracuda were common in the bay too, and after dinner, from the pier, we watched large bull sharks cruising slowly around the pilings, hunting.

Ponds and swampy areas attracted the most dragonflies, but crocodile tracks and trails dotted the mud everywhere. Typically, crocodiles look torpid, but I kept alert, my machete in hand, as I tramped through the low brush. I avoided wading because I didn't want to stumble on an underwater den and felt I could move faster on land. Not that it would have helped. A crocodile's muscular legs could run faster than mine for short sprints, so I realized I couldn't outrun one if it were hungry and determined. I doubt my machete could have stopped it either, but having it along felt reassuring. I had not yet had a close shark encounter, but I would have preferred a shark to a close-up crocodile.

Sean had lived most of his life in South America and spoke Spanish like a native. He was worldly and somewhat aloof, and slicked his hair back with pomade, looking shined and polished as if he had just stepped from a salon. Even in the jungle, he looked neater than the rest of us. Sean hired a peon to help him find the spots shown on his aerial photos because he needed to ground-truth the land use for his mapping project. He was never talkative, and a bit difficult to get to know. After a long day of hot, tiring fieldwork, he returned in a foul mood every night, even less talkative.

This upset Barb, who appeared interested in him but was making little progress. She didn't care for me much and seemed somewhat uptight, even in the office. Sean's bad mood didn't help the situation. The three of us weren't bonding well, but we had our own projects, and exhausted from the terrific heat and humidity, we were all in bed by 8:00 p.m. We awoke by 5:00 a.m. every day, and in the early mornings, I felt more alive and energized than I'd ever been.

Taking my cue from Sean, I hired a peon who showed me a swamp I never would have found on my own. I caught two very unusual species there. The first had a black thorax and an abnormally wide, bright red abdomen with white lateral stripes. It flew at the speed of light, and I spent three hours stalking it. It was wily and escaped from my net five frustrating times before I accidentally captured it while swinging at something else.

The wings of the second species had oddly rounded ends and heavy black pigment on the distal third. Dr. Donnelly, the expert from Rice, believed these were two new undescribed species of an entire genus never before found above the equator! Both were holotypes, single physical examples of a new species on which the species description is based. That was exciting! To formally describe a new species, however, we needed additional corroborating specimens, or isotypes, and I had run out of time. I had no time to return to Osa to search for more.

We spent much of our last morning collapsed in a small shady spot against a schoolhouse wall, drenched in sweat, shirts sticking to our backs, energy levels at zero. A chorus of student voices above our heads droned multiplication tables as we awaited the avioneta to San José. It never arrived. Later, the pilot said he couldn't find the small ball field that doubled as an airstrip. *How could he miss it? The jungle covered everything else. Surely, he didn't expect a paved landing strip and airport?*

We made alternative arrangements to take the 3:00 a.m. boat to Golfito, with a connecting flight to San José. This left us an unexpected free afternoon to walk the beautiful shell-covered beach. Thick mangrove clusters covered parts of the coastline, their stilt-like roots providing a protective nursery for many juvenile fish and other creatures. They also stabilized and protected the shoreline from wave erosion. Today, with coral reefs dying, their shade may also cool shallow waters, protecting corals from bleaching.

We edged around a large mangrove clump and arrived at the river. The field boss's words echoed in our ears. "Don't swim in the river; adolescent bull sharks come upriver at high tide." Too hot and sweaty to care, we jumped in the river for a swim, clothes and all.

It was a blessing the avioneta never arrived. After dinner, we found our way to the boat dock and stretched out to sleep on the hard floor of the small wooden boat terminal. At 3:00 a.m., a sputtering motor interrupted our fitful sleep, and a small ten-passenger boat pulled up to the dock. That's when we realized our unexpected boat trip to Golfito might be special. The sea around the idling motor was glowing. Millions of tiny bioluminescent plankton in the water glowed a beautiful turquoise-silver when disturbed. Sharks were gliding gracefully through the water around the pilings, their bodies coated with iridescent silver bubbles, and their passing left glowing bluish trails in their wake. Small fish zipped through the water leaving streaks of silver-blue.

The stifling afternoon air had cooled to a comfortable, light balmy breeze, so we stood outside on deck at the rail. Overhead, without the reflected glow of civilization, the cloudless ink-black sky blazed with uncountable thousands of jewel-like stars, appearing close enough to touch, while the boat ride treated us to a spectacular show of bioluminescence in the bay. In the distance, breaking waves outlined the shoreline in glowing turquoise froth, and the motor churned up a wide turbulent glowing wake behind the boat the entire trip around the peninsula to Golfito. Sean eventually went below deck, and Barbara followed, but I stayed outside watching the amazing light show. I've never seen anything so spectacular since.

Despite the previous turbulent avioneta ride to the logging camp with Holdridge, I appreciated the avioneta more the following week. Elena and Lucia, two Costa Rican students, and I would join OTS scientists in the small town of Villa Neily, and drive to their tent camp somewhere in the Premontane Wet jungle near San Vito close to the Panamanian border. They seemed out of their comfort zone anywhere except San José, and were afraid to use the avioneta, so we all caught the 4:30 a.m. bus for a tedious nine-hour drive.

Like most local buses, ours felt stifling. People, packages, and a few chickens crammed every inch inside and overflowed onto the roof. We sat jammed tightly together motionless and uncomfortable on the sticky, red-vinyl back seat, sweating profusely. I envisioned us melting together, fused at the hip. After several hours, almost everyone on the bus developed motion sickness. During the tedious drive, I silently cursed crowded buses, the heat, people afraid to fly, and vowed never to ride the bus again if an avioneta were available.

We disembarked onto a street-long strip of small buildings and sat in the cantina having Cokes, awaiting OTS. After two hours, we realized there was a miscommunication, but we had no way to contact them in the jungle. The town had no telephones, but Elena found someone with a short-wave radio to call the office, and the office radioed OTS. They said we would have to spend the night in Villa Neily; they would arrive tomorrow. That was problematic.

From the way people talked, we gathered Villa Neily had an unsavory reputation. The characters hanging around the streets did nothing to dispel that impression. The main business seemed to be brothels, and we received many covert appraising stares from the locals. As the day wore on, Elena and Lucia became increasingly uncomfortable and nervous for their physical safety and reputations.

When they realized we wouldn't be rescued from Villa Neily until the next day, their drama went into overdrive. They adopted the manner many upper-class Spanish matrons affect to convey that a situation is beneath their station. True drama queens, every gesture and overly loud comment, told anyone within earshot that ordinarily *they* would never frequent a place like this. *Perhaps they intend to telegraph a message that we aren't available, but I doubt we look the type in our sweaty field clothes.*

At first, I found their actions somewhat amusing, but their non-stop posturing became tedious. Convinced their virtue was at stake, they clung to each other like glue, even walking the 30 feet from the dining room to the bathroom together, arms linked in a show of solidarity, their rigid backs radiating indignation. It seemed to me their airs, loud talk, and histrionics continued to draw attention to us, producing the very thing we wanted to avoid.

Now, late in the afternoon of a very long day, we were without reservations, and lodging prospects in the small town weren't promising. After a long search, we located a small vacant room above the cantina, devoid of anything but a tiny, rather dirty bed. Throwing our backpacks down, we squeezed in for an uncomfortable night. Using my pack as a pillow, I slept on the floor.

The following morning, an OTS jeep pulled up to our "hotel." Elena and Lucia marched out to the jeep, exuding indignant outrage. They heaved their gear into the jeep while voicing loud and vigorous complaints to the driver and everyone within earshot about their ordeal in weathering dangerous Villa Neily. I was embarrassed to be with them. The driver, no doubt ignorant of yesterday's mix-up, ignored them, threw the jeep in gear, and hit the accelerator.

After an hour of bumping over potholed roads, we arrived at the jungle camp, and settled gratefully into our tents, a welcome change from the cramped room above the restaurant. I spent days wandering through the jungle and looking for dragonflies, but finding mainly butterflies. Elena hauled around her bulky wooden plant press, collecting new tree ferns and *Heliconia* flowers. Each heavy thick-stalked fern frond measured five to six feet long, and required folding several times before she could stuff it into the plant press. Heliconia's large, colorful waxy flowers were also impossible to press flat, and made the already heavy plant press even more unwieldy and difficult to carry. She couldn't haul it far, so I doubted she would go off the path or far from camp.

After dinner, the myrmecologist, who had been searching for new army ant species, invited me to join him in his search since most ants are more active at night. I hoped we might see some on the march. We didn't but, in the morning, we found large cat tracks all around our tents. We assumed they were jaguars. Jaguars are crepuscular, i.e., especially active around dawn and dusk, so I felt relieved we had met none while ant hunting.

I'm sure thankful I zipped up my canvas tent fly last night. Should I be more watchful for big cats while alone in the jungle? Holdridge never warned of them. Perhaps because they were elusive and somewhat rare, I never saw a sign of them other than footprints. On reflection, that was probably a good thing.

After several days in the tent camp, OTS dropped us off in San Vito. Elena and Lucia took the early bus and began the nine-hour ordeal back to San José, but I'd had more than my fill of the bus. I spent a leisurely day in San Vito collecting and talking with Vincent, an interesting farmer from Idaho. When he learned Wayne's project focused on *huaqueros,* or grave robbers, he invited me to come to dig Mayan graves on his farm. It certainly sounded interesting. With more time, I would have loved it but I would have to be content with buying pre-Colombian pots the huaqueros brought to sell in the office for a few dollars each.

Later that afternoon, I grabbed an avioneta to San José with relief. *At least my next trip should be more comfortable than Villa Neily.* Wrong.

- *Eleven* -

Parasitos and Huaqueros

Nicoya Peninsula 1965

I
T WAS 6:00 A.M., AND WE WERE ALREADY ENCASED IN dust. Tom, Liz, and I were headed north to the small squatter villages of San Juanillo and Marbella on the coast of the Nicoya Peninsula. Holdridge suggested I join them because I had no dragonflies from the Tropical Moist Monsoon life zone yet. Despite the Land Rover's closed windows, dust somehow wafted inside and enveloped us. I could taste it even breathing through a bandana, and I tried not to envision it coating my lungs. The jarring potholes made the tedious ten-hour drive slow and uncomfortable, and Tom bottomed out with such regularity it seemed almost intentional.

I decided Liz and Tom were the easiest people to travel with, because they could roll with the unexpected. Despite their tendency toward constant bickering, they weren't flustered when things went awry, so I hoped this trip would be easier than the drama in Villa Neily.

Tom and Liz were studying *parasitos*, or squatters, a significant problem on large properties with absentee landlords. Once parasitos moved onto a property, they settled in, built houses and gardens, and claimed the land. The landowner then faced a complicated, expensive, and convoluted process to evict them.

"We visited this area before, to observe the squatter problem first-hand, meet with the squatters, and gather their perspectives. This is a five-day follow-up visit," Tom said.

The long, hot trip to Nicoya progressively worsened as the day wore on. The highway was still unpaved in parts, and the density and size of car-eating potholes made it impossible to avoid hitting them. Oncoming cars roared past us, pounding the potholes and raising clouds of fine dust that hung in the air, blanketing our Land Rover.

Liz and Tom bickered, argued, and picked at each other on every imaginable topic the entire trip. I sat in the back seat, attempting to block out their exhausting arguments, but without success. Ten very long hours later, about 4:00 p.m., mentally and physically exhausted, we arrived at the small squatter settlement of Marbella. I hoped at least now we could relax.

It was the first time I'd seen the squatters' squalid lifestyle. The few small houses were all constructed of scrap wood or boards, with palm frond or tin roofs, and we appeared to have the only vehicle. We stopped first to visit a low house Tom and Liz had previously visited.

"We took pictures during our last visit that we want to share with them," Liz said.

The small two-room structure housed ten people. They cooked over a small inside firepit, a shallow depression in the dirt floor encircled with rocks. The firepit seemed to be the centerpiece of the house, and in a desire to beautify it, they had covered the stones with a mixture of ashes and water, baked it into a smooth, hard covering, and painted the edges blue. The people were difficult to understand because their vocabulary differed from that of San José, but they were pleasant and hospitable, and offered us instant coffee.

They were delighted with the pictures Tom had taken. They were the only pictures people had ever seen of themselves, and everyone crowded around, pointing, laughing, and wanting more photos taken. This time Tom brought a polaroid camera. The girls ran off giggling to change into their best clothes for a photography session. Although not in the same league as Peace Corps projects, as far as goodwill went, Tom's one gesture probably equaled a year's worth of Peace Corps work.

After visiting, primping, and picture-taking, we drove to the small group of buildings calling itself San Juanillo. We planned to stay at the only room in town, the space above the *pulperia*, a local grocery/restaurant/hotel all in one.

"No need for reservations," Tom said. "No one ever goes to San Juanillo."

Right. We arrived to discover a group of huaqueros occupying the room over the pulperia.

This was terrible news. *Huaqueros*, or grave robbers, ran a thriving and lucrative illegal business robbing Mayan gravesites and selling the artifacts. They cared only for the money the artifacts could bring, and they destroyed the sites, taking anything of value but collecting no archaeological data to accompany their finds. Mayan sites littered the countryside, and huaquero digs were so ubiquitous we could identify them from the car window. Now it seemed they had found some sites nearby. And they occupied the town's only available room.

"Let's go eat in the pulperia," Tom said. "We can discuss our options over dinner."

"I'm game for anything with a roof," I said.

"You could use the local schoolhouse, since school is out for vacation," someone suggested.

Liz agreed. "It sounds better and safer than sleeping outside." We drove over to check it out after dinner. The one-room hollow-block school, the best construction in town, even had a rusty tin roof and a glass window. Even without lights, water, or a pit toilet, the school's walls and roof made it appealing.

"Interesting door," Tom said. Several misshapen boards nailed together passed for a makeshift door, and the handle was a piece of driftwood. It didn't fully close and had no lock.

Looking around, Liz said, "Let's move off the floor."

"Good idea," I said. "There's bound to be rats running around. And it's getting dark."

Fifteen small desks sat on the compacted mud floor. We pushed them together into the middle of the room to make an elevated rectangular sleeping platform. We had no blankets, pillows, or towels because we had expected to stay in the pulperia, but nights were warm, and at least being off the floor reduced our chance of encountering rats. The desks were small, hard, slanted, and wobbling. It would be difficult to move or even turn over with the three of us crammed uncomfortably close together and balanced on the desktops.

Will we be able to sleep at all on these things? This could be a long five nights.

Tom immediately plopped his duffel bag in the middle of the desks, staking out a position between Liz and me. I envisioned him returning to the office with a leering grin, telling everyone how he had slept with two women on the trip, perhaps even embellishing a bit. When he went outside to visit the open-air "facilities," I moved his duffel bag to one side, placing Liz in the middle. She smiled, amused.

"Wha….?" Tom stopped mid-word, but the sound of surprised dismay in his voice when he returned confirmed my suspicion. He looked at his new duffle bag location, unsure who had moved it. We let him wonder.

We brought only a few snacks, so we were forced to take all our meals in the pulperia. Every meal was identical: a plate of rice and beans and a *refresco*, a sticky-sweet drink resembling lemon Kool-Aid. Although not very good, it killed the taste of the water, which we learned only later, came from a sluggish gray stream running alongside the line of houses. They said they filtered and boiled the water, but it didn't look like it.

While Liz and Tom interviewed *parasitos*, I went out with my net, and quickly attracted a following of curious villagers, including Don Pedro, a visiting local advisor. I explained my project, and he directed me to a clean freshwater stream and a small pond near the beach. The cool sea breeze felt refreshing after the hot, stagnant air in town. *They ought to build their houses and get their drinking water here.* However, they were illegally squatting, so perhaps staying inland made their presence less noticeable.

Don Pedro was right; I saw quite a few dragonflies, but all the vegetation grew in the middle of the pond. I would have to spend most of my time standing thigh-deep in water if I wanted to catch anything. People warned me about leeches, protozoa, worms, and other water parasites, and I vaguely considered what kind of bad news might be lurking here. Although surprisingly cold, the water looked clean and relatively shallow. I waded in slowly, poking the bottom with a stick, checking for quicksand. Over the next several hours, I caught five new dragonflies and emerged with nothing more than a plethora of unknown small red bumps covering my legs.

For lack of anything else to do, we spent our free time hanging out in front of the pulperia, waiting for mealtime. Many unemployed men hung out there too, and they pulled us into their drunken conversation. We were the town's only diversion, and they were quite interested in Tom and Liz's squatter project. Obviously, we were rich *gringos,* so they spent much of their time hitting us up for money and requesting loans. It did no good to protest that we were poor students because to them, we *were* rich; we had decent clothes, watches and shoes, and even a car, which seemed of particular interest to them.

Every day, the desks grew harder, and the pulperia food less edible, but our last night provided some excitement. We went to bed at about 8:00 p.m. as usual, because without lights, we had nothing else to do. Around 11:30, I awoke from a fitful sleep, hearing odd noises and crunching leaves. A light flashed outside the window near the car.

I thought someone was trying to steal the car, or at least the gas, and felt relieved Tom had brought the keys inside. I got up quietly, grabbed my machete, and peered out the window, but the light moved off, and I saw nothing more. I considered going outside alone for a closer look but thought the better of it.

Tom woke up and saw me with the machete. "What's going on?" he whispered.

I whispered back. "Someone was outside nosing around the car; I saw a flashlight. I think he left."

"We should check it out! If we lose the car, we're in big trouble."

"It's still there. I debated whether to wake you guys, but he's gone."

"We should go outside and check to be sure the car's OK." He grabbed his machete.

The two of us crept out silently, leaving Liz, now awake and machete in hand, guarding the useless door. We checked around the Rover but saw and heard no one. Except for a few other night noises, we thought the night had finished without incident.

We left San Juanillo in the morning, looking forward to an uneventful trip back. About ten miles away, we stopped in the small town of Sta. Cruz, praying it would have a gas station and, hopefully, at least an egg or bread for breakfast. While we waited for someone to turn on the gas pump, four or five men strolled over to admire the Land Rover. They carried baskets and said they were going shrimp hunting. They struck up an animated conversation with Tom and ran their hands over the Rover's smooth hood, asking lots of questions.

We also met Don Pedro from San Juanillo. "I'm here to report a murder," he said. "Someone was brutally decapitated near the San Juanillo school early this morning."

We all exchanged glances. Everyone knew we were staying in the school-house, so we told Don Pedro about the incident the night before. We had little information to shed light on the murder and didn't know whether the person nosing around the Rover was the murderer or the victim. Several town officials joined us, and a great discussion ensued about the murder.

"The murderer had to be either a drunk or a huaquero," someone said. Those terms weren't necessarily mutually exclusive, and the huaqueros weren't exactly reputable, upstanding citizens.

"I heard the huaqueros in the pulperia have discovered a new cache of Mayan artifacts near San Juanillo. They'd probably silence anyone who discovered their dig location," an official added.

"Then the murderer looked for a place to spend the night and came to the school, expecting it to be empty. Seeing your car parked outside, he hesitated to go in," someone else volunteered. Everyone agreed. That was their theory, and the motive seemed plausible.

No one seemed anxious to confront the huaqueros, and everyone with any authority appeared satisfied that since they had identified a probable motive, they had solved the case. I doubt they even searched for the murderer. We never heard anything more about the murder or the victim.

We gassed up and began the long return drive to San José. About a mile out of town, we saw the shrimp hunters from the gas station, trudging along the road. As we passed them in a cloud of dust, they all began running down the road after us, yelling, waving, and trying to flag us down.

"They asked me about a ride earlier," Tom said as he pulled over. "I promised we'd give these guys a ride. They've never ridden in a car before."

The gas station group, now increased from five to nine, were all excited that Tom had magnanimously agreed to give them their first car ride. *At least that explained their interest in the car; I was worried that they planned to steal it.* Liz and I weren't thrilled about this, but we weren't consulted. The nine men quickly swarmed around the Rover. Five crammed themselves inside with the three of us, all piling atop one another, and four others scrambled onto the back, sides, fenders, and top, hanging on wherever they could find a handhold. With twelve of us in and on the Rover, we looked like the typical overloaded local bus, with people hanging out on all sides.

Everyone talked at once, laughing with excitement as the overloaded Rover moved ponderously down the road. The wild ride was short-lived. Within a mile, Ted bottomed out in a big pothole. With a loud metal-on-metal squeal and a heavy *clunk*, the car jerked to a halt and died. Everybody climbed out. We stood around staring at the Rover, now oddly unbalanced on one side. Ted opened the hood. The shrimp hunters all crowded around, peering inside with interest, and everyone ventured wild and uninformed guesses about the problem. They'd never been in a car before, but now everyone was an expert. "Maybe it's this?" (The battery.) "How about that?" (The fan belt.) But it was obviously a spring.

Unable to help, the men good-naturedly thanked us for the ride, happily waved goodbye, and resumed their walk down the road, discussing their experience with animation. They were thrilled with the ride, but now we were stuck with a broken vehicle. We couldn't drive it back to San José, so we restarted the engine and limped grindingly back to Santa Cruz, the only town within reasonable distance having a prayer of being able to fix it.

The gas station was clueless; they only sold gas, and shops were closing for siesta. Three long hours later, shops reopened and we found a greasy closet-sized metal shop owned by a small grease-covered man with some knowledge of cars. After much discussion, he concluded we had broken *la maestra*, the mainspring. This was a terrible place to break down. Santa Cruz was the next closest place to nowhere.

The shop owner didn't stock parts and said ordering a new spring would require several days. That felt unacceptable on many levels. He reluctantly agreed to try welding the spring together. Perhaps, if we drove slowly, we could make it to San José before it broke again. Between the three of us, we had just enough cash left to pay for the welding, and in late afternoon, we finally began the extended, dusty return home. This time were even slower, but at least it was quiet; Liz and Tom were too tired to argue. We finally arrived at the office early the following morning, exhausted.

"How was the trip?" one of the new students asked.

"We broke the mainspring on the Land Rover and someone got beheaded outside the schoolhouse we stayed in yesterday."

Tina had seemed timid and slightly uneasy in the culture from day one, and when we came to the beheading part, she became almost hysterical and refused to hear anything more.

"That couldn't happen. You're making it all up! That just couldn't happen!" She shook her curly hair vehemently, holding up her hand as if to ward off the vision, refusing to believe someone could have their head cut off. Considering everyone here ran around with machetes, it seemed rather logical to me.

Nothing on the entire trip had been comfortable: neither the lodging, the food, nor the long drive. Once we were again sleeping in actual beds and eating decent food, the uncomfortable and inconvenient trip became just another interesting field story, but San Juanillo hadn't finished: I soon came down with a hideous case of dysentery.

- *Twelve* -

Looking Ahead

San José 1964

MOST PEOPLE WERE TALKING ABOUT GRADUATE school, but I had been too busy to give much thought to it. I knew science required an advanced degree, but I had no money, and neither my parents' vocabulary nor their bank account included graduate school. Costa Rica taught me that significant steps may require giant leaps into the unknown. If you try to analyze or understand every detail first, the door may close and the opportunity may pass.

My small detail was lack of money. I had zero, and grad school would be expensive, but I took the GRE exam and requested applications anyhow, without a clue how to pay for it.

One morning Tom poked his head into my office. "You're going to grad school, right? Where are you applying?"

"Probably Texas A&M and the University of the Pacific, in California. How about you?"

"I'm applying to Stanford, Harvard, and the East-West Center in Hawaii." Perhaps he thought to impress me, but all I heard was "East-West Center."

The EWC! Why hadn't I remembered that? I hadn't heard the name or given it a single thought since Dr. Welty mentioned it my freshman year. It had been buried so deep in my brain that despite discussions on grad school and marine biology, it took Tom's specific mention to dredge it up into consciousness. Tom would continue in anthropology, so I wouldn't have given his mention of the Center a second thought if Dr. Welty hadn't previously connected it with marine biology.

"Why there? I thought the Center focused on marine biology."

"No. It's associated with the University of Hawaii. The Center's main function is cultural interchange, so grantees can major in anything. It's international, like a Rhodes Scholar, and the government pays for everything. And you spend some time in Asia."

That grabbed my attention. *Maybe I could dive there, too.* Hawaii didn't feel nearly as far away or unattainable now as it had only three years earlier when I was still Midwest-focused. Costa Rica had opened my world.

"That sounds great! Think it's too late for me to apply?"

"I don't know, but I'll give you the address." I sent for an application the same day, hoping it wasn't too late. An application arrived by return mail. I solicited recommendations from Drs. Welty and Holdridge and sent the application off quickly.

Soon a letter arrived from the U.S. State Department, asking me to come for an interview at the Embassy in San José. *Why did a graduate school application need an interview? And why the State Department?* That seemed odd, but I dug out my one skirt for the occasion.

At the American Embassy, a thin, nondescript man in a light tropical suit took me into a large room, strangely empty except for two card-table chairs. *Don't they even have a decent conference room here?* He gestured to a chair, peered at me over wire-rimmed glasses, and without cracking a smile, asked me some generic questions.

"How do you like Costa Rica?" and "What are you doing in the jungle?" He asked where I lived and how I liked living abroad. It felt more like an interrogation than an interview. He neither asked nor told me anything about Hawaii, the EWC, or Asia. *Does he know anything about the Center or the University?*

He rather casually asked, "Have you ever had a security clearance?" *Security clearance? Why would I need that?*

I said, "I don't know," but I had a feeling the EWC was going to do one. Then I flashed on the obnoxious FBI men at the Glen Ellyn boathouse, who told us they would start files on everyone attending the Mao movie. *Do I actually have an FBI file, and if so, what does it say? Could it compromise a security clearance?*

He paused and looked down, studying his hands. Then, staring intently into my face, out of nowhere, he said, "How do you feel about the Vietnam War?"

War? I seldom read the Spanish newspapers, but the paper contained little Stateside news in any case. Back home, the war would remain low on the public radar until about 1968. In late 1964, I was totally unaware of it. I had no idea what answer he wanted, but the Government seemed to take this war seriously, and I sensed my answer would be significant. *What does he want to hear? Should I be for it or against it?*

"I don't know. I've been in the jungle for months; I don't know what's happening in the States." It was true; at that point, I didn't even know we were at war, but it didn't seem like a good idea to admit it.

"Well...I guess that's a good answer," he grunted. He peered at me over his glasses again and seemed satisfied.

A *"good answer?"*

Fortunately, I had such solid and supportive mentors. A few weeks later, the same day Tom was accepted at Stanford, I received a special delivery letter of acceptance from the EWC, thanks mainly to Welty and Holdridge's recommendations. The grant included a semester of field study in Asia, and I discovered later that they wanted grantees they thought could handle a solo Asian experience. Without Costa Rican experience, the Center might not have given me a second glance.

Clint looked visibly upset. "You never told me about this."

"Yes, I did," I said. Later, I realized I hadn't told him I applied, because the whole process had happened while he was feeding pigs at Dr. Hunter's jungle cabin. He wanted to get married after Costa Rica and hoped I would remain close at Texas A&M while he finished his last year of college. We didn't seem to be on the same wavelength. We'd discussed marriage, but I'd never agreed to get married so soon, and I'd twice declined a ring.

My parents, who had never questioned or commented on my graduate school applications at all, now said little about my acceptance. I don't think they could comprehend it. They couldn't process the idea of Texas; Hawaii was off the map. Only Holdridge and Welty seemed pleased.

In retrospect, if I hadn't chosen coral reefs for my term paper in my freshman year, Dr. Welty would never have made his offhand comment about the Center. And I could look past Tom's anthropology focus when he dropped the name three years later only because I previously knew about it. Without Dr. Welty's apparently hand-picking me for Costa Rica, I wouldn't have had experience abroad, which I suspect factored significantly in the Center's selection. And fortunately, Tom had been there to bring the East-West Center back into my consciousness. A fortunate string of events? Possibly but, in retrospect, I could see God's fingerprints all over the steps leading me to the Center. It would change the direction of my entire life.

We were now nearing the end of our time in Costa Rica. I had almost forgotten the mysterious lack of information that initially seemed to envelop the Costa Rica program. Now I was about to find out.

- *Thirteen* -
The Pieces Finally Come Together

<u>Monteverde 1965</u>

L ATE ON A MISTY AFTERNOON, HOLDRIDGE AND I
drove up a narrow and muddy, bone-jarring road through ethereal
mists of the Monteverde Cloud Forest to the top of the continental divide,
at 3,500 feet elevation. In this magical Tropical Montane Forest, a low
layer of misty cloud hovered at canopy level most of the year, eclipsing
the sun, and the green ridgetop trees glowed like emeralds from the continual moisture.

The clouds and mist form because the humid Atlantic trade winds
carry moisture-laden Caribbean air over the land. As the air is forced up
over the high continental divide, it condenses, producing swirling mists
interspersed with drizzle and dazzling intermittent sunshine. This creates
a magical and misty, cool and unique cloud-forest ecosystem. Like Osa, it
is one of the world's biodiversity hotspots, supporting one hundred species of mammals, one hundred twenty species of reptiles and amphibians,
four hundred different birds, twenty-five hundred plants, and thousands
of insect species.

Les had said, "I'm going to quickly check out something in the cloud
forest. Why don't you come along?"

"Great! I love it there, but my project's essentially done; it's a bit late to
add any new species."

"You probably won't catch any. Bring a poncho, its rainy season."

He was right. I saw no dragonflies that day, but I was about to learn the answer to something I had wondered about since Beloit.

Now mid-afternoon, we sat alone at a small wooden table in an isolated cantina atop a mist-enshrouded mountain, overlooking the vast, lush and hilly, green canopy. We were relaxing over beer and watching the wisps of cloud swirling below us. Our time was drawing to a close, and we were reminiscing about the year. *I'm going to miss this magical place.*

Holdridge seemed to be weighing something in his mind. Then he smiled. "I've had a breakthrough in my life zone research," he said.

"I wondered what you were doing out there while I was catching."

"Did you ever wonder how your research might be used?"

"Yes, I did. I thought just making a collection for taxonomic purposes was a bit too simple but, once I got started, it was interesting enough just collecting them. But I did wonder about how you just happened to have contacts at the Smithsonian and Rice, and why the Smithsonian cared about dragonflies."

He began telling me about a new way in which the life zone model could be used predictively. At last, I learned what I believe was responsible for the program's almost secretive lack of information during the application process. I also began to understand how my project, OTS, and the Smithsonian involvement, had tied into the life zone model and what was behind it all: Vietnam. There it was, again.

As far as I can remember, it went something like this: the Vietnam War was ramping up, and the Army lacked information on actual ground conditions for much of northern Vietnam and Laos. GPS systems and satellite photos didn't exist, of course, but the Smithsonian contained an extensive collection of dragonflies from Vietnam, with data on their collection locations.

"Costa Rica's life zones and topography are similar to Vietnam's, so if we could find dragonfly species in Costa Rica similar to the Vietnamese species in the Smithsonian, someone could correlate your species and their life zones to their dragonfly counterparts in the Smithsonian and estimate the probable Vietnamese life zones and likely environment for various areas." The model would, of course, provide expected altitude, temperature, precipitation, humidity, and other data for each area.

"But there's something more specific. The model can now be used to estimate things like the expected number of trees per hectare and the type of soils in each life zone. This will allow the Army to determine whether an area can support tanks or only ground troops, and similar information."

I didn't process everything he said at the time, but I was fascinated. I'd often wondered what he did in the jungle while I collected. Now I realized he was probably generating supporting soil and vegetation data for this expansion of the model.

My information provided only a piece of the puzzle. He didn't mention other people and groups involved, but I imagine at least the Dr. Slud's bird data, and maybe even tree ferns and ants, also fit there somewhere.

Dr. Slud's obituary states that he "assisted the Army on biological classifications for military environments, to predict plant formations and distributions of birds."[5] I assume this referred to his work in Costa Rica. That also explained the military-looking OTS tents and supplies, the oblique references to the Army that I sometimes heard around the office, and the reticence of OTS field staff in discussing their work. It was also possibly one reason why the National Science Foundation seemed interested in Holdridge's theory and funded the program.

This expansion and use of the model were fascinating; I wish now I had asked more questions. At some point, perhaps believing he might have revealed a bit too much, Les said, "You should keep this quiet." And until now, I have. Today, almost sixty years later, GPS systems and satellites make the model archaic and obsolete for that type of use.

Later, I realized with surprise that a piece of life had come full circle. During WWII, the Navy placed Dad in Naval Intelligence and sent him to Pearl Harbor to make rubber invasion maps. He interpreted black and white aerial photographs using stereo-pairs, a unique set of glasses that converted two-dimensional photographs into three-dimensional images. From those, he constructed large three-dimensional rubber maps of various

Pacific islands. The maps were colored, topographically accurate and to scale, and he modeled every building, tree, road, airfield, and land feature from the photographs onto the maps in intricate detail. His maps were critical to the war effort because the Navy needed an accurate representation of ground conditions to plan land invasions and identify bombing targets.

The Life Zone theory took a more scientific and sophisticated approach to planning invasions than dad's detailed rubber maps. Yet, both served the same objective: to provide the military with a better idea of the terrain our troops would be invading. The only difference was that my project involved another war, 20 years later.

For all the life zone model's biological sophistication, it didn't appear reconnaissance of inaccessible areas had made much tangible progress in the 20 years between WWII and Vietnam. It would require satellites and GPS systems of the future for that. Aside from the methodology, the primary difference seemed to be that dad knew why he did what he did, while I remained totally in the dark.

Then the program began winding down in earnest. They allotted us ninety minutes for final oral presentations, but most of us finished in less than an hour.

"I want to present on the first morning to get it over with," Clint said. I did too.

"Who are all these people? No one introduced them."

The unfamiliar audience didn't speak Spanish, so I presented in English, and everyone but Tom and Liz followed suit. They droned on for four and a half hours in fractured Spanish.

"Aren't you glad we went first?" I said later. "By the day's end, most of the audience were glassy-eyed, and looked like they desperately needed a siesta or a good cup of coffee."

And then we were done. It was the most enjoyable thirty credits I ever received.

I had visited all of Costa Rica's eleven life zones, collected in 61 locations around the country, and caught hundreds of specimens representing

65 dragonfly species. Tom Donnelley, the taxonomist from Rice University, told me I'd discovered holotypes of two entirely new species of an entire genus never before found above the Equator, both from the Osa Peninsula.

It was only in writing this book that I discovered that although I recorded those species descriptions in my diary, those pages with descriptions were missing in the copy of my research paper (mailed to me a month after I left). I know I included them in the original manuscript. Publishing is essential in science, so now I have questions. *Who removed those pages, and why? Did someone ever return to Osa, find additional specimens, and claim credit for their discovery?*

That wouldn't be very professional but, if someone did, I hope they gave me credit for the holotypes. It's decades too late to get excited about it now, or to try to determine if additional specimens (the isotypes) were ever found to validate my holotypes. Were the two species ever described and named? In hindsight, now it's small stuff.

Initially the move from the pension to the house had been positive. Clint and I built large new cages for the Señora's parrot and rabbits, the kids learned some English, we all played chess, and one day, I realized with surprise that I had become fluent in Costa Rican Spanish.

The last couple of months things became increasingly difficult and stressful. The year of mourning had ended, and Amaya shed her mourning clothes. Now she could party. Doña Isabella burdened herself with the arduous task of chaperoning her, and began guarding her like Fort Knox.

"Is it just me, or is Doña Isabella beginning to drive you crazy?" I asked Liz.

"It's not just you. I feel like she's always watching us. It's getting very uncomfortable."

"Maybe she thinks we aren't good role models for Amaya."

"Maybe, but I can't see that having Tom and Clint over occasionally should cause problems."

We were seven years older than Amaya, but now Doña Isabella became a self-appointed chaperone for Liz and me also. Her ponderous and omnipresent, black-draped bulk hovered in the background, her alert eyes clocking our every movement in and out. She didn't try to control us, but she discouraged Tom and Clint's visits. Dr. Shook, Kim, Clint, and I had played bridge on weekends, but now she didn't want us playing in the house anymore either. Everything felt uncomfortable. *Poor Amaya.* I couldn't imagine living under a system like this.

When she realized Liz and I would soon be leaving, Doña Isabella began searching aggressively for replacement renters. I returned from Osa to find a third student in our room, and Isabella was considering adding a fourth. She justified this because when Liz and I were in the field, our beds were empty, but we still left our belongings in the room, and we paid for the room whether we were there or not. They made extra money from us too, because although we paid for food, we were hardly ever home to eat. This unexpected invasion of privacy was disruptive and uncomfortable.

Soon, not content with adding one person, Doña Isabella also brought in Ellen, an adventurous middle-aged American woman who traveled around the world, financing her trip by giving viola concerts. She moved into Amaya's room, so Amaya used Doña Isabella's bed and shared Liz's closet, and Isabella moved into our room, using whichever bed was vacant. *This is becoming really annoying.*

Sleeping arrangements changed daily, depending on who was home, and playing musical beds became irritating and confusing. When everyone was home, Amaya and Doña Isabella shared a room, something less than fun for Amaya, I'm sure.

We knew taking in boarders was a necessary inconvenience, and a loss of face for this previously affluent family. We also understood they needed to look ahead, because when our program ended, losing Liz and I would substantially decrease their income. Still, we didn't appreciate sharing sleeping arrangements with other people, never knowing who our room-mates would be for the night.

When Ellen moved on, Doña Isabella replaced her with two teachers. We had increased from two to five boarders. On rare days when everyone was home, twelve people crowded around a dining table for six, and we were immersed in fractured Spanish as everyone tried to practice their conversation at once. I assume the teachers stayed in our room, because I slept in Amaya's room my last three nights. This last straw cut my final tie to the house. I was ready to leave.

Costa Rica had given me what I needed: a year full of amazing adventure. It had opened my world. For the first time, my head and immediate career path felt focused and grounded. Now Clint and I planned to drive his VW van back to Texas, and his parents flew down to San José to drive back with us. We never knew whether they wanted to chaperone us, evaluate their potential daughter-in-law, or take a vacation. But I had to give them credit; they were the only parents that ever came to visit.

Before we left Costa Rica, they wanted to see Irazú Volcano. Clint and I had gone there once before, when it wasn't erupting. Familiarity breeds complacency.

- *Fourteen* -
An Explosive Goodbye

Irazú volcano June 1965

I MET CLINT'S PARENTS JUST AFTER RETURNING FROM my last trip to La Selva, and I wasn't dressed to impress. I was darkly tanned, with my hair like straw, sun-bleached almost white, and scraggly from months without a haircut. As his mother scanned my men's work shirt, clean but stained khaki field pants, and heavy leather field boots, I could almost read her mind: "*This* is my future daughter-in-law?"

It was noontime in a cheap motel, but she looked dressed for a cocktail party. A scoop-neck black dress and a heavy gold necklace set off her waved blond hair and careful makeup. *Are Texans always so dressy? I hope she didn't dress up on my account.* Belatedly, I realized she had. Perhaps I could have made more of an effort for a good first impression myself, but impressing people had never been high on my totem pole.

This may not go too well, I thought. No doubt she felt the same.

The gray, overcast sky was somehow fitting a visit to Irazú. The view from San José didn't do the two years of volcanic devastation justice. As we drove into Cartago, we passed a giant *lahar*, or mudflow.

"What's this huge mess?" Clint's dad asked.

"It's a lahar. They say it's a half-mile wide and five miles long," I said. "Last year, thick volcanic ash buried 186 square miles of the mountainside, and December rains eroded it, creating this giant mudflow."

The mudflow picked up trees and boulders as it roared down the mountain, burying people, livestock, and houses in Taras district. We all stared at it, trying to imagine the terror of being caught up in a lahar.

"How many died?"

"They never determined the number dead, and recovered very few bodies, but 400 houses are under there somewhere," Clint said.

This was one of forty-six separate lahars occurring between 1963 and 1965. Many families still lived on the volcano's slopes, in the potential path of additional lahars. They were justifiably terrified but, trapped, without money or the ability to relocate.

As we neared Irazú, we began seeing bedraggled trees, their leaves drooping under the weight of the ash. Gray and blackened ash began collecting along the roadside, and the ash grew coarser and the piles deeper. As we ascended the crater, gradually ash and rock began burying fences and trees, and piled several feet deep along the road. The government had obviously attempted to keep the road clear for a while but, eventually, the task became overwhelming, and they quit trying. Ash began burying the road.

"It's so gloomy here," someone said, and the gloom seemed to have its own weight. Not even a sliver of blue sky relieved the grayness of the cloudy day. We continued climbing, following tracks of previous vehicles atop the ash-covered road.

"Well, we're not the first ones here, so it must be ok," someone said. The gray ash now covered everything, producing a monochromatic landscape vaguely shaped like trees, houses, and fence rows.

"I feel like we're trapped inside a black and white movie. I can almost hear the doo-doo, doo-doo music of the *Twilight Zone*," I said.

As we climbed higher, a cold mist began penetrating everything. The crater was totally quiet; not even a bird cry or insect buzz broke the silence. The magnitude of the disaster and gloomy atmosphere affected everyone in the car. Conversation dwindled as we stared out at the bleak gray landscape. I thought, *Dr. Tosi's house is buried under here somewhere.*

"If Government officials were worried about public safety, wouldn't someone stop us?" Clint's mom asked.

"Well, there aren't any roadblocks, checkpoints, or warning signs," his dad said. "It must be OK."

The fine ash and small rocks gradually become piles of cinders and large chunks of rock, and as we approached 11,000 feet, the van labored a bit under the altitude. About a half-mile from the crater vent, large rocks in the road made driving impossible.

"This is it; we can't drive farther," Clint said, parking the van. Without discussion or a plan, we all got out and continued upward on foot. Eventually, we encountered a weathered board sign hanging at a skewed angle on a battered piece of broken gate, about 300 yards from the crater. It said simply, 'Observation Point.'

"This looks like the official stopping point," I said. Given the condition of the sign, and the amount of ash and rock lying around, we were already much too close. Still, we encountered no warning signs or other barriers, so we all cavalierly circumvented the battered gate and strolled idly toward the crater without a second thought.

When not erupting, the crater appeared safe/. We knew the predominant direction of the ashfall was toward San José, on the opposite side, but the enormous rocks we passed on the way up indicated the volcano ejected heavy-duty material in all directions. But Irazú wasn't erupting at the moment. We never considered the possibility of shifting wind, poisonous gasses, or being hit by large rocks like those covering the road we had just ascended.

We were far too close, but the lack of signs or barriers conveyed a false sense of safety. We were not the only people to circumvent the barrier. Car tracks and footprints in the ash showed others had been there before us.

Doña Sofia knew where we were going. "*Peligroso*," she said. "My friend was hit on the head by a falling rock twenty-five days ago, and he's still unconscious in the hospital." But she didn't try to warn us off.

We didn't even discuss our approach. We walked along like a bunch of lemmings, perhaps each assuming someone else actually knew what they were doing and, at some point, would say, "Wait a minute; don't you think we're getting too close?" or "Isn't it about time for the eruption?" But nobody did. We continued as if on a beach stroll. Familiarity with the predictable daily eruptions gave Clint and me youthful confidence, and his parents seemed to have confidence in Clint's judgment.

What were we all thinking? How close would we have gone? Would we have continued to walk like robots right up to the edge and peer inside the crater? Maybe. Clint and I had done that before. Perhaps we assumed it would provide some advanced warning of an eruption. It didn't.

From far off, eruptions seem slow and silent. It's quite a different experience on the crater. Fortunately, before we walked much closer, suddenly without warning, a tremendous hissing and boiling directly below our feet shattered the silence, followed almost immediately by a deep and deafening rumbling, like a boiling cauldron. We had no time to react except to cover our ears.

Then, with a crashing, ear-splitting roar, an explosive rush of dense grey clouds of superheated steam and ash burst from the vent with incredible force, shooting thousands of feet into the sky, directly in front of us and straight over our heads. Sharp popping and cracking of exploding superheated rock punctuated the deafening hiss of released gasses and steam as thousands of tons of rock pulverized into ash. *It sounds like the simultaneous collision of several freight trains.* The noise made talking impossible.

We watched for ten or fifteen minutes, almost trance-like, awe-struck at the untamed power of nature, as the wind carried tons of ash toward San José. *We're lucky it's blowing away from us.* Then, as the wind began shifting, a pea-sized rock fell right in front of me, and other small rock fragments began dropping like isolated hailstones around us. That brought us back to reality. "Let's go back!" Clint's mom mouthed, making wide-eyed gestures toward the van, and we beat a hasty retreat.

We had driven over piles of ash and rock on the way up. *Obviously, with so many rocks on this side of the crater, eruptions aren't entirely predictable. We should have realized that.* We were less than a quarter-mile from the crater's edge. If we had continued much further toward the edge, or the wind had shifted more quickly, we would have been enveloped in hot, steaming, poisonous gasses, hit on the head with rocks, or buried in choking ash. It seemed a rather dangerous way to accomplish Goal #38, Watch a Volcanic Eruption.

We weren't the only people foolish enough to get so close, and many others didn't fare as well. No one told us that a Costa Rican Physician and a Hungarian visitor had died the previous year, and fifty others were injured when approaching the crater during an eruption. In a second incident the same year, seven others died under similar circumstances. We were unhurt, but incredibly naïve and reckless.

***

A week later, Clint, his parents, my parrot Pepino, and I piled into Clint's VW van, said goodbye to Costa Rica and started a month-long trip back to Texas. I bought Pepino in the market six months earlier, for only C25, about four dollars. "*Regalado*," a gift, the Señora said. I hadn't planned to buy a parrot, but she looked so sad and bored in her small cramped cage in the market that I felt compelled to rescue her.

"She'll learn many words," the owner said, although her vocabulary never exceeded "*hola*."

Now Pepino rode in the back of the van, her cage perched precariously on top of the luggage, squawking hola, shedding feathers, scattering seeds all over the van, and otherwise endearing herself to Clint's mother.

We spent a month driving up through Nicaragua, Honduras, El Salvador, Guatemala, and Mexico, stopping whenever something looked interesting. With our luggage, Pepino, and all my butterflies and insects, the van was overloaded, but Clint's parents took it all in stride, and the trip was an excellent chance to get to know them better. Once she shed the cocktail dress, I found I liked his mom, although I'm not sure how either of us felt about my ability to fit into the Texas culture. I learned her view when Clint reported he overheard her on the phone with his sister, saying with disdain, "Well… she collects *bugs*." Not an auspicious sign.

At the U.S. border, we encountered the mother of all traffic jams. Long lines of cars inched their way up to the border. Thousands of day workers walked up, flashed their work cards at the border station attendant, and with barely a change in stride, poured through the border and crossed into the U.S. The pretext at screening seemed almost laughable.

The contrast between sides of the border was stunning. One moment we were on poorly maintained streets with nondescript stores, buildings needing paint jobs, dilapidated cars, ragged children, and drab surroundings, and the next, we were on clean, well-maintained streets with newer cars and modern, maintained and landscaped buildings. Blue water from motel swimming pools glistened in the sun and even McDonald's golden arches felt welcoming.

An almost tangible aura of lightness, promise, and hope filled the air. *I can see why the U.S. holds such an allure for the third world. I haven't missed the States in the slightest, but I can appreciate the sense of order and organization of life here.* I felt surprised; I hadn't expected it would feel so good to be back.

When I returned to Glen Ellyn, my parents relaxed. Reassured I would be at the university in Honolulu, rather than in a jungle somewhere, Dad canceled my Costa Rica life insurance policy. He even began to reminisce about his war days in Honolulu.

But eventually, he asked, "Why do you keep talking about Asia?"

"The Center sends me to Asia for my second year. Don't you remember? I wrote you about it." It hadn't registered. As it sank in, he leaned his head in his hand, looked down, and said, "Oh. My. I didn't realize…." I had assumed he would be interested, or excited, but he stood stunned and wordless. As usual, I couldn't read him. *That's it? Is he dismayed or just overwhelmed? When he was younger, he had been an excitement seeker; why couldn't he be excited about this opportunity?* Perhaps he couldn't fathom it. Or was he just regretting he had canceled my insurance?

A few weeks later, Clint flew to Chicago to visit. Now, excited about Hawaii and Asia, I felt even less prepared to settle down. I'm sure he could sense that, and perhaps he could feel me beginning to slip away. After a few months in Hawaii, we broke up.

EAST, WEST, AND THE CENTER

(1965–1967)

Jefferson Hall, East-West Center

"The goal of life should not be to arrive at the grave in an attractive and well-preserved body, but rather to slide in sideways, chocolate in one hand and a latte in the other, body thoroughly used up and totally worn out, screaming, "WOO HOO, what a ride!"

– author unknown, slightly altered

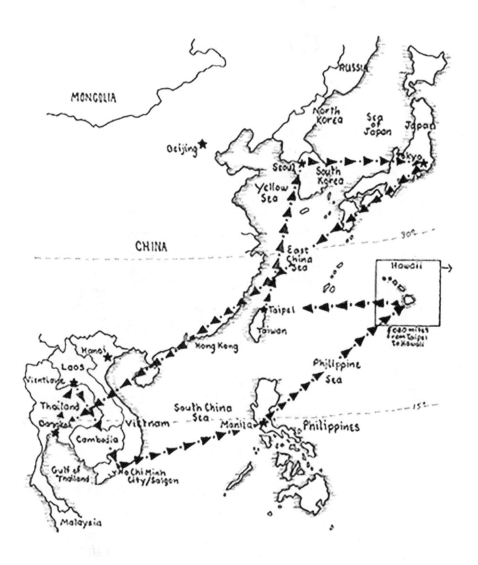

Asian Field Study

- Fifteen -

Paradigm Shift

Honolulu, HA 1965

H AWAII IS ONE OF THOSE PLACES THAT'S BOTH A location and a feeling. Its unique aloha atmosphere tugged at us even while we were still airborne. As the plane circled to land, Hawaiian chants and a beautiful ukulele adaptation of *Over the Rainbow* lured everyone to the windows. As we gaped at the lush green mountains, the beginnings of the sunset reflecting on the blue water, and the white sand beaches full of surfers and paddleboarders, my seatmate turned to me and said, "Toto, I don't think we're in Kansas anymore."

On the plane to Hawaii, I met a pretty red-haired girl wearing a small EWC pin like mine, and a friendship started before we reached the East-West Center. Laura's small Indiana town was quite similar to Glen Ellyn, and we both were excited about the change. Neither of us could have imagined how Hawaii would intertwine and change both of our lives.

None of the Asian nor American grantees arriving at the East-West Center had any idea how greatly it would impact our lives. Congress established the Center in 1960 to promote cultural interchange between people of the United States, Asia, and the Pacific Islands. That goal was amazingly successful.

The EWC experiment built incredible bonds and life-long friendships among the grantees, particularly those attending in the mid-1960s, and resulted in an astonishing number of interracial marriages. Many

American grantees would move permanently to Asia, and many Asians would eventually become U.S. citizens. The EWC exploded my worldview, and its impact still shapes my life and incoming email every day.

As we deplaned, Hawaii's unique warm, soft breeze enveloped us with the sweet smell of pikake and plumeria. Two grantees met our plane, recognized our EWC pins, and draped purple orchid leis around our necks. As we drove us past the Ala Wai boat harbor and through downtown Waikiki to the Center, the ocean glowed with the remains of sunset, and evening lights from beachside cafes and bars were beginning to sparkle and reflect on the water. Excitement and promise called out to us from the beach, the open-air bars, and cruising convertibles on the street.

Laura and I were immediately captivated. I remembered dad's painting, and sensed I was coming home. *How did Dad feel, arriving here after Pearl Harbor's devastation?* I hoped someday he would be able to return and experience a more welcoming arrival.

The university's low, yellow concrete buildings, lush green tropical plants and spacious, palm-sprinkled lawns bore little resemblance to ivy-covered mainland schools. We turned up Manoa Valley on East-West Road, toward the twenty-one acres of dorms, Kennedy Theater, and Jefferson Hall that made up the East-West Center campus. When Dr. Welty offhandedly mentioned it in 1961, construction had barely begun but, by the time I arrived, the campus was completed and housed about 500 students, slightly more Asians and Pacific Islanders than Americans.

Laura and I were both staying in *Hale Kuahini*, the House of Women, an unremarkable three-story dorm. My small, non-descript second-floor room held pairs of single beds, small desks, bookcases, and closets. A pile of folded bed linens awaited me on a bare mattress. Not seeing my roommate, I made the bed and fell asleep at once.

The following day I ditched my travel dress, put on Bermuda shorts and sandals, and wore little else for the next two years. I began letting my blond hair grow long again, and quickly regained my dark Glen Ayer and Costa Rica tan. The laid-back island environment felt like home.

I found my way to Jefferson Hall, looking for breakfast. The iconic modern building with tall ceilings, long glass windows, and graceful arches projected an airy, open feeling. In the back, a large covered lanai ran the entire length of the building, and overlooked a beautiful Japanese garden, complete with a stream and large, brightly-colored white, orange, and black koi.

Jefferson was the heart of the Center, and a gathering place, because it housed three things important to the students: student mailboxes, a spacious lounge with a piano, and an international cafeteria serving a mixture of Asian, Pacific Island, and American food. It tried to satisfy food preferences of students from 30-50 nationalities, an impossible task.

Our stipends paid for everything from transportation, room, board and tuition to an Asian field study. Our grants had only three requirements: Asians not fluent in English studied English, while Americans studied two years of an Asian language; Asians spent a semester or more on the mainland while Americans went on an Asian field study; and everyone had to room with someone of a different nationality. *I wonder what nationality my roommate is. I hope we can communicate enough to relate.*

I returned from breakfast to find my new roommate, Pheng, from Laos. She looked dressed for a party, in an elegant *sinh*, the traditional long, wrap-around silk tube skirt with a broad, ornately embroidered hem; a long-sleeved, cuffless white blouse; and a long matching silk sash that draped over her shoulder and down her back. Her long black hair, pulled into a tight bun, accentuated a round, moon-like face.

She looked so formal and exotic, I wondered how we could relate, but I soon found she dressed up only for class, and once in the dorm, she took down her bun and relaxed in pants and a tee shirt. Her English was fluent, if not always grammatically correct. We rapidly became good friends, and often cooked dinners and attended beach picnics on group dates together.

Pheng had been at the Center for a year, and through her, I became connected to the Laotian and Vietnamese groups. There I met Mai Phuong, a small thin Vietnamese girl whose small stature camouflaged a determined personality and a hidden will of iron, and her boyfriend Sengphet, a personable, gregarious guy from Laos. He was politically astute and used an American name because he thought Americans found it easier to pronounce. He had previously been a foreign exchange student in the States, spoke four languages, and was somehow related to Pheng. We would all become lifelong friends.

I was one of only two American grantees at the Center studying marine biology. American students tended to major in Asian languages, international relations, political science, or similar fields, and many later often joined the State Department or Foreign Service. Someone told me, "One of the Center's worst kept secrets is that it's considered a training ground for the State Department and CIA." There might have been a grain of truth in that, but only because the intercultural exposure led many to gravitate toward the Foreign Service or State Department after graduation.

Foreign governments were watching the new institution. I had been there about two weeks when a friendly woman about my age approached me, claiming to be a student. I asked her where she was from. She hesitated, then said she was Russian, not one of the countries at the Center. She asked about my background and major and seemed quite interested in learning about the Center but gave away little of herself. She subtly mined me for information but soon, apparently deciding I had nothing of value, she disappeared, and I never saw her again.

Surprisingly, my first encounter with blatant male chauvinism was in Hawaii, of all places. A few days after classes began, I found a note in my mailbox from the biology department chair, asking me to come see him. I went to his office to find a well-padded, middle-aged man, self-assured and somewhat pompous. I couldn't help comparing his unsmiling face and thin, unsmiling lips with Carl Welty's broad grin. He said he just wanted to chat, but soon he leaned back in his chair, fixed his eyes on me, and challenged, "Why are you here? Did you come to find a husband?"

"What?" The outburst astonished me. *What brought this on?* "I left someone on the mainland to come here to study marine biology."

He picked up my transcript, waving it at me. "Well. It doesn't look to me like you even have enough credits to be admitted here," he challenged.

"What??" I could feel my blood pressure rising. "What are you talking about? I have almost twice the biology credits required!" I reached for the transcript and pointed to the top. "Did you see these four AP credits for advanced biology?"

"Oh, I missed those."

"How about these 30 credits for my year of Costa Rican fieldwork?"

"Well…." He trailed off, unwilling to apologize or admit he hadn't looked at it carefully. "Hmm. Well, I guess they admitted you. So. You know you're taking up a slot here many other people would love to get." By other people, I assumed he meant men. "So. Make sure you make the most of it. Don't want you to go running off and getting married." He made no apologies for his assumptions or arrogant attitude.

The assumption that all women would get married and sit home wasting their degrees begged for a nasty retort. Many retorts rested on the tip of my tongue, but I stifled them with effort, clenching my teeth to keep my mouth shut,

"Do you need anything else?" He didn't.

"Good," I said, and left his office fuming, not knowing what annoyed me most, his attitude or the blatant, unabashed way he manifested it. After the acceptance and support of Welty and Holdridge, I never expected to encounter this attitude, let alone from a department chairman. I suddenly realized the department had few women graduate students, and I hadn't seen a single female professor.

Women in science fought an uphill battle, and white males dominated marine biology. Like Blacks, who had to be better than Whites simply to be considered equal, women had to work harder than the men just to prove themselves worthy. Many people believed science was a man's field, as if female brains weren't capable of complex thought.

In the Sixties, many older women weren't yet in the general workplace, and fewer still worked in scientific fields. But I was pleased to hear from Mom that Jean Wallace, our old Glen Ellyn neighbor, had helped her get a job as a librarian at Elmhurst College. Mom was finally spreading her wings a bit, and although not a student, she was finally at a college.

A few weeks later, the chairman called a mandatory meeting of the entire department. We assembled, wondering about the reason for the meeting. Privately, I hoped he was announcing his resignation. Instead, he gave us a fiery lecture on morals. One of the women, and he actually named her, had dropped out because she had the nerve to get pregnant. Hands clenched, red-faced, he strode up and down in front of the blackboard, his clipped tone measured and hostile. "She's wasted her education and taken up a slot someone else could have used. Women don't belong here; they always get pregnant!" He had no censure for her boyfriend.

He lurched into a long tirade, ranting about her morals, our morals, and morals in general. "None of *you* better be fooling around! You are here to study. Many people wish they had your chance. Don't mess it up." He became so worked up I wondered if he would start foaming at the mouth.

I speculated about the real impetus for his rant. *Who made him the self-appointed Morals Police? Was he angry because she had "wasted" a slot, or did he simply have a low opinion of women in general?* We all sat there looking sideways at each other and rolling our eyes as his tirade continued for 20 minutes.

"Any questions? Well. So. OK then." He turned and strode out, radiating self-righteousness. Attitudes toward women here didn't seem any better than those on the mainland.

My ichthyology class was taking a trip to the Biological Marine Station in Kaneohe Bay, on Oahu's windward side. As our boat pulled up to the dock, we passed a young guy cleaning out his marine samplers. I stopped to see what he had collected.

"I've just returned from doing research on Eniwetok Atoll, he said."

"Wow! It sounds fantastic. I'd love something like that. How did you get to go there?"

"Yeah, it's great. I don't know if you could go there, though."

"Why not?"

"They don't have facilities for women…you know, no separate showers and that kind of thing." They could easily remedy that, but Eniwetok either never considered the possibility women might want to go there, didn't want women there, or no one had forced the issue yet. I sensed an uphill battle looming.

One reason for our visit was a giant sixteen-foot tiger shark. It lay sprawled under a roof on the cement pier, the largest shark any of us had ever seen. The large mouth sagged half open, showing impressive teeth, and its black lidless eyes gazed out in a dark, vacant stare, giving an impression of malevolence I knew it hadn't possessed.

We ran our hands over the sandpapery skin and bent down to peer in the open mouth, curious to see the multiple rows of teeth. I knew it was dead, but it still looked so alive I couldn't bring myself to touch the head. I noticed no one else could either. I never expected to be that close to a giant tiger shark again, but twelve years later I would meet a bigger one, and the next one would be live.

Tiger sharks are one of the three main species responsible for shark attacks, second only to the great white shark in their number of victims. They're voracious hunters and more aggressive than great whites. Someone asked, "Have you done a stomach content analysis?"

"No, not yet. We're waiting for the authorities to come before we cut it open. See this?" He pointed toward the side, where a large protruding C-shaped curvature pushed out against the stomach wall. A brief chill ran through me. That's why they waited; it was the unmistakable curve of a human iliac crest. I heard later that it belonged to the headless torso of a missing local fisherman.

Kaneohe Bay was my first ocean snorkel. The bay was almost pristine, and the supersaturated colors and diversity of the organisms gave me an amazing high. I had been waiting for this since my Racine Quarry scuba dive in 1961.

Soon many of my classes had fieldwork at the beach. In the rainforest, most animals were camouflaged or hidden but, on the reef, many things were in plain sight, and many organisms like corals, sponges, and tube worms couldn't hide, because they were sessile. Vast schools of reef fish swam through the clear waters, and the seemingly unlimited variety of large invertebrates from brittle stars to octopi, sea cucumbers, and starfish, put me on sensory overload. Reefs were still almost pristine, and thanks to my classes, now I could identify many of the organisms. I couldn't wait to get diving again.

But in the four years since Racine, diving had matured as a sport. Now my homemade certificate wouldn't pass the laugh test. Local dive shops required comprehensive NAUI or PADI certification courses. I would need to find a class and get properly certified. I hadn't brought my heavy cold-water scuba gear to Hawaii, so I'd have to buy all new dive gear. I was cash-poor, had no transportation to and from dive classes and dive sites, and my heavy class workload left little spare time. I realized with disappointment that my circumstances didn't yet mesh with the coincidence of time, transportation, and monetary investments diving required. But my classes provided so much water work they satisfied me for the moment.

I returned from class one morning to find unfortunately I had missed a telephone message from Holdridge. He was passing through Hawaii on his way to Southeast Asia. He didn't say where, but given his research, I assumed he was headed to Vietnam, perhaps to ground-truth his theory.

The Center's Kennedy Theater periodically sponsored International Nights, where different cultures showcased their native dances, songs, and skits. Filipinos, one of the larger groups, produced some of the best artistic productions, so Laura suggested we attend Filipino Night.

One scene opened with two barefoot Igorot headhunters wearing only red and black woven headbands and Igorot G-strings. They were holding spears and awaiting a bamboo litter carrying a tribal princess. The tall one looked solemn and fierce. The shorter, stockier one had such oversized calf muscles, I easily visualized him running long distances barefoot through the mountains of Banaue. I would never have guessed one was a physics teacher and the other a future bank officer.

Several weeks later, Laura suggested we study for exams at Waikiki. Studying at the beach is an oxymoron, but we brought some books anyhow and drove Laura's sporty Mustang convertible, top down, to Queen's Surf. We lay on our woven grass beach mats, making a pretense of studying while tanning and listening to Laura's radio. She had already jettisoned her Midwest mindset and wore a new green and pink floral bikini that would have been scandalous in her small Indiana hometown. By comparison, my pink and white plaid two-piece suit, almost daring in 1965 Chicago, looked old-fashioned in the expanse of bright bikinis.

A shadow fell across our books, and we looked up to find two Asian guys standing over our beach mats. Ed, a somewhat padded Japanese-American with a dark surfer's tan and a wide, somewhat lecherous grin, wore Hawaiian jams hanging to his knees and sprinkled pidgin in his sentences. I guessed him to be local. His friend Carlos, a short, somewhat stocky Filipino, also darkly tanned, had impressive, sculptured calves. His accent indicated he was an international student.

Ed said, "Can we listen to your radio?" Without waiting for a reply, they tossed down their beach mats next to ours and flopped down on the sand.

Inwardly, I groaned. *Oh great. A beach pick-up.* But Laura appeared interested in Ed, who worked in a university dorm near the Center. Carlos turned out to be an EWC grantee. I eventually realized he was one of the Igorots holding spears at the cultural night. He looked better in a swimming suit than the G-string.

Ed asked Laura out. Not knowing him, she hesitated, then suggested that the four of us could double. Carlos and I weren't interested in each other, but we agreed to go along to accommodate Laura and Ed. And that's how Laura and I met Ed and Carlos. The four of us became good friends. Laura and Ed soon became inseparable, and Carlos and I found we had good chemistry too. We shared a love of swimming, outdoor sports, and travel. We were both excitement-seekers, and working on Master's degrees.

Carlos and Ed shared the Green Beast, a dilapidated 1952 Dodge, and divided up use days, allowing us to get off campus a couple of days a week. We joined Ed and Laura at concerts, movies, and picnics, and spent our free time at the beach and nights sitting in the Hilton Hawaiian Village listening to Hawaiian music, dancing, and nursing single expensive drinks all night to make them last.

The sun-drenched, carefree days passed seamlessly from summer into winter. Carlos would graduate next June, a year ahead of me, and the EWC grant required Asians to return home for at least two years after graduation. We had fun, but the future seemed too complicated and uncertain to get serious.

Carlos asked me to do his friend Raul a favor and buy him a gun to bring back to the Philippines. He didn't say why he wanted one, but guns were common, and it didn't appear to be a big deal. Hawaii required a gun permit from the Honolulu Police. Raul, a non-citizen, couldn't get one, so I found myself in the Honolulu Police Station, getting fingerprinted and registering for a gun.

The policeman asked patronizingly, "Why would a pretty little thing like you want a gun?" I hadn't given any thought to that, but made up a story on the spot about wanting to shoot doves. It made no sense, but they didn't inquire further. After fingerprinting and registration, I walked out, and handed Raul my gun. I forgot all about it until I saw him on TV five years later. He was stirring up trouble.

After Christmas, everything sped up. I would leave for Asian field study in August, so I had only eight months to find a major advisor, decide on a thesis topic, plan my field study itinerary, and cram two years of intensive language training into the 12-week summer session. Then I would go to Asia, gather whatever information I needed for my thesis, return to Hawaii, and spend the spring semester writing it.

I needed a thesis advisor, and approached Dr. Gosline, my ichthyology professor. "Well, I don't usually take women. It's a waste of my time. They usually get married and don't continue in the field."

Here we go again. Didn't guys get married too? Why are these stereotypes still so entrenched here? But perhaps because he had a daughter about my age, he relented and agreed to become my advisor.

I was intrigued with the morphology of fish otoliths, the small stones in the inner ears of fishes, and it seemed a good research topic. Gosline suggested focusing on the basal percoid fish families and using my field study to collect them. Flush with funding, the Center allowed us total control over our field study itinerary and duration, and since every country had fish, justifying an eight-country travel itinerary was easy.

After hearing one grantee spent an entire year in Nepal studying erotic temple art, I realized EWC's primary objective was probably to get us comfortable in an Asian setting; what we accomplished on field study appeared incidental.

Summer arrived, and with it, significant changes. I invited Pheng to visit my parents during her field study but her advisor said she was returning to Laos. *Did she ever plan to tell me? Or one day would I realize she had quietly left without telling anyone?*

Carlos completed his Masters and returned to the Philippines, where he had a job awaiting him at Citibank. With my two closest friends gone, it felt lonely at first but, once I started intensive Thai, that filled every spare moment.

Almost immediately, the empty bed in my room attracted attention, and a woman from downstairs approached me. "I'm about to leave on field study, and my Nepalese roommate, Sanjiya, doesn't want to room alone. Can she room with you?"

"Sure," I said. And that pulled me into the group of students from Nepal and India.

Sanjiya was more flamboyant than Pheng. Her striking colorful sari set off a great figure, and she wore her thick wavy long black hair in a heavy ponytail. Her dark skin and kohl makeup around her dark eyes set off a dazzling white smile, and she used lip liner to make a perfectly round *tika*, a colored dot on her forehead, varying the color to match her sari.

Although shy at first, she soon opened up, and we got along well. Like many Asian girls, the casual ease of American clothes attracted Sanjiya, and as time passed, she began casting an eye at my pants and dresses. We were about the same size. Eventually, she said, "Do you think I could wear one of your pants sometime?"

"Sure. No problem."

"Maybe the Indian boys wouldn't like it, though."

"Why do you care what the Indian boys say? And why should they care what you wear? You're Nepalese, not Indian." But I knew the groups were close, and she didn't want them talking.

"Western clothes are kind of revealing."

"That's a cultural thing. From a Western perspective, your low-cut blouse shows an inch of stomach that seems more provocative than my pants would ever be."

Nevertheless, she tried the pants, liked them, and bought herself a pair of tight black capris and a bright, floral Hawaiian blouse to wear around the dorm. Eventually, she ventured to wear them outside within the EWC campus too. No one appeared upset, and if the Indians disapproved, she didn't let on, but, like Pheng, she continued to wear her saris to class.

Then I received an invite to an international party. Sanjiya asked, "Do you want to wear one of my saris?"

"That would be fun, thanks! You'll have to help me get it on though."

Getting into the sari turned out to be less complicated than I expected. The colorful thin sari material is lightweight, but there are six yards of it and an exact way to wrap it. I first put on a cotton underskirt. Sanjiya wound the sari material loosely around the underskirt two or three times and I tucked it into the waist of the underskirt all around to hold it. Then she folded seven or eight wide pleats and tucked them into the front of the underskirt and arranged the remaining material into four pleats, draped them over my left shoulder, and left the remainder hanging down my back.

Without hooks or fasteners to hold it together, it took a bit of practice to master making it loose enough to walk in but tight enough to prevent it from unexpectedly deconstructing. It was worn with a short, scoop-neck blouse exposing an inch of stomach above the sari skirt, and felt quite elegant yet comfortable.

Now, knowing Asian customs, I wondered what favor she would request in return for the loan of her sari. From Pheng's stories, I knew requests could be outrageous in proportion to the original favor, but what Sanjiya proposed didn't sound excessive. She said, "Maybe I could borrow one of your dresses sometime."

"Sure," I said. She never mentioned it again.

A couple of weeks later, walking through campus on a Friday afternoon, I saw someone walking down the sidewalk wearing a blue floral dress that seemed vaguely familiar. I thought, *I have a dress of similar material* but, not recognizing the girl, I didn't give it another thought. A block later, I saw more familiar material walking by on someone else.

That's like one of my dresses, I thought.

No, I corrected myself. *It IS my dress!* A third dress walked by, and then another. I realized my entire closet was parading by on the sidewalk, and I smiled, realizing I was repaying the sari favor. When I returned, I checked my closet. Sure enough, every single dress had disappeared. She hadn't left me even one. Sanjiya had mustered enough courage to wear a dress that showed legs but, wanting the comfort of numbers, she had convinced all her Nepalese and Indian friends to wear one too, and everyone wore them out together.

She had hadn't even hinted this might happen, so I wondered how long they would be gone, but I didn't ask. *I just hope I won't need one until they come back.* One by one, over the next week, clothes mysteriously began reappearing in the closet, and then having had their fling, everyone went back to their saris. But Sanjiya continued to wear her pants around the dorm, and never once mentioned the dresses.

***

Fast forward to the 50th EWC reunion/conference in 2010, and I was on a panel discussion about the EWC experience. There, I discovered Sanjiya had a hidden side. I stood at the podium looking out with some nostalgia at so many almost-familiar faces in the audience, now gray-haired and 45 years older.

"Since neither Pheng nor Sanjiya is attending the conference and therefore unable to defend themselves, I'm going to share some roommate stories of life in the dorm." When I told the story of the Nepalese girls and the dresses, the audience roared with laughter.

After the panel, a distinguished Indian man looking vaguely familiar, took me aside, opened his wallet, and pulled out an old worn, color picture of Sanjiya from 1966. He still had it. She stood on the beach, flashing her beautiful smile and wearing a bright floral two-piece bathing suit! It astonished me. It was very modest, more like shorts and a halter top, but it showed legs, and I remembered all the fuss about wearing tight pants. *Was he why Sanjiya had worried about what the Indian boys might think?*

To be wearing that, I assumed she must have been quietly dating. It surprised me because I never saw her with a boy, and although she had occasionally mentioned him, she had never mentioned dating. She had quietly lived a double life right beneath my nose. I didn't know she had ever even gone to the beach, let alone owned a swim suit.

How many other girls had been doing the same thing? And how had the EWC experience impacted them when they returned home? Their degrees undoubtedly helped their careers, but did the American experience make their lives easier, or did it create internal and cultural conflicts? Were they now in intercultural limbo? And then I remembered meeting Pheng in Laos, on my field study, back in 1966, and how she had coped with her memories of Western exposure.

- *Sixteen* -
A Friendship for Life

NOW SUMMER WAS ENDING, MY TWO YEARS OF INTEN-
sive Thai were completed, and I was about to leave for field study.
Solo travel in Asia wasn't scary for me; it was exciting. In Costa Rica, often
I'd found the best way to travel was alone, because people would start
conversations and drag me into unexpected places and adventures I never
would have experienced if I'd been accompanied.

I planned to spend the bulk of my field study in Thailand, but assuming
I would never return to Asia, I planned to visit eight countries along the
way. I would also visit families of Pheng, Mai Phuong, Carlos, and Akemi,
a Japanese pen pal from high school days.

Field Study: Japan, August 1966

Japan was my third country on field study, and Akemi, and I were
headed into a liquor warehouse. In 1958, only 12 short years after WWII,
my high school Latin teacher announced the Government was establishing
a pen-pal program to promote good post-war relationships between the
States and Japan. Impulsively, I signed up and began corresponding with
a girl from Niigata. Now, thanks to the EWC, after eight years of correspondence, we had finally met.

We had never exchanged pictures, so we were both excited to meet.
Akemi was pretty and stylish, a head shorter than I, with glowing skin
and a friendly smile. She must have labored over her letters because she

had an extensive writing vocabulary but, once we met, we discovered a vast gap between her writing, speaking, and listening vocabularies. She had memorized many English phrases describing the sights we would see in Japan, but I soon realized she understood little of what I said. I reduced my speech to essential nouns and verbs, without intermediate words or long sentences, and somehow, we communicated. We laughed a lot, and both felt quite at ease from the start.

She brought me home to Niigata, quite an honor because Japanese rarely entertain visitors at home. I expected an apartment, but the family lived in a liquor warehouse because Akemi's father worked there as a live-in security guard. We entered a small side door in the metal warehouse and walked down a narrow aisle flanked on both sides by tall stacks of whiskey cases. A single room bordered on all sides with shoji screens sat amid the stacks. Sliding open a screen, she ushered me into a pleasant living room with tatami mat flooring and a small TV with a large piece of convex glass over the front, presumably to enlarge the screen.

Once inside, although windowless, it felt like a regular house, except looking up, I could see the warehouse ceiling. A narrow path between stacks of gin and vermouth led to a tatami-floored bedroom, similarly enclosed with shojis. Another bedroom, the kitchen and bathroom were similarly spaced. The unusual arrangement was comfortable, and probably larger than the average Japanese house, but I thought, *I hope I don't need to get up in the middle of the night; I'll get lost on the way to the bathroom. I almost need a map to go from one room to another.*

Neither her parents nor her younger sister spoke English. Only twenty years past, WWII still loomed fresh in older people's minds. Like American vets, her father had many leftover issues from the war, and he obviously felt uncomfortable meeting me. He greeted me stiffly, with a formal bow, said a few tight-lipped words I assumed to be a polite greeting, and disappeared. *Was he ashamed of Japan's part in the war? Or did he feel uncomfortable because he felt I was still "the enemy?"* I never saw him the rest of the trip.

Another path, through stacks of rum, led to a shoji-enclosed bathroom, complete with a huge wooden tub of steaming water. As the honored guest,

I was the first to use the bath. I tentatively poked a finger in the nearly scalding water and quickly jerked it out. *How could anyone stand that temperature?* I couldn't even keep a toe in there. Dipping a washcloth in the water, I waved it around to cool, took a sponge bath, and splashed some water on the floor to make it appear I had used it.

Family pictures were the ice-breaker. Everyone knows Americans have big cars and houses, but they were amazed to see the yard. They had never imagined yards because most Japanese homes don't have them. Everyone sighed over Carlos' picture because he resembled some famous Japanese movie star.

In the States, WWII was behind us, but it was still very fresh to those in Japan. Through Akemi, they asked, "Was your family hurt by the war?"

"Only my uncle John; he was killed in Normandy."

Like many Germans, Japanese appeared to have guilt over the war, and hearing this, they seemed to feel personally responsible for his death. "So sorry, so sorry...." they said over and over, bowing and apologizing so profusely I felt embarrassed.

Finally, I said, "Governments make war; people don't. The war is over. Akemi and I weren't part of it." They understood some of that, relaxed, and the apologies stopped.

Japan, the world's fourth-largest island country, includes 6,852 islands, and Akemi had arranged an elaborate tour of Honshu, the largest. She bought tickets and made all our reservations in advance. It must have been expensive, but her mother adamantly refused any reimbursement for my tickets. They were ashamed and embarrassed about the war, and perhaps this was their way of making reparations and saving face. I decided not to force the issue, hoping I could repay it at some point, although with limited vision, I assumed I'd never return to Asia.

The following day, we embarked on a week-long trip around Honshu by train, overnight train, ferry boat, and taxi. Asia's population pressure manifested first at the train station. The shinkansen, or bullet train, put American trains to shame. Its long-nosed aerodynamic engine looked sleek and modern. Lightning fast, it could reach almost 200 mph, and was punctual almost to the second.

Capacity was another matter. Professional 'pushers' disregarded the maximum capacity signs on the walls and prodded and shoved people into the train until we could scarcely breathe. Just when it felt positive they couldn't possibly squeeze in another person, the pushers somehow shoehorned in more. We were trapped without personal space, unable to move or shift position, touching people on all sides.

Trains were notorious for gropers, and people withdrew into themselves, avoiding eye contact with those around them. *Gee, this sounds fun. Will being a foreigner make me a target for gropers, or keep them away?* The Japanese women would stand stoically and quietly bear it, but I was prepared to cause a scene, which would have embarrassed Akemi. Luckily no one groped.

I was the only *Gaijin* and blue-eyed blond head on the entire train, so I became an object of interested scrutiny by anyone who managed to look up. Although only five foot six, I was taller than almost everyone else and I realized I could see the length of the car. I'm a numbers person, so I automatically began counting heads. Based on the recommended capacity stated on the wall, the car had filled to nearly 300 percent capacity.

We traveled around Honshu for ten days, talking and laughing a lot, neither completely understanding the other. We traveled to the ancient cities of Nara, Osaka, and what felt like every temple in Japan; visited Atami and Hakone, a mountainous area with volcanic hot springs; and drank liters of beer in small *ryokans*, or Japanese inns. Akemi apologized for not staying in expensive western hotels, and she didn't believe me when I said I preferred the quaint and interesting traditional ryokans.

After ten whirlwind days, I left for Hong Kong, owing Akemi a big debt I doubted I could repay. We both thought we would never meet again, unaware that we had just cemented the roots of a lifelong connection that would pull in four generations of our families.

Field Study: Hong Kong, September 1966

To me, Hong Kong represented the epitome of the mysterious orient. I was excited, and expected the unexpected. Luxurious goods from all over the world flowed through Hong Kong's duty-free port, and today it's still considered one of the world's great shopping meccas. *On my small per diem, I can't do much shopping, but it will be fascinating to window-shop these exotic stores.* Assuming I wouldn't return, I wanted to see and absorb as much as possible.

As we descended towards Kai Tak airport, I looked out the windows, expecting an exotic scene, but was surprised to see the shoreline and mountainous slopes of Hong Kong Island jammed with tall, surprisingly modern skyscrapers, their windows glowing in the remains of twilight. The plane descended abruptly onto a runway near the ocean's edge and screeched to such an abrupt stop that I half expected the plane to end up in the water.

I found a taxi to the Chungking Guesthouse, a budget hotel on the Kowloon peninsula. "It's not much, but it's within your $10 per day budget," my EWC advisor said. *She was right about that.* My small, poorly lit, windowless room held little more than a bed, but the location matched my needs.

Only a street or two away, Kowloon's high-end stores and expensive hotels sold Dior, Chanel, Coach, and other duty-free luxury items, but I wasn't interested. I wanted to see things uniquely Chinese, and the Guesthouse suited me perfectly. Dropping my two heavy Samsonite suitcases in the room, I left to explore and find dinner.

The Guesthouse on Nathan Road sat on a crowded side street, in a maze of small shops overflowing with exotic produce from all over Asia. Luxurious bolts of shimmering silk and brocade; carvings of ivory, jade, rosewood, and quartz; sandalwood, lacquered and intricately inlaid boxes, heavy gold jewelry, Japanese scrolls and screens, delicate porcelain, and antiques of every type jammed the shelves. Herbalist stores held shelf after shelf of glass jars filled with everything from traditional herbs to dried seahorses, powdered rhino horns, snake gall bladders, and bottles of liquor containing scorpions, snakes and other creatures.

Aggressive, turbaned Sikh tailors in skinny, shiny pants seemed everywhere. They worked in pairs, one waiting inside the store, and the other outside, accosting and literally dragging people in off the street. Their tailor shops could make a beautiful suit in one day.

Down narrow side alleys, bamboo poles holding flapping laundry extended out from every upper story window, an inventive adaptation to an environment without clothesline space. Old women squatted on the street chewing betel nuts, bright red saliva dripping from their mouths as they spat and sprayed the sidewalks. The sounds of shuffling and clacking ivory tiles indicated backroom mahjong games in progress.

I found a hole-in-the-wall restaurant, ordered a noodle bowl, and bought a copy of Chairman Mao's Little Red Book, *Quotations from Chairman Mao Zedong* to mail home as a curiosity, but Customs apparently confiscated it. I remembered the FBI at the Glen Ellyn boathouse movie. *Did a note about the book end up in my FBI file too?*

At dusk, the streets and stores lit up in a light display rivaling Las Vegas; blinking neon signs plastered every conceivable space. In English, the signs would look hideous and tacky but since I couldn't read the characters, they didn't look like advertising, they just looked exotic. Everything about Hong Kong was fascinating. I couldn't imagine anywhere more different from Glen Ellyn.

Hong Kong Island and the Kowloon Peninsula became a British Crown Colony after the 1842 and 1860 opium wars, and later Britain leased China's New Territories, which included 200 outlying islands. Everything would return to China in 1997. Under British colonial rule, Hong Kong had become a global financial center and enjoyed a capitalistic system and political freedom not found in mainland China. Although still 30 years distant, people already viewed 1997 with trepidation.

Europe and Asia blended here, taking some of the best from both worlds. I had expected Hong Kong to look old and Chinese, but the tall modern skyscrapers were Western, and the British rule imposed some order on what might otherwise have been simply another chaotic Asian city. Skinny-legged traffic policemen in baggy khaki Bermuda shorts and red knee socks directed traffic, people queued up obediently, and transportation adhered to schedules.

The streets surged with churning humanity that scarcely abated even late at night because large families crowded into small apartments, sharing beds in shifts. Those not sleeping roamed the streets, regardless of the hour. The interesting street sights were the only thing that kept me from feeling claustrophobic. With a population of 8,532 per square mile, it was one of the most densely populated places in the world. And population was growing. By 2020, it would double to over 16,000 per square mile.

The gray, cheerless and sterile Guesthouse dining room held only five Formica tables, so guests often had to share tables. I was considering the day's possible adventures over a breakfast of rice noodle soup and fish balls when Randy, a young nice-looking photographer, sat down and struck up a conversation. His genuine, friendly smile and unusual brown eyes, so light they almost looked amber, somehow put me at ease right away.

"I'm touring Asia, hoping to sell travel photos to *National Geographic Magazine*," he said, pointing to a large, black, foam-lined case he lugged around. It was loaded with cameras, an impressive assortment of zoom and wide-angle lenses, straps, filters of all kinds, a tripod, rolls of film, and several other pieces of unidentifiable paraphernalia. He had invested thousands of dollars in equipment, so he carried it with him everywhere, even to breakfast, never letting it out of his sight. We decided to explore Aberdeen Harbor together.

In 1966, ferry was the only way to reach Hong Kong Island. We walked a few short blocks under a slightly overcast sky to the busy waterfront and, for about $1 HK, boarded the green and white Star Ferry from Kowloon to Hong Kong.

Seating looked chaotic on the open-sided lower level. Some benches faced forward, and others backward. The forward-facing benches were all taken, so we sat awkwardly facing backward. People smiled. We watched people enter, flip the seatbacks over the benches, and convert them to forward-facing seats. Feeling foolish, we stood up and flipped our seatback over to ride facing forward. The windy, scenic ride across the choppy gray water of Victoria Harbor took perhaps ten or fifteen minutes. Then we hopped on a red double-decker bus to Aberdeen.

At our first glimpse of Aberdeen Harbor, I could see Randy already composing shots in his head. A massive floating city of over ten thousand sampans, houseboats, junks, and fishing vessels covered most of the large harbor. A few boats looked varnished and well maintained, but most hadn't seen a coat of paint in decades, and were so weathered it was difficult to ascertain their original colors.

A few graceful Chinese junks glided across the water, catching the wind with large distinctive sails, but most boats were small, flat-bottomed wooden sampans with unique squared ends, used mainly for fishing or transportation. They lacked keels, masts, and sails and normally motored, steering with a rudder. Low, rounded metal roofs provided limited shelter, and many housed live-aboard families.

Fishing boats slipped in and out of the harbor, their decks piled high with stacks of buckets, fishing gear, wire cages, coils of rope, wicker baskets, iron-banded kegs, and odd-shaped bundles tied up with rope or covered with old tarps.

The boats jammed side-by-side, each linked to its neighbors by wide boards placed across the bows of adjacent boats. This provided a make-shift boardwalk allowing people not moored directly alongside the dock to access their boat. Boats moored closest to shore paid for this privilege by losing privacy because a constant parade of people walked across their bow at all hours of the day and night. Owners moored farther out had more privacy but might have to cross over a dozen or more boats to reach their own. The scene was in constant motion, and people scurried from boat to boat like so many crabs. *I can't imagine living in that maze of humanity.*

We walked along the cement sidewalk lining the harbor's edge, watching the busy panorama. "I don't know where to start, there are so many good photo ops," Randy said. He set his camera case down on the sidewalk, selected a lens, and began almost obsessively snapping pictures, trying to capture the many facets of the colorful, bustling scene.

What appeared to be two immense Chinese Imperial palaces floated majestically in mid-harbor. Large electric signs on top advertised them as floating seafood restaurants, and small boats plied back and forth from shore, ferrying people to the restaurants. Their ornate, lavish decorations and garish colors glistened in the sunlight, a stark contrast to the dingy poverty of the sampans. Color and activity saturated the scene. Randy excitedly snapped picture after picture.

Seemingly out of nowhere, a wooden motorboat materialized alongside our sidewalk, and a raspy voice broke into the picturesque scene. "You wanna go restaurant?" A stout woman wearing wide black trousers, a white Mandarin-collared blouse, and a woven conical bamboo hat, grinned toothlessly, gesturing to a wooden seat behind her. I was tempted. I knew Randy was itching to get closer to action on the water.

"No restaurant, only harbor ride."

"You wanna go restaurant? Only seven Hong Kong dollah," she persisted.

"No restaurant. Ride around." We gestured at the harbor, making circles with our hands. "How much, one-half hour?"

We bargained back and forth over the length of the trip and the price, reaching a price satisfying both of us. She nodded and motioned to the seat. We could have bargained her lower, but she probably needed the money, and it let her save face. I didn't want to bargain too shrewdly because for Westerners, bargaining is a game but, for locals, it can be the difference between eating or not that day.

We climbed in, and for half an hour, she motored us slowly up and down the small channels among the boats, giving us an intimate glimpse into life on the water. In such tight quarters, people lived out their lives in front of the community. Old men sat on deck smoking, playing cards or mahjong in their pajamas, while women hung clothes on makeshift clotheslines strung from every available part of the boat. Small children squatted on deck, staring out at the busy harbor. Some came running to peer curiously at us over the sides of their boat, but adults continued their daily living as if we were invisible.

A man relieved himself off the stern of his boat, oblivious to everyone around him. People mended nets, washed clothes in small tubs, or cooked pots of rice on small grills. Smells of grilling fish sometimes wafted temptingly over the water, reminding us of approaching lunch. Sometimes we heard a Chinese radio chattering away, a fight between neighboring boats, or an occasional splash, indicating someone had thrown or dropped something overboard. Trash disposal, I assumed. The harbor looked like a floating garbage dump.

The harbor water was anoxic and beyond disgusting. Floating garbage, sewage, and formless black lumps floated about on the oily black water. In some areas, bubbles of hydrogen sulfide belched up to the surface. *This harbor is lifeless; nothing could live in there.* Small ragged children ran around, jumping and balancing on the boards between boats. *How many curious unattended children had fallen overboard and drowned in the filthy water?*

Some of the world's poorest people lived here, and while I wouldn't have wanted to live in such a place myself, yet I sensed a feeling of community here. Life somehow felt very real compared to the islands of comfortable padded and sanitized suburban existence back home.

Eventually, we found ourselves near the immense Tai Pak floating restaurant. The woman gestured and asked again, "You wanna go restaurant?" Now we realized she probably received a commission for each customer she brought them.

Primed by the proximity and smells from the small grills, we decided to try the restaurant, hoping it wasn't too expensive. There would certainly be space; it was said to seat 2,000 people. She motored us up to the short dock, and we entered the multi-floored palatial restaurant through a large, elaborately doorway of gold dragons and intricate designs. Pictures of Queen Elizabeth, Churchill, Eisenhower, movie stars, and famous people lined the walls, attesting to its popularity. Like everywhere in Hong Kong, it was crowded, and business was brisk, but we found an empty table.

The Chinese place a premium on fresh seafood, and an efficient waiter guided us to a giant aquarium filled with large, bored fish swimming in endless circles around the tank. We picked out two for lunch. The waiter expertly dipped in a net, hauled out our selections, and whisked them off to the kitchen. At our table, we ordered drinks, vegetables, and noodles and waited for the fish. They arrived quickly, crispy and hot. We enjoyed a leisurely lunch for another hour, people-watching and speculating on the contents of unusual dishes being carried past our table.

Suddenly Randy began frantically searching around his chair. I lowered my chopsticks and stared at him. "What's wrong? Are you OK?"

"My camera stuff is gone!" He spoke with disbelief, his face ashen. "Did you see me bring it in?" I had to admit I hadn't.

"Oh. No," he said softly, running his hands nervously through his hair, as reality sank in. "I think I left it on the sidewalk. How could I *do* that?" He berated himself, yet was still half disbelieving. "I have thousands of dollars of equipment. It's been over two hours. There's no way it's still there."

"Come on. We still have to go look," I said. We waved frantically to catch the waiter's eye, threw money at the bill, hailed a boat, and rushed back to shore. Unsure where he had left it, we disembarked at the nearest point and walked hurriedly along the shoreline, anxiously scanning the sidewalk for a black case.

We soon spotted it about 100 yards ahead, lying open on the sidewalk, its contents displayed, tempting those passing by. Randy's huge sigh of relief reflected amazement. "I can't believe it's still here!" I sped up, but he grabbed my arm. "Hold on. Slow down. Let's see why no one's taking it." We slowed our walk, watching people react to the case.

One after another, people strolled by, stopped, and looked in, assessing the contents. Then they glanced furtively around to see who was watching. Seeing no one but still suspicious, they straightened up. But then, unable to help themselves, they looked greedily into the case again. It had to be some kind of trap; nobody would accidentally leave something so expensive displayed there. And with a last lingering look, they left without touching it.

Amazing. It was still intact. Anywhere else, the case would have developed legs the minute he turned his back. Randy walked over, closed it, and picked it up with an audible sigh of relief. "I'm a wreck," he said. "How about going to the Peak for tea?"

We caught the bus back to downtown and, by trial and error, bumbled our way to the Victoria Peak cable car. The small, ancient cars jerked, swayed, and creaked their way 1,811 feet up an almost vertical incline to Victoria Peak, the tallest point on Hong Kong Island. Our ancient, rusty car seemed so frail I was almost afraid to move for fear it would detach from the cable before reaching the top.

A small German beer garden perched on top, a stone wall and some flowering shrubs peacefully enclosing a few cheap, oil-cloth covered tables. A tiny peek-a-boo view of Kowloon, Victoria Harbor, and the steep green mountainside below was possible from between the bushes outside. In the far distance, a forest of tall, pencil-thin towers with tops immersed in a brownish ozone haze, marked the border of mainland China. An amazing view. *Why doesn't the garden take advantage of this?*

As dusk approached, lights began flickering on all over Hong Kong like so many fireflies. A few strings of outdoor lights randomly draped overhead created a warm glow in the comfortable atmosphere, making the perfect end to a fascinating day. I loved it and thought I would come here again if I ever managed to return to Hong Kong, not dreaming I'd return here twice within less than a year. However, progress was coming to Hong Kong, and soon neither Aberdeen Harbor nor the Peak would be the same.

In five days, I would leave for Thailand. Every country had its share of discomfort and uncertainty, but Thailand, my longest stay, would be the most unique.

- Seventeen -

Let the Wind Blow

Field Study: Bangkok, Thailand 1966-1967

THAILAND, MY MAJOR DESTINATION, PROVED TO BE many things: uncomfortable, challenging, and frustrating, yet often beautiful, fascinating and awe-inspiring. Small temples and villages dotted the beautiful countryside, interspersed with remnants of jungle, a contrast to humid, sprawling, and dusty Bangkok. I planned to stay with a Thai friend's family for several months, collect fish for my thesis, and work out of the Fisheries Station in Yanawa district.

The large, once-green wooden house on Bangkok's Sukhumwit Road had seen better days. It was set back from the street at the end of a lane, and still had old trees, remnants of a rather unmaintained lawn, and a few flowering shrubs. In a neighborhood of more modern houses, it seemed a throwback to the bygone era of relaxed, more rural lifestyles.

The family relationships felt strained. The four people in the house passed each other silently, like monks in a temple, living together but hardly speaking and maybe not even liking each other much. Fortunately, everyone seemed comfortable talking to me, but my less-than-fluent Thai limited our conversations to the superficial, making any in-depth connection difficult.

Kuhn Chalerm, the father, was a professional, and he looked the part. He was trim and distinguished, intelligent and pleasant, but he rarely spoke little more than a sentence or two to anyone. He spoke some English,

159

although he didn't speak enough for me to ascertain how much. He talked about karma and Buddhism, but I couldn't identify with it. In Buddhism, working to accumulate good karma increases your chances of reaching nirvana, a state of nothingness. But nothingness wasn't something I aspired to attain.

Once when I expressed my thanks for letting me stay with them, Chalerm said, "I add good karma by having you." But helping people only to increase his own karma seemed self-serving rather than altruistic, and made me wonder how he actually felt about having me there.

He asked if I would act as hostess and help serve the visitors when he entertained. I was happy to help out because his wife, Kuhn Boonsri, Chalerm's total opposite, disappeared when visitors arrived. I found it difficult to imagine them as a couple. Her slovenly, ponderous bulk shuffled around the house in a shapeless shift, her flat, cracked feet stuffed into old flip-flops or slippers. She spoke no English and seemed to hold to many old superstitions.

Almost immediately, Boonsri asked if I had a boyfriend. She seemed relieved when I said "Yes, in the Philippines," but she periodically reminded me I needed to *"su trong fahn,"* (be faithful to my boyfriend.) At first, I thought she felt concerned for Carlos, but then I realized she was very possessive of her son Aroon, and just worried I would steal him and whisk him off to America. She guarded him like Doña Isabella had policed Amaya. If she saw us even casually talking, she immediately invented errands for him. One of the relatives later warned me: "Be careful; she'll be very upset if she sees you and Aroon talking."

Boonsri didn't need to worry. Aroon, a university student, was friendly and about my age, but I never saw him except at dinner, and when he was home Boonsri ordered him around non-stop like a maid. Calls of "Ar-ooooon….., Ar-ooooon…." seemed to echo incessantly through the house. He patiently put up with her, keeping his feelings carefully hidden, but he rolled his eye at me in exasperation.

An eye infection had left Aroon blind in one eye, and apparently the other was badly damaged, because his thick heavy glasses magnified his eyes to the point that they threatened to overtake his whole face.

Boonsri didn't believe in doctors, but she had a smooth, round, magical black stone that could be placed on any dysfunctional body part and cure anything. I gathered it had initially treated Aroon's eye. Unfortunately, the stone wasn't up to the eye infection, and he lost his vision. But I provided proof of the stone's power. Boonsri loaned it to me once when I had an ear infection. Sure enough, it cured my earache, although I imagine the doctor's ear drops helped a bit too.

The daughter-in-law lived in an attached apartment above the carport. Oddly, I never saw anyone interact with her or her young son even once. We got along well, and she went out of her way to make me feel comfortable. Sometimes we went out to eat, horseback ride, or play tennis at her club, and perhaps understanding life on my side of the house, she offered me breakfast in her apartment but, not wanting to impose, I usually ate breakfast somewhere on the way downtown.

My thesis involved fish, and the new fisheries station in Yanawa provided me with lab space for doing fish dissections. It employed about 50 people, and most were friendly and around my age. Most exciting of all, more often than not, the building's toilets actually worked. That was a major plus; the ones at home seldom worked well because water service was unreliable and sporadic. One day I realized I had subconsciously been planning my daily activities based on the location of working toilets.

Bangkok couldn't supply water to the entire city at once, so water service rotated from area to area. Because we couldn't predict when to expect water in our area, a bathroom tap remained open all day in our house, with a giant Chinese ceramic jar beneath it to catch water whenever it happened to come on. Sometimes, no one noticed when the water came on, so they didn't turn off the faucet once the jar filled. Occasionally walking past the bathroom, I saw the water on, the jar overflowing, and precious water flowing down the drain. *If everyone did that, no wonder Bangkok had a water shortage.*

Obtaining fish for my thesis was challenging. I had no way to catch them, so I bought fish at the covered pier next to the fisheries station, where the ocean trawlers docked. I needed to leave home at 4:30 a.m. and go by taxi, to arrive by 5:00 a.m.

Although dark for at least another hour, the noisy bustling cement pier swarmed with people pushing handcarts and dollies. Buyers unloaded boxes and stacked large wicker baskets, bantering loudly back and forth over the rattling of chains and clanking of metal trays. A few dim overhead lights illuminated the busy scene and reflected off misty morning raindrops splashing into the dark, oily harbor water. Steam rising from the freshly washed cement dock caught the light and dissipated upward into the misty night.

A vague fishy, saltwater smell mingled with the aroma of fresh sweet buns, fried fish, soup, and noodles. Vendors wandered through the crowd, hawking their specialties, reminding me I needed breakfast.

I often bought my breakfast from the soup man, who carried his entire store on his back. Two large, heavily loaded wicker baskets hung from the ends of a long bamboo pole balanced over his shoulders. The weight bent the bamboo into an arc that bounced slightly as he carefully maneuvered down the street. One basket contained assorted plastic bowls, chopsticks, and a large, heavy tub of hot water. The other held a large kettle of hot soup. I had difficulty imagining how he could even carry this load, let alone balance it from a pole while navigating the crowded streets.

His soup, a flavored broth with organ meats and vegetables, varied somewhat from day to day but normally contained pieces of liver, tripe, intestine, and other unidentifiable organs mixed with fish, mushrooms, some soft leaves, bok choy, and a green bean or two. The hot and surprisingly flavorful soup cost only one baht, about 5 cents.

In spite of his difficult work, he always looked happy. He recognized me, grinned, and automatically handed me chopsticks, reached into the basket for a bowl and ladled in some soup. I fished out the solids with the chopsticks, drank the soup from the bowl, and returned them. He swished them swiftly once through the hot water and placed the bowl and chopsticks on the pile, ready to hand off to the next customer. *The soup is good and seems safe, but the dishwashing methodology sure leaves something to be desired.* Yet I never became sick.

It was still dark when the large trawlers began arriving, their nets bulging with fish. Long metal arms swung the heavy nets over the pier and poured the night's catch into a massive pile on the cement dock. The daily catch, a grab-bag of jumbled species, ran the gamut from giant tuna to smaller reef fishes and even an occasional small shark or stingray.

Buyers swarmed over the giant mound, rapidly sorting the fish into rope or wicker baskets by species. Thankfully, a biologist from the fisheries station volunteered to help me select the fish I needed because most of the Thai species were unfamiliar. He picked a basket and pawed quickly through the pile, grabbing fish. Within half an hour, the massive mound was entirely sorted and sold. Regardless of the species, someone would buy it. I brought my fish back to the lab and placed them in jars of formalin.

My thesis required fish dissections, and I dissected a few fish at the fisheries station, but it seemed easier to bring the fish back and dissect them in Hawaii. I didn't come here to spend all my time in a lab. I wanted free time to sightsee and visit with my returned Thai friends and other classmates passing through Bangkok on their own field studies.

Sometimes, I battled the dust, humid heat, and ever-present flies to wander the streets and visit one of the magnificent temples. Their shining gilded spires and golden *chedis* pierced the dusty ozone haze above the dingy roofs of the nondescript surroundings, and glowed in the sunlight, making them easy to spot. Most downtown buildings looked much alike to me, and since I was unable to read signs, sometimes I used the temple spires to help navigate parts of the city.

Thai temples were the most exquisite and ornate temples I had ever seen, and guaranteed to put any visitor on sensory overload. They provided exotic islands of fantastic architecture and color amid the drab surround-ings. The uptilted roofs, often covered with thick orange, green and yellow ceramic tiles, topped walls covered with hundreds of thousands of small, intricate tiles. Every inch, inside and out, was decorated in exquisite detail with gold leaf, stones, and small tiles. The ornate detail in the temples extended to the furnishings, pavilions, statues, and other structures in the temple complex.

The centerpiece of each temple was a giant serene Buddha. Wat Po housed Thailand's largest, a reclining Buddha an astounding 150 feet long and 50 feet high, entirely covered with gold leaf, except for soles of the sixteen-foot feet, which were inlaid with mother-of-pearl. Rows of bronze and gold-covered Buddhas lined the walls. Gongs, giant demons, ornate mythical creatures, frescoed walls, altars, and other objects filled the tem-ples, everything ornate and all undeserving of being dismissed with so little description.

When Boonsri talked of her temple, I expected something like that.

Despite her possessiveness of Aroon, Boonsri had a kind heart, and one day she invited me to accompany her to her temple. In contrast to the beautiful intricate temples, whose visitors seemed to be primarily cam-era-laden tourists, Boonsri's relatively small, simple temple seemed more authentic. Only worshippers filled her temple, and I was the only *farang*, or foreigner. Large, smoking incense coils hung from the ceiling, sending clouds of incense wafting through heavy, dark wooden beams in the dimly lit temple. Saffron-robed monks glided silently through the passages.

In the front, facing outward, a large, rather plain bronze Buddha sat in a lotus pose, surrounded by various plates holding offerings of rice balls, fruit, a few cigarettes, sometimes money, and other gifts. We paid a few baht, and in return, we each received a lotus flower, an incense stick, a postage-stamp-sized piece of thin gold leaf, and a chopstick-sized piece of wood covered with writing. Boonsri bowed to the Buddha. We placed the lotus flowers in a large water pot nearby, lit the incense sticks, and poked them into a sand-filled urn at the Buddha's side. Later I saw someone col-lect the flowers from the water pot, and wondered if they would be resold.

We looked for a suitable smaller Buddha statue to place our gold leaf. People placed the gold leaf on the Buddha depending on which part of their body needed help. The Buddha we chose wore the most gold leaf on his stomach, so I gathered that many worshippers had stomach problems. I had the beginning of my ear infection, so I patted my square on his ear. We brought our sticks to the fortune teller, who added them to a number of his own, shook them up in a tin cup, dumped them out like a game of Pick-up-Sticks, and read our fortunes. Mine was generic and non-specific.

Chalerm's comment about working for good karma had made me suspect everyone's motives, and now I couldn't help wondering, *Did Boonsri invite me only to build some good karma?* Then I decided perhaps she simply wanted to give me an experience, and I gave her the benefit of the doubt.

A week later, I was having lunch with a returned EWC friend, when she said "Do you want to visit my palm reader? He's near here, and very good."

"Sure. I'd like that." I didn't believe in palmistry, but at least it was based on a system, unlike seances or crystal balls. We weaved our way through a narrow lane and down a sidewalk crowded with palm readers, fortune tellers, astrologists, reflexologists, and diviners of tea leaves and entrails. In contrast to those sitting along the sidewalk amid their cloth zodiac signs and astrological charts, her palmist was a professional.

We found his closet-sized shop and entered to find a dignified, gray-haired Chinese man sitting on a stool, hunched over a heavy leather volume filled with palm prints. Stacks of oversized leather-bound books filled his small shop, floor to ceiling. They contained decades of readings, attesting to his methodical and precise recordkeeping.

He inked our right palms, pressed them carefully on empty numbered pages, and scrutinized the prints thoughtfully through his wire-rimmed spectacles. He predicted a long life, two children, marriage to a foreigner, and extensive long-distance travel in my future, all relatively safe bets for any young single foreigner in Bangkok. But then he mentioned I would be married in September, which I found interesting since I wasn't even engaged. In case I ever wanted to revisit my reading, he annotated the highlights on a slip of paper for me as he talked, and recorded the volume number and date of my print, using the Buddhist calendar year (2509 B.E., or Buddhist Era, based on Buddha's death year.) Palmistry seemed to have no scientific basis, and he said nothing exceptional, but his accuracy turned out to be 100 percent.

The exchange rate was 20 baht to the dollar, so foreigners spending dollars lived cheaply. The EWC gave us $10 per diem, but since I stayed free with my friend's family, I could live on about thirty cents a day. I spent one baht each way for the bus, one or two baht for breakfast, and one baht for lunch, although being a spendthrift, I often spent two, so I could have a coke with my lunch, something my co-workers thought quite wasteful. I ate dinners at home.

Boonsri cooked simple, healthy, and rather generic meals; rice, fried fish, a soup or a cooked vegetable, a fresh lettuce salad soaked in bright purple potassium permanganate to kill bacteria, and sometimes a bit of watermelon for dessert. She never cooked noodles or any dishes I considered particularly Thai. I contributed by washing the dishes and grinding the small hot red chili peppers to make *Nam Prik*, the hot chili pepper sauce accompanying every meal.

Dinnertime was almost wordless, punctuated with only an occasional request to pass the food. The silence became more uncomfortable each night. Aroon and I, both students, had many things to talk about, and he wanted to practice English, while I wanted to practice Thai. But with Boonsri, any conversation would create fallout, so we remained quiet.

One afternoon, after more than a normal number of demands, in a minor fit of rebellion, Aroon suddenly said on the spur of the moment, "Let's go movies." We timed our escape to avoid Boonsri's sharp eyes, and sneaking out with a mixture of guilt and glee, we ran outside and down the long driveway laughing, pleased with our escape.

A few weeks after I arrived, a relative appeared unexpectedly and conveniently at dinnertime. Kasem came from his work at an oil company, and despite the oppressive heat, he wore a suit. Short and well-padded, jovial and outgoing, Kasem laughed loudly, smiled broadly, and talked non-stop through dinner, seemingly oblivious to the absence of other conversation. I found it a relief. Then he began returning every night for dinner, which eventually began to annoy Chalerm, who told me, "This is not polite." But perhaps it relieved Boonsri, because Kasem's monologue passed for dinner conversation and prevented me from getting my clutches on Aroon.

Thai was more challenging to pick up than I expected. In Costa Rica, I learned Spanish words daily because even without knowing the meaning, I could read them, pronounce them, glean meaning from the context, or remember to look them up later. But not Thai. I lacked proficiency at reading characters, and Thai sentences have no spaces between words, making it difficult to identify individual words, so I couldn't pick up words by reading. Conversation was the easiest way to learn. Kasem knew a smattering of English and was very patient. He did more for my conversational Thai than anyone else in Thailand.

Thai grammar is simple. Thai doesn't conjugate verbs or have first, second, or third person endings like Spanish or French. It differentiates tenses by adding time words, so putting a Thai sentence together is somewhat like speaking pidgin English. Translated literally, you say, "Today I go store, yesterday I go store, and tomorrow I go store." Once you learn some vocabulary and how to place the adjectives and adverbs, it's relatively easy to make a sentence.

Unfortunately, what the listener hears might be vastly different from what you thought you said, because Thai has five tones, and each syllable has a tone. A slight difference in tonal pronunciation can be the difference between saying "tiger" and "shirt," and the tones are so subtle they often strain the Western ear.

I went around for weeks saying what I thought was "excuse me," only to learn I somehow missed a slight difference in pronouncing an 'o,' and I was actually saying "let the wind blow." No wonder people smiled whenever I said it. They knew what I meant and never tried to correct me. When someone finally pointed out my mistake, I still couldn't distinguish the sounds, although they repeated the difference to me several times. I knew I would never say it correctly.

Before I left Hawaii, several Thais had warned me about cultural rules relating to feet and heads.

"Be sure to remove your shoes before entering a house," one friend said. That was simple.

"Never point the bottom of your foot at anyone; it's insulting," my Thai teacher said. That was problematic, particularly when sitting uncomfortably on the floor at a low table, because it seemed impossible not to point my soles somewhere. When I broke that rule, if I knew them, people lifted an eyebrow and quietly nodded toward my feet. Even with cushions, positions on the floor were uncomfortable, and I could count on breaking that rule almost every time.

"Keep your head lower than royalty," someone else said. *Fat chance I'll need that one.* Then I bumped into Chinda, an EWC grantee now returned to Bangkok. We met for lunch, and afterward, she asked, "Would you like to meet my mother?"

That seemed odd, but I said, "Sure." When we went to her house, I saw the head rule in operation.

Chinda's mother was royalty of some sort. "When you meet her, be sure to keep your head lower than hers," Chinda said.

A maid let us into the old style, once-elegant house, and left us standing in the entry while she disappeared, presumably to ask Chinda's mother if she would receive visitors. Then she returned, and guided us to a large, somewhat dim, tall-ceilinged room, where her mother sat placidly cross-legged on a simple raised platform like a Buddha. She did not rise or speak in greeting. We walked in, heads low, hunched over in deference, hands steepled in front of us, and greeted her mother with a deep *wai*.

The two of them acted like strangers; they exchanged no smiles or hugs, and I sensed little feeling of connection between them. They talked briefly, using High Thai, a formal language above my comprehension. Then we said goodbye and backed out, making sure to keep our heads lower than hers. The whole scene felt anachronistic. *I can understand <u>my</u> need for deference, but this is her <u>mom.</u>* I couldn't imagine ever being so formal with my mom, even if she were queen. I couldn't decide whether Chinda was modeling for me how to act with royalty or whether they interacted that way even in private. However, it soon became a non-issue when Chinda married an American grantee and moved to Hawaii.

And then there was the monk rule. "Never touch a monk." They took monk-touching quite seriously. Monks were commonplace because at some point in their lives, most Thai men become monks for a few months to intercede for a sick family member or other pressing problems. *This rule sounds simple enough; their long saffron robes should make monks easy to spot and avoid.*

On December 9-20, 1966, Bangkok was hosting the Fifth Asian Games, so my bus from the office was more over-crowded than usual. Like the Japanese shinkansen, people jammed the bus to over-capacity. A tidal wave of people poured in, shoving and carrying me along to the back of the bus. To my dismay, I found myself jammed in beside a young monk. Neither of us could move an inch. Horrified, people began pointing and motioning for me to move. There was nowhere to move, but they continued to point, becoming increasingly agitated.

Ti nai kah? Mai dai. Where? I can't, I protested. But that wasn't sufficient. They wanted us separated. I was undoubtedly making him unclean, but touching his robe was unavoidable. The monk avoided looking at me but made no effort to move either.

I hoped someone would say *mai pen rai*, a common expression essentially meaning "never mind," or "it doesn't matter." It covers a multitude of situations, but no one was assuring me with that. They were becoming visibly more upset and more vocal by the moment. I began to wonder if I would disrupt the whole bus, maybe even cause a riot. The monk stared ahead, expressionless, pretending not to notice.

I had spectacularly broken the "don't touch the monk" rule and couldn't wait to leave the bus. When some people began exiting at my stop, as a little space opened up, I elbowed and shoved my way to the front, telling everyone to "let the wind blow," as I determinedly plowed toward the door. I wondered briefly how the monk would get decontaminated.

The entire city spruced up in a flurry of excitement for the Asian games. This major production attracted over 2,500 athletes from 40 countries and featured 16 sports in 142 separate events. Every light post flew colorful banners announcing the games, and advertisements plastered every size-able inner-city billboard. The official song of the games was in English, the only common language, and it continually blasted from loudspeakers on the street. Today the games rival the Olympics, with almost forty sports, including an unusual variety of obscure martial arts competitions, yet the Asian Games are still virtually unknown in the West.

Kasem invited me to *Muay Thai*, or Thai boxing. I'm not a boxing fan, but it turned out to be quite entertaining. Thai kickboxing uses kicks, knees, fists, and elbows, and the fighters are so proficient at extremely high kicks it looks almost like a choreographed ballet.

A week later, we went to the racetrack, and it began dawning on me these were serious dates, and he was working hard to impress me. When he learned I planned a visit to Chiang Mai in northern Thailand, he insisted I stay with his widowed mother for a couple of days. I much preferred to be on my own, but I saw no easy way out. In retrospect, this was serious. *Now I was meeting his family.*

One night as my departure from Bangkok approached, he caught me off-guard. Without preliminaries, he suggested (roughly translated), "Maybe we married. I come States. We no sleep together. Divorce when I get green card." *Wow. I didn't see that coming! And so romantic. Such a deal. Put my life on hold for three years so he could get a green card.* It wouldn't be much of a bargain for me, but it would be a windfall for him; people often paid ten thousand dollars for such an arrangement. I'd have been a pretty cheap date if he could have pulled it off. I doubt he expected me to agree, but I guess he felt it worth a try.

My stay in Bangkok had not been particularly comfortable. The unpredictable water, often non-working toilets, and hot, humid, dusty and fly-filled days were uncomfortable. The nights were filled with the drone of mosquitoes. They came through the screenless windows in droves, because the old, warped, wooden shutters did little to keep them out. Bangkok was the most humid place I had lived, and I was perennially bathed in a mist of sweat. I also missed English conversation. Yet, people had been kind and helpful, the culture was vibrant and fascinating, and many experiences would remain burned in my memory.

A week before I left, I received an air letter from Laura, now on field study in Japan. She was cutting it short and returning to Honolulu to marry Ed. Her parents had exploded, because Ed was Japanese American. Despite the distance and cost, her mother called, ranted, wrote nasty letters, even came to Hawaii, threatened to disinherit her, and called again. It was ugly, excruciating, and gut-wrenching for everyone.

"They believe mixed marriage is morally wrong; how can you fight that?" Laura asked. She and Ed married before I even returned from field study. Her parents didn't attend and refused to acknowledge Ed or engage with him. Laura stood firm, saying if they wanted to see her, they had to accept Ed. They remained estranged for years until grandchildren, the best mitigation for prejudice, finally brought them around.

Laura's small Midwest hometown town came from the same mold as Glen Ellyn. I didn't know whether anything would come of my relationship with Carlos, but I never seriously considered the possibility that my parents might be upset.

Then, hauling my jars of fish, I set off for Laos, excited to visit my old roommate, Pheng.

It will be interesting to meet Pheng at home in her own environment and see how she's readjusting after two years exposure to the West in Hawaii.

- *Eighteen* -
Shadows of the Past

<u>**Field Study: Laos, January 1967**</u>

L AOS WAS A YOUNG COUNTRY IN 1967; IT HAD GAINED
independence from the French Colonial Empire in 1953, only 13 years
earlier. Smaller than the state of Michigan, it had only 2.3 million people. A
civil war had already divided Laos into a Communist portion in the North
and East and a Royalist portion in the South and West. Pheng lived in
Vientiane, the southern capital.

Pheng and a friend met me at the small airport, and we drove to a restaurant for lunch. Before leaving, they pestered me until I used the restroom.
Their persistence should have been a clue for me. Then we toured the city. It
was difficult to think of this as a capital city. Everything was small, old, and
primitive. The two-story building where Pheng worked looked taller than
almost everything except the defining symbol of Vientiane, the Patuxai
war monument.

The large square Patuxai resembled the Parisian Arc de Triomphe in
general shape and size, and straddled a wide walkway in the downtown
park. It looked something like a hybrid between a Disneyland castle and St.
Basil's turreted Cathedral in Moscow, although the tall arched entrances
on all four sides and five ornate turrets were obviously Lao. It was only four
years old, and possibly the largest structure in Laos at that time.

Laos constructed the Patuxai with American-donated cement intended
for an airport expansion. I doubt the gift was altruistic. The Vietnam

war was expanding, and I suspect the U.S. wanted an airport expansion more than the Laotians did. However, locals apparently thought Vientiane needed a unique symbol more than a larger airport, and Patuxai filled that function well. Since the country lacked almost everything, I wondered how the U.S. viewed diverting airport cement to a monument, but it provided something the Laotians could be proud of. *If I were Laotian, I might prefer the Patuxai to an airport expansion too.*

As we started toward Pheng's house, she and her friend discussed plans for the next day. It jolted me to realize I understood much of the conversation; I hadn't known Thai and Laotian were so similar.

"That sounds like a good plan," I said, startling Pheng, who had left Hawaii before I began studying Thai. Another stop, again urging me to use the restroom, and her friend dropped us off in Pheng's village, a couple of miles from downtown.

Her small rural village of perhaps twenty unpainted board houses sat peacefully along the banks of the Mekong River. The clean, hard-packed ground around the homes supported little vegetation, although a few bananas and coconut palms provided touches of edible greenery. A few thin dogs ambled around or slept lazily in the sun, and stray chickens scratched around in the dirt under the houses, hoping for an occasional bug or worm. It was tranquil, showing no trace of the civil war occurring in the North.

Like all the other houses, Pheng's house of weathered boards and rusty tin roof sat elevated on posts. Nearby, a young-looking man and woman wearing long printed cotton sarongs tied under their armpits stood chest-deep in a small but deep waterhole, swishing nets through the muddy water. Beside them, on the bank, a couple of two-inch minnows swam around in a small yellow plastic bucket.

The pond was liquid mud. *How could any fish survive long in there?*

Pheng introduced us, and as I steepled my hands in the traditional *wai*, I realized these were her parents, and the fish were dinner.

The house had several rooms, and Pheng's seemed to be the largest of all. Given its size and adjacency to the entryway, I guessed perhaps it had once been the main family room. Possibly they gave it to her either as an honored person who had been abroad, or because she was the only daughter. Since we had been roommates for a year, I assumed we would share the room, so we could talk and reconnect, but wanting to give me privacy, she spent the night with her younger brothers. *Why?*

I glanced around the bedroom with interest. The wood-planked room looked twice the size of our Hawaii dorm room. Its shuttered, glassless and screenless windows kept it breezy and cool. The only furnishings were a small wooden chest of drawers, a futon, and a pillow, which turned out to be quite comfortable. A turquoise two-piece swimming suit, mask and snorkel decorated the wall above the futon like prize fish.

As with Sanjiya, I had no idea Pheng even owned a swimming suit, much less a two-piece. And a mask and snorkel? I knew she couldn't swim, and I couldn't imagine it. *When and with whom did she go to the beach?* We had joined group parties and dates together, and she had occasionally mentioned a Laotian man I knew, but if she had dated him, she did it quietly.

Now I finally figured out why the girls had been so insistent I use the restaurant restroom. I saw no bathroom or outhouse but, not wanting to lose face, she let me figure it out. The Mekong River was only a few hundred feet away, and I assumed the whole village used it both for bathing and as a latrine. *I'd better have a spot selected in advance in case I need it.* I decided to walk down to the river and unobtrusively scout out a private place for later use.

I no sooner emerged from the house than a gaggle of seven or eight elementary school children appeared seemingly from nowhere and attached themselves to me. They swarmed and jumped around, clamoring for attention and loudly chanting repeatedly, almost in unison, "Hello. Hello. What you name? Where you from?" proud to show off their few phrases of English. I told them my name was Joan, eliciting a titter of merriment that puzzled me until I remembered that in Thai, at least, the word 'Joan' means "thief."

They walked me down to the river, sticking to me like appendages. Everything I did seemed fascinating to them, and I knew I'd have no privacy on the river or anywhere else, at least until dark. The importance of the chamber pot in the bedroom hadn't fully registered with me when I arrived. *That explains why Pheng gave me a room to myself.* Now understanding, I returned to the house.

The following day Pheng was working. We walked down the front steps and around the back of the house to an old blue car I hadn't noticed the day before. I assumed we would drive it to her work. Pheng walked over, made a show of kicking the tires, and pronounced them good. She got in, sat down, turned the key, and started the car. She turned the lights and windshield wiper on and off and revved the engine loudly. Then to my surprise, she turned it off, got out, and we walked out to the road and flagged down a tuk-tuk.

These motorized rickshaws and tricycles originated in Bangkok but quickly spread throughout Asia as a substitute for taxis. Their name derives from the loud "tuk-tuk" sound of the engine. Most have three wheels, an open, sheet-metal body with side curtains, metal or canvas top, and a cloth seat accommodating two normal-sized people. Often the cab is powered by an attached motorcycle. Although noisy and polluting, they provide a cheap, open-air ride.

We climbed in and rode into town. "Whose car was that?" I asked, confused.

"Mine."

"Then why don't we take it?"

"I don't drive it anymore." Like many Asians, although she may have had a driver's license, I doubt she had formally learned to drive, because Asia had few if any, driver education courses. I saw no other cars in the village. She never owned a car in Hawaii, but now, apparently, she wanted the prestige of a vehicle. Then the story got murky. Pheng had driven the car once or twice until she hit something or someone. She didn't elaborate, and I didn't ask. It caused a big loss of face, and now she didn't drive anymore, but she didn't want to part with the car either, so it sat, gassed up, a rusting status symbol in the yard. *Does she realize the gas in the car will eventually go bad? And how will she handle that?*

I felt sad for her. The car, swimming suit, mask, and snorkel were symbols and nostalgic reminders of a life she once lived for a short time, but now so far removed from her current life that Hawaii must have seemed like a fantasy. *Had the EWC been a good thing for her?* I wondered how Pheng viewed her Hawaii experience. I'd never seen her crack a book all year. *Had she ever regretted not finishing her degree and perhaps parlaying it into something more? Did my intrusion into her present bring up buried shadows of the past she had put behind her? Did I revive good memories or only make her feel loss? The contrast was so great. Could she ever feel satisfied in Laos again after exposure to the West in Hawaii?*

She had asked me nothing about our friends or the EWC. She seemed to have walled off that part of her life, and I hesitated to reopen that door.

To prevent an Asian brain-drain, EWC required Asian grantees to return home for two years before returning to the States. And many later returned, using the Hawaii degree to change their lives and become productive U.S. citizens. For Pheng, that chance had vanished, at least for the moment.

With Pheng at the office, I wandered Vientiane, bought some material in a local open-air market, and walked along the bank of the Mekong, using Thai with some of the farmers growing taro and other crops along the bank. We were both surprised we could communicate. Foreigners were a novelty, and the farmers proudly showed me their fields and explained their crops.

That night after dinner, we had a surprise; Sengphet's parents came to visit. Somehow, they learned of my visit. I had forgotten Sengphet was Pheng's relative. The 'bamboo telegraph,' Asia's counterpart to the grapevine, was apparently alive and well in Vientiane.

In Honolulu, Mai Phuong and Sengphet were planning to marry, and his family wanted to know all about this Vietnamese woman. What was she like? Did she come from a good family? How well did I know her?

Would they like her? Would she fit in? Behind the questions were possibly things left unsaid: Why not a Laotian girl? And what prestige, wealth, or connections could Mai Phuong bring to the family?

Although I knew little about Mai Phuong's family, I told them what I could about her, assured them we were good friends, and that she would be an excellent match for Sengphet. I don't know whether this reassured them, but it turned out to be more accurate than I knew. Of course, Pheng was good friends with both Mai Phuong and Sengphet but, oddly, she never contributed a word to the conversation.

The EWC produced scores of intercultural marriages. In Hawaii, mixed marriages were almost the norm, and none of us perceived racial or intercultural differences as barriers. It was easy to forget perhaps the rest of the world didn't feel the same way. Almost uniformly, everyone's parents seemed to feel intercultural marriage posed big, even monumental, stumbling blocks fraught with problems. They appeared unable to see that usually the main problem was not different races and cultures, but their own attitudes and ingrained prejudices.

I enjoyed the quick three-day reunion with Pheng and was thankful for her presence because it made things much easier for everyone. Her brothers and parents seemed shy about interacting with me, but we ate all our meals out, so I never saw them for more than a minute. Although they undoubtedly understood Thai, they spoke no English and probably had little or no previous contact with Americans. It could have been uncomfortable for all of us without Pheng there. Then, hauling my jars of fish, I left Laos to visit Mai Phuong's family in Saigon. It was the last time I saw Pheng.

*****

Pheng lost touch with everyone, but I eventually heard she escaped Laos when it fell to the Communists. Recently Sengphet said he heard she now lived in Los Angeles.

Field Study: Vietnam, January 1967

When I arrived to visit Mai Phuong's family in Saigon, now Ho Chi Minh city, Vietnam was celebrating Tet, the Vietnamese lunar new year. Tet is usually joyful, as people celebrate the past year and try to ensure good luck in the coming year. This year it felt subdued.

Mai Phuong's parents were charming, educated, and spoke English well. The family roots were in the beautiful and historic Imperial City of Hue. Her mother's family had lived in the royal Forbidden City, where the king and his family had lived, before the monarchy dissolved. Her father, an influential physician, had established the first medical school there.

Sporadic fighting made life increasingly difficult and unsafe in Hue, but things were still relatively normal in Saigon. Although I'm sure the war never left their minds, no one mentioned it. In addition to her numerous brothers and sisters, the big house overflowed with relatives, and I realized a visitor at this time had to be an inconvenience. Giving me a room meant somewhere else became even more crowded.

The family was warm and welcoming, and the big family dinners, around a long table that must have seated at least fourteen people, were filled with talk and laughter. One of Mai Phuong's family had married an American. They gave me a city tour, and paraded me around Saigon to visit several of Lo's relatives.

Of course, everyone questioned me about Sengphet. I told them I had met his parents in Laos, and they had the same questions about Mai Phuong. Fortunately, the two countries were geographically close and similar in culture, so I sensed this marriage wouldn't meet the parental resistance Laura and Ed's had.

Saigon's layout and elegant buildings reflected the French influence, and even the leaden sky, continual rain, and Saigon's subdued, somber mood couldn't conceal the city's charm. The stores were open, with business as usual. American women were a rarity, and I received a few curious looks as we went through the city, but it felt safe and I sensed no hostility.

Mai Phuong's mother surprised me with a generous and unexpected gift, a beautiful turquoise silk Ao Dai, the long, graceful Vietnamese dress slit up both sides to the waist, and worn over wide black or white trousers. To my surprise, it fit perfectly.

"It's beautiful! How did you know my size?"

Her mother smiled. "Mai Phuong sent me your measurements." Then I remembered Lo had measured me several months before I went on field study, "In case you ever want to buy an ao dai." I never realized she sent the measurements ahead to have one made for my visit.

Had I been less oblivious and truly understood the magnitude of the war, I wouldn't have visited at that time. I felt grateful I had only burdened the family with three days. Unfortunately, now leaving was problematic. I couldn't confirm my flight to the Philippines. The airlines cancelled my reservations, made six months earlier, when the military tied up all the planes. The prospect of being stuck there indefinitely wasn't good news. I finally called the EWC contact at the U.S. embassy, and a spot miraculously opened on a small cargo plane.

The war hadn't visibly impacted Saigon yet, but its presence had reached the airport. A sense of urgency permeated everything, and the bustling airport overflowed with scurrying trucks, jeeps, military vehicles, and planes of every conceivable type. I counted eight small aircraft in a landing pattern moving like an assembly line, landing within seconds of each other with very little air space between them. My plane was stacked up in a similarly long line, awaiting clearance for take-off, and we were airborne within three or four minutes.

The strictly utilitarian flight had no regular seats, and I was the sole passenger. I wondered what strings EWC had pulled to get me on. Hastily loaded cardboard boxes, rope-bound containers, pallets, and crates of miscellaneous odd-looking metal parts were jumbled together and jammed into the plane's stripped-down interior. I carefully maneuvered between boxes, pulled down a wall seat, and strapped myself in for the three-hour flight to Manila. A stretchy nylon net containing large round orange plastic spheres looking like bomb casings rested against my feet.

The Philippines would be my last stop before returning to Honolulu, and I planned to visit Carlos' family for a week. We hadn't seen each other in almost eight months, and were able to correspond only sporadically, so I wasn't sure what to expect of either Manila or my relationship with Carlos.

- *Nineteen* -

Meeting the Family

C ARLOS AND I HAD BEEN CORRESPONDING FOR EIGHT months, but even with the speed of the relatively new "air mail," an exchange of letters took several weeks, and I had been moving around Asia for six months. We had exchanged only a handful of letters the whole time.

A grinning Carlos picked me up at the airport, and we took up right where we had left off eight months earlier, as if we had never been apart. Unlike Pheng's Laotian EWC contemporaries, who were still all studying in Hawaii, the Filipinos in Carlos' group had now returned to the Philippines. They had bonded well, and the EWC was still very much alive for him.

I expected Manila to be a poorer version of Hawaii or Tahiti. Some of its 7,106 islands no doubt looked like that, but sprawling Manila had no pretty palm-treed swimming beaches. Manila didn't have an island lifestyle either; its cathedrals and Spanish remnants reminded me more of cities in Costa Rica. On the large island of Luzon, it was possible to live inland and never even see the beach.

Maintenance seemed an unknown word in Manila. Broken, potholed streets and sidewalks were typical. The city lacked sewers and other basic infrastructure; raw sewage ran through *esteros,* or canals, and emptied untreated into Manila Bay. Drainage was poor, and some areas routinely flooded in the rainy season. It looked old, dingy, and in many parts, trashy. None of the countries I had seen in Asia looked this dilapidated. *This used to be an American territory? We helped Japan rebuild after WWII. Perhaps we should have tried harder to help Manila rebuild.* Yet as a group, Filipinos were some of the happiest people I had ever met. They faced any discomfort and adversity with the comment *"Bahala na,"* or roughly, 'What will be, will be.'

Many people lived in abject poverty. Small children, often piggybacking even younger children, swarmed the streets, walking through lines of dense traffic, begging or hawking single cigarettes and sticks of gum. They offered to guard your car or wash the windshield, and you declined their help at your car's peril.

The ultra-rich existed alongside pockets of poverty. Their tall, ugly concrete-block walls, topped with broken glass and barbed wire to discourage prowlers, gave no hint of the large, opulent houses and beautiful landscaping hidden inside.

In cities like Chicago, San Francisco, Paris, and London, large fires had catalyzed redevelopment by destroying large sections of old vermin-filled buildings and poor infrastructure, allowing for large-scale urban renewal and construction of planned cities more suited to modern living. WWII leveled most of Manila, but unfortunately, Manila rebuilt without taking advantage of the opportunity to plan and upgrade. Privately, I thought, *Whole sections of Manila could benefit from a large controlled burn.*

Like Laos and Vietnam, the Philippines was a young country. It had gained independence from the United States in 1946, only twenty years earlier. Unlike other Asian countries, four centuries of Spanish colonial rule, followed by four decades under the United States, had both heavily influenced the culture. The Spanish legacy included beautiful old cathedrals, Catholicism, and Spanish inclusions in the Tagalog language. Americans left the significant legacy of English and a veneer of democracy.

Schools were taught in English, and most people spoke English as a second or third language, giving them a considerable advantage over other Asians in the international business arena. Tagalog, the national language, incorporated so many Spanish and English words I could often follow pieces of the conversation. No matter how nice they were, other Asian cities felt foreign to me, but Western influence produced so many similarities to Costa Rica that the Philippines felt comfortably like coming home.

Carlos' family lived in Paco, a residential but increasingly commercialized section of Manila. They were comfortably unconcerned with appearances, but Carlos said, "We painted the inside of the house for the first time since WWII in honor of your coming."

His father, Victor, a lawyer who had retired from the second highest position in the Bureau of Internal Revenue, was probably the only person in the BIR who had never accepted a bribe. He was a risk-averse and somewhat introverted personality, conservative and practical, bureaucratic, and frugal to the extreme.

Carlos' brother, Mario, was a down-to-earth and unpretentious farmer, and Mario's wife, Fe, ran a small store and supported several small charities.

Carlos' mother, Solita, former Dean of Business Administration at Philippine Women's University, had recently retired. She was twenty years younger than Victor, and in many ways his total opposite. Her small, thin, energetic presence increased the energy level of any room she entered. She refused to dwell on anything negative and she could find the positive side of any situation.

Solita was an outgoing and fearless entrepreneur, and dove into any new business opportunity, even without having any relevant prior experience. Although she had never worked in a bank, now she was establishing a rural bank in Pagsanjan (pronounced Pahg-sahn-hahn), a historic and picturesque provincial town 60 miles south of Manila. She divided her time between Manila and Pagsanjan, and eventually, the whole family would be moving there. The Cabrezas were pragmatic, unpretentious, and hospitable, and I immediately felt at ease with them.

As Carlos and I drove to Pagsanjan to visit Solita, Manila's tall buildings slowly changed into clusters of small stores. Noise and traffic congestion decreased as taxis and buses morphed into motorcycles and tuk-tuks. Coconut lands and rice paddies appeared, and life slowed down. Rural farmers even began appropriating portions of the highway to spread out their tarps of drying rice, and traffic simply swerved around them.

Pagsanjan projected an aura of quaint natural charm. A few large Spanish-style houses had survived the war, and many smaller old-style dwellings retained wood latticework and flat, translucent capiz shells rather than glass window panes. Rural life seemed simple and slow-paced compared to Manila, but crowing roosters, noisy motorcycles, and tuk-tuks woke everyone early. By 6:00 a.m., the town bustled with traffic and commerce, because it was a tourist destination.

Solita's rural wooden house resembled thousands of others in the province. Built in the old style and elevated on posts, the broad, slightly asymmetrical floorboards allowed glimpses to the ground below, where dogs, cats, and sometimes a chicken or two, ran around. The maid cooked outside in a so-called 'dirty kitchen' instead of an inside kitchen, a Filipino custom I neither understood nor learned to appreciate.

Solita used the main, multi-purpose room for everything from work to dining, family meetings, and entertaining, but Solita prioritized bank development over comfort. It contained only a large dining table, chairs and a cabinet. A long, strictly functional fluorescent light fixture suspended from the ceiling emitted a cold, rather dim light at night. *This room just begs for a comfortable chair, a picture, a reading lamp, or a woven mat on the floor to make it feel homey.*

Woven grass *banig* mats on the floors replaced beds in the three small bedrooms. I was pencil-thin, with little personal padding, and I found the banig hard and uncomfortable. But wood latticework on the screened windows provided a semblance of privacy, and the rooms were cool and airy.

Pagsanjan's primary asset is a beautiful waterfall. Below it, the Pagsanjan river flows through a deep, jungle-lined gorge, over seven sets of small rapids, and into the town. Shooting the rapids is the town's main tourist attraction. For a nominal sum, barefoot boatmen, or *banqueros*, paddle pairs of people upstream to the waterfall in slim, canoe-like *bancas*, hopping in and out of the bancas at each set of shallow rapids, to push them upstream over the rocks. Their bare feet have memorized the placement of every large underwater boulder, and they know exactly where to step without even glancing down. After visiting the falls, the bancas shoot the small white-water rapids back downstream into town.

Before returning with Solita to Manila, we took the banca ride through the narrow jungle gorge, hearing birds and occasional monkey chatter. The falls were beautiful. This was more how I expected the Philippines to be. I'm not a big-city person. *Living in green, restful, rural Pagsanjan would definitely be preferable to urban Manila.* Unfortunately, most jobs were in Manila.

The following day, wanting to be hospitable, Fe took me to see Makati, a new, emerging city being carved out of rice fields a few miles south of Manila. My first view of Makati was startling. In early 1967, Ayala Avenue, the main street, ran through large rice fields. Only a single row of tall, modern buildings lined Ayala on each side, looking strangely out of place in the sea of rice. Makati reminded me of Oz's Emerald City which seemed to float among the poppy fields, uncluttered by dirty urban sprawl. A modern city created out of nothing.

Makati was everything Manila wasn't. Makati's tall modern buildings, clean and unpotholed streets, and colorful tropical landscaping generated excitement. Its vibrant promise attracted people and money, and most companies wanted to relocate there. Already five new villages with huge luxurious houses were in various stages of construction. With a rapidly increasing population of 114,000, it was already on track to become the Philippines' financial and business center. The bright contrast to dirty downtown Manila seemed almost schizophrenic.

Makati was the new future of the Philippines, and within less than a decade, it would build up and out. The sea of rice fields would explode into a sea of new, modern high rises, bursting at the seams with block after block of tall buildings, megamalls, supermarkets, theaters, restaurants, and the International School.

My upcoming return to Honolulu was looming as a make-or-break moment for our relationship. Carlos and I had already been apart for eight months. And now, after only a week's visit, we would have another eight-month separation while I finished in Hawaii. I would probably never return to Asia, and the time and distance from Manila to Chicago via mail and airplane were too great to sustain an indefinite long-term relationship. The telephone was too expensive, and letters took several weeks each way. The distance complicated anything requiring serious discussion.

Not making a decision is a decision in itself, and if one of us wasn't proactive, we would likely never see each other again. The week was passing quickly. Finally, hearing nothing from Carlos, I said, "Is this relationship going anywhere or not?" And although we hadn't seriously discussed the future, we became engaged the next day.

When we wandered into the *sala* and announced our engagement to his parents, they greeted us with blank and confused stares, and offered neither congratulations nor hugs. In fact, they showed almost no emotion at all. *How should we interpret this? Are they displeased? Upset? Worried?*

Carlos had never mentioned the possibility of an engagement to his parents; this had caught them completely off-guard. It was unexpected, and now they were simply trying to process it. Later I realized their normal reaction would be low-key in any case, because they weren't huggers or effusive people. For better or worse, they were emotional clones of my parents.

We should have realized even after they processed the idea, they still wouldn't be excited. Filipinos had no problem with mixed marriages; they were common in Manila. But they knew that sooner or later, most people who married Americans moved to the States, and Solita had assumed Carlos would eventually become president of her new Rural Bank.

Always the pragmatist, Victor asked for our handwriting samples. Then he studied the writing and pronounced us compatible. Although I put no stock in handwriting analysis, when comparing our scripts, it surprised me to see they were almost identical. I wondered how he would have reacted if they were very different.

Victor appeared satisfied. "I can die now, since I've seen who Carlos will marry."

What an odd thing to say. I wondered if he had a terminal disease. Later I learned this was simply his way of marking important events off his own private goal list.

Only the grandmother, Lola Guida, overtly voiced reservations. Families expected, or at least hoped, that marriage would enhance the family's economic and social standing. "What can she bring to the family?" Lola Guida asked.

Not much, it turned out, except a hefty student loan.

I would drop the same bomb on Mom and Dad, with the added postscript that I was moving to the Philippines. To me, this was merely an incidental fact. I gave no thought to their upcoming reaction, naively assuming they would have little problem with it.

- Twenty -

Breaking the News

Glen Ellyn, IL 1967

I RETURNED TO HAWAII AND WAS DEBRIEFED BY SOME men in black who seemed very interested I my feelings and experiences in Vietnam and Laos. The war was ratcheting up, and I assumed they were CIA.

I also wrote home about our engagement. I would have preferred telling them in person but, in 1967, overseas telephone calls were exorbitant. Even at Beloit, my parents only called me once a year. They had never called me in Costa Rica or Hawaii, but I rather hoped they might make an exception this time. They didn't. Knowing how Laura's parents reacted to her marriage, I should have known this would shake my Midwest family to the core, but now viewing things through Hawaii's multicultural lens, I hoped they could bridge this gap and be pleased for me.

After three weeks, I received a relatively neutral letter from Mom. She asked a few questions, and her flat tone lacked excitement, but she didn't try to talk me out of it. Then there was Dad. I never received a single letter from him all six years, through Beloit, Costa Rica, Hawaii, and Asia. He seemed to think it my duty to write but, apparently, it never occurred to him I might like hearing from him. He let Mom do all the work. Now, after a month, I received my first-ever letter from him.

"Your mother took to her bed worrying about this," he wrote, with more comments in a similar vein. *'Took to her bed?' That sounds like anachronistic hyperbole. And worrying about what, exactly? Marrying an Asian? That they hadn't met Carlos? That I'm moving to the Philippines?* Then realization dawned. *It's not Mom who's most upset; it's you. You're trying to manipulate me by playing a guilt card. Worse yet, you're blaming it on Mom.*

My brother Phil, still living at home, relayed various comments to me. "Dad talked about you 'ruining all our generations of good English blood,' and said 'Hawaii moonlight must have gone to her head.'" Dad's pride about our good English blood had always seemed pretentious; now, I also found it small-minded.

I wasn't the first family rebel to take an ax to our pristine WASP family tree. After WWII, Aunt Connie's marriage to an Italian Catholic created a flood of family criticism. They seemed to perceive Quentin as a threat to the family's Protestant history and English genetics. Then Uncle Phil returned from college with a young bride from rural Georgia. The family's rigid mold didn't accommodate people from the South easily either.

Those created slight family tremors, but a few years later, Uncle Phil's move to California created a family earthquake. The only male heir on mom's side was deserting the family for the ends of the earth. They believed they would never see him again. Now, sixteen years later, I was marrying an Asian Catholic and moving to the Philippines, four times as far away.

I bet Dad, at least, is also worried about what people will think. Old fashioned prejudices still abounded, particularly in the Midwest.

In the 1800s, all but nine states had miscegenation laws. Their original intent was to prevent Black-White marriages, although some states expanded them to include Native Americans, Filipinos, Asians, East Indians, and Native Hawaiians. When we became engaged, our marriage would still be illegal in sixteen states. Not that I cared.

In June 1967, a Supreme Court ruling finally overturned the remaining state laws, but mixed marriages were a rarity, and many people like Laura's parents still violently opposed them. Even 13 years later, the 1980 census reported only three percent of marriages involved interracial couples.

But within decades, attitudes changed rapidly. Between 2008-2010, twenty-two percent of new marriages in Western states, fourteen percent of marriages in the South, and thirteen percent in the Northeast were mixed ethnicities. The Midwest had changed least, with only eleven percent. *The times they are a-changin',* [6] Bob Dylan sang. And they were, but not as fast in the Midwest as elsewhere. No one gave Carlos and me a second glance in Hawaii, but we would draw stares in Glen Ellyn.

Meanwhile, I finished my fish research in Honolulu and presented it to my committee. *The morphology of otolith-air bladder connections in basal percoid fish families* wasn't exactly a top draw. Outside of my committee, few students came to listen. After only a few questions, Dr. Gosline fished into a hidden cellophane bag, draped a purple orchid lei around my neck, and pronounced my research accepted. I had completed the last hurdle.

I returned to Glen Ellyn for ten weeks before leaving for Manila. Once home, Dad renewed his efforts to dissuade me from getting married. "Your children will never be accepted here," he said.

Maybe that's true, if everyone thinks as you do. Even in 2010, forty-three years later, Glen Ellyn would remain eighty-seven percent White.

"But we aren't living here," I reminded him. "We're living in Makati. Over there, American mixtures are not only accepted but considered desirable." His face registered shock. This appeared to be new information for him, but I had told them this in my letter. *Hadn't it penetrated at all? Or had he assumed I would come to my senses once I came home?*

"I don't have money to send you there," he said as if that closed the discussion.

"Never mind. I have enough."

Obviously, rather than trying to understand the situation, he was focused on refocusing me. A few days later, he tried another tack. "You're a strong person; I'm only worried you'll be in a relationship where they won't treat you well. A lot of cultures treat their women like chattel." He obviously didn't understand Philippine culture. *Why doesn't he ask questions? He doesn't try to understand my choice; he just tries to attack it.*

"The Philippines is a matriarchy. If anything, women have more opportunities over there than here. I haven't found the male establishment here very welcoming to women in science."

He looked surprised. Then he looked down and almost seemed to deflate. Finally, he said the first thing that made sense. "It's just so far away," he said with a sad sigh.

Possibly nowhere but the Midwest would have felt acceptable to them, yet dad had made it pretty clear he thought we would not be accepted there.

Later, I realized he and Mom believed I was walking out of their lives forever. But if this was their primary concern, why didn't they just say so, for heaven's sake? They seemed unable to start the conversation, and didn't realize it might have helped if we had one. They never mentioned their fears, and they weren't something I took seriously because the last three years abroad had opened my world. Globally, things were changing rapidly, and people in my world were very mobile. In my parent's world, things still moved at glacial speed.

To his credit, Dad finally decided to contact the Cabrezas. "Can they read English?"

Good grief. "Of course, they can. They both have Master's degrees from the States." It shocked him; they were better educated and more travelled than he and Mom. He labored obsessively over a letter to the Cabrezas, and Solita wrote a similar letter back. I hoped it assured them I wouldn't be living in a small hut herding cows and carrying firewood on my head.

Carlos sent Mom and Dad a package of wedding invitations to send to their friends, even though we didn't expect anyone to attend. The invitations listed both sets of parents, a style not yet common in the States, surprising and pleasing Mom and Dad. Their friends remarked on it with interest, too.

Mom and Dad didn't make even feeble attempts to see if they could somehow attend the wedding, and I didn't bring it up because I knew they couldn't afford it with three kids in college and Grandfather about to enter a nursing home. Yet a thought still crossed my mind. *If I were getting married in Glen Ellyn, wouldn't they somehow have found a way to scrape up money for a wedding?*

In the Philippines, the man's family pays for the wedding, so their cost would be only a trip to the Philippines, much cheaper than an Illinois wedding. We might have at least discussed the possibility. We might have had a simple beach wedding in Hawaii, a halfway point everyone could have enjoyed. Having both families meet would have gone a long way toward making Mom and Dad feel more comfortable about everything. Who knows? We might even have decided to live in Hawaii; I'd already had two unsolicited job offers there in some weird new field called computer programming. None of us considered these options.

However, I had a lot of company; almost all of my EWC friends were now in intercultural marriages. And as far as I knew, none of their parents had attended their weddings either.

Physiologists say people's brains aren't fully formed until age 30. At 24, I was proof of it. In August, with a remarkable lack of reflection on possible consequences that today seems truly reckless, I packed up my life into two heavy, hard-sided suitcases, several boxes, and an old trunk from Dr. Townsend, my invertebrate class professor. I was traveling to Manila by ship because air freight was too expensive. The trip cost $750.

The night before I left for the Philippines, we sat watching *Guess Who's Coming to Dinner* on TV as Spencer Tracy and Katherine Hepburn struggled with their daughter's marriage to a Black man. Somewhere upstairs, a radio played Peter, Paul, and Mary, singing *"I'm leaving on a jet plane, don't know when I'll be back again."* They both poignantly capsulized the moment and the times. Mom turned and left the room.

Young and self-absorbed, I had no idea what I was doing to them by leaving. Our generations were so different, and our viewpoints came from such different positions. In my EWC world, everyone I knew traveled all over. Manila might or might not be a permanent relocation for me, but I had no doubt that I would see them again, and probably in the not-too-distant future. But they felt this was a permanent break. Generations of the family had lived in Glen Ellyn. No one had ever left Glen Ellyn except Uncle Phil. My parents couldn't even envision visiting him in California; the Philippines might as well have been Mars.

I hadn't tried to soften the blow of my announcement because I honestly didn't think they would be that concerned. I dropped the bomb of our engagement by letter without warning, returned home after graduation for ten weeks, then packed up and left. We could have at least talked about their fears and our differing viewpoints, and attempted to see each other's views. It might have eased the blow or even opened the door to looking at other options, although dad's comments about 'your children not being accepted' backfired, and helped slam the Midwest door, at least. Strangely, he worried about mixed children but said nothing about a mixed marriage. Perhaps he knew arguing that would be a non-starter.

The following day, hauling Pepino's travel cage, I left for Manila to get married. *Shouldn't this be a moment for last-minute advice? For things we had always meant to say, assurance I could come home any time, promises to send pictures, stay in touch, wishes for good luck…something?* Mom and Dad were quite upset, but outward calm prevailed. Never emotional people, now they wouldn't, or perhaps couldn't, release their emotions. They closed down. Well trained, I followed their lead. I had experienced warmer send-offs leaving for a semester at college. We drove into the brown ozone haze around the airport with little conversation. *We still haven't learned to respect the environment.*

I'm sure they questioned whether I would ever return to the States or even see or talk directly with them again, but they never once brought that up, and self-focused, I gave that serious question little credence. Mobility was my new normal, while my parents had never even been on a jet. How fast things were changing, both for me and the U.S. culture.

However, I had been traveling on U.S. Government dollars for the last three years. I hadn't yet realized how difficult travel might be when earning pesos.

THE PHILIPPINE YEARS

(1967–1973)

"Two roads diverged into a wood. I took the road less traveled by, and that made all the difference."

– Robert Frost

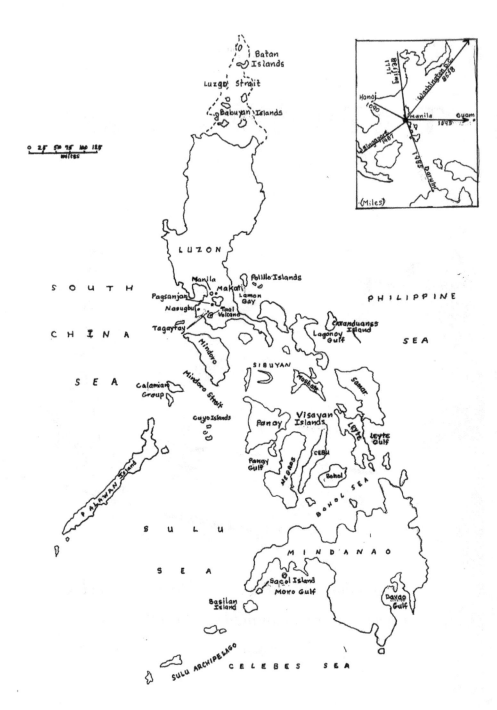

The Philippine Islands

- *Twenty-One* -
Cruising "Steerage"

At Sea, July 1967

Hauling Pepino's parrot cage, I flew to Honolulu, and boarded the President Wilson, an American President Lines ship, for a two-week trip to Manila. I stood at the rail, looking down at hundreds of well-wishers crowding the dock below, shouting and waving goodbye to passengers at the rail. Ship's officers were passing out rolls of colored streamers to the passengers, who held the loose end and threw the roll down to someone ashore. I had no one to throw it to, but I accepted a blue roll anyhow and tossed it into the crowd.

The crew secured the gangway, hauled in the lines, and cast loose the cables. As the ship's horn blared, and the engines revved, the boat eased away from the dock and out of Honolulu. The long streamers connecting people on the ship to those on shore began to stretch, finally pulling apart, leaving a tangle of broken streamers in the water.

The symbolism brought it home. Based on a week's visit to the Philippines, I had essentially jettisoned my life, family, friends, and country and made an almost impulsive leap into the comparative unknown. For the first time, the enormity and finality of my break cascaded over me. Possibly I would never return, never see any of them again. Amid all the merriment on board, suddenly feeling totally alone, I stood at the rail and sobbed.

The rich had taken luxury cruises since at least the Queen Mary and the Titanic in the 1930s, but in the 1960s, few ordinary people cruised for fun. The ship had First Class and Economy class, but Economy should have been called Steerage. My class didn't cruise for a luxury vacation; we traveled to reach a destination. No fruit baskets, flowers, or bottles of champagne decorated our cabins. We weren't locked in, but rope and signage separated us from the First-Class cabins, their dining room, and the single tiny swimming pool. Conditions were uncomfortable at best, unsafe at worst.

The steward directed me downstairs to a small, long narrow cabin below the waterline. It had no porthole and, as I recall, held ten people. *I wasn't expecting luxury, but this feels like a dungeon.* I later learned the military had initially commissioned the ship as a WWII troop carrier, but when the war ended, they converted it to an ocean liner. Or at least they converted first class. The economy cabins still stashed us like cordwood in narrow submarine-style bunks on both sides of the room.

The aisle between the bunks measured three feet wide at best. We had no luggage storage, so our bags sat on our bunks during daytime. At night, our luggage clogged the aisle. Curtains and a small light in each bunk created an illusion of privacy, which helped somewhat, but bunks crowded so closely above each other that sitting upright was impossible. The top bunk lay less than three feet from the ceiling. It was definitely not for the claustrophobic.

A dim ceiling light lit our dingy, featureless cabin in the daytime. At night, a red low-watt bulb hung above the single washbasin and mirror at the far end of the cabin, swinging back and forth on a naked cord as the boat rolled with the waves. Getting up at night meant navigating the luggage obstacle course to the cabin door, and walking down a long, dimly lit corridor to reach a couple of toilets down the hallway.

Our entire cabin bolted from the room as early as possible in the morning and stayed out as late as possible at night, returning only to sleep.

Most people kept to themselves, except for a few bits of polite conversation. Maryann, the only cabin-mate I connected with, was a rather chunky Haight Ashbury hippie from San Francisco who wore mid-thigh skirts and strappy Jesus sandals that wound around her leg nearly to the knee. In this Sixties era of free love, she quickly solved the space problem for herself by spending her nights in an officer's room, which, although small, looked much nicer than ours.

Pepino spent her days in a First-Class open-air pet cage on the top deck, but the cage provided little shelter, so I brought her in at night, further crowding the cabin. During the day, she lived well, and one day I found a huge bowl of Bing cherries in her cage.

Dining was unpleasant, because a nauseating odor of hot grease and garbage perpetually wafted up from the kitchen below into our hot, stuffy dining room. The food was remarkably unmemorable. Our daily desert was the choice of an apple or orange; we had no other fruit or anything resembling a real dessert. Pepino's Bing cherries were obviously First-Class leftovers, and Maryann and I finished any cherries she didn't eat without second thoughts.

One night, as the wind was picking up and the ship began heavily rolling, I remembered Pepino was still topside in her cage.

"I forgot Pepino. I've got to get her. I can't leave her out there in a storm."

"I'll come along with you," Maryann said. I was very glad she did.

The animal cages sat atop a square, windowless structure on the stern. An inside stairway allowed First Class passengers easy access to their animals, but the crew locked it at dusk. The only alternative, a narrow vertical metal ladder on the wall, led from the deck to the cages on the roof. Nothing lit the area; the ship obviously tried to discourage people from coming back here.

The moonless black night felt heavy and oppressive, and the gusting wind carried the feel of an approaching storm. The boat rolled heavily side to side, plowing determinedly through rising seas, as we fumbled our way to the stern.

Maryann considered herself a bit psychic. "This place doesn't feel good to me," she said.

"Me neither," I said. "But it's just the dark, messing with our heads. You'd think they'd have a light up here." Mainly by feel, we groped our way precariously up the vertical ladder, fumbled around to locate Pepino's cage, and transferred her into her small travel cage.

I attempted to descend the ladder, but carrying the swinging cage left only a single free hand to grip the ladder, and to move down I needed two hands. A solo descent was impossible. With difficulty, we shared the ladder, descending each narrow step together, one step at a time. We slowly inched our way down the ladder by feel, passing the swaying cage back and forth between us on each step, as the boat labored through the waves.

Maryann breathed a sigh of relief when we reached the lighted portion of the ship. "Phew. That place had bad vibes. I felt really uncomfortable up there."

"Me too. I'm glad to be out of there." It was more than just a lack of light; a dark uncomfortable atmosphere had permeated the area but, running on adrenalin, I had pushed the feeling down to focus on retrieving Pepino.

Later in the bar, Maryann mentioned our topside visit to her ship's officer friend. He looked horrified. "Oh no! Don't ever go up there. It's very dangerous. That's where the animals working below decks go outside at night for some air. They're not allowed out during the daytime."

He sounded so arrogant I challenged him. "You call the below-deck staff animals? That's pretty demeaning."

"They *are* animals," he said. "You're very fortunate. They're never allowed on deck, never mix with the passengers, never see women…" He let the thought hang in the air. After that, I never forgot to bring in Pepino.

The comment about below-deck staff never mixing with passengers wasn't entirely accurate. Two days later, one of our cabin mates was about to take a shower in the free-standing metal shower stall in the hallway, when she saw a thin wire snaking through a small hole bored in the front wall. A tiny sliver of soap plugged the hole, but someone had gone behind the shower with a wire to reopen it. Grabbing her towel, she quickly went behind the shower and caught a peeping Tom crouching with his eye to the hole. Seeing her, he promptly threw a towel over his head and fled down the hallway. Perhaps the officer's comment about animals wasn't so off-base after all.

At 6:00 a.m. every morning, the ship held an outdoor Continental breakfast buffet on the bow. The minute it opened, our whole cabin poured out onto the deck to escape the claustrophobic cabin and avoid the horrible dining room. As I piled a paper plate with fruit and sweet rolls, I heard, "Good morning, Miss Hadley."

Surprised, I turned to see a young, white-jacketed steward. "How do you know my name?"

"All the passenger's pictures are downstairs on a big bulletin board. We have to memorize everyone's name." He grinned. "The early morning buffet is where we catch most stowaways."

That explained why the dining room required us to sit in an exact assigned seat every meal; they could more easily identify stowaways.

"It's easier to avoid being caught up here. Stowaways sneak out in the morning for the buffet, load up on breakfast, and disappear below deck. We memorize your pictures so we can spot anyone who doesn't belong here."

A similar system operated in the bar at night because stowaways emerged for complimentary appetizers. That explained why the boat required multiple pictures when we bought our tickets; they plastered our faces on bulletin boards all over the inside of the ship.

The days at sea passed with mind-numbing sameness. Only First Class could access the ship's small swimming pool. The ship provided no movies or other activities to pass the time, but a so-called library in the bar contained a dozen dog-eared books and a couple of well-used board games. Two Spanish-speaking Chinese interested in learning English found a Scrabble game in the library. Once they realized I spoke Spanish, they pressured me into joining them. They used Scrabble to increase their English vocabulary, and filled the board with three and four-letter words. Every time I placed anything longer, they asked me to stop and explain its meaning. It was painful.

A group of young Mormon missionaries were transitioning to the Philippines and I asked them a few naïve questions about Bible prophecy. "In Revelation," they said, but had no definitive answers. They apparently weren't in missionary mode until the boat docked.

Maryann and I spent most of our days sitting on the deck lounge chairs, reading or staring at the endless rise and fall of the rolling waves and the churning wake as the ship sliced through the water. The highlight of our day was watching sea birds, fish, and an occasional shark fight over the kitchen garbage tossed off the stern. At night, the small smoke-filled lounge provided a live band and bar, but our class, at least, had no regularly organized entertainment. It was a long two weeks.

The ship stopped for day layovers in Yokohama and Hong Kong. Since I had been there ten months earlier on field study, I felt very comfortable going ashore. Maryann and I always disembarked, but the chubby mother and daughter in our cabin wouldn't leave the ship, and tried to discourage us.

"Surely, you're not getting off? The cities are too dangerous. Especially Manila." Even the lure of Hong Kong's exotic shopping couldn't pry them from the ship's safety. They made the six-week round trip from California without ever setting foot on land, frying themselves sunbathing on the hot metal stern, while the rest of us went ashore to explore the cities. They returned home with deep tans, undoubtedly bragging about their "Asian cruise."

I couldn't imagine it. Spending money for a vacation of horrible meals, dull days, and cramped nights was bad enough; missing the few offshore diversions available on the entire trip seemed pathetic.

"You can't live your life in fear of what might happen," I told them, but they chose the monotony of safety over the highs and lows of living.

I was relieved when the boat docked at the Port of Manila. They were horrified I was going ashore, and when I said I planned to live there, they were speechless. Yet, for six interesting, challenging, and often eventful years, I did.

- *Twenty-Two* -

Cultural Initiation

Manila, Philippines 1967-1968

THE PHILIPPINES WAS AWASH IN GUNS. EVERYONE carried a gun. Carlos and Victor met my boat at the Port of Manila, and Carlos brought his gun. I never knew he owned one, but I soon discovered it came with us everywhere, even to the movies or the market. I don't know how well Carlos could shoot it, but even for show, with everyone toting a gun, I began to understand why my cabin mates thought Manila was too dangerous to disembark. It felt like the Wild West.

Carlos bought his gun in Arizona when he and his friend traveled around the States during their EWC field study. Seeing a gun shop, on impulse, both decided to buy guns. Bringing guns on planes wasn't a problem.

Raul and the gun I bought for him in Hawaii were already in the Philippines too, and Raul was beginning to stir up trouble.

The following day, we returned to the Port to collect my stowed luggage, now offloaded onto the dock. "The Port's known for thefts and muggings," Victor said. So, naturally, we brought the gun. Carlos stashed it inside my heavy leather purse.

A surging mass of humanity milled around on the dock, searching for their luggage, offering to help carry bags, or hoping for opportunities. I hugged my purse under my arm, gripping the strap tightly as we pushed through the crowd. Almost immediately, someone shoved me so hard from behind that I almost fell. I chalked it up to the jostling crowd, but when it happened again, I pulled the purse in front of me. The bumps stopped.

As we wandered around, searching for my luggage among the giant piles off-loaded on the dock, a loud parrot screech split the noisy air. Somehow, Pepino had spotted me among the throngs of people, and began calling me at ear-splitting volume. Following the loud, raucous squawks, we spied her small travel cage perched precariously atop my small pile of luggage. Grabbing my trunk, boxes, and Pepino, we fought our way through the crush of humanity to our 1955 Chevy.

Back in Paco, I opened my purse, and saw light inside. *Light in my purse?* Puzzled, I looked at the outside. On the end, two large slashes formed a V-shaped gash in the leather. Penetrating the thick, stiff leather would have been difficult, no matter how sharp the knife. *No wonder the bumps were so hard.* I had moved my purse just in time. Another few seconds and I would have lost my passport, all my money, and the gun.

"It's lucky you didn't realize what was happening and turn around or you probably would have been knifed," Victor said.

Maybe my cabin mates were right; Manila was a dangerous place. I had been targeted within the first minutes on the dock and escaped loss only by a fluke. *I wonder how many of my fellow passengers had been targeted and victimized?* Welcome to Manila.

We would be married two weeks after arrival, so I had little involvement in wedding planning, but I felt OK with that. I wasn't one of those girls who spent years dreaming about their wedding. I didn't understand Filipino weddings anyhow.

A well-known bridal shop in Manila was custom-making my dress, and this became my first minor culture clash. They had no ready-made dresses, only designs. The dressmaker refused to use the silk I bought in Hong Kong and showed me elaborate designs with beads and trains. I equated simple with elegant but, to the shop, simple was just plain, and they wanted elaborate.

"I don't want beads or a train," I said.

"You are advertising our shop," they said. "You need one of these styles."

Shouldn't the dress be about the bride, not the shop? But with the wedding ten days away, we had no time to argue or shop around. They were lucky I wasn't a typical bride. I saw the dress for the first time the night before the wedding, and although not my style, its train and beads were beautiful. Fortunately, it fit, because it was too late for alterations.

In Glen Ellyn, Mom had asked about my dress, but not focused on it myself, I told her, "I'll buy one in Manila. I have no idea of Filipino styles, anyhow." In hindsight, helping me buy the dress could have been a meaningful way to involve her, and I could also have gotten a style I liked. At least we could have discussed it, but she never said anything more about it, and remained so quiet and guarded that I didn't think it mattered to her. Communication didn't seem to be our family's strong suit.

The Cabrezas weren't practicing Catholics, but traditional Filipino weddings were Catholic with Filipino twists. Two days before the wedding, Carlos and I visited the priest to discuss the final wedding arrangements. The priest seemed surprised to discover I wasn't Catholic. Matter-of-factly, he said, "Then I can't marry you."

"It's a bit late to tell us now! The wedding is two days away. We've sent the invitations and ordered the catering. Everything is finalized."

He shifted uncomfortably in his chair. "Would you agree to convert to Catholicism?"

"No." I didn't tell him I had no church affiliation, but my having grown up in a church seemed enough to satisfy him.

"Would you agree to raise your children Catholic?" He looked hopeful.

"No. I don't believe in forcing religion on anyone."

Fortunately, he agreed but, unwilling to give up, he almost pleaded. "Would you at least agree to expose your children to it?"

"Of course." *How could they not be exposed to it, with the whole country Catholic?*

He sighed softly and caved in.

Driving home, we spotted a familiar face on the street. It was Dave, a marine biology friend from the EWC, in Manila on his field study. He looked surprised. "What are you doing here?"

"I've moved here. Carlos and I are getting married in two days. Want to come?" To my surprise, he did. He was soon getting married himself to my Thai friend, Samsi. *Score another mixed marriage for the Center,* I thought.

Solita arranged a wedding in the historic Malate Church, a 400-year-old baroque stone cathedral in downtown Manila. The only time available on eight months' notice was a 6:00 a.m. mass, so a breakfast reception would follow at a family friend's restaurant. Dr. Llamas, aka Lolo Sendo, Carlos' Grandfather, was giving me away. He insisted I arrive in his expensive Cadillac, with a massive bouquet of white lilies and roses on the front bumper. The flowers were late, and he refused to leave without them.

"Don't worry," he said. "You're the bride; they can't start without you." But yes, they could. We almost missed the wedding altogether, because the regularly scheduled morning mass had only one appropriate place to insert a wedding. And I was late. We arrived at the church with literally one minute to spare. The priest had just told Carlos, "If she doesn't arrive within the next two minutes, we'll miss the proper place to insert you into the mass. I'll have to cancel the wedding." Given my negative answers to his questions about conversion, perhaps he secretly hoped for that.

I had no idea what to expect. I assumed the organist would play Wagner's Bridal Chorus, but apparently not when the wedding is part of the mass. I stood in the large, ornate stone doorway, looking at the backs of hundreds of mantilla-covered heads in morning prayer, hesitating and wondering when to enter. *A rehearsal might have been helpful, here.* Lolo Sendo firmly gripped my elbow and propelled me in the door and down the aisle. Carlos, waiting at the altar, looked visibly relieved.

Filipino women came dressed to impress, laden with expensive showy jewelry and wearing *ternos,* the national dress with oversized vertical 'butterfly' sleeves. Many ternos were elaborately embroidered silk, *jusi or* raw silk, or *piña,* a translucent cloth made of pineapple fiber. The men wore either suits or Barong Tagalogs, loosely woven formal embroidered shirts of jusi, worn outside, over the pants.

And then there was Dave, the only representative from my side. He was traveling on field study, so naturally he had no dress clothes. His bushy red beard attracted attention because few men sported beards then, and he wore a suitcase-wrinkled white shirt looking as if it had been slept in, without a coat or tie, and paired with jeans and tennis shoes.

My parent's absence already provided juicy tidbits for the gossip mill. Now people decided Dave, the only other American present, must be my brother. His casual appearance further fueled speculation. If they were aware of the gossip, to their credit, the Cabrezas never mentioned it.

In addition to the maid of honor and best man, Filipino weddings have a Principal Sponsor, someone who has played important role in the couple's life and joins in the prayers of blessing. Four Secondary Sponsors also have a part. The Candle Sponsor lit two candles, symbolizing our individual lives; Carlos and I would later blow out the single candles and together, light a third candle in the middle, signifying our new unity. The Coin Sponsor brought a pouch of thirteen blessed coins for Carlos to pass to me, a promise to provide for our future family. The Veil Sponsor placed a large veil over Carlos' shoulder and my already veiled head, and the Cord Sponsor draped a cord around us on top of the veil, another symbol of unity. They were big on unity.

The mass droned on, and we had been kneeling forever. The hot, humid air felt difficult to breathe. Whether it was the early ceremony with little food, the hot, heavy beaded gown and long gloves, the feeling I couldn't breathe under the veil, lack of sleep, stress, or all of the above, I began feeling queasy. With horror, I thought, *I think I'm going to be sick!*

As the priest droned on, I knelt at the altar, agonizing over strategy. *What do I do? Which is worse: stay here and get sick at the altar? Or leave in the middle of the ceremony to hunt for a bathroom?* It seemed an impossible choice, but my body solved it for me. For the only time in my life, I slowly slumped over against Carlos and apparently fainted. Luckily, I was already kneeling.

Our Principal Sponsor, Dalia, who for some reason carried around smelling salts, hopped up and poked them under my nose. Someone propped a chair under me, and we finished the ceremony. The priest droned on uninterrupted, as if nothing was happening. I had no idea I had even fainted, although, at some point, I realized I was sitting on a chair I didn't recall having been there earlier.

This incident added fuel to the active gossip mill. Now everyone was sure I was pregnant, which conveniently explained why my parents sent my "brother" to attend the wedding in their place. For several months afterward, people dropping by the house, probably hoping for a gossip tidbit, never failed to ask with apparent innocent interest, "When is the baby due?"

"What baby? We aren't having children for at least a year." They were shocked.

They looked disappointed as the hope for juicy gossip evaporated. "Are you sure you're not pregnant?" Or, hopefully, "Maybe you had a miscarriage?"

Filipino culture centers on having children, so people responded to my comments with concern and disbelief. They wanted to pop out as many babies as possible as quickly as possible. Everybody asked, "Is something wrong? I know a good doctor." Carlos was getting those questions at work too.

Irritated, I shut off the questions. "I'm on the pill." This statement brought disbelief because the Church held the culture in a firm grip. Birth control pills were illegal in the Philippines. "Well, they're not illegal in the States," I said. That stopped the questions.

In actuality, we had never even discussed the possibility of children. In a culture so child-oriented, Carlos just assumed them, but they weren't even on my radar. We never discussed many things before getting married because we were continents apart during our entire engagement, connected only by letters taking two or three weeks each way.

Some wealthy friends of ours took the baby thing very seriously. After they married, they immediately bought an enormous house, furnishing it with thirteen beds. When I asked, "Why so many beds?" the wife almost glowed.

"We're going to have twelve children," she said, her voice swelling with pride and anticipation. I tried to nod with appreciation as we toured her seven bedrooms but, privately, I was appalled. I firmly believed in Zero Population Growth, and the Philippine growth rate of four percent per year was one of the highest in the world. This growth was unsustainable, and I felt they were being irresponsible. I became claustrophobic just thinking about it.

In 1967, the Philippine population approached 32 million, and the average family had eight children, a Malthusian nightmare in the making. Our friends contributed to this, popping out eight babies in quick succession. She didn't make it to twelve, but she gave it a good try.

Thankfully, things began changing. By 1993, the average number of children per family dropped to 4.1, and in 2017, to 2.7. Unfortunately, as many feared, by 2018, the Filipino population had tripled to 96 million. It's currently on the cusp of an exponential rise, because the average Filipino age is only fifteen.

I entered the Philippines on a tourist visa but, to live there, I needed an Alien Certificate of Registration, or ACR, and the application had to be obtained abroad after marriage. Hong Kong was the nearest location. As I prepared to depart, our wedding Sponsor, Dalia, approached and asked me to hand-carry a letter to Hong Kong for her.

"Can't you just put it in the mail?"

"No. It has to be hand-carried." That should have been a clue.

When I arrived in Hong Kong, I called the telephone number on the envelope and reached someone who picked it up and brought me a fat letter for Dalia. I threw the letter in my purse, obtained my ACR, and returned to Makati.

Dalia called me almost immediately on arrival. "Do you have a letter for me?"

"It's here somewhere. I'll bring it over in a day or so." She pestered me non-stop, but wouldn't drive to come get it. We finally drove it to her house to stop her calling.

"Did you open it? Did anyone ask you about it?"

"Of course not. Why would they?"

She slit open the letter with a letter opener and pulled out a folded blue paper covered with clay. Embedded in it were dozens of diamonds. She smiled happily to herself. I was shocked, and exceedingly angry.

"You used me! I'm immigrating! What if I were caught? This could have banned me from future entry, if not worse!"

She was complacent. "Don't worry; we would have bailed you out. We have people in the Customs." That introduced me to the amoral world of the nouveau riche and over-privileged. Dalia's husband had made his new fortune by acquiring a logging contract for Philippine mahogany and other hardwoods.

Like Costa Rica, jungles were under attack here too. Logging, charcoal production, and clearing for farmland were destroying entire ecosystems for the benefit of a few individuals. It was another sad example of the 'progress' that so disturbed me in Glen Ellyn.

Carlos found us a mother-in-law apartment in Makati's Magallanes Village and returned to work. I began job hunting. Most of Carlos' family and friends were educators, so when I started looking for work, they assumed I would teach. A few non-teaching biology jobs probably existed, but I didn't know where to find them in a strange culture, and no one suggested alternatives.

I'd never aspired to teach and had taken no education courses, but the Philippines didn't require them. A Master's degree from the States opened doors, and I began teaching high school biology at the International

School (IS) in Makati. It amused me to discover Tony the Humorless, the stern physics teacher in the classroom next to mine, was the barefoot man standing with Carlos at the EWC cultural night holding a spear and wearing an Igorot G-string. Now that I knew him, I realized how truly out of character that was for him, and wished I had a picture; the other teachers would have loved it.

To my surprise, I loved teaching. The students had an average IQ of 125, and were incredibly motivated. Their parents, mainly diplomats or ex-pats, were also interested and involved. My only problem was commuting. Carlos dropped me at school in the morning, but he wasn't off work until 5:00 p.m. The school followed tropical hours of 7:00 a.m. to 12:15, so I was on my own. My complicated trip home involved walking to the highway, then waiting along the dusty highway for a jeepney or bus, more walking, a second jeepney, and then a tuk-tuk ride. The perhaps three or four-mile trip took over an hour in the height of the energy-sucking, mid-day tropical heat. I arrived home every day wilted and exhausted.

Sunday family dinners are a Filipino tradition. I enjoyed the dinners, but not the hot ten-mile drive to Paco in our old, non-airconditioned 1955 Chevy, in bumper-to-bumper traffic, and dusty air laced with high lead levels and unregulated vehicle emissions. Drivers abruptly cut people off, passed on the right, parked on the sidewalks, barreled through intersections, and flashed their lights to claim right-of-way. The trip, almost an hour, was mentally and physically exhausting.

Paco's hard wooden furniture became uncomfortable within minutes. After lunch, Carlos joined Solita for a long siesta while I sat alone, reading uncomfortably on a hard bench in the humid sala or staring out the barred window at Lolo Sendo's banana trees next door, and wishing I were home. Weekends were my only free time, and I needed them for mundane things like shopping, cleaning, and personal down-time. I began to resent wasting so much time sitting idly in Paco.

I knew nothing about cooking, American or otherwise, so while everyone napped, I began using the siesta time to shadow the Cabrezas' cook and to shop in the old, unrefrigerated Paco market. It definitely wasn't an American supermarket, but most American ingredients were either unavailable or exorbitantly expensive anyhow.

Tediously bargaining for each item was time-consuming. I learned the basic Tagalog bargaining phrases, the expected prices, the names of the local vegetables, the best local food brands, how to tell old fish from fresh, and dog or water buffalo meat from beef.

Like most local markets, Paco was old and dirty. When it rained, the market often flooded. Then I waded up to my calves in filthy dark flood-water to shop, wearing rubber flip-flops to preserve my good sandals. The floods picked up water from the esteros, so water quality in the flooded market rivaled Hong Kong's Aberdeen Harbor. I'm amazed I shopped there, but no one suggested an alternative, and not knowing where else to go, I simply accepted it.

After several months of spending most of every Sunday in Paco, I told Carlos "I've had enough Sunday dinners. I need my weekends." And he agreed. We discovered the Greater Manila Food Terminal, cleaner and closer to home than Paco, and it didn't flood, but shopping for the week's food still required an entire morning. Without Paco's *lavandera*, we needed to wash our own clothes, but our apartment had no washing machine, and Makati had no public laundromats. I broke down and did something I swore I would never do: I hired a day maid to clean the house and do the washing.

Around the same time, what may have been the nation's first two modern supermarkets opened in Makati. To the locals, they were novelties, but the foreigners greeted them with relief. In the States, I had taken supermarkets for granted, and hadn't appreciated their usefulness. Since I shopped in the local markets, I had put supermarkets out of my mind. Now, I looked at them through new, local eyes.

Rustans and Makati supermarkets sold everything from canned and packaged products to fresh dairy products, frozen foods, and even some imported items. I could buy diverse things like packaged cereal, ice cream, fresh milk, bread, frozen peas and ready-made deserts all in one store, rather than having to go to several different stores to find everything! Not having to bargain for each individual item saved time too, and having a shopping cart certainly beat schlepping multiple heavy shopping bags around for several hours. The supermarket's variety made meals less complicated and more varied, too. I realized with surprise how much my mindset had changed. In the States, I had taken supermarket convenience for granted.

Meanwhile, back in the States, things were exploding. The 1968 Vietnam Tet offensive ratcheted up the anti-war sentiment. Hundreds of new, massive and violent anti-war demonstrations flared up across the country. The news filled with demonstrators chanting, "Hell No, We Won't Go!" "Make Love, Not War!" and "Hey, Hey, LBJ: How Many Kids Did You Kill Today?" Men burned their draft cards, and some moved to Canada to avoid the draft.

The hippies, free-love, the drug culture, and Jesus movement all blossomed in California, while the rising Women's Liberation and Civil Rights Movements stirred more social unrest. Murders of high-profile Civil Rights leaders Malcolm X, George Rockwell, Robert Kennedy, and Dr. Martin Luther King heightened unease in those turbulent, divisive times. The States seemed to be imploding. From my vantage point in Asia, America seemed even more messed up now than when I left.

Analysts believe the Civil Rights Movement and its leaders threatened the status quo of white male privilege and supremacy. That seems likely. The population had diversified, but the leaders hadn't. White males still dominated every sector of life.

Soon the war became more personal. Rheumatic fever in high school had exempted my brother Phil from the draft, but Steve went to Vietnam. Consistently stoic, Mom rarely mentioned his absence, but after being smoke-free for a decade, she took up smoking again. Dad bragged about Steve. "*My* son didn't wait to get drafted. He's not a draft dodger. *He* enlisted."

Alcohol had dulled dad's logic, and he seemed to make no distinction between WWII, a defensive war, and Vietnam, a war of aggression on a people who simply wanted freedom and unification after centuries of European subjugation. He also didn't seem to process that Steve didn't enlist to be patriotic; he knew he would be drafted soon, so he enlisted, because enlisting shaved a year off of his service time.

EWC had widened my perspectives. Vietnam wasn't some distant Asian war far from our shores; it had become personal. I thought about Mai Phuong's family in Saigon and Pheng and Sengphet's families in Vientiane, all unwillingly entangled in a war my country brought to their cities.

For two years, the newness of the culture was challenging, interesting, and engaging. I studied Tagalog, took Chinese cooking lessons, prepared for my classes, and began applying the key to successful living I discovered in Costa Rica: *don't compare*. Immerse yourself in whatever situation you're in, and be content with it. If there's no hot water for a shower, don't look with longing at the time when you did; appreciate how nice a cold shower is in the tropical heat. Don't long for a supermarket when you have only a flooded market. If you remember a meal or a tradition you can't duplicate, don't dwell on it; create a new one. *Slow down, and live in the present situation.* You can still look toward future change, but accept the present for what it is, day by day, and avoid comparisons with what you don't have.

This attitude worked as well for me in the Philippines as it had in Costa Rica. Yet, Carlos and I both missed traveling and being near the ocean, and the new culture had now become routine, but traffic and poor roads made local weekend outings difficult, and earning pesos hindered our ability to travel anywhere. Then, what seemed to be an exciting travel opportunity opened up.

Twenty-Three

You Can Always Make Another One

Hong Kong, October 1969

T HE LAST PLACE I EXPECTED TO SPEND A PROMISING holiday was in a Hong Kong hospital, paralyzed and attached to a heart-lung machine.

In June, the bank had offered Carlos an excellent six-month opportunity in Hong Kong. and he planned to return in mid-November. I was pregnant without a family or support system in Manila, but the baby wasn't expected until the end of January. In early October, I took a week off work to visit Carlos in Hong Kong.

The second night in Hong Kong, I left dinner with severe abdominal pain. By early morning, it was agonizing. The hotel called a doctor, who diagnosed a ruptured appendix, and requested an ambulance. An hour later, it finally arrived, whisked me outside on a stretcher, and siren blaring, maneuvered through the crowded streets to the hospital. The delay should have alerted us to the potential misunderstanding between the British doctor and the Chinese hotel staff. The doctor assumed we were going to the British hospital, but the Chinese hotel staff had called a local Chinese hospital. Few people at the Chinese hospital spoke English, and my British doctor spoke no Chinese, but after a challenging gesture-filled discussion, the hospital doctors understood I needed an appendectomy, not a Cesarean. My request for them to save the appendix was probably not helpful in an already confusing conversation.

When my situation progressed to include labor contractions, the doctors were unable to operate, so they proposed administering curare, a neurotoxin, to cause muscle paralysis and stop the contractions. Curare would also stop my heartbeat and respiration, so they would connect a heart-lung machine to provide oxygen and keep my circulation going.

Hospitals had used curare since 1942, but all I knew was that South American Indians used curare on their poison arrows. Curare sounded like some weird Chinese medicine, and this seemed archaic, not to mention dangerous. Questions swirled in my drugged haze. *Is this a standard procedure? How does it work for pregnant patients? How would curare affect the baby's heart or other organs? The baby has no heart-lung machine.* I had no choice but to assume the doctors knew what they were doing. But did they?

Curare was unpleasant but not painful. Although awake and alert, I lay mute, eyes closed, powerless to move even an eyelid for the first time in my life. Relinquishing total control over my body was uncomfortable, but losing the ability to communicate was worse. Trapped inside myself, I felt incredibly isolated. Yet my brain was unaffected and fully awake. *Is this how patients in a coma feel? Can they still think?* It seemed almost like an out-of-body experience.

Knowing I could still hear, the doctor explained the procedure before the anesthetist placed the mask over my face to put me under. However, since I couldn't respond, he had no way of knowing whether I was under or not. I wasn't.

A sharp point pierced my abdomen, slicing smoothly down the stomach. I'd done enough dissections to visualize the procedure. The brain, unaffected by curare, reported on happenings in the rest of the body almost as though it floated unconnected to my body. *That's the first cut to get through the skin*, the brain informed me with detachment.

"I can feel this!" I shouted, but the scream stopped in my brain. Nothing vocalized. Curare blocks the motor nerves, causing paralysis, but it doesn't block pain. It hurt, but the feeling of total helplessness was worse. There was no escape, and no control. *Perhaps POWs feel like this when at the mercy of their captors*, I thought.

I lay there, immersed in pain, eyes closed, hearing fragments of Chinese and English conversations but unable to move or say anything, hoping the anesthesia would kick in. An English voice said, "We can probably save the mother, but I don't know about the baby." That certainly wasn't something a patient should hear. Yet somehow, through it all, I felt as if an unseen presence was assuring me everything would be OK.

Then three scalpel pushes and pulls that felt more like sawing. *They need a sharper scalpel,* my brain observed dispassionately. *Now they're into the body cavity. Now, something's poking inside. Am I going to feel the entire operation?* Finally, anesthesia kicked in, the brain stopped analyzing. Mercifully, everything faded.

The scratchy extraction of the breathing tube awakened me. The room was jammed with dual sets of Chinese and English doctors, obstetricians, surgeons, nurses, and anesthesiologists. Once I could talk, I said, "I felt the whole thing, you know."

The doctor's face registered shock. "You felt that?"

"Yep. It took two cuts to get in, didn't it."

He went pale. "I'll have to speak to the anesthesiologist about this."

Too late, I thought.

He offered an excuse. "Maybe you're one of those people immune to anesthesia." I doubt it; I imagine the curare made it difficult for the anesthesiologist to determine when I was entirely under, and perhaps he tried to keep anesthesia light out of concern for the baby.

My first words to Carlos were, "If I'm ever in a coma, always keep a radio or TV on in my room, even if you think I can't hear it. It might be the only stimuli I have."

I asked to see the appendix. The doctor produced a baby food jar with a long yellowish tissue inside. "It looks pretty normal to me," I said.

He squirmed slightly. "Yes, it is but, when we cut you open, we found your abdominal cavity filled with black fluid. We assumed the appendix had ruptured, but when we cleaned everything out, it looked normal. Since we were already in there, we decided we might as well take the appendix out anyway."

"What caused the fluid?"

"I don't know. I've never seen anything like it."

That was disconcerting. I wish they had analyzed the fluid. Without knowing the cause, I assumed it could reoccur, but it never has.

I figured my ordeal was over, but the Chinese hospital operated differently from the English hospital. They provided a bed. Period. No food, water, or patient care. I had never been in a hospital before, and didn't know what to expect. I assumed this treatment was normal after an operation. My doctor stopped in only the next day, and once a day, a nurse peeked around the door for a minute, but no one checked the stitches, spoke, or asked me a single question. Carlos came by after work every day and assumed everything was fine.

They told me I could leave on day three, and offered me a bowl of thin watery soup. I had received no IV or fluids for three days. No wonder I felt so incredibly thirsty! They said, "Drink the soup slowly," but unable to control myself, I removed the spoon and gulped the entire bowl down at once, only to vomit it up thirty seconds later. Eventually, we learned that patients' families were responsible for providing the patient's food and most other care in the Chinese hospital. It would have been helpful if someone had told us this up-front.

Later, I realized how fortunate I was to be in Hong Kong with Carlos when this happened. In the middle of the night, alone in Makati, I might have waited, and by morning, I might have been in no condition to get help. The Cabrezas now all lived in Pagsanjan, several hours away. We had no phone, so I would need to use the pay phone at the village gate, although its functioning was always problematic, and I was in no condition to drive our stick shift car to the village entrance.

Manila, November 1969

In Manila, four weeks later, the stitches barely out, I returned to a hospital again, this time in Manila, to deliver Lisa, supposedly ten weeks ahead of schedule. The obstetrician watched me struggle for over 30 hours, saying we couldn't have a cesarean delivery because the hospital was "over their quota for the month," as if babies responded to hospital quotas. Finally, he said, "I think you need a cesarean, but the hospital needs permission first. Who can provide it?"

"I can."

"No, it needs to be someone else. Where's your husband?"

"Still in Hong Kong for another week."

"How about your parents?"

"In the States."

"How about Carlos' parents?"

"In Pagsanjan, but the phone usually doesn't work. This is ridiculous. Shall we ask the janitor?"

He reluctantly gave in and operated, and this time I had enough anesthesia.

Lisa arrived, a startling blue-gray color, bald as a billiard ball, with an elongated bumpy head, having struggled with anoxia during the prolonged labor. But somehow, in my fuzzy mental state, she still looked perfect. They whisked her away to oxygen, and fortunately, she had no permanent brain damage.

The hospital contacted Pagsanjan, Solita and Victor came to the hospital, and Solita called Carlos in Hong Kong. Victor said, "I can die now since I've seen my granddaughter."

Carlos called, asking if he should return a week early. Knowing I was a new, first-time mom recovering from two major operations alone, in a foreign country, you would think he wouldn't have to ask. For my part, I should have explained my situation, but my thinking was still fuzzy. "You're almost done. You might as well stay and finish up."

Realistically, there was no way I could cope alone. We had expected to have another ten weeks to prepare. I had planned to wait to buy things until Carlos could help with the preparations because driving a stick shift while fighting Manila traffic, and carrying heavy loads while pregnant was difficult. We bought a stroller and playpen in Hong Kong, but I didn't yet have formula, bottles, diapers, baby clothes, or food. We had no phone, no live-in maid to run errands or to help watch the baby, and with two healing scars and stitches, the doctor told me not to drive. Solita asked if I wanted to come to Pagsanjan, but my doctor was in Makati, and I had no baby things. None of us thought this through.

When the hospital learned we hadn't finalized a name, they refused to release the baby. We couldn't decide on a name over a long-distance call, so I provisionally named her Carla to get released. The hospital was adamant; she needed a middle name, and the nurse pushed hard. "You have to name her Maria. Everyone names their baby Maria," she insisted.

"We don't," I said. Following the Spanish tradition, I gave her my family name, and the hospital let us leave. Fortunately, my friend Lori stepped up, bought diapers and formula, and took us home with her for a few days.

Once Carlos returned, we drove to the Manila Registrar and changed Carla's name to Lisa. It had been a rough two months, but now we were three.

Lynn wrote, "It's killing Mom, not being able to see her first grandchild." But it didn't seem like that to me; they never even called, telegrammed, or asked for a picture, let alone visited. Eventually, however, a letter arrived with a check to start a bank account for Lisa.

Several weeks later, to my amazement, Mario and Fe said, "Do you think we could adopt Lisa?"

I stared at them. "You're not serious?" But they were. They had two boys and, for some reason, thought they couldn't have a girl.

"You can make another one," Fe said. "Anyhow, she'll still be in the family."

Make another one? Like making a cake? Give away a child with no more thought than giving away a puppy? Without thinking of how it might affect the child's life or complicate family dynamics? The suggestion seemed preposterous.

"I don't think so," was all I could manage.

Glen Ellyn, IL August 1971

Nineteen months later, our son David arrived, a fat Buddha-like baby, with a full head of black hair. Thankfully, this time lacked drama and arguments about cesareans. Now we were four.

David was only six weeks old when the bank offered Carlos an around-the-world travel award. This was a rare chance to visit Glen Ellyn, but dragging a newborn around the world for six weeks seemed a terrible idea. We reluctantly left him with Fe and Mario, but brought Lisa, because I knew my parents would be upset if they didn't see at least one grandchild. After four years of marriage, they would finally meet Carlos and Lisa.

During those four years, *National Geographic* had published two articles on the Philippines. One featured the Igorot headhunters of the Banaue region, and the second featured the Tasaday, a stone-age tribe recently discovered in the Mindanao rainforest. Tasaday lived in caves, used stone tools, and wore leaves for clothes. I'm sure the articles stirred up my parents' lingering questions about my life there.

Intellectually, they knew Carlos had been at the University. They had corresponded with Solita before our wedding, seen the pictures, and received my letters, yet they still apparently comprehended almost nothing about our life. *They rarely ask me any questions. Either they don't care to learn, or it's somehow too foreign for them to relate to.*

They never sent us any pictures of themselves, either. When we arrived, I was shocked and saddened to see how much Mom and Dad, now almost sixty, had aged. Suddenly they had more wrinkles and gray hair, and moved more slowly. Of course, it hadn't happened overnight, but I hadn't been there to watch the gradual changes. *How quickly time had passed, and how far our lives had diverged!*

Once they met Carlos, Mom and Dad relaxed. Dad began praising him so effusively that I finally said, "You can tone it down. I think he's great too; after all, I married him. But he's just a normal guy."

I couldn't help thinking: *Dad seemed so relieved. What was he expecting? A naked headhunter?*

Then, seeing Lisa, and perhaps regretting his former comment that "Your children will never be accepted here," Dad set about to rectify it. "It's all different here now," he said. "Only last month, a Japanese family moved in right across town."

One family. I laughed. They lived far across town, yet everyone knew about it. That showed how unusual it was. Not that much had changed. People still stared at us on the street, seemed confused about who to give the bill to in restaurants, and looked at us sideways, trying to decide whether we were a couple. That he still remembered his comment made me wonder. *Had Dad spent four years thinking perhaps his statement had dissuaded me from returning home?*

In 1971, mixed couples were highly unusual. The following week, we saw a young Black and White couple at the Brookfield Zoo. As we passed on the sidewalk, we all locked eyes, and then everyone smiled as if we were part of a small secret fraternity. We were. We still sense a unique camaraderie with other mixed couples and share a bond that's hard to describe, regardless of the mixture. Perhaps it's because we share common experiences and issues related to intercultural or interracial differences.

Our families seemed to focus on the difficulties we would face. Yet we seldom stumbled over intercultural or interracial problems. We fought about normal issues, like how to squeeze the toothpaste tube, or who to invite to dinner. Today, half a century later, people are more accustomed to mixed couples, but we still encounter people who can't relate to, or don't like, the idea.

Our visit thrilled my parents but, now that we had shown return was possible, it only made them want to see us more. We'd just arrived, and already they were asking "When are you coming back?"

I assumed they meant coming back to visit, and I knew it could be a very long time with the four of us and peso salaries. The bank paid for this trip. We couldn't have done it. And they, earning dollars, never seemed to consider finding a way to come see us.

I eventually realized they meant, "When are you *moving* back?"

"Mom, we have a life in the Philippines; we're settled. Our jobs are there, and we've just built a house. We're not moving right now."

Then Dad tried a new tack. He would show me how much better life was in the States. For the first time, he showed some interest in our life. "How much did your house cost?"

"You can't compare, Dad. Dollars mean nothing. It's a peso economy."

But he seemed unable to grasp what that meant, and he pushed. "What's that in dollars?"

"In dollars? About fifteen thousand."

He almost sneered. "Fifteen thousand? What can you build for that?"

"A lot. Don't you understand? It's not a Stateside economy. A bag of cement costs fifty cents there. Laborers earn maybe two dollars a day." Either alcohol had ruined his logic, or he simply couldn't imagine it. He dropped the subject.

We had two weeks to catch up before going on to Europe. Although it was still challenging for them to relate to our life there, at least they felt more comfortable about it, and I was pleased to see they liked Carlos.

Manila, August 1971

After six weeks, we returned to Manila, and drove to Pagsanjan to pick up David. "Everyone thinks he's so cute and mestizo looking," Fe said. "I have a friend without children. Do you think you could give him to her?" Because again, "You can always make another one."

She was still at it. And she was serious. *What made her think we would actually hand over our newborn child, to someone we didn't even know?* The Philippines had plenty of orphans, but her friend wanted a mestizo child. Ironically, she apparently valued dad's 'good English blood,' even if I didn't.

I couldn't wrap my head around it anymore this time than when she wanted Lisa. *Does she think I'm a baby machine? Who would give away their child?*

A lot of people, it turned out. This apparently wasn't as unusual as I thought. When I mentioned this at school, a co-teacher said bitterly that her parents gave her away when she was a baby because they couldn't afford an eighth child. She grew up an only child, having almost no contact with her siblings. Now, in her thirties, she said it had ruined her entire life, and she still questioned why she had to be the one given away.

Large families and unwanted children were an acknowledged result of the national birth control ban. Two years later, the government out-maneuvered the Catholic Church, and for nearly a year, the national policy made such an about-face that stores dangerously handed out free birth control pills with boxes of tampons.

When we had decided to build a house, Solita gave us money to buy a lot, believing giving children an advanced inheritance when they're young and need a leg up is better than waiting until they're so old it's too late to affect their lives. Most people in the Philippines couldn't afford to own homes because banks didn't give residential loans. Fortunately, Citibank made home loans a perk for its officers.

Friends had urged us to buy a lot in one of the new high-class subdivisions in Makati because it would quickly appreciate value. However, almost overnight, Makati had become a large city. We weren't expecting to leave the Philippines, so having an oversized, more rural lot farther out, despite a longer commute and lower long-term appreciation, felt worth it.

Marcello Green Village lay on the edge of a large fallow field, perhaps ten miles from downtown Makati. It wouldn't be anything like the open fields, swamp, and woods of 1950s Glen Ellyn, but at least a large yard would allow the kids to play outside, and Marcello's air quality was much healthier than Makati's. Our new house had more space, and our maid became a live-in.

The empty field next door still supported wildlife, and one day the maid came in, excited. "Mam, there's a snake under my bed!" I went into her room and peered under the bed, wondering how she had even noticed it. A coiled three-foot Philippine cobra stared out at me miserably from the corner. I don't mind snakes; I just don't like to be startled by them. I couldn't fathom how it got in, but it obviously had to go. I remembered the red-hooded cobra in Costa Rica, killed because of me, and thought, *It's my time to pay it back.*

Before the gardener could go after it with his machete, I edged the cobra out from beneath the bed with a broom. It wasn't in a fighting mood; it was just scared and wanted to go home. When it slithered out, I pushed it toward a wastebasket that was lying on its side. When it entered, I carefully upended the wastebasket over the snake and pushed in its remaining tail. Then carefully slipping a piece of cardboard under the upside-down wastebasket to close the bottom and keep it inside, I carried it out into the field and released it away from the house. As it moved out into the grass, I thought, *life for a life; debt paid.*

The maid soon convinced us to hire her cousin to help with child care, and she became the cook. I realized we had now become a typical help-dependent Filipino family. I never really felt comfortable with maids, but had to face the fact that without child care and American appliances, we needed them.

Maids freed up my time. Lori was spiritually searching, as I was, and she offered to share many interesting articles and pamphlets on beliefs and cults that she had collected. Once we returned from Glen Ellyn, I took her up on her offer. It took me in some strange directions.

- *Twenty-Four* -
The Faith Healer

Manila, 1971

IT'S BEEN SAID THAT WE ALL HAVE A GOD-SHAPED HOLE in our souls, a place only God can fill. We can try to fill it with material things and activities, but they can never satisfy for long; something feels missing. I had a hole like that, and I was trying to fill it. My friend Lori, a lapsed Jehovah's Witness, was too, and we worked our way through Lori's collection of materials by the Witnesses, Herbert Armstrong, the Assemblies of God, the Mormons, Dianetics and Scientology, and the Seventh Day Adventists. I delved into near-death experiences, tarot cards, astrology, astral projection, levitation, ESP, auras, chakras, out-of-body experiences, channeling spirits, and Edgar Cayce. You name it, we read it. Nothing filled the hole, although I found materials on Edgar Cayce particularly interesting.

Edgar Cayce went into trances to diagnose illnesses. He also interpreted dreams and gave "readings" about people's past lives. He often referenced Christianity, and it all sounded interesting and benign. I couldn't define what I was looking for, but Cayce's best-selling books, a blend of healing, reincarnation, dreams, and past lives, intrigued me. I also learned about spirit writing, where people allowed something or someone to use their hand to write messages. Some people who had "spirit guides" or "channeled" spirits reported having written songs or entire books that way.

I decided to try spirit writing, but something deep inside warned me against it. A thought came; *What if the spirits aren't who they pretend to be?* Lori said the Bible gave dire warnings about this, so to cover my bases, I casually asked God for protection from anything evil. I also asked for discernment, although that word wasn't in my vocabulary yet.

I sat at my bedroom desk, pencil in hand, opening myself up to whoever or whatever wanted to use my hand. After a few minutes, I was almost ready to give up, when suddenly the muscles in my arm began twitching, and the pencil started moving. I felt a chill run through me, and goose bumps rose on my arm. Something inside my arm seemed to be testing my muscles as if learning to control the pencil. *Almost the way one might maneuver a robot.* I realized I had no idea who or why something would want to interact like this, but my unease increased. *If I allow something to manipulate my arm, would it want to take over more of me at some point? Could I become possessed, like someone's robot?* I dropped the pencil.

When I told Lori, she was horrified.

"Don't ever do that! It's so dangerous! I have so many articles about people who became involved in the occult. Many experienced terrible things, and some even died." She was so adamant about the danger I stopped the spirit writing before it got off the ground.

Later, sitting at home, I remembered missionaries on the ship saying the Bible had prophecies in Revelation. *Prophecies sounded interesting; maybe I should read them.* I dusted off my confirmation Bible and flipped to Revelation. I found some precise hair-raising predictions.

A third of the earth burned; one-third of the ocean dead; the fresh water poisoned. Wars, famines, fires, huge hailstones, demonic attacks. A third of humanity destroyed. I didn't understand all the imagery, but many things sounded like actual future events. *Scary things seem to lie ahead for some group of people.* The who, where, and when, were unclear, but I had one main takeaway: *I don't want to be around when this all comes down.* I could relate to the people in Revelation. I thought, *I'm pretty good, compared to some people I know. No one's perfect.* But I knew I could be better. I rather generically asked for forgiveness.

Meanwhile, stories about faith healers began appearing in the Philippine papers and generating heated debate. Some people swore they were genuine; others believed, and in many cases proved, some were fakes. And there were many fakes. Today, YouTube is full of them. I was on the fence about the faith healers, but Edgar Cayce's healings sounded genuine and benign, so when I had a chance to see a faith healer in action, I jumped at it.

On a Monday morning, Mrs. Baranga came into the IS teacher's lounge, excited because a faith healer had removed a large lump from her shoulder. He operated without instruments, anesthetics, or antiseptics, yet the unusual surgery was painless. She pulled her blouse down to show us her now-flat shoulder, with only a thin scar.

The Science Department wanted to see this man. The following Saturday, Carlos and I joined a group of IS faculty visiting the faith healer. Dr. Blanche worked mainly from home, but on Saturdays, he held office in a small room on Mabini Street, an older part of downtown Manila. We arrived early, but already, milling people filled the room. Some came hoping for help, but many simply came out of curiosity.

Dr. Blanche, a nice-looking, middle-aged man, dressed simply in a short-sleeved white tee-shirt and pants. I assumed Doctor was merely a title of respect, because he certainly wasn't a regular doctor and no diplomas or certificates adorned the office walls. His small, stuffy, white-walled operating room contained only a flat table covered with a clean sheet and a small pillow, and a filing cabinet holding a few small bottles of alcohol, cotton balls, rolls of cotton, a glass, and a spoon.

He had no appointment system; he just looked over the crowd and beckoned someone forward. A man complaining about vision in his right eye lay down on the table. Without preliminaries, Blanche went to work. He stuck his right hand into a can of something looking like Crisco, and gouged out a white, marble-sized lump with his index finger. He spread the man's eye open with his left thumb and forefinger, and carefully but steadily pushed his right index finger with Crisco into the eye. I stood right next to him, and had a clear view. I winced as the finger slipped in up to the second knuckle. He didn't double up his finger. The finger and Crisco passed right through the tissue into the back of eyeball socket. When he withdrew his finger, the Crisco remained inside.

Common sense and human physiology both argue against this because muscles and tissue attach to the eye all around the socket. *If a grain of sand in the eye hurts, what about an entire finger?* Yet the man registered no pain whatsoever. We waited, watching him. After a couple of minutes, Blanche said, "It's coming back now," and held the man's eye wide open with a thumb and forefinger.

I gazed at the eyeball, watching the lump of Crisco slowly slide around from behind the eyeball of its own volition, nowhere near Blanche's fingers. The irregular white glob had become smooth, flattened, gray, and discolored. Blanche wiped it out with a cotton ball. The man blinked, looked around, said he could see better, thanked Dr. Blanche, hopped off the table, and left. There was no logical explanation.

Next, a thin woman complaining of stomach pain lay down on the table. Blanche palpitated her stomach.

"You have an abscess. I'm going to drain it."

Exposing her abdomen, he slowly pushed his fingers through her skin. I stood next to him, staring at his hand, as his fingers slowly slipped through the skin up to the top knuckle. They weren't doubled over; they were definitely inside. As he gently probed, a whitish pus-like liquid began seeping out through individual pores on her stomach, and formed droplets that pooled in a depressed area on her stomach. Blanche spooned a couple of tablespoons of liquid off of her stomach into a small glass and wiped her off with a cotton ball. The woman got up, thanked him, and walked out. It was startling and unquestionable.

Surgeries were his most impressive procedures. Next, a woman with a lump on her arm lay on the table. When he planned to cut open the skin, first he swabbed some alcohol on the area, his only concession to antiseptics. Then holding his index finger six to ten inches above the body, he pointed it toward the site to be cut and moved his finger through the air in a quick slicing motion. A thin red line of blood appeared on the skin below. The cut, so thin it looked like a paper or razor blade cut, scarcely bled. *Somehow, either Blanche focuses his energy like a laser beam, or he's not the one doing the cutting.*

Pushing his fingers into the cut, he removed a piece of tissue. *That ought to hurt.* Yet, the patients lay there, unflinching, apparently feeling nothing. The lump, noticeable before, had disappeared. Significantly, Dr. Blanche put the tissue into a small jar, and said, "Possibly this is cancerous; have it biopsied." He wasn't concerned a biopsy would identify it as anything other than human tissue.

Now he was red in the face, and sweating profusely. "I'm tired. I can't do any more today," he said with regret.

The following Saturday, many of us returned to watch him again. This time someone complained of vein problems. The cure was visually startling, although it made a certain sense. First, he used his finger to make a cut above a large vein in the lower leg. He placed a large peso coin near the cut, placed a small alcohol-soaked cotton ball on the coin, and covered everything with a small glass. The peso merely supported the cotton ball; I presume anything similar would work. Tilting up the edge of the glass, he stuck a lighted match briefly underneath. The cotton ignited with a small pop, and he pressed the glass tightly down onto the skin. It burned for only a few seconds until it used up the oxygen under the glass, creating a vacuum. We watched the skin swell up under the glass, and slowly pull the edges of the cut apart.

A thick red substance slowly began oozing from the cut, accumulating inside the glass. *A clot? Cholesterol? Why was it red? Perhaps it mixed with blood?* After several minutes, when perhaps a tablespoon or two of this substance had oozed out, he removed the glass, breaking the vacuum. The cut closed on its own, so clean it needed no stitches. He wiped the area off with alcohol.

We returned several weeks in a row to watch various operations. I was one of the few who didn't mind seeing blood, and who had questions, so

Blanche beckoned me to move right beside him at the operating table for a close view.

"How do you make the cuts?"

"I can't really explain it, but there's nothing special about my finger…I could even use your finger to cut. Do you want to help in an operation?"

Of course, I said, "Yes!"

A woman with a lump lay down on the table. Covering my hand with his, he pointed my index finger and guided my hand to perhaps six inches above her arm, then moved it in a small quick downward motion. A thin line appeared on the woman's skin, and a tiny amount of blood seeped out. My finger made a cut! Blanche reached in, removed some tissue, and put it in a small jar for biopsy.

Our hands were nowhere near the skin when we cut. As usual, the thin cut resembled a laser cut. I hoped to feel heat, power, or something pass through my finger when he used it, but I felt nothing. When Carlos expressed amazement, Blanche said, "Do you want to do one too?" and he used Carlos's finger for the next operation.

Were these surgeries simply sleight of hand or even intentional fraud? It didn't seem so, and if so, to what end? Blanche, a humble, mild-mannered man, never requested money. He said he had received the gift of healing as a young man and didn't want to spoil it. He accepted a few vegetables or gifts of cotton and alcohol to use in his 'surgeries,' but he certainly wasn't getting rich from this. Several things also persuaded me he was genuine. He never did more than three operations a day; then, red in the face, dripping in sweat, he would announce he was too tired to do more procedures. You can't fake sweat. He expended a lot of energy, which is often the case with psychic phenomena.

He couldn't hide bags of blood in his armpit and send fluids down into his hand via a tube or some similar trick. He worked in a short-sleeved tee-shirt without surgical gloves, his hands and arms completely visible. Once, at someone's suggestion, he spread his fingers, turning his hands for inspection before operating. The patients left satisfied. The operations left scars. And he didn't fear the biopsies would turn up non-human tissue and reveal him to be a fake.

After watching him several times, Patsy, a fellow teacher, wanted to visit Blanche at his home in Mandaluyong. She asked me to come along. Her husband was a doctor, so I'm sure she didn't tell him our destination. I'm equally sure he would have labeled it dangerous quackery and opposed the visit.

Somehow, she had obtained Blanche's address. After school, we drove through the congested Makati traffic, and with much effort, we found his crowded *barrio* in nearby Mandaluyong. The maze of crowded, narrow streets lined with tiny, yard-less houses and huts swarmed with people, skinny dogs, and noisy vendors. Streets narrowed, and congestion increased. Afraid of becoming boxed in and unable to turn around, we parked the car, and wandered down small alleys, asking directions. Everyone knew of Blanche, and eventually we located his small wooden house.

He invited us into his living room, which doubled as an office. Patsy lay down on a table that occupied most of the small space. She had leg cramps at night. He did his usual cutting procedure, placed the glass, created a vacuum, and drained out a sluggish red substance.

While waiting for the substance to finish oozing out, I asked Blanche, "How did you learn this?"

"When I was a boy, someone who also did this told me someday I would be able to do it too. A few years later, I could. I really don't know how I do it." I had read similar things about other healers.

"Does it work better on people with more faith?"

He laughed. "No, I don't need faith to cure you. I'll cure you whether you have faith or not. But," he added, "operations work better on good people." That was interesting; it implied his operations didn't all work equally well or produce similarly lasting effects.

"How do you know if someone is good or bad?"

"I can tell by their colors." He didn't define good or bad or elaborate on the colors. This fascinated me. This mild-mannered man, who I'm sure had never read about auras, talked about them, yet he didn't use the term *aura*. But he was seeing something. Because living things have energy, the concept of an aura made total sense to me.

When Patsy's treatment finished, I asked, "Do you feel any better?"

"I don't know. I'll know later tonight at home."

Then Dr. Blanche turned to me. "Now, what can I do for you?"

"Nothing. I'm only along to accompany Patsy."

He looked me over as if scanning me. "No. There's something wrong with your elbow." Two years earlier, I crashed trying to ride a unicycle, and slammed my elbow on the pavement. The pain was sporadic; some days, it throbbed; other days, it felt normal. At the moment, it felt fine. I wasn't favoring the elbow, so he had no reason to think I had a problem.

"Really, it's fine."

"No, it's not. Something's wrong inside." He took my elbow in his hands, massaging it for about 30 seconds. "That should fix it," he said, dropping my arm. Patsy gave him 20 pesos for some cotton and alcohol. We thanked him and left. Several months later, I realized my recurring elbow pain had never returned after the afternoon at Blanche's house.

A month later, we returned to the Mabini St. office one last time. While we waited for Blanche to arrive, a hard-looking, heavily made-up woman, and a thin seedy-looking middle-aged man with a skinny mustache and a loud plaid suit, seemed to be taking charge. They weren't aware we had been there often before, and the woman came over and began telling me stories of Blanche's miracles. Her eager eyes darted around like a bird of prey as she told me how Blanche had pushed some cotton through someone's skin. "And it didn't even show up on the x-ray!"

I never saw him push anything into anyone that remained more than a minute, and he certainly had no x-ray machine in his clinic. Despite the bizarre things we had seen Blanche do, what she said didn't make sense. Unable to let that pass, I said, "I don't think most cotton shows up on an x-ray." The woman gave me a sharp glance, stared hard, and turned away to corner someone else.

The woman seemed to be taking charge. When Blanche arrived, she opened a large Bible, and announced "Now we will all say the Lord's Prayer before he operates." It felt contrived, if not almost blasphemous. My fraud detector lit up; everything about these two felt phony. I sensed they had attached themselves to this humble man hoping to make money. It was confirmed when they passed a plate for donations at the end of the session.

Blanche had told me faith or belief didn't matter, but he had no objections to the prayer. He never asked for donations because he said his healing had been a gift. *Why isn't he bothered by these people? Blanche must realize they are soliciting donations. Does he receive any of the money? They seem like con artists. Can't he tell from their colors what type of people they are? Why doesn't he confront them?* I wish I had pressed him about this. We never returned, and never found out anything more. It was the last time we saw or heard anything about him.

***

Today, fifty years later, I have a theory about his healings. Humans clearly exist in four dimensions of width, length, height, and time, but physics superstring theory states that the universe contains at least ten dimensions, many involving gravitational, magnetic, and spatial distortions too complex for most of us to grasp. Theologians agree that other dimensions exist and that spiritual beings inhabit some of them. Heaven probably exists in another dimension, for example.

The scriptures mention the resurrected Christ's ability to pass through walls. This seems similar to Blanche's ability to move his hands through a person's body. Perhaps they were both somehow accessing another dimension, which to us three-dimensional people, seems to be bending our laws of physics.

It seems likely the occult works by accessing different dimensions too. Blanche seemed to focus energy, sending it through his finger to make the cuts. How can you explain that? None of us, including Dr. Blanche, had any idea how he did it. I couldn't explain how he did it, but I never doubted its reality. None of us did. I just don't believe he was the one doing the cutting.

Dr. Blanche's acts were impossible for a regular person. I believe something beyond the realm of our physical laws, as we understand them, worked through him from another dimension, and Blanche, a willing channeler, allowed his body to be possessed or used for 'good,' as Edgar Cayce and many psychics and spiritualists do. The real question is, who or what was the source of his power?

I believe his power was occultic, not God-given. The immediate results of his cures appeared to be for good. Still, occultic activity always has an ulterior motive, and that's one reason the Bible warns so strongly against any involvement with it. It also talks of evil's ability to appear as good.

I'd been searching for a visible, tangible sign of the spiritual realm, and Dr. Blanche had supplied it, even used my finger. The healings were an intriguing curiosity, but they didn't fill my spiritual hole.

Prophecy, not faith healings, became the hook God used to finally reel me in. As Chuck Missler said, "A fisherman cleans the fish after the fish are caught.[8]" In my case, He began baiting His hook a few weeks later, although the 'cleaning' would take several more years.

One of my IS students came up after class. "I think you might like this book. It's pretty interesting." And she handed me *The Late Great Planet Earth*, by Hal Lindsay, a Christian writer. It focused on prophecy, mainly the book of Revelation. I'd never had a student give me a book before. She was right; it was interesting.

On May 14, 1948, against all odds, Israel, the Jewish national homeland, was re-established in one day with the signing of an agreement, fulfilling seemingly impossible prophecies in Isaiah, Ezekiel, and elsewhere. More remarkable, after 2,000 years of dispersion, the Jews still retained their identity as a people. Now they were returning to Israel from all over the world.

Israel's re-establishment fulfilled a foundational Biblical prophecy on which most of the yet-unfilled 'end-time' prophecies depend. Lindsay's book became almost an instant classic and sparked a national revival of interest in Bible prophecy. It was one of the first of a flood of modern books on it. Lindsay also removed some of the mystery from Revelation. His book caught my interest more than any other books, magazines, or tracts I had read, and helped focus my reading and spiritual searching.

However, I didn't have as much time to read as I had hoped, because local and national events were becoming increasingly complicated and challenging.

- *Twenty-Five* -
Bomb Threats

Manila 1971-1973

B Y 1971, AFTER FOUR YEARS IN THE PHILIPPINES, I was becoming restless and dissatisfied with life. International School students had initially challenged me to dig deeper into topics I only *thought* I knew well, but, after several years, I could grab my notes, rush to class, and lecture without preparation. Teaching had become painfully routine; the challenge was gone. And so, it seemed, were marine biology and travel.

Carlos and I both loved traveling, but peso salaries circumscribed our ability. By Filipino standards, both IS and Citibank paid well, and living and spending pesos in the Philippines had allowed a good life. But the peso was devaluating, and converting pesos into dollars, shrank my salary to only $125 a month, making travel outside the Philippines prohibitive. Carlos' pay, although better than mine, was similarly limited. Neither of us had considered this problem when we chose to settle in the Philippines. Even one return plane ticket to Chicago would cost over two years of my salary. Maybe my parents were right; in our current situation, I might never be able to see them again.

The excitement had disappeared from my life, leaving a vague feeling of incompleteness and dissatisfaction. There were few diversions, and I envisioned a life of routine stretching into retirement, with little chance to indulge either my love of travel or the ocean. I was only 28 and, unless something changed, I pictured retiring in my sixties, probably still living in the same house, still teaching at IS, and having spent my life sidetracked from marine biology and travel. It was depressing.

But the winds of change were blowing. IS expanded its curriculum, and asked me to teach new semester courses in marine biology and physiology. Teaching something new, always a challenge, relieved the boredom, and I regained some connection with the marine environment, if only in the classroom. Introductory marine biology and physiology textbooks weren't available, so I had to develop my own curriculum and lab exercises. That would become an unexpected future blessing.

The marine biology class highlight, a three-day field trip to Hundred Islands Marine Area, attracted the principal and several interested parents as chaperones. It became a big hit with the students. Word spread, and the Girl Scouts and other groups also began asking me to lead ocean field trips. This inspired Willa, one of the parents, to establish a summer camp on the small island of Balesin during summer break.

Willa taught life-saving and water skills, and she invited me to join her, and teach marine biology. The camp became quite popular, although the students complained of our 'onerous' rules: no soft drinks, no electronic devices, aka radios, and no maids to pick up after them. Physically reconnecting with the ocean became a lifeline. After several years of holding my breath, I began to breathe, and teaching felt fulfilling again.

Brother Alfred, the science department chairman at De La Salle University, originally came from Lisle, IL, a town next to Glen Ellyn. Despite his being twice my age, his long white cassock seemed in non-stop motion, and energy and ideas swirled in his wake. We clicked, and had similar teaching philosophies. Somehow, he heard about the physiology and marine biology classes, and he asked me to come teach at De La Salle.

Filipino students generally learned by rote memory, and he wanted them to learn to think, so he wanted no textbooks, only lab exercises, and he talked about dissecting pig hearts, eyeballs, and other interesting lab possibilities. I liked his approach, but declined, because De La Salle, was on Taft Avenue in downtown Manila, a long commute. Undeterred, he pestered me with calls, sent a priest to IS to convince me, and even appeared unannounced at our house in Marcello to plead his case. He was persistent. Eventually he wore me down, and I agreed to teach marine biology and laboratory techniques during the summer. I became De La Salle's first female teacher. Soon he also pulled me into teaching afternoons after IS, during the school year, and then he began pushing for full time.

Meanwhile, the 1972-1973 International School year became chaotic. Students were restless and unmotivated, and drug use increased. School discipline was lax, and the administration seemed impotent. As summer break approached, some enterprising students discovered if the school received a bomb threat, school would evacuate until the fire department bomb squad arrived to perform the impossible task of searching the entire school for bombs.

The first time the office received a bomb threat, classes jerked to a halt, and everyone quickly poured into the athletic field. We stood sweltering in the blistering tropical sun, sweating, and swearing until the bomb squad arrived and searched the building, a process taking well over an hour. The ruse worked well, so predictably, we began receiving daily bomb threats. The school knew these were pranks but felt unable to ignore them, so day after day, the calls continued, and everyone slowly shuffled out onto the athletic field to await the bomb squad.

One Friday, about 10:00 a.m., marine biology class was in the middle of fish dissections. Thirty large fish lay spread out on the lab tables in various states of disarticulation when the bomb squad ordered an immediate evacuation. This time their search seemed more thorough than usual. Noon was approaching when they announced the All Clear. Since it was Friday, and school normally ended at 12:15, the principal told everyone to go home for the weekend, and turned off the air conditioning.

On Monday, the whole high school wing was complaining about an unbearable stench permeating the school. Wrinkling my nose at the horrible but unfamiliar odor, I walked down the hall toward the teacher's lounge with no idea it involved me. As I passed the marine biology door, I remembered the fish. *Oh no.* With a sinking feeling, I cracked open the classroom door. The smell hit me like a blow. Thirty fish still lay on the lab tables, where they had been marinating in the tropical heat for three days. Holding my breath, I rushed to open the windows.

The unsalvageable dissections immediately went into the garbage, but the lingering odor permeated everything. People connected the smell with the lab, but within an hour, before there could be much discussion about it, another bomb scare sent everyone into the athletic field. This time the high school at least, went thankfully, appreciating the fresh air. The incident got lost in the chaos, and even the stern, eagle-eyed department head never mentioned it.

IS also began a series of mini courses. On the surface, an anthropology mini-trip to Sakol Island, a small island in Mindanao, the southernmost region of the Philippines, sounded interesting. But it was incredibly ill-conceived. Mindanao was Muslim, and even in 1972, it was a perennial trouble spot, and considered dangerous and unfriendly to non-Muslims. Foreigners were routinely kidnaped and held for ransom, yet this was apparently the administration's idea of a good place for a field trip. They hired Andi, a former Peace Corps worker, to lead the group. She supposedly had familiarity with the area and knew the language. As Senior Class Advisor, they asked me along as the chaperone.

Our group of fifteen flew first to Basilan Island, a large island off the coast of Mindanao. Andi had never briefed us on conditions in Sakol, but now arriving in Basilan, she said, almost off-handedly, "You should probably go to the market here because you might want to bring some extra food to Sakol."

It's a bit late to tell us that now, I thought, and she only gave us about ten minutes to shop. None of us took her suggestion of buying food seriously. The school had scheduled the trip, and our host families were supposed to feed us. Students thought more in terms of snacks, and bought a few candy bars and bags of chips.

Thinking perhaps these were food presents for our hosts, I bought a *ganta* of rice, about two pounds. Surprisingly, people in Basilan seemed to be speaking Spanish, not Tagalog or English, and I could easily bargain in the market. Andi asked, "Where did you learn Chabacano?"

"Chabacano? I was speaking Spanish." The two sounded so similar that I hadn't even noticed. *Good. At least we should have no problem communicating in Sakol.*

The bamboo outriggers of our motorized ocean bancas bounced heavily through the choppy waves slapping the boat as we left Basilan and ploughed through churning seas to Sakol, a tiny island on the Sulu Archipelago, where we would spend several days. The students consumed most of their snacks on the boat before we even reached Sakol.

It surprised me that Sakol would agree to visitors, because it was common knowledge that Sakol's sole revenue-generating activity was smuggling American cigarettes into the Philippines from Borneo and the Asian mainland. The lack of any viable business on Sakol bore this out; the town was only a handful of simple, weathered board houses and a small *sari-sari* store roughly the size of a small bathroom, constructed of flimsy, weathered plywood and a palm-frond roof. Its small inventory contained only bottles of hot Pepsi, a few small packages of cigarettes, chips, gum, and candy bars. Fortunately, at least Andi brought along cases of water.

Tina and Flora, two of my former students, roomed with me in the Muslim Datu's house. When we arrived, an older woman in a hijab and long dress silently appeared and wordlessly led us to an empty room. Without a word or smile of welcome, she pointed to two mats on the planked floor of an otherwise empty room, and left without making eye contact.

The Philippines has perhaps twenty major languages and dozens of dialects but, whatever the village spoke, it wasn't Tagalog, English, Spanish, or Chabacano. We had no way to communicate with the Datu or the family, although communication became a non-issue, because both the family and any vestige of hospitality were invisible. We never met the Datu or any children, and it was the last we saw of the wife except for perhaps thirty seconds on our last night. So much for interacting with the Muslims.

Either they ate elsewhere, or they perpetually fasted, because we never saw the family and they never offered us anything to eat or drink. They supplied a floor, period. Dinnertime came and went, and all the meals on the second and third days as well. From the complaints I heard, students in the other houses were having similar problems. We were all on an obligatory fast. We finally complained to Andi.

"Really?" She seemed surprised. "They were paid to feed you." She, at least, must have been eating something. "I'll try to talk to them."

Try? Contrary to our expectation, she couldn't speak any common language with the Datu either. If she had worked in Mindanao as a Peace Corps worker, how could she have accomplished anything without speaking the language? She had provided us no advanced information on what to expect or what we might need, and I don't recall her explaining anything about Muslim life or planning any activities.

She told us to bring bathing suits so we assumed we could swim, but waves crashed directly onto the sharp lava and coral rock fringing the island. Even crossing the rocky beach to the water's edge was difficult, and required shoes to avoid shredding our feet. With no sand beach, entering the water was too dangerous.

Meals and swimming, the two most enticing activities, were lacking. Andi might also have suggested we bring house gifts, but I didn't feel upset about that omission since we had paid for non-existent food.

The unfriendly Datu, at least, obviously didn't like visitors, but greed won out over privacy. He wanted our money. I assumed the school paid him in a lump sum. *Did any of it trickle down to the other families, or did he keep it all for himself?*

Perhaps people existed mainly on seafood because we saw no crops or animals except a stray chicken or two. We saw no boats either. *How could they go to Borneo for cigarettes without boats?* I assumed they must be hiding a big part of their life from us.

We had nowhere to buy anything except the sari-sari store, and my kitchen pantry looked like a Costco warehouse compared to that. Eventually, a couple of families understood they should provide some food. But not the Datu.

I bought rice, but we had no idea where or how to cook it. We didn't feel comfortable snooping around the house looking for cooking utensils, matches, and dishes, and no one was ever available to ask. The occupants were invisible. Perhaps they felt non-Muslims somehow contaminated them. Other students weren't raving about the quantity or quality of the food at their houses either, although a couple of families finally provided something small. Not ours.

After day two, usually around noon, our conversation somehow always came around to food. We fantasized at length about our favorite foods, and spoke longingly of pepperoni pizzas thickly covered with mushrooms and cheese. Thick, juicy hamburgers with fresh lettuce and tomato, crispy bacon, and dripping melted cheese. Crunchy fried chicken. Salty, crisp French fries. Mounds of cold ice cream, dripping with hot fudge and smothered in whipped cream.

On our last night, the Datu finally decided to feed us. We never received an apology for our lack of food, but the wife silently materialized again. Wordless and unsmiling, she avoided our eyes as she held out a battered empty, lidless pot, and pointed to a rusty propane burner. She left one small raw egg and two small two-inch minnows to share between the three of us, and disappeared. Didn't she even have the grace to feel embarrassed about our treatment?

Thankfully, I had rice from the Basilan market! We hunted around for a match to light the rusty burner, boiled the egg and tried to cook some rice, which proved difficult without a lid. Tina contributed a small bag of Cheetos from the sari-sari store.

We sat on a bench at a tiny wood table, staring at our dinner. It came to about two bites each. We debated how to divide the small egg and tiny fish three ways. Should we each take one item, or should we try to cut everything in thirds? Should we include the heads and tails? Everyone wanted the egg, so we awkwardly divided it into thirds, but minus heads and tails, dividing the now one-inch fish three ways seemed so ridiculous that I donated my portion to the girls. We joked about our concentration camp meal as we ate dinner but, despite the undercooked rice, none of us had ever felt so hungry.

The next day, we reboarded the outrigger without breakfast for the long return trip to Basilan, and then Manila. At the Manila Airport, a group of parents waited excitedly at the gate for their children. The students disembarked, and totally ignoring their waving parents, charged *en masse* to the airport's Jolly Bee hamburger stand, leaving a line of bewildered parents standing at the gate.

***

Problems in the southern Philippines worsened over time, and the Muslim extremists continued to kidnap and foment unrest in the south. Unfortunately, the extremists were only one aspect of the Philippine problem; chaos was escalating throughout the country. Life first became uncomfortable, then difficult, then frightening.

- *Twenty-Six* -
Living with Chaos

Manila 1968-1973

W HEN I ARRIVED IN 1967, THE PHILIPPINES WAS touted as Asia's 'shining star of democracy', but typhoons, earthquakes, tsunamis, and volcanic eruptions continually threw the young country off-balance. In an average year, twenty typhoons pounded the Philippines, and of those, four were generally heavily destructive, flattening houses and destroying crops. It was difficult to move forward when year after year, storms wiped everything out.

Poor public policies on deforestation and the government's inability to construct or maintain sewers, storm drains, and other basic infrastructure, compounded typhoon impacts. Manila routinely flooded, leaving potholed roads and sidewalks filled with holes and loose stones. When the city flooded, trucks couldn't transport food, and people panicked, immediately hoarding anything available.

In 1972, a powerful typhoon blew down concrete walls and uprooted enormous acacia trees in the Makati villages. Torrential rains caused the most severe flooding in recorded history, leaving potholes and cracked pavement, large sections of washed-out highway, and 775 confirmed deaths. Once again, downtown Manila was underwater, in some places so deep that when Carlos attempted to drive home from work, he discovered our VW bug actually floated. Seeing an opportunity for extra money, several enterprising boys appeared and pushed the floating car to higher ground while he kept his foot on the gas to keep the engine going.

Earthquakes were also common because the Philippines was part of the Ring of Fire, a volcanically active region associated with tectonic plate movements. About seventy percent of world's volcanoes and ninety percent of the world's earthquakes occurred along the Ring of Fire. Its 452 volcanoes circled the Pacific Basin in a horseshoe, stretching up the east coast of Asia past the Philippines, Japan, and Korea, across the Bering Strait to Alaska, and down the west coast of North and South America. The Philippines routinely experienced earthquakes of magnitude six, seven, and infrequently, even eight, on the Richter scale.

Filipinos were resilient and accustomed to natural disasters, but human elements immeasurably increased people's misery. President Marcos' regime became infamous for corruption and extravagance, and his greed for power and money appeared boundless. Graft and corruption escalated under his presidency, and he began amassing a fortune of unprecedented scale on the backs of the citizens.

One innovation was Imelda Marcos' birthday fund, a thinly veiled extortion project to collect money from businesses and individuals all over Manila on her birthday. The proceeds supposedly went to civil improvement projects, like the Filipino heart center, but people joked about how much of their contribution went to finance Imelda's famous 5,000-pair shoe collection. The donation was supposedly voluntary, but the Palace suggested the amount of contribution, and it could be costly: one bank forked over ten million pesos one year.

As President Marcos began printing extra money to buy votes for his reelection, inflation and currency devaluation rose dramatically. The amount needed to pay back my student loan fluctuated with the exchange rate of the peso. When I arrived, the exchange rate was 2:1, and paying off my $3,000 loan would require P6,000, about ten months of my starting IS salary. Then peso appeared to go into free-fall, and began devaluing before our eyes. As the peso devalued, my loan increased astronomically. The exchange rate began rising; from 2:1, it became 5:1, then 11:1… 21:1… 35:1, and eventually stabilized at 45:1. The value of a peso, worth 50 cents when I arrived, had plummeted to about 2.2 cents.

When the peso devalued to 11:1, my student loan had risen to P33,000. Salaries didn't keep pace with inflation, and we couldn't have paid it; it was already more than Carlos and my annual salaries combined. Solita saw what was coming, and graciously paid it off before it became worse. Thankfully, she paid it when she did, because by the time the peso stabilized at 45:1, my $3,000 dollar debt would convert to a whopping P135,000, more than the original cost of our house. I would have had to default on my student loan.

Rising prices spurred hoarding. We watched supermarket staff walking the aisles daily with acetone and a marking pen, erasing yesterday's prices and replacing them with today's higher ones. The only certainty was that tomorrow's costs would be higher than today, so paradoxically, the only way to save money was to spend it as fast as possible.

Survival became difficult for the average person, but families living near the poverty line suffered the most.

Under Marcos, bribing became ingrained as an accepted way of life. The president set the tone, and corruption flowed down to all levels. Public servants had innovative ways of soliciting bribes, and every service seemed to require kickbacks. People grudgingly excused this because they understood many people couldn't survive without bribes.

Businesses had "fixers" whose job was bribing officials to expedite official paperwork. When I visited Carlos in Hong Kong, as an alien, I needed an exit clearance. The Fixer in Carlos' office offered to get my papers signed for me, but I was adamant. "I'm not paying any bribes for this routine service."

He smiled and shook his head. "Then be prepared for a long delay. And bring ten copies of all your exit papers, marriage certificate and Alien Certificate of Registration. Don't ever give anything original."

I started the exit process. It required many signatures, and every desk seemed to lose my papers, awaiting a bribe. "I have another copy," I would say. They reluctantly signed, and passed me on to the next desk, to wait hours more. After two days I arrived at the last desk in the multi-step process. Then they lost my passport. I had no copy of that.

"It doesn't seem to be here. We'll have to look for it. Come back tomorrow."

I exploded; I was leaving in two days. I resorted to a threat. "It had better be here tomorrow, or I'll have to involve Senator Benitez (Solita's cousin.)" When I returned, the passport miraculously surfaced. I'd paid no bribes, but I wasted three days. My resolve was broken; next time I would use the Fixer.

The policemen were quite creative. They stood on street corners with traffic-light manipulators, watching cars pass through the intersections. When a car approached mid-intersection, they switched the traffic lights from green to red, ticketed it, and then offered to let the driver off for a fee. Experiences like that so conditioned our responses that even today, fifty years later, when Carlos approaches a green light, much to my annoyance, he slows down, because he is still unconsciously expecting traffic-light manipulators.

In my case, because thievery had become so rampant, even today whenever I misplace something, no matter how insignificant, my first instinct is still to think, *OK, who stole it?*

Although our jobs both paid well, the spiraling price of goods forced us to change our eating habits. I began changing what I usually bought; we ate more fish and less beef, then switched from beef to pork. I began cutting out treats like frozen peas. Yet we fared better than many. It's difficult to explain the suffocating feeling of inflation when you don't know where the downward spiral will stop. In 1974, the inflation rate rose to an astronomical thirty-six percent.

Many people lived on the edge, their diets reduced to rice and a few dried fish. The malungay trees outside our fence had soft, edible leaves, and people broke off so many branches they reduced our trees to sticks. People went door-to-door begging to work without pay, simply for room and board.

Our gardener, hired to work one day a week, kept pressing us for more work, until he eventually worked for us six days a week. He arrived early, so the maid fed him breakfast in addition to lunch, and he began staying late, so she provided him dinner too. Then he asked if he could make a garden in the field outside our fence to grow vegetables to take home. One day, realizing the maids seemed to have a lot of 'visitors', I began counting. During the course of one day, I counted fifteen people silently entering the kitchen door. The maid was feeding them. But how can you refuse someone a cup of rice?

The difficulty of life undoubtedly helped the communist guerilla insurgency gain strength in rural areas. In 1969, a Maoist group called the New People's Army (NPA), the military faction of the Communist Party, began attempting to overthrow the government by protracted guerilla warfare. They promised people a better life, and many had little to lose.

The NPA stifled initiative and new business development because if anyone looked prosperous, the NPA appeared, asking for protection money. Projects that could have benefitted the local economy were never initiated. Mario didn't repair the bank fence for fear of looking prosperous, and he avoided putting new land into production or starting any new business for the same reason. Once I asked Mario why he didn't replant a few coconuts in his yard, but he said "If I do that, the NPA may think it's a coconut farm."

The government, unable to protect the people from this extortion, took advantage of it. The Philippine Army offered to protect people from the NPA for a fee. "But we can only do so much," they said, and encouraged our rural bank to continue paying off the NPA. Caught in the middle, people paid both sides. The bank paid protection money to the NPA, but they continually demanded more. Finally, Solita refused to pay more, and they threatened to burn down the bank. Mom just shrugged and said, "I guess I need to increase the bank insurance."

Mario paid P1,000 a month to the NPA for his agri-business, but it frustrated him, because he said, "I know the NPA will use my money to buy weapons that make the rebels even stronger, but I have no choice." He didn't pay the Army directly, but he provided favors, loaning them vehicles or occasionally paying for their visitors at the Pagsanjan Lodge.

The NPA continually demanded more money, and at one point, when Mario resisted, they even kidnapped him for a short while. He never gave us details, and they never demanded a ransom, so perhaps it was only a threat to prove what they could do.

Eventually, the kidnapper surrendered to the Army and then, in a bizarre twist, he asked Mario to be *Ninong*, or godfather, for his newborn child. Possibly the kidnapper considered this insurance because a Ninong is expected to take care of the godchild if something happens to the parents. At the very least, the child will visit every Christmas, expecting a sizeable gift of money.

The kidnapper's 'insurance' paid off; someone killed him within a year. Then his young widow began appearing from time to time asking for help, and Mario always provided it.

Some NPA were tough guerilla fighters, but others often seemed more like children playing at war. Whether they expected to benefit or were pressured into joining, even some of Solita's employees were NPA.

When my sister Lynn visited the Philippines, we wanted to hike to the bubbling mud springs near Los Baños, so Mom offered us a car and driver. "Take Jerome. He knows where they are." Almost as an after-thought, she added, "Don't talk politics in the car. Jerome is NPA."

That surprised me. "Are there many NPA on your staff?"

"Four." She didn't seem bothered by this; she had employed them for years.

We started for the bubbling mud. Somewhere near Los Baños, we drove off into the brush until bamboo and jungle vegetation became too thick. Jerome stopped the car, and pointed toward an overgrown trail. "It's down there," he said. "I'll stay and watch the car."

We climbed out and started down the trail. The path dwindled, gradually vanishing into thick vegetation. Unsure where to go next and not wanting to get lost, we returned to the car.

Jerome was gone. We called his name loudly several times, with no answer. I was becoming concerned, when the vegetation parted and he emerged from hiding.

"I thought you were going to watch the car?"

"I worried about the NPA. If they find it, I thought maybe they steal it."

"But I thought you were NPA?"

"I am," he readily admitted. "But some NPA not so good as others."

Since he brought it up, this was an easy opening. "Why did you decide to join them?"

He shrugged. "They say we would have a better life."

"Do you?"

He shrugged again slightly. We all got in and drove home. Life was a struggle, but Filipinos were resilient and seemed able to rise above everything.

Soon after his reelection, on September 23, 1972, President Marcos proclaimed martial law. Being President wasn't enough; he wanted to be Dictator. Using the communist threat and other things as a pretext, he used the Army to seize the government, and extended his time in office another 14 years.

The first clue of the coup came on September 24, when Carlos' primary addiction, the Sunday newspaper, didn't arrive. TV and radio silence were deafening. Marcos shut down seven TV stations, eleven weekly magazines, sixty-six community newspapers, and 292 radio stations in a total news blackout. He even shut down the Manila Electric Company, Philippine long-distance telephone, and three Philippine airlines.[8] He wanted total control.

Patsy called me, scared. "What's going on? Do you think there's been a coup?"

"Maybe. We don't have newspaper, radio, or TV."

We could only wait and speculate. As we talked, we heard a click. "Someone's listening in on our call," she said.

The power grab was widespread and well-orchestrated. Marcos abolished Congress and outlawed political parties. He used the army to seize the news media and immediately arrested hundreds of people, from political opponents, journalists, and student activists, to farmers and religious workers. He had a large hit-list, and anyone opposing him was fair game. A friend's cousin, one of hundreds confined for a while at Camp Crame, said he never knew why they imprisoned him in the first place, but thought it was because he hadn't contributed to Imelda's birthday fund.

Fear gripped the country. Everyone was uneasy, not knowing what to expect.

Around 3:00 p.m. a few selected TV and radio stations returned to the air. When newspapers returned, the more vocal columnists were conspicuously absent.

A few months earlier, we had seen Raul, the man I bought the gun for in Honolulu, on TV, standing atop a platform at a big rally in Plaza Miranda, waving his arms and calling for people to string Marcos up by his heels in the Plaza. If he wasn't already on the Marcos hit list before, this undoubtedly put him there. He became one of seventy-seven people who disappeared without a trace.

Marcos promptly confiscated all private guns, set up road checkpoints, and established a 10:00 p.m. curfew. Armed security guards and metal detectors became permanent fixtures at the entrance of every building, even supermarkets. We all had to wear building-specific photo IDs for our work places.

The general climate of fear produced a few upsides. Reckless drivers now drove more responsibly, careful to follow all the rules. People waited their turn instead of cutting in line, and walking down the street or going to the movie without being surrounded by guns prominently displayed in belts and back pockets was a welcome change too.

Little remained exempt from Marcos' greed. Even the stone age Tasaday tribe featured in my parents *National Geographic* was later "declared to be a gigantic hoax perpetrated by the corrupt regime of Ferdinand Marcos for political and financial gain.[9]"

Every business seemed to be affected to some extent. Even IS. Imee Marcos, the President's daughter, wanted to attend Princeton, but Princeton required a diploma from an American-accredited school, so Marcos approached IS to enroll her for her senior year. We were happy to have her, but the first day of class she arrived with several armed bodyguards who patrolled the school corridors with automatic rifles. Rifles didn't mesh well with the school's anti-firearm policy so IS told the bodyguards to leave. Marcos refused to let her attend without security, so IS said Imee had to leave.

Marcos retaliated, threatening to change the IS school year to coincide with the Filipino school year, June through March. Changing the school calendar would be a disaster for IS because our calendar coordinated with other international and Stateside schools to allow a seamless transition to other schools and U.S. colleges in September. Outflanked, IS caved in, and Imee joined the class of 1973. As a compromise, teachers would tutor her at Malacañang Palace, and it would notify us when to come.

Going to the Palace several days a week would be inconvenient, but it became a non-problem. My department head said the Spanish teacher was the only person who ever made it inside. He apparently spoke to Imee for a short time in Spanish and pronounced her proficient. As far as I know, no one else ever set foot in the Palace, or provided a grade.

Imee sat with the class of 1973 at graduation, President Marcos gave the graduation address, and Princeton accepted her. She is now a Philippine Senator. During the recent election, opponents charged she had faked four college degrees, including Princeton. I have no idea about that, and I do know she attended Princeton. But I admit I would be curious to see her senior-year high school transcript.

- *Twenty-Seven* -
Following Our Gut

Manila 1973

B Y 1973, THE COMBINATION OF INFLATION, MARTIAL law, corruption, traffic, typhoons, earthquakes, lack of diverse opportunities, and difficulty of peso salaries all coalesced into a giant lump of frustration. We also worried about the kids, now two and four. Even if we could afford to send Lisa and David to IS, we couldn't give them Stateside vacations, fancy houses, U.S. clothes, Polo Club memberships, and other advantages most ex-pat students took for granted. We couldn't even afford to visit Chicago on our peso salaries, let alone travel or send the kids to college in the States. We needed to earn dollars.

We could permanently move to the States, but we both felt quite rooted and settled in the Philippines. An international assignment paying dollars wouldn't permanently sever any ties, yet we could travel and save some dollars. Citibank offered Carlos a two-year assignment, with a choice between Brunei, a Muslim country on the north coast of Borneo, and Guam, a U.S. territory in the middle of the Pacific.

Brunei sounded more exotic, although as a foreign woman in a Muslim country, I couldn't work, and might not even be allowed to drive. Guam sounded like a desolate and barren military outpost. Its small size meant that anyone who wanted culture and diverse activities wouldn't find them there. "If your marriage is rocky, Guam might finish it off," Citibank said.

Then I was challenged and tempted. The IS science department chairman moved into administration, and the principal offered me her job. For two years I had also been teaching summers and afternoons at De La Salle University in Manila. Now Brother Alfred was retiring, and he offered me his job as department chairman. Either job would be a career opportunity coming only once in a decade. Yet both would lock me into school administration, and likely be a death blow to any dreams of marine biology. An international move, although a big unknown, might open up unseen opportunities.

Carlos was supportive, and willing to forego our move if I wanted to accept either job, but following my gut, I turned down both offers in favor of a short-term, two-year stint on tiny Guam, a questionable island with unknown opportunities. Most people said I was foolish to pass up two such good, secure job opportunities for the unknown. Maybe. I didn't burn any bridges, saying, "We'll be back in a couple of years."

Everyone laughed, but I truly believed it.

As we prepared to leave, we hauled Pepino down a crowded aisle in Kartimar public outdoor market, shopping for a travel cage. The pet store had a lone male Central American *Amazona* parrot, and as we passed down the aisle, somehow it recognized Pepino by sight, and called out. It was love at first screech! Both parrots began excitedly calling loudly back and forth, their deafening, raucous squawks echoing through the market. They created such a ruckus that the owner came running from his store in alarm expecting a robbery. He stopped short when he saw Pepino.

"We're looking for a parrot travel cage," I told the owner.

"I don't have anything like that," he said. "But I'd like to buy her." And he immediately fished a $100 bill from his shirt pocket. He gestured to the male, promising "I'll only sell them as a pair."

I was torn. We'd been together since Costa Rica, almost ten years. But Guam's strict six-month isolation quarantine for incoming birds would be very difficult for her, and here, she could avoid that, and finally have an appropriate companion. I didn't even bargain. We moved her into his big cage, and calm returned to the market. I told him to be sure to feed them some scrambled eggs and bacon occasionally, and he was astonished. I hope he did.

Without the internet or libraries, and only a limited bookstore, we had no idea what to expect of Guam. Then, a Manila Times story provided our first glimpse. Hunters had just captured a Japanese WWII straggler who had been hiding in the Guam jungle for 28 years. I had envisioned Guam as a flat hunk of barren coral rock, but apparently it had jungle and coral reefs! There could be ocean, travel, and unknown adventures. I began getting excited about the move.

Carlos went to Guam three months ahead of us to house-hunt, while I remained in Makati to finish the school year. Career-wise, the move was a huge gamble. I had bypassed two outstanding opportunities in Manila that might never come my way again, for a two-year jump into the unknown. But in my gut it felt right, and it turned out to be one of the most important decisions of our lives.

My parents and I, 1943

Me, Lynn, Steve and Phil, 1954

Me and Steve with my favorite pet guinea pig, Easter, 1955.

Our group at the Tropical Science Center, 1964. Dr. Holdridge, top row center

On the crater during Irazu's eruption, 1965

Near Waikiki Beach, 1965

Carlos, 1964.

Carlos and I at Queen's Surf, 1966

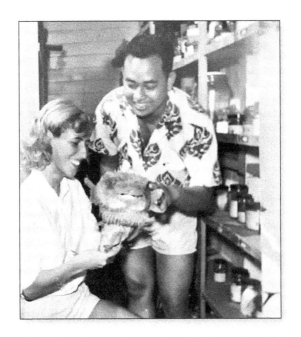

Examining a puffer fish at the marine station with Surapol, a Thai grantee, 1965.

Our Wedding, Manila, 1967

Victor, Me, Carlos and Solita, 1967

At the Rural Bank of Pagsanjan, 1969. Fe and Mario, Victor and Solita, Carlos' brother Lito, and me. Bottom row: Fe's two sons, and Carlos holding Lisa, 1969

Mom and Dad, 1971

Lisa and David, around 1975

Goal #8: finally completed in Nepal after twenty years

In Federal Way, 1982. Mom, Aunt Connie, Lisa, me, David, Carlos and Georgie

The heron at home, sunbathing on the dock, 2021

GUAM:
"WHERE AMERICA'S DAY BEGINS"

(1973-1979)

"Man cannot discover new oceans unless he has the courage to lose sight of the shore."

– Andre Gide

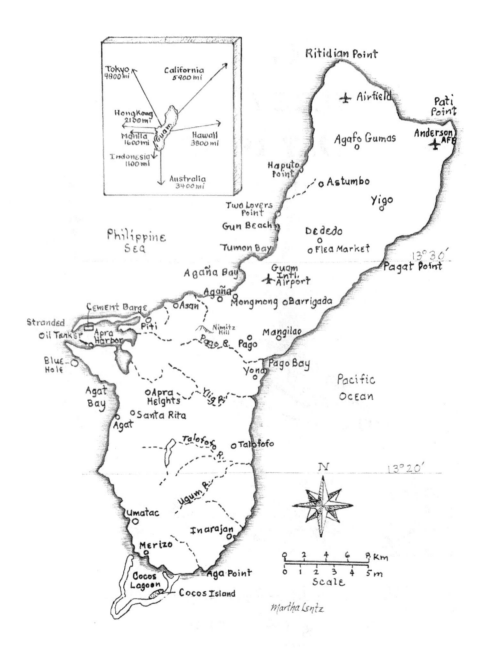

Territory of Guam

- *Twenty-Eight* -
A Foreign American Culture

Guam 1973

W E WERE FINALLY BACK ON AMERICAN SOIL, SOME-
what. Guam lies on the cusp of nowhere, approximately 6,000
miles from the U.S. mainland. It proudly claims to be "where America's
day begins" because it lies across the international dateline. Although
the largest, most southern island in the Marianas Islands archipelago,
it's a mere speck in the ocean, only 212 square miles, about one-sixth
the size of Rhode Island. From the air, its shape resembles an exploded
kidney bean.

Successive Spanish, American, and Japanese occupations, followed by
waves of Filipino and Vietnamese immigration, create an exciting mix of
cultures, all overlaid with a veneer of American culture.

Guam is a strategic U.S. military hub in the Western Pacific, and the
military occupies about 28 percent of the island. Anderson Air Force Base,
the most critical U.S. airbase west of Hawaii, claims much of the limestone
plateau on the island's northern tip, and naval presence includes the Naval
Station and other facilities at Apra Harbor, and the Naval Command for
the Marianas.

Carlos picked us up from the airport. Even at night Guam felt like a
sauna, and the humid tropical night air felt thick and heavy as a blanket.
The average temperature hovered around 81°, and the humidity beat

anywhere I'd ever lived. Despite moving from the tropical Philippines, I would sweat three months straight before adjusting to the humidity.

Rows of glowing yellow reflectors in the smooth asphalt road winked up at our headlights. I'd never seen reflectors before, and I'd forgotten the quality of American infrastructure. Everything looked clean and maintained compared to Asia's potholed streets.

We passed the new, self-proclaimed "World's Largest McDonald's." It lacked a drive-through window because people preferred eating inside to escape the heat, and it sold Guam red rice in addition to fries as a concession to local tastes. American fast-food hadn't overrun the planet yet; even the Philippines had no McDonald's. Once Carlos discovered it, he ate there often, with the zeal of a new convert. It was the sole American fast-food chain on the island, but simply seeing it provided a welcoming sense of familiarity.

Carlos had worked hard to make the house habitable before we arrived, but his assessment of "not very nice" seemed charitable. It was an outrageous $450 a month dump, but it was the only available house he saw during his three months of living in the Guam Hilton, so he grabbed it. Little distinguished it from the other small concrete block houses in Tumon Heights. The sharp coral rock in the yard wasn't child-friendly.

"Poor we, we have no friends and no place to play," Lisa said. That didn't bode well.

The owner, a local Chinese prostitute, had previously rented it to a Filipino band. "They must have owned dogs because the house crawled with ticks," Carlos said. "I used almost a dozen cans of Raid."

He must be exaggerating. How could there be that many ticks? I discovered later he hadn't exaggerated. Since we were barefoot in the house, it's a wonder we didn't all develop pesticide poisoning, but it didn't smell, and the year we lived there, we never had a single bug because anything wandering in under the door expired on the spot when it hit the carpet.

Despite Carlos' cleaning, the lime-encrusted, impossible-to-clean bathroom, filthy carpet squares, and kitchen counters covered with ugly contact paper, all looked tacky. A stand-alone tin shower stall decorated the end of the kitchen, and we speculated about the potentially interesting contents of a kitchen drawer, apparently sealed shut. Several months later, finding a crowbar, I pried it open, hoping to find something interesting. I did. It was a paper plate full of mummified fried chicken. The drawer wasn't locked; it was just totally filled from top to bottom with the most luxuriant growth of *Rhizopus* mold I had ever seen. Thousands of filamentous hyphae had cemented the drawer shut.

Our second day Carlos said, "Let's explore the island." A single road with one stoplight circumnavigated the island, tracing the shoreline, and only one road bisected the island. What a contrast to Makati's traffic jams and air pollution! The scenic, mountainous southern half contained most of the jungle, and all of the rivers. Small rural villages with unique names like Talofofo, Mangilao, Merizo, Umatac, Agat, and Yona, hugged the coastline.

The sun shown in the bright blue, haze-free sky, and a warm breeze blew off the ocean. I suddenly realized how much I had disliked working in the noisy, crowded city Makati had become. Guam felt like a vacation, and I felt a weight lifting. We all liked this laid-back place already.

Guam was a living WWII museum. War relics littered the hills, the beaches, and underwater, reminders of the fierce battles my Uncle Quentin and Aunt Connie must have witnessed. Yet they had never spoken of them. A decrepit Quonset hut sat along the roadside; a fleet of rusting tanks remained frozen in time on a mountainside near Mangilao; gun emplacements hid in small caves along the cliffs and beaches; a broken, barnacle-encrusted tank rested on a reef, and a coral-encrusted sunken Japanese zero lay in shallow water offshore. Apra Harbor bottom contained everything from sunken German, Japanese and American ships to full boxes of ammo, a torpedo, and a wide variety of military litter. The war left toxic environmental legacies everywhere, but no bones; Japanese bone hunters had repeatedly returned searching for soldiers' remains to carry home to Japan.

At the war's end, about 1,000 Japanese soldiers remained hidden in the jungle, ordered to fight to the death and never surrender. All but a handful died within a few years. Only a few weeks before we arrived, two Talofofo hunters had captured the last surviving Japanese straggler. Sargent Yokoi had lived in the jungle, seven feet underground in a three by nine-foot hideout with a concealed trap door, for 28 years. The last six years he had lived alone, after watching his original group of five or six die off one by one. Bustling activity at Naval Station, Anderson Airbase, and the international airport convinced him WWII continued; he just assumed the war had moved on to another part of the world.

His emotions must have been quite mixed. He expected to be jailed or executed but, instead, he became a celebrity. He had worked as a tailor before the war, and now received several offers of employment from clothing stores, and a large number of marriage proposals. His only wish was to return to Japan and meet the former Emperor Hirohito, but the emperor declined to meet him. Perhaps he felt ashamed because the Americans had demoted him from a god to a mere mortal after the surrender. Unable to cope with Japan's pollution, industrialization, and modernization, Yokoi emigrated to Australia.

Like Guam, the Philippines are islands, but Luzon was so large that living inland in Makati, Pagsanjan, or Marcelo didn't feel like island living. Weeks could pass without seeing the ocean. It was miles to a decent swimming beach, and traffic was terrible, so we went to the beach perhaps once a year, and never just on a whim. But in Guam, we couldn't miss the ocean because we drove along the shore daily.

Guam looked much like I assumed Hawaii had fifty years earlier. Buried memories of Hawaii flooded back, and I felt a surge of hope and anticipation. No matter where I worked, I could finally reconnect with the ocean. With a surprising wave of nostalgia, I realized how much I'd missed island life. Although we had moved for dollar salaries, I sensed we had gained much more; we had gained a new lease on life.

- *Twenty-Nine* -

A Heaven-Sent Job

<u>Agaña 1974-1977</u>

AFTER SETTLING IN, I BEGAN JOB HUNTING. I SAW NO marine biology jobs, but I had enjoyed teaching in the Philippines and could teach on Guam. But I hadn't realized Guam had difficulty finding local teachers, so they brought teachers from the U.S. mainland on two-year contracts. They had already filled most positions months earlier.

I sat home several months, feeling discouraged. Surprisingly, I gave no thought to the opportunities I had left in Manila, but I wondered, *Can I take two years of this?* As I sat on the couch in our dreary Tumon Heights living room watching the kids glued to Big Bird hopping around the TV, suddenly a quiet voice inserted itself into my thoughts. "Try the Academy of Our Lady of Guam." I knew it wasn't my thought, and I didn't question a voice in my head, but the suggestion surprised me. I knew about the Academy, a private Catholic girl's school run by the Sisters of Mercy in Agaña, because the town plaza behind the school constantly swarmed with young children in checkered uniforms, running and laughing among the palm trees. I thought it was an elementary school, so hadn't even considered it.

The thought persisted. Digging out the phone book, I looked up the Academy. For once, the telephone worked. I talked with the acting principal, Sister Joshua. Feeling somewhat foolish, I asked, "Do you happen to have a high school?" To my surprise, they did. Hopeful, I asked, "Do you happen to need teachers?"

Sister Joshua's following words weren't encouraging. "Well, actually, we don't right now; it's the middle of the year. Although…" She paused. "We do have two needs, but they're quite specialized. I don't suppose you teach biology?" She asked with a slight tinge of hopefulness.

"Yes, I do! I've been teaching biology at both International School and De La Salle College in Manila. Do you need a biology teacher?"

"Yes, we do, but they're specialized courses. What did you teach?" She wasn't going to give away what kind of teacher she needed.

"Physiology and Marine Biology. And of course, general biology."

The pause on the other end of the phone lasted so long that I wondered if she was still there. When she collected herself, in a voice tinged with awe, she said, "It's *exactly* what we've been praying for!"

"Well," I told her, "I've been praying for a marine biology class."

Interestingly, the Academy had never offered either course before, and no one understood how or why these classes could have been advertised. Yet now, two full classes of expectant students awaited a non-existent teacher.

She sounded apologetic. "There is a problem," she said carefully, as if afraid to scare me off. "We weren't expecting these classes, so we have no curriculum, materials, lesson plans, or textbooks for either course." *That's odd. The students obviously knew about the classes. Why didn't the administration?*

"I don't suppose you could…?" She let the question hang in the air unfinished.

Both IS and De La Salle's lack of texts and materials the years before had forced me to develop materials and lab exercises from scratch for exactly those two classes. They had prepared me perfectly. I jumped at it. "My classes in the Philippines had no materials either, but I have all my materials and notes. When would you like me to start?"

"Can you come down today? The new semester starts tomorrow."

What perfect timing! No one understood how the Academy could advertise two such specialized classes without having any teaching materials or teachers in mind. They certainly couldn't count on finding those specialized teachers on the island, especially mid-year. Yet somehow, they had announced both classes, students had signed up, and now the administration appeared blindsided. God orchestrated everything, solving their needs and mine, almost to the hour.

The next day I started at the Academy, and loved it from the beginning. The Sisters of Mercy was a progressive Catholic order originating in Dublin, with about half the sisters from Guam, and half from Ireland. With their short veils and solid light blue, short-sleeved, knee-length dresses, they looked and acted more like lay teachers. Most lived in a convent adjacent to the school. The sisters didn't earn regular salaries, but the convent provided their support, and they received $120 a month. Next to their salary, the lay teacher's salaries looked reasonably good, yet the $5,000 salary was half that of the public schools, and despite the pleasant school atmosphere, the low pay usually caused frequent turnover of lay faculty.

The Academy's finances were tight. With a nod to the concept of large families, the more children a family enrolled, the cheaper the tuition. While people paid $200 a month per child at St. Johns, a private Episcopal school, the Academy charged $80 for the first child, $50 for the second, and $20-$30 each for the rest. This was a bargain for Guam's large families; the average child probably paid only about $40 a month. Worse, the sisters extended unlimited credit. I understood one high government official owed over a year's tuition. He could certainly afford it but, apparently, no one had the temerity to demand payment.

In contrast to the public schools, my classes contained students who truly wanted to learn, and had parents who cared about education. The girls were quiet, interested, polite, and bright.

The semester finished quickly, and the following year I found myself with five classes; three general biology classes, marine biology, and physiology. It required three different preparations, but nothing new to prepare for. I displaced Sister Frances, the previous biology teacher, who stopped speaking to me. They found uses for her elsewhere, including placing her in charge of the teacher's lounge.

She became the Lounge Policeman, insisting we pour all the coffee grounds from the large coffee urn in the teacher's lounge down the sink every day to "clean out the drain." It was impossible to convince her this was a bad idea or that nothing but coffee went down the sink, so there was nothing in the drain to clean out. Day after day, at her insistence we poured several cups of coffee grounds down the drain. Amazingly, it never clogged up, but Sister Frances knew why: it was because we poured in all those coffee grounds.

The Academy's lab supplies consisted of one Bunsen burner, two test tubes, and a couple of beakers. At the end of the year, Sister Luke, the new principal, said, "Would you be willing to draw up some plans for a new laboratory?"

I gladly agreed, and over the summer, they added sinks and gas jets, and bought Bunsen burners, microscopes, slides, beakers, Petri dishes, and pipettes. Now we could do some lab work. A lab assistant and double periods for lab would have also been nice, but supplies were a significant improvement, and unlike IS, I had few lab reports to grade.

Learning the students' names was challenging. With the same long, straight black hair, brown skin and eyes, the girls all looked superficially alike, and everyone wore the same blue and white checked uniform and saddle shoes. It seemed like nearly half the class was named Perez.

But some students always stand out. Even in a culture of large people, Inez was large. This presented a problem because lab space was tight, but the problem solved itself when the class chose lab partners. She teamed up with Maria, a girl short enough to have difficulty doing experiments on the lab table. Together they creatively solved the problem: Maria sat on the lab table so she could easily reach the experiments, and Inez had more space on the floor. Maria, exceptionally bright, also helped Inez finish her lab experiments, so it became a win-win for everyone.

Most Guamanian girls were relatively slim until they reached about eighteen. Then, like many Pacific Islanders, they began adding weight, and by age 25, many were heavy. So, when we studied the digestive system, this seemed like a perfect place to analyze what we ate. I had the entire sophomore class weighing and counting calories for a week.

The calorie table from my Joy of Cooking cookbook didn't have Guam in mind. Every day the girls found things not listed there. How many calories in a beetle nut? In finá denné? In fruit bat? But we estimated the best we could, and at the end of the week, we all compared notes. Inez said she ate only 1000 calories a day. We went over her menus: breakfast (none); lunch (orange juice, one apple, one slice of bread (200-300); dinner (very little). Then I saw her in the cafeteria at recess. Maybe she never ate much at meals, but she more than made up for it on break. Her tray overflowed with packages of potato chips and candy bars, a hamburger, and a sugary soft drink.

"Did you count those calories? I asked.

"Oh, I didn't realize snacks counted." But she learned quickly, and a week later, she told me happily, "I've lost two pounds!" That was a good start; I was proud of her.

Unexpectedly, a genetics project generated great enthusiasm. Guam has large, extended families, and family connections are significant, so the girls became interested in making family tree diagrams. Strong family ties and oral tradition kept relatives' names fresh in everyone's mind, and they made extensive trees going back several generations, usually farther than Filipinos or Haoles could.

When the students compared their trees, inevitably, the same names began appearing on many of them. Everyone became so excited that we linked all the charts and pinned them up on the wall. Not unexpectedly, much of the class was related, and many of the class discovered new relatives. Regardless of how much they grasped the actual mechanics of genetics, it became one of the most popular units I taught.

I also decided to include a unit on birth control because so many students were pregnant by graduation. I didn't know how this would go over in a Catholic school, but pragmatic Sister Luke agreed, as long as I didn't advocate anything but the rhythm method. I didn't push any particular method, but I provided some statistics on the success of various types, and soon girls began coming in with additional questions before class. The sisters wisely turned a blind eye to all of this.

On May 1, Flores De Mayo, the Academy honored the island's patron saint, Our Lady of Camarin. This commemorated the day a statue of Mary washed ashore on Guam and began performing miracles, although people seemed a bit hazy on exactly what they were. Our Lady usually resided in the Agaña Cathedral adjacent to the Academy but, on Flores de Mayo, she moved into the Plaza de España, and the entire school turned out to decorate her. There were leis and flowers, speeches and eulogies, and even a Maypole. The happy, colorful ritual gave Catholicism a unique island twist.

After Flores de Mayo, the school year devolved into chaos, mirroring the last months of IS in Makati. Anonymous callers plagued the island's schools with bomb threats, hoping to leave school early. The calls were obviously false alarms, but policies required the school to evacuate until the Fire Department came to search the building. We lost two or three hours every time this happened, and the Fire Department went on overload, scrambling from school to school.

But unlike IS, the sisters were pragmatic. After a couple of days, they began leaving the office phone off the hook so no one could call in. It undoubtedly went against policy, but they reasoned that we couldn't receive threats if we didn't get a call, and classes could continue as usual.

The convent sponsored a big end-of-year Mongolian barbecue in the Plaza for the teachers and spouses, and there the sisters met Carlos. When they discovered he majored in economics, they quickly corralled him into teaching a consumer economics class. Like the Philippines, Guam didn't require teacher certification. This widened the pool of possible specialty teachers, because teachers could be professionals in their field; they weren't required to be education majors.

I loved the Academy and taught full time for another year, until I discovered the Guam Environmental Protection Agency (GEPA), a young government agency, was hiring. I had been waiting since Glen Ellyn for people to wake up to the need for environmental protection. Now, this new field had finally acquired some legal teeth, and it was exploding and generating jobs.

When the school year finished, I moved to EPA, but the sisters persuaded me to return one period a day the following year, to teach marine biology. EPA agreed to this because the deputy administrator, a former Guam science teacher, knew how desperately Guam needed science teachers.

I would finally be able to work where I felt meant to be: around the ocean and focused on the environment.

- *Thirty* -
EPA, Guam Style

<u>**1975-1979**</u>

A**S A CHILD IN** 1950S G**LEN** E**LLYN,** I **WATCHED AS** progress, seemingly intent on asphalting the entire surface of the planet, destroyed the fields, polluted the air and water, littered the land, and filled the wetlands. Nothing mitigated the destruction. As long as environmental protection laws, public awareness, and citizen involvement were still future, environmental quality would continue to spiral downward.

In 1969, Ohio's Cuyahoga River caught fire. That shocking incident helped ignite public environmental awareness, and stimulated the swelling clamor for environmental protection. Earth Day and the Environmental Protection Agency (EPA) were both established the following year. With new laws, the environment finally had a fighting chance.

In 1975, I joined Guam EPA as an enforcement officer. GEPA was only three years old, still small and un-bureaucratic, with a technical staff of twenty-five. We were badly needed. Untreated sewage discharged just off the reef edge in Agaña, and hundreds of improperly constructed septic tanks leached effluent into the drinking aquifer. WWII had left a substantial toxic legacy, and most Air Force wells showed trichloroethylene contamination. Several hundred abandoned 55-gallon drums in the jungle near Orote Point sat in a large pool of a heavy tar-like substance that had been slowly oozing across the shoreline and into the water for decades. An unidentified rusting drum on the bottom of Apra Harbor sat in a large sandy circle, ominously devoid of any sea life, leaking unknown toxins into the water. New contaminated areas were continually being discovered.

Digging or clearing anywhere turned up so many unexploded shells, grenades, and mortars that the military maintained a special ordnance disposal squad just to deal with them.

Thousands of unexploded phosphorus tracer bullets littered the hillsides. As they rusted through, oxygen contacted the phosphorus core and they ignited, starting hundreds of fires that left bare, unvegetated scars in the grassy hills. Old Army jeep trails across the mountains, now rutted, became eroding patches that enlarged with each rainy season, and eventually, much of the soil ended up on the reefs.

To reduce erosion, after the war, Americans seeded the island with tangen-tangen, a nitrogen-fixing shrub. At first glance, it appeared to be a good choice for revegetation and soil rebuilding, because it spread with astonishing speed, but it kept regrowth of the lush native vegetation at bay. Nearby Rota, with fewer battle scars than Guam, provided a glimpse of how Guam had once looked, and I wondered how long the land would need to recover from the ravages of WWII. (About 60 years, as it turned out.)

The shaggy reddish hair and beard of my new boss, George, a former Ohio farm boy and recent Vietnam pilot, disguised a precise, methodical personality. All of his actions were agonizingly slow and deliberate. He took a long time to produce a report but, when he did, the first draft was usually flawless. He was an avid scuba diver, and equally meticulous with his diving. George assisted the Coral Reef Marine Center with their scuba classes, and when I told him about my bogus diver certification at Glen Ayre, he encouraged me to become properly certified. The EPA lab could use extra divers, so I could dive for work, too.

After ten years, I finally had the coincidence of time, money, transportation, and easy ocean access. I bought a new shorty wetsuit, all new gear, and became NAUI/PADI certified. Guam's warm, 82° water, amazing 200-foot visibility, and diversity of organisms made spectacular diving. Giant green moray eels grinned toothily from their holes; graceful manta rays glided smoothly through the water; and rafts of motionless, five-foot barracudas hung slack-jawed near the surface. Giant anemones, clownfish, sea turtles, colorful fish, and soft and hard corals covered the reefs. Once, four giant humphead wrasse the size of small refrigerators burst over the reef terrace edge, and unconcernedly munched on corals right beside us. With every dive a treasure hunt, diving quickly became my obsession.

George's methodical, deliberate habits made him a perfect first dive buddy. Before a dive, he planned entrance and exit, depth and time, and carefully checked each piece of equipment as he precisely packed it in his dive bag. After a dive, he repeated the procedure, carefully washing everything off, and stowing it in precise order. These meticulous procedures could stretch an hour boat dive into four, but they made him a very safe diver, something I appreciated after my dangerous peat bog and Racine quarry experiences in the Sixties.

Before 1970, people commonly parroted the mantra "dilution is the solution to pollution," and Guam's untreated sewage discharged offshore on the edge of the reef terrace. Now the new Clean Water Act (CWA) required primary sewage treatment, and Guam began constructing its first sewage treatment plant. Someone with a dubious sense of aesthetics and a lack of community planning had decided the beach in downtown Agaña would be the perfect location for it.

The project involved blasting and dredging the existing Agaña channel to accommodate the new sewer outfall and filling six acres of reef flat to create an offshore platform for the treatment plant. Aside from total reef destruction on the platform site and inside the channel, the blasting killed anything unfortunate enough to be in the channel at the time. It also generated an incredible amount of coral-smothering silt. The irony that compliance with the CWA had caused such an environmental mess did not escape me.

George and I stood on the edge of the Agaña channel watching a dredge remove chunks of blasted reef from the channel to provide fill for the platform site, appalled at the devastation of what had been nearly pristine reef only a week earlier. Plumes of silt billowed from the channel and an occasional dead fish floated to the surface and out to sea.

George frowned. "Someone should go see what's happening down there."

"I think there's a lot more fish impact than we're seeing. If blasting ruptured their swim bladders, lots of dead fish are on the bottom."

We returned to the office to devise makeshift sediment traps, tying tin cans at intervals along a rope and marking each can with a flag. We placed the traps on the bottom, across the width of the channel, anchoring them to the channel wall.

Two days later, once the blasting stopped, although the dredging continued, we returned to measure the sediment in the traps. As we submerged into the turbid channel, brownish silt swirled so thickly in the water that we could barely see six inches in front of our masks. Yet it felt relatively safe, because although we couldn't see anything, it wasn't dark, unlike the frightening black Illinois peat bog. *It feels like we're diving inside a swirling chocolate milkshake.*

Today, the dredge was ripping out blasted coral chunks. As long as we stayed near our sediment traps, perhaps 150 feet down-channel from the dredge, we weren't in danger of becoming dredge material ourselves, but the dredge sounded like it was working directly above us. The loud crunching and scraping sounds of the dredge, magnified underwater, were definitely unsettling, and we couldn't see anything. I tried not to imagine the dredge's heavy iron bucket scooping us off the bottom. *Let's just hope the dredge doesn't move.*

Working by feel, we groped along the rope to sediment trap number one, along the channel edge. It overflowed with sediment. By placing our faces practically on the trap, we could see sufficiently to measure sediment depth. We moved to trap number two. After some excavation, we found the entire trap buried under several inches of sediment and made a futile attempt to measure its depth. Undaunted, we moved toward trap number three, in mid-channel. The silt layer was so thick we couldn't even find the rope or the flag marker, let alone the trap. Then something bumped my left fin. George was on my right, so that seemed odd. *I must have kicked something.*

As we groped around trying to locate the trap, a wispy stray current of clean water displaced the turbid cloud around us, exposing a few feet of clear water below an overlying layer of dark, sediment-laden water. In the middle of a small, colorless patch of silt-covered bottom, less than ten feet away, a large grouper flopped frantically and erratically on the bottom. A gaping, crescent-shaped hole almost a foot across marked where its stomach used to be. The attack had just happened. As we stared at it, the fish gave a final twitch, flopped over sideways, and died in front of our eyes.

We had only enough time to stare wide-eyed at each other before the current shifted and the sediment cloud rolled back, enveloping us in the swirling brown cloud. I'm not sure what George was thinking, but questions swirled through my head like the silt in the water. *The shark was right here. Where is it? Will it return for the rest of the fish? What size shark makes a bite that large? Does it know we're here?* Probably. *Can it tell the difference between the fish and us? Does it even care?* A shark couldn't see through the silt any better than we could, but they operate mainly by vibration and smell. *Did the fish provide a lucky distraction from us, or did the fish draw the shark into our vicinity? Were our movements fish-like enough to attract him?* Something had sharply bumped my fins once. At the time, I hadn't given it much thought.

The foolishness of diving in zero visibility amid a bunch of dying fish suddenly hit us. Focused on sediment, we'd given no thought to how attractive dead and dying fish might be to sharks. It suddenly seemed an excellent time to end the sediment study. Quantifying the tremendous siltation damage was pointless; the channel required a sediment boom. Monitoring the extent of the silt plume on the reef flat would be more productive. We quietly groped our way along the rope to shore, trying not to disturb the water. As we climbed out, George said, "You bumping me down there was a bit unnerving."

It wasn't me.

One Monday morning, a new time clock with punch cards appeared on the wall outside the administrator's office. The administrator had decided staff weren't putting in a 40-hour week. I certainly didn't know anyone like that; most technical staff worked over 40 hours, but our overtime was never noticed, much less appreciated.

The administrator hadn't a clue how much we worked, and the clock quickly became an irritation. He instructed us to punch in at 8:00 and out at 4:30, saying he would monitor it daily. The clock particularly annoyed field people because unexpected problems often made field time challenging to estimate. People grumbled privately, but no one overtly protested; the administrator came from an Asian culture where he was not accustomed to being questioned. He became the time clock policeman and made a show of checking the clock every morning, irritating us even more.

The following week, George and I joined Tory and Izzy, two biologists from the lab, and drove to Agaña Bay to inspect the existing sewage outfall and check the status of the sewage treatment platform construction. We arrived to find five or six frustrated Department of Fish and Game biologists treading water in a big circle inside the treatment plant platform site. They enthusiastically waved us over.

"We could use some help here. There's a large sea turtle trapped inside the platform site." Trucks were continuing to fill the platform with dredged material from the channel, and if not rescued, the turtle would soon be buried.

Catching the turtle was challenging. Fish and Game had left their office before considering how to catch it, and they arrived without a net. Now high tide forced everyone to tread water, but the water was too silt-filled to see anything. We swam out to join the circle surrounding a sizeable floating sea turtle. Sensing a confrontation, the turtle dove through the silty water to the bottom. It remained down for five or ten minutes. Eventually, it surfaced for a breath but, seeing us, it quickly grabbed a breath and resubmerged.

It was impossible to see where it went. Whenever it surfaced, we tried to grab it quickly before it dove again, but we were never quick enough.

After several rounds of surfacing and diving, the turtle remained down so long that just when we thought it had escaped, it came floating limply, belly-up, to the surface. Then it began to sink.

Someone shouted, "It's passed out. Grab it before it drowns!" Three people dove for it, clamped down on the edges of the shell and brought it to the surface. Holding its large limp head out of the water, someone blew in its nose to resuscitate it. When it recovered, they turned it over, floated it out beyond the platform area, and released it outside the reef.

We returned to the jeep, launched our Zodiac, and motored out to begin the sewer outfall inspection. The turtle had put a serious crimp in our inspection schedule. By the time we pulled into the office parking lot, it was almost 4:30. We still needed to wash down the boat, motor, and trailer, which would require nearly an hour. Tory checked his dive watch. "Well, it's 4:25…" We looked at each other, all thinking the same thing. Frustration with the time clock had reached the action level.

"It's time to go home," Izzy said. "I guess we'll have to finish this tomorrow." We went inside, carefully punched out, took our dive gear to our cars, and went home smiling, leaving the unwashed boat, motor, anchor, and trailer sitting in the Agency parking lot. Fortunately, no one stole them overnight.

The following day, at 8:15, the administrator emerged from his office, checked the clock, and called us in. His tight lips and clipped words telegraphed annoyance. "What are the boat and trailer doing in the middle of the parking lot?"

George answered with a straight face. "When we returned, it was 4:30. We already put in our eight hours, so we thought it could wait, and we'd do it this morning."

The administrator took a long, hard look at each of us, trying to read behind our innocent faces. "Get it out of there," he said, with an edge to his voice. He turned on his heel and disappeared into his office without another word. He rarely acknowledged an error but, to his credit, at 11:00, the time clock came down. It was the last anyone mentioned work hours.

Vehicles were in short supply on Guam, and most were in bad shape. Cars passed from owner to owner, driven until they fell apart. Then they were patched together and resold. The salt air played havoc with anything metallic, and every week my used VW bug sprouted new rust spots. I painted red and black enamel ladybugs over the rust spots to prevent the car from collapsing into a pile of rust.

Soon, layer upon layer of ladybugs decorated the outside, but I gave little thought to the inside. After diving, I usually threw my wet dive gear on the floor in the back to wash later at home, without much thought about salt inside the car.

Now, promoted to Territorial Water Quality Planner, I needed to inspect a proposed subdivision site in Piti. It was near our house, so I decided to stop there on my way home. I turned down a rutted dirt track winding through coconuts and jungle. About a quarter mile down the track, the car shuddered slightly, and I heard a loud thud. A large black metal box in the middle of the road stared back at me in the rear-view mirror. *How could I have run over something that big without noticing it?*

Stopping the car, I walked back and moved it out of the road to avoid hitting it on the way out. It was an ancient, crusty battery. Turning it over, I saw a piece of masking tape on the side. It said 'Cabreza.'

Cabreza? It can't be mine. The car was still running after I passed it. Even then, it didn't register. Maybe I shouldn't have turned off the engine. Climbing back in, I turned the ignition key and listened to dead silence. I looked under the back seat to check for the VW battery and stared down at the dirt through a gaping hole where the floor used to be. The battery was gone. My wet, salty dive gear had rusted out most of the floor. I brought the battery back to the car, left the car sitting in the middle of the track, and hiked back to Marine Drive to find a phone and call a tow truck.

At least I'm lucky it didn't fall out in the middle of Marine Drive and cause an accident. Next inspection, I'll take the office car; it's in good shape.

Not for long. A week later, the deputy administrator appeared at my desk, a pained but slightly bemused expression on his face. "Come outside; I want to show you something." Curious, I went outside. He pointed to my new agency car, now on the opposite side of the parking lot, with what remained of its right tail light firmly embedded in the rear door of my new boss's car. "I wanted to leave it here so you could see it."

The car had rolled across the slightly sloping parking lot. *Oh no. I must have forgotten to set the hand brake.* Fortunately, my boss's car was old. Unfazed, he said, "Give me $30, and we'll call it good. I'm taking it in for some other work this week anyhow."

The deputy said, "PUAG (Guam's Public Utility Agency) is in charge of government vehicles. Send the car over and have them fix the tail light. It should be an easy fix."

It should have been, but weeks dragged by, and the car still hadn't returned. After several follow-up calls without a response, the administrator called the PUAG director. This produced results. The next day the deputy appeared at my desk waving a letter.

"PUAG 'surveyed' your car (i.e., deemed it unusable) and sold it at auction. As the owner, we're entitled to two-thirds of the value." He grimaced, waving a check for $26.67.

"They sold our new car for $40.00?" Unbelievable. Someone bought our new car at auction for almost nothing.

The administrator was apoplectic. "This is outrageous. The damage was minimal." and sent a vitriolic letter demanding an explanation, but I don't believe he ever received one. EPA bought another car.

PUAG periodically sold excess government equipment at auction, and someone at PUAG seemed to have quite a racket going. A few months later, George bid on three jeeps in a PUAG auction. They were almost new, except all three mysteriously lacked a battery and four tires. Not usable in this condition, rather than buy parts, PUAG put them up for auction. George placed a very low bid. To his surprise, he was the highest bidder. Whoever he outbid probably expected to be the only bidder and greedy, submitted a ridiculously low offer. Now George only needed to order the missing parts. Before he could do that, another auction advertised three batteries and twelve tires among the auction items. He bid on those, won again, and became the owner of three new jeeps for almost nothing.

Soon I became chief of the Safe Drinking Water program. We were conducting water meter surveys when I received a new temporary employee. I assigned him to the water meter survey, and he used my new agency car to drive around the island reading water meters. One morning, he sheepishly appeared at my desk. "The car is stuck."

"Stuck? Where is it?"

"In the Malojloj swamp."

"The swamp? What's it doing there?"

"I heard there was a pile of stolen water meters in the swamp and thought I'd go, get them back, and surprise you."

"Water meters?" I sounded like a parrot. His story seemed contrived, but odd things were always happening on Guam, and it was barely possible someone was stealing meters to sell as scrap metal. Copper telephone wire sometimes suffered the same fate.

I called my drinking water counterpart at PUAG. "Hey Ray, have you heard anything about missing water meters?"

"No. Why do you ask?"

"My agency car is stuck in Malojloj swamp because someone went in there looking for them."

"No idea about the meters, but I'll have someone go tow your car out."

A few hours later, he called again. "Your car's stuck bad. And sinking. It's up to the top of the hub caps. We thought we could get it out with one of ours, but now ours is stuck too. I'll send our tow truck out tomorrow to get them both out." I stifled the impulse to ask why he didn't do that in the first place.

The next day he called again. "Now our tow truck is stuck in the swamp too. I'm calling a commercial tow truck." A lot of potential scrap metal seemed to be accumulating in the swamp.

On the fourth day, with much difficulty, the towing company hauled all three vehicles out of the swamp, and a muck-encased car appeared in the parking lot. I was half surprised they hadn't surveyed it due to mud damage. At least PUAG absorbed the towing bill.

Around 5:00 p.m., everyone had left the office but Sierra and me, and I was about ready to go. Sierra, an uninhibited and unconventional California free spirit, always oozed cheerfulness. She came over to my desk, happily waving a rolled brown stub of marijuana. "Hey, look what I found in my desk! This is high-quality stuff. Want to try it?"

"I've never tried it. I missed the drug scene; it hit right after I left college."

"Wow. Then you have to try it! The butt is the most concentrated part."

"I don't think I'd appreciate it. You keep it."

She looked at me incredulously. "Come on...you don't know what you're missing. No one else is here."

I'd never had much desire to try it or gone out of my way to look for it, but I hadn't attempted to avoid it either. Nobody had ever offered me any. Now here it was.

"OK. I'll try it. Might be interesting." She lit up and passed me the joint. I inhaled a big puff, held it a bit, and blew it out.

"How do you feel?"

"I don't feel anything."

"Try it again, and take a really big puff. Sometimes first-time users don't get high right away."

I took a big puff. Still nothing.

"Nothing?"

"Nope. I think you're wasting it on me." I handed it back.

"Let me try." She took several big puffs. "I guess you're right. It must be too old. I don't feel anything either." She returned it to her desk.

Suddenly she perked up. "Hey, I have an idea! C'mon. Let's try something!" She grabbed my arm, walked me around the corner past the administrator's office, and contemplated the xerox machine. Without warning, she pulled down her pants, hoisted herself up onto the machine, sat down, hit the button, and xeroxed. Giggling, she grabbed a thumbtack and pinned the picture up on the nearby bulletin board.

"It can surprise everyone when they come in tomorrow! Do you think they'll know who did this? Hey, why don't you make one too? Maybe we can even have everyone make one and pin them all up on the board and try to guess who's who!"

So much for not being affected by marijuana. It would take a bit for people to recognize what they were looking at, but it was interesting to envision the administrator's reaction and the ensuing fallout once he figured it out. As she left to drive home, I returned to the bulletin board, tore down the picture, and stuffed it in the trash.

I turned out the lights and left to go home. It was pouring. I hoped Sierra's driving was better than her present judgment because rainy season was accident season on Guam roads. The asphalt roads contained coral rock, which became unusually slippery when wet. I started home in rush hour traffic, passing three accidents in the first two miles. Cars were hydroplaning on the asphalt, and Marine Drive looked like a game of bumper cars.

Traffic ahead was slowing for our traffic light. I braked, but the car's steering and brakes were unresponsive. It continued forward with a mind of its own. Pumping the brakes, I lay on the horn, trying to warn the vehicle ahead, but my slide continued unabated, and unable to turn, I slammed loudly into his car, crumpling both our bumpers.

We stood in the driving rain surveying the damage. "Oh, it's only the bumper," the other driver said, looking at the mangled remains. "No problem. It's an old car." He got back in and drove off.

I continued home, surprised to beat Carlos, who usually arrived first. Then our rarely-working phone rang. "I slid off the road, hit something, and crumpled the hood. The car isn't drivable. It's in the shop. Can you come downtown and pick me up?"

"I just rear-ended someone on Marine Drive. My bumper's crumpled, but it's drivable. I'll be right down." I climbed back in and started toward downtown, taking the steeper but less crowded road over the mountain.

Too late, I remembered a short steep curve and discovered neither traffic nor speed were necessary to have an accident on Guam's wet asphalt; you only needed to be moving. The car began sliding toward a big tree on the curve. Again, the brakes and steering were useless. Helpless, I slid sideways in slow motion and smashed into a large tree, denting the right door. Sigh. *It's only a door. At least it still opens.*

Between us, three accidents in one afternoon set a family record. Fortunately, we were both uninjured, although the cars looked a bit trashed. I realized we were developing an island mentality; like the driver I rear-ended, we took the new dents in stride. I was learning not to sweat the small stuff.

Although I now worked at GEPA, I continued to teach one period of Marine Biology or Physiology at the Academy. Toward the end of the year, I felt the marine biology class needed a field trip to the ocean. I thought it would be easy, a no-brainer. We wouldn't go into open water because I knew they couldn't swim, so what could possibly happen?

Thirty-One

Rogue Wave

Gun Beach 1976

I TOOK A DAY OFF FROM GEPA, BECAUSE I WANTED THE adventurous girls in my marine biology class to experience what they had been studying in class all semester. The class needed a field trip, but we had an obstacle. Although surrounded by water, few Guamanians could swim. They loved beach picnics, and some fished or boated, but most never went in the water beyond their knees or had any idea what lay beneath the surface. I assumed none of the girls could swim or even snorkel, so going into open water was out of the question.

I selected Gun Beach, a beautiful palm-lined bay, so-named because of a large WWII gun emplacement installed in the tall rocky cliffs along the shore. I told everyone to bring a mask and snorkel, but no fins, because we wouldn't swim.

Gun Beach seemed the perfect location. On some beaches, the water continually deepens as you go farther from shore, but Gun Beach had a classic shallow reef flat extending out from the shore for several hundred feet. The reef flat ended in a sharp coral rock ridge, or edge, and then plunged down almost vertically into deeper water. Even at high tide, the ridge was never more than a few feet deep. It was a perfect location for non-swimmers. The girls could lie down on the shallow reef flat, hold on to the ridge, and look over into 20 feet of crystal-clear water without going into it.

The big day arrived. We walked along the beach, identifying beach zones, ripples, swash marks, and other beach features we'd learned in class. We compared the organisms found at different tidal elevations on the cliff, and did some sand-grain studies.

At that time, Gun Beach contained almost no normal coral-based sand. The entire beach consisted of billions of foraminifera, tiny calcareous planktonic organisms. As a result, practically every grain had the same cream-colored spherical shape and size. It was beautiful and unusual sand and felt very clean because the large grains contained little powdery material. I'd never seen anything like it.

And of course, we ate lunch. No respectable Guamanian would ever bring a sandwich to the beach; every beach outing becomes a fiesta. The girls planned an elaborate menu for our field trip, complete with red rice, barbecued chicken, potato salad, and unique local dishes. Then the highlight: we walked out to study the reef itself.

We were lucky; it was slack tide, the water smooth as glass. The high tide hadn't begun receding, so I easily floated out over the sharp reef ridge and into open water. From there, it was easier to explain the various features the girls were seeing.

Although they had lived their entire life on Guam, it was the first time most of them had ever looked beneath the water's surface. They peppered me with excited questions:

"What's the long black thing?"

"Is the one with fat spines dangerous?"

"Are those spots supposed to be camouflage?"

And inevitably, "Is it edible?"

The water was calm and beautiful. Eventually, six girls approached me. They begged. "Can we come and float out over the reef edge with you?"

"Can you swim?" I asked.

"Oh, yes," they assured me. "We can all swim."

In saltwater, everyone is buoyant as long as they stay horizontal, and the sea was smooth without a wave. Somewhat against my better judgment, I said, "OK." They effortlessly floated above the jagged reef margin to join me in 20 feet of water. We floated out there for perhaps half an hour, absorbed in the profusion of colorful fish, coral, and algae below.

Suddenly, with a tinge of panic in her voice, one of the girls said, "My mask is leaking!" She stopped floating and ripped it off. Once vertical, she began to sink. I floated her on her back while I treaded water trying to fix the strap, but now, nervous, she refused to wear it. We needed to head in.

I looked shoreward and, for the first time, realized that while we had been floating, absorbed in the underwater scene, the tide had been rapidly ebbing. The jagged reef edge we had so effortlessly floated over before, now loomed out of the water, several inches above our heads. Small swells were beginning to slap against the sharp coral edge and suck noisily back out. There was enough wave action that anyone trying to climb over the edge would repeatedly be slammed against the razor-sharp coral rock. With bare feet and hands, there was no way we could climb over it.

How could I have forgotten the tide change? My lifeguard training hasn't prepared me for this.

Once they took their eyes off the bottom, the other girls noticed the building swells and stopped floating too. Once they became vertical, they began sinking. They clustered around me, awkwardly treading water. I could feel the tension rising, and several girls teetered on the edge of panic. As we bobbed on the surface, slowly but surely, the swells nudged us closer and closer to the jagged reef.

Our options were limited. The reef edge had a cut where the undersea cable came ashore, but now, as the tide ebbed, a strong rip current exited the reef flat there. The girls couldn't fight that. The nearest place to reach to the beach without fighting our way over a sharp coral ridge or against a rip current was likely Ipao Beach, perhaps a mile down the coast. The girls would never make it. Horrifying visions of trying to explain to six sets of parents and Sister Luke how I drowned their daughters on a field trip floated through my head.

There was no solution.

The swells continued pushing us closer and closer to the jagged reef edge, but now the girls were unwilling to move farther out. Staring at the jagged edge, perhaps ten feet ahead, in desperation, under my breath, I said, "God, please help us!"

Within only seconds, one of the girls pointed behind me in terror, her eyes wide with fright. "Mrs. Cabreza, *look!*"

I turned and looked up at a gigantic wall of water now bearing down on us like a freight train. From the bottom of the wave trough, it towered at least eight feet above our heads. I had time for only one overwhelming thought before the wave reached us: *We're toast.*

Waves begin to build in height when they 'feel bottom.' As depth gets shallower, water is pushed up and waves become taller, until eventually they become top-heavy and break. But this wave, still moving over deep water, wasn't breaking. As it approached, it pulled us all smoothly up the front side of the wave, lifted us high above the sharp coral ridge, and rolled on over the ridge, depositing every one of us gently and safely inside on the shallow sandy reef flat beyond, where it dissolved in a mass of froth and foam. None of us received even a scratch. The successive waves were all small again.

Now sitting in a foot of water on the reef flat, we stared at each other incredulously, and then, we all began laughing. The mixed emotions of surprise, relief, and exhilaration that result from a narrow escape, flooded over us.

I said accusingly, "You told me you could swim!"

They all smiled sweetly. With an innocent face, Maria said, laughing, "We lied."

Carmen chimed in. "We were afraid to go out, but we wanted to try it, and we knew you'd take care of us." Oh my. What a flattering but misplaced vote of confidence! I'd come close to drowning half the class.

A rogue wave had rescued us. Rogue waves are a known, but rare and unpredictable, phenomenon. These single giant waves arise without warning, seemingly out of nowhere, and arrive onshore with sufficient force to overturn boats and wash unsuspecting beach walkers or fishermen out to sea. Then the ocean is calm once more. Rogue waves often drown people, but this wave had saved everyone. It was the only rogue wave I ever saw or heard about in my almost seven years on the island.

We waded back to shore, finished the remains of lunch, and waited long enough to ensure school had ended before starting back. The girls returned home sunburned and excited, with a great new adventure to tell. I knew they would probably never venture over the reef edge again, but the field trip was successful, because I knew their view of the ocean and their island would never be the same. For my part, I learned not to take everything students tell me at face value.

Was the wave timing simply a lucky coincidence? Some would say so, but I don't believe it. It was a single wave, in the precise location, precisely when we needed it. I know people tend to see what they want to believe, but I think God had our backs on that one.

- *Thirty-Two* -
Gifts From the Hill

Nimitz Hill 1975-1979

A s Carlos' two-year assignment drew to a close, the bank recalled us to the Philippines, but we weren't interested in returning to peso salaries, traffic congestion, air pollution, and the general uncertainty of living under a dictatorship. In the Philippines, jobs and commuting had occupied most of our time and even simple tasks like shopping were time-consuming tedium. In Guam, jobs occupied part of our lives, but we found time for the beach, mountain hikes, and vacations to the Philippines or neighboring islands. We spent weekends playing outside, not trapped in Makati's urban jungle. We certainly hadn't saved enough for the kids' college educations either, one of the main reasons we requested an international assignment in the first place. The people who laughed when I said we'd return in two years were right.

I was a U.S. citizen so we could stay, and the bank agreed to change Carlos to local hire, but we paid a price. We lost the bank's free semi-annual trips to the Philippines, and the bank stopped paying our rent and the children's school tuition.

We both lost our Philippine pensions and social security contributions. Although we still owned our house in Marcelo, we were essentially starting over financially but, in our early thirties, those peso losses were insignificant unless we intended to eventually move back. We never even discussed that possibility; subconsciously, I think we both viewed this as a permanent life change.

We slowly discovered another considerable disadvantage of local hire. The Philippines required overseas Filipino citizens to pay income tax on money earned abroad, even though they had already paid taxes in the host country. If Carlos returned home to visit, he would not be allowed to leave again without paying income tax on his Guam income. Previously the bank had paid those taxes, something we had never recognized.

This difficulty became a blessing in disguise. The unfairness of this double taxation prompted Carlos to apply for U.S. citizenship. With an American spouse, in those days, he received citizenship within a couple of months. Lisa and David were technically Filipino too. Automatic citizenship required either being born on American soil or having two American parents, but they were born in Manila to only one American parent.

The American Embassy in Manila had wisely advised me to register any children with the embassy at birth, which now saved us a mountain of red tape. After Carlos obtained citizenship, now with two American parents, they were processed automatically within a month.

Once we decided to stay, renting seemed foolish. We bought a house in Nimitz Hill Estates, a new subdivision high on Nimitz Hill. Our back yard abutted the grassy mountain, providing the kids an extensive outdoor playground. However, it also produced several unpleasant surprises. I discovered our first 'gift' from the hill when I returned from work one day to find Lisa, David, and several neighborhood kids bouncing an old grenade on the street.

"We want it to explode, like in the movies," they said. They had found it on the hill behind the house. It was hard to envision our yard as the scene of horrific battles three short decades earlier. *How do you convince kids of the danger when throwing grenades in the movies often looks more like a game?* Horrified, I confiscated it, but I knew hundreds of pieces of ordnance still littered the hillside.

The hills behind our house were also the new home to African land snails, *Lissachatina (Achatina) fulica*. In some countries, their enormous shells can reach up to 7.8 inches long and 3.9 inches tall, but Guam's rarely exceeded four inches. Japanese soldiers brought the giant snails over for food in WWII but, invariably, some escaped. They encountered few predators, and populations multiplied rapidly. I assumed our dry mountain would have some, but I didn't expect hordes.

One morning, as I glanced out the front window, the grass looked odd. *What's the matter with our yard?* "Carlos, come look at this. Does the lawn look strange to you?"

"It looks a little ragged."

We went outside. "Didn't we have something planted here?" A closer look near the house revealed only a few ragged stubs, the remains of a once-lush *Coleus* bed. The entire front flowerbed had vanished, overnight. Although I saw none, it had to be snails.

That night after dark, we went outside into the yard. Giant snails ranging in size from quail eggs to tangerines now covered our postage-stamp yard so thickly it was difficult to walk without stepping on one. Only two days ago there were none. It was mystifying. We'd occasionally seen a few, but now an entire army had arrived in what appeared to be a massive, coordinated invasion. This required action.

We gave the kids flashlights and trash bags and announced, "Tonight, we're having a snail hunt. Let's have a contest to see who gets the most."

"Yuk," Lisa protested. "I'm not picking up those." David wasn't thrilled either.

"Grab the top of the shell. It's not slimy."

Once they got into it, they wandered around picking up, counting, and dumping snails into the bags. At twelve hundred snails, we quit for the night, exhausted. The harvest filled our large garbage can to the brim. Then antennae began appearing over the top, and they all began crawling out. I knocked them back in, poured in some snail bait, and slammed on the lid.

The following morning, I peeked into the garbage can, and found it cemented solid with hardened, bright yellow slime and dead snails. The stench was already overpowering. The garbage man took one look and hauled the whole mess to the Ordot landfill. We bought a new can.

We caught 500 more the second night, around 60 the third night, and less than a dozen the fourth. All this from a small lot, perhaps 60 x 100 feet, most of it covered with house and driveway. Unfortunately, the mountain behind the house had an unlimited supply, and since the snails are hermaphrodites, every snail produces eggs; the population would rebound in no time.

We gave up growing herbaceous plants like *Coleus* and replaced them with some rather unusual orange and purple varieties of thorny bougainvillea. The snails weren't interested in those.

Within a year, the bougainvillea had nicely filled out. People often admired our yard because we had made an effort to grass it and plant shrubs, while many others did nothing but mow their weeds and maybe plant a palm or two. The yard and bougainvillea looked beautiful until our neighbors had a fiesta.

We returned from a short vacation on Saipan to find our new trash can overflowing with piles of paper plates and large chunks of rotting turkey. More plates and plastic forks lay scattered around the yard. Our next-door neighbor drifted over, and I gestured in bewilderment at our front yard. "What happened?"

"The Pangilinan's had a big fiesta while you were gone. I guess people liked your yard."

I guess. Not wanting to sit on the Pangilinan's barren dirt front yard to eat, people moved across the street to picnic on our green front lawn. I didn't mind. But then, admiring our bougainvillea, they broke off branches to take home, presumably to plant in their own yards. Our beautiful bushy bougainvillea now looked like an insane pruner had come through with a chainsaw. The damage to the plants was small stuff – they would regrow quickly in a few months, so I concentrated on the positive. With luck, if some of the branch-breakers lived on our street, maybe they would beautify their own yards with it.

The hill behind us harbored several other surprises besides grenades and snails, but it took us a while to realize it. Our golden Labrador puppy, Georgie, liked lying next to the wall on the cool kitchen floor. After about a year, I noticed a long black line above her, along the top of the kitchen wall, where it joined the ceiling. I stared up at it. It appeared to be tiny sand-grain size black spots. *Dirt? Mold? Why only there?* The wall had a few spots too, right above Georgie. I peered closely, and realized with surprise the spots were slowly making their way up the wall, headed for the ceiling. Thet were bugs of some kind but, less than pinhead size, I couldn't even determine what they were.

I dragged a ladder into the kitchen and climbed up to look. A solid mass of these things had concentrated in the junction between wall and ceiling. A couple of them were large enough to identify. Yikes! Baby ticks! Masses of them. Literally thousands of them. The numbers were astounding. Backing down the ladder, I ruffled my hand through Georgie's blond fur. Her skin looked as if she had rolled in a pepper shaker. Had they been adults, the sheer numbers would have dehydrated her. Belatedly, I appreciated all of the work Carlos did on the Tumon Heights carpet before we moved. I thought he exaggerated when he said ticks covered the carpet, but maybe it warranted all of those cans of bug spray after all.

Our ticks rode in on Georgie, ate a microscopic meal, and once satiated, they dropped off and climbed the wall until they hit the ceiling. At some point, when they became hungry again, they would begin raining down on us.

I climbed up the ladder with bug spray, wondering how long they had been hanging out there unnoticed. Because Georgie liked lying in the same spot, at least they were all concentrated in one place. An ocean swim seemed the easiest way to de-tick her, and de-ticking became part of our weekly beach excursion.

Grenades, land snails, and ticks. I hoped we were done with the mountain's surprises. Yet within three years, we would discover two more, and those would both be poisonous.

- *Thirty-Three* -

Flea Markets, Fruit Bats, and Fiestas

1973-1979

G UAM'S TWO MAIN SOCIAL ACTIVITIES WERE FLEA
markets and fiestas. Shortly after we arrived, Filipino friends excitedly informed us about the Saturday flea market operating in an abandoned Navy field near the USO. It operated from 5:00-11:00 a.m. but most of the action was over by 9:00 a.m. The military initially established it to help their personnel sell unwanted belongings before leaving the island, but it became a gift to everyone because unless you were lucky enough to have PX privileges, except for Mark's small department store, the flea market was the only place on the island to buy anything. Koreans and Filipinos were particularly avid market fans because they could find things not even available in their home countries. People anticipated Saturdays like Christmas.

I was amused to find the same people who criticized Americans for being materialistic often filled their own houses to overflowing with flea market bargains. One friend devoted an entire room in her house to storing her newly acquired bargains: used Halloween costumes, dishes, clothes, toys, dozens of puzzles, Christmas ornaments, curtains, furniture, and other flea market treasures.

"Look at these neat pans," she said, showing me a special pan for cooking hot dogs, with parallel grooves and ridges on the bottom, presumably to keep them evenly spaced while boiling. Another pan had oval hollows on the bottom for making hard-boiled eggs, spacing apparently being essential for proper cooking. I tried not to laugh.

After a year, realizing their house was overstuffed with unused bargains, she began a new set of flea market trips, selling off everything she had hoarded for the last year. She bargained well, making a profit on most of her sales. And it was all tax-free.

Many military families had traveled around Asia, amassing interesting items and trinkets that often ended up in the flea market after their novelty wore off. Oriental rugs, vases, Japanese scrolls, screens, Thai bronzeware, wood carvings, temple rubbings, and similar objects were so common that sometimes the market looked like an oriental bazaar. Some residents made a living doing buy-sell in the market, but they avoided these because their resale value was slight.

Haoles normally didn't engage in buy-sell business or even purchase much, but we enjoyed browsing, and occasionally we found unexpected and unusual treasures. I discovered a carved wooden doll wearing a suit of armor constructed of 500 old corroded Chinese coins, carefully tied together with string.

"My husband bought it in Cambodia during the Vietnam War, and he probably doesn't want it anymore," the woman said. I bought it for a dollar. She was happy to unload it, and if nothing else, I felt the old coins made it a bargain. I'd never seen another like it and wondered how her husband would react once he discovered she'd sold it.

Like this sale, transactions were always win-win because both the buyer and seller celebrated their good luck. The seller thought, "Hallelujah! I can't believe someone actually bought my old piece of junk," while the buyer rejoiced over a new-found treasure. In my case, the doll actually was a treasure of sorts. I recently saw a pair of similar coin dolls listed online for $600.

Although the military established the flea market to sell unwanted second-hand items, enterprising Filipinos soon began bringing in stacks of new Filipino-made clothes, tapes, records, and other merchandise. The military, not in the retail business, forbade this practice, but found it impossible to police the sales or keep them out. In exasperation, they shut down the flea market.

The entire island went into mourning, and the boy scouts, who made twenty-five cents on each admission fee, lost their primary money maker. Soon, an enterprising Indian stepped into the void, rented the abandoned Harmon Field airstrip, and opened up a new flea market. He charged $2-$7 admission for sellers and fifty cents for lookers, and promptly raked in several thousand dollars. The flea market was back in business.

Once we settled into island life, our interest in the flea market waned, but we would see a quite different side of it six years later when we became sellers.

Fiestas were Guam's most popular social events, and any excuse would do: a holiday, birth, death, christening, birthday, first communion, someone coming, someone leaving, or if all else failed, simply to have a party. Everyone pitched in. Fiestas always filled several food tables, and the more people, the better. The number of attendees usually exceeded the actual invitees because hosts expected people to bring along extra guests, and guests usually contributed something too.

Fiestas were high-priority social obligations, and families sometimes went deeply into debt for one. My co-worker, Nico, had lost his two front teeth, and the considerable gap greatly affected his speech and appearance.

"I've debated getting new teeth, but I think I'd rather spend the money on my daughter's christening fiesta," he said. All four years I knew him, he never replaced his front teeth. Somehow, on Guam it seemed a logical choice.

Fiesta staples included chicken kelaguen, barbecued ribs, red rice, taro, yams, eggplant, potato salad, and finá denné, a hot dipping sauce made with soy sauce, lemon, onion, and red chilis. Fiesta food mirrored Guam's multicultural population, and usually included Filipino, Korean, Vietnamese, and Chinese dishes like lumpia, bean-filled buns, adobo, pancit, and kimchi.

With so much food, no wonder so many people approached obesity by age 30. Many Pacific Islanders were so large that in 1973, the Hilton actually posted a sign in its elevator saying, "Capacity: Ten people, five Samoans, or three Tongans." I doubt the sign ever offended anyone because many South Pacific cultures admire fat; it indicates prosperity.

My Tongan EWC friend had a lovely figure by Western standards, but about six months before returning to Tonga, she told me, "I'm way too thin. I won't look attractive there unless I gain some weight," and she began working hard to gain at least thirty pounds before returning. This thought was comforting for those of us that like to eat.

The definition of a real fiesta seemed difficult to pin down, Vaguely, it meant hordes of people, loud live music, and overflowing beer and food, all gathered under a canvas, old parachute, or large tarp. Guamanians seemed to feel possessive about fiestas, and they were quick to point out when one wasn't real. According to Guamanians, we Haoles had trouble getting them right.

One Monday, a co-worker was discussing a weekend Haole fiesta. "How did it go?" I asked. She shrugged, a bit of disdain tinging her voice.

"The food was good, but it wasn't a real fiesta."

"Why not?" I naively assumed anything with food was a fiesta.

"They didn't serve Guamanian food."

"No chicken kelaguen?"

She rolled her eyes indignantly. "He didn't even have potato salad!"

I laughed. "Potato salad probably isn't Guamanian. We eat it in the States all the time. I bet it came to Guam with the GIs in WWII." She looked shocked, and I doubt she believed me.

Fruit bat, *Acerodon sp.*, is one of the few genuinely Guamanian dishes. These rabbit-sized mega-bats have a face resembling a fox and a five-and-a-half-foot wingspan. Unlike most bats that eat insects, fruit bats eat fruit and nectar. Fortunately for the fruit bats, the custom of inviting them to fiestas was dying out. In 1973, few fiestas served them anymore because bats were nearly extirpated from Guam and had to be imported from Saipan at $17 per pound (1973 dollars.) Because fruit bats were so expensive and challenging to get, younger people hadn't learned to like or expect them, so bats were in less demand, hopefully allowing the small bat population a chance at recovery.

I saw my first and only fat fruit bat at a large Citibank fiesta held under a massive parachute on the beach. As I canvassed the variety of food arranged on the table, the food coordinator approached and said proudly, "We even have a fruit bat." Knowing its rarity, she radiated pride. "Have you ever seen one?"

"No, but I'd like to!"

Taking my elbow, she guided me over to a large black iron pot and removed the lid. I peered in. An entire giant bat, its matted fur still intact, sat in a pool of coconut milk, milky eyes bulging from their sockets, and a fat, very human-looking tongue protruding somewhat obscenely from its mouth. It looked agonized and surprised to be there.

The startling expression prompted me to ask, "Was it dead when it went in?" I hoped it had been killed and degutted before going into the pot.

She wasn't surprised at the question, but, not being the one who brought it, she said, "I don't know." The answer to both my hopes was probably no. Most recipes indicate that bats were traditionally washed and thrust alive into the pot, fur, viscera, and all. I didn't want to dwell on it; it seemed appalling and unnecessarily inhumane, not to mention a bit unsanitary.

Often the bat is served as soup, and after cooking, it's chopped into pieces. Later, the food coordinator offered me a furry bit. "The fur is the best part," she assured me. I almost gagged at the thought. I'd eaten everything from fried crickets and dog to snake, tepezcuintle, and duck embryos, but fur had to be an acquired taste. I simply couldn't force myself to eat it.

I took some meat but said, "I think you should save the fur for someone who appreciates it." The dark meat tasted somewhat like chicken. It certainly wasn't tasty enough to pursue a species to the brink of extinction. My bat soup recipe specifies one bat will serve two Chamorros or fifteen

Haoles. With the fur on, I guessed the fifteen Haoles would happily let the two Chamorros have all of it.

Each year Guam EPA celebrated its anniversary with a large fiesta. Work ground to a halt for two days while we built barbecue grills in the parking lot, scrounged supplies, and in general, lived up to the reputation of nonworking government employees.

The food coordinator approached me. "What are you bringing?"

"My Aunt Connie's casserole, a vegetable and rice dish with a good topping."

"Really?" The same dishes repeatedly appeared at every fiesta; she sounded excited at the thought of something new. "What's in the topping?"

"It sounds weird, but it's good. It's a mixture of celery soup, mayonnaise, mustard, curry, and cheese."

"Mayonnaise and mustard?" She grimaced. "I've never heard of something like that."

I assured her people liked it, but I could see she thought it would be horrible and was merely too polite to say so.

On fiesta day, I brought the casserole. After eyeing it, she finally decided to try some. Surprised, she took a second helping. Later on, she came up to me. "I didn't think anyone would like it," she admitted. "But it's really good. Can I get the recipe?"

"Sure." I smiled, knowing my Aunt Connie would be pleased. Connie had never returned to the Pacific after the war, but now her casserole had. I imagined it appearing at the next fiesta, and the recipe being passed around until it became a Guamanian Casserole and a regular at island fiestas. Right near the 'Guamanian' potato salad.

My boss and Sierra were both leaving EPA, and I volunteered our house for a going-away party. As Haoles arrived, they plopped their food down on the table wherever there was space. The table looked acceptable to me, but several Guamanians stood there discussing it. They finally approached one woman to ask, "Is your dish pork or chicken?" On learning it was pork, they moved it to a slightly different place on the table. Then, unable to stop themselves, the women began rearranging everything on the table. To my untrained eye, it made no difference but, once they established the standard table order, they all stood back surveying the table with satisfaction.

To the uninitiated, a fiesta table may simply look like a big food table, but there's a definite order for placing the food so everyone can quickly locate their favorites. The first part of the table always holds the starches, prominently featuring Guam red rice, followed by chicken, beef, and pork, then fish, kelaguen, vegetables, salads and soups, and deserts. After much debate, a Connie's casserole ended up with the starches.

The office now had thirty people, so we expected perhaps fifty guests, but almost eighty people showed up. Later, our neighbor across the street said disparagingly that ours wasn't a real fiesta because we didn't have enough people. I think she felt insulted we hadn't invited them, but it never entered my mind to do so. I naively thought it was an office party but, to the Guamanians, it was a fiesta. As neighbors, I think they expected to be invited but were reticent about dropping in because we weren't Guamanian. One of the guests also said it was a "very Haole" fiesta, but she couldn't define why, although it seemed to revolve around having canned music instead of a live band.

Gov Guam's employee picnic at Ipao Beach was the biggest fiesta of all because the government employed almost ten percent of the island, and everyone brought their entire family. Each agency had an assigned location under the coconut trees along the beach. Saturday morning, the beach swarmed with employees rapidly assembling large, palm-frond covered booths. Enormous tubs of ice and beer appeared, and 55-gallon drums, cut in half lengthwise, morphed into giant barbecue pits.

Agency staffs intermingled, but each agency held its own party; this was one fiesta that discouraged outsiders. Usually, adding a few people wouldn't be a problem but, that day, instead of taking tourists to a regular restaurant, at least a dozen large Japanese tour busses just happened to time their Ipao beach stops with lunchtime and dropped off several hundred tourists at Ipao beach to scrounge for a free Authentic Guamanian Lunch.

I don't know whether tourists found free lunches with a sympathetic agency, but they didn't find any with us. We were a small agency, and couldn't feed hundreds of additional people. The planning director creatively stationed himself beside the food line and tactfully asked people if they had a ticket. Of course, there were no tickets, but the tourists didn't know this, and generally, they simply said no, and wandered off down the beach to search for lunch elsewhere.

The governor arrived with much fanfare, and arrogantly parked his car on the beach, a known violation. A zealous policeman gave him a ticket, and was fired two days later. This created a great uproar, with groups for and against the governor vocally weighing in on both sides. I never heard whether the policeman got his job back.

***

The governor flouted the law in other things as well. A few years later, he was convicted on ten counts of bribery, corruption, witness tampering, and obstruction of justice, stemming from fraud involving a $60,000 kickback related to establishing a scrap metal facility at the commercial port.[10] After a failed appeal to the U.S. Supreme Court, he faced a four-year sentence in a federal minimum-security prison.

In 1990, three hours before he was scheduled to leave for prison, he drove to the Chief Kepuha statue at the Paseo Loop, wrapped himself in a Guam flag, and set up signs saying, "I regret I have only one life to give to my island." Then he shot himself in the head with a .38 caliber pistol. His actions were hard to understand, but they seemed a bit drastic. Bribes and kickbacks are common in Asia, so perhaps it was easy to justify the corruption, forgetting the reality that Guam was part of the broader U.S. justice system.

- *Thirty-Four* -
In the Eye of the Storm

Nimitz Hill 1976

MAY 21, 1976, WE WENT TO WORK, UNAWARE THAT within hours, eighty percent of the buildings on the island, including our house, would be damaged or destroyed, and that we would be without water for three weeks, and without electricity for almost a year.

Every year typhoons caused flooding in Manila, leaving thousands homeless, so we expected the same thing in Guam. Each year typhoon warnings sent Guam scurrying to stock up on radio and flashlight batteries, candles, LP gas and charcoal for the barbecue. People stored food and water, stowed loose objects that could become flying projectiles, and placed typhoon shutters on their windows. We prepared for the worst, yet experienced only wind and hard rain. After four years of what we considered false alarms compared to Philippine typhoons, we became blasé. We never boarded our windows and hardly even bothered to prepare anymore. We regarded typhoons more as a chance to get off work.

Naval Air Station and Fleet Weather Central on Nimitz Hill provided plenty of advance warning, and Radio and TV announcements informed everyone of any storm systems approaching the island. Permanent signs at base entrances announced the current typhoon signal. Usually, the signs showed Signal 4, normal weather conditions. Signals 3, 2, and 1 indicated the likelihood of a typhoon within 72, 48, or 24 hours.

Around May 14, Fleet Weather Central announced, "A small tropical storm is developing in the Pacific." At that point it was still unnamed and caused little concern. Over several days, once wind speeds increased to over 74 mph, FWC upgraded it to typhoon status, and named it Typhoon Pamela. It appeared to be headed for Guam. Once it acquired a name, people began taking it seriously.

"Maximum wind speed of Pamela is now over 100 mph, and Fleet Weather Central has upgraded it to a super typhoon," the TV announced. Old-timers, remembering Typhoon Karen in 1962, began preparing for the worst. Those still living in wooden, tin-roofed houses prepared to move into the schools for safety. Despite all the warnings, we weren't overly worried because our walls and roof were constructed of solid concrete slabs.

About 10:00 a.m. on May 21, Guam upgraded to typhoon signal 2. Most businesses closed, and EPA sent us home, but I didn't feel any particular urgency. Happy for an afternoon off, I stopped at McDonald's before going home. Carlos and the kids arrived home early too. Wind and rain began picking up. We finally realized this typhoon could be more severe than most, but now it was too late to do much except store water.

"Bring everything portable inside," I told Carlos. "And we need to store water." We dragged the garbage can, a heavy boat anchor, barbeque, wrought iron patio furniture, and anything else we thought might become airborne into the enclosed carport.

The heavy leaden sky produced a premature twilight, and I dug around for candles and matches while I could still see to find them. I filled some pitchers and the bathtub with water too, in case we lost electricity. If that happened, the well pumps stopped, and water would drain from the pipes.

The rain steadily increased in intensity. Then, while hundreds were moving to the safety of the schools, with a sudden burst of enthusiasm, somehow Carlos decided this was an ideal time to weed the yard. "I'm going outside to weed. It's easier to weed when the soil is waterlogged." He pulled on a rain jacket and went outside into the wind and rain.

I watched through the window as he went to the side yard, bent down, and started weeding. This rain wasn't much worse than a typical rainstorm.

Once again, Guam has overreacted, I thought. But the typhoon hadn't arrived; this was just the prelude.

Abruptly, without warning, the storm made landfall. With a tremendous crash, a violent wall of wind and rain slammed the house full force. Instantly, the whole island lost electricity. Wind funneled up the gully behind the house, shrieking, howling, and gusting erratically, as rain smashed against the house and glass sliders in sheets. In the time it took to light a candle, things went from hard rain to chaos.

I looked out the window but now saw only a wall of water, an opaque white-out. I couldn't even see the house below us, less than 30 feet away. Carlos was gone. *He needs to come in, now. Perhaps he's moved to the backyard?* But I couldn't see anything outside. Belatedly, I realized this wasn't an ordinary typhoon. It began to feel like a storm of almost Biblical proportions.

The bedroom window screens flew past the sliding doors and disappeared, followed by pieces of what looked like our avocado tree. Everything was airborne. *Thankfully we moved the wrought iron furniture into the enclosed carport, or it would be gone.*

Inside the house, uneasy thoughts swirled in my brain. *Where's Carlos? Surely, he's not crazy enough to stay out in this?* I assumed he would return any moment, but he didn't. After a few minutes, my thoughts changed from *Why doesn't he come inside?* to *Does he need help?* My unease ratcheted up, and my stomach began to tighten. Through the window, I could see nothing but a wall of water. I wouldn't even know where to start looking in such limited visibility, and I felt conflicted, because I couldn't leave the kids alone in the house.

A tense ten minutes later, I heard a loud pounding at the front door. Cracking it open, I looked down with relief, to see Carlos on his hands and knees.

"The wind's too strong; I can't stand up," he said, crawling inside, shaken and streaming water.

"What were you doing out there?" *Where were you? I couldn't see you anywhere!"*

"It blew me off the yard," he said, somewhat dazed. "I went over the retaining wall and down into the Tedtaotao's back yard."

Nimitz Hill houses on our street were terraced on the hillside, with each yard perhaps eight to ten feet above the one below it. Vertical concrete retaining walls stabilized the hillside between houses. When the typhoon made landfall, the initial blast lofted him into the air, blew him over the retaining wall, and threw him eight feet down into the yard below.

"Wow! You were lucky it dropped you in their soggy back yard rather than slamming you against their house or concrete driveway!"

Miraculously unhurt but, unable to stand against the wind, he crawled to the front sidewalk on his hands and knees, and groped his way along the sidewalk uphill to the house.

Our house stood at the top of a natural drainage channel, and winds exceeding 200 mph funneled straight up the gully toward the house unopposed, gathering force as they came. With nothing to block it, the full brunt of the wind slammed the living and dining room sliders and the master bedroom window. We had initially liked our house because, unlike other houses, a double set of sliding doors faced the ocean. In a storm, this became a liability.

"I think we're going to lose the sliders. The glass is bending!" I never realized glass could bend but, when the wind strength increased, the glass in the sliding doors began bowing inward. I watched as the rubber weather stripping between the glass and the frame peeled out and blew away. The glass bowed inward so far that, if I had dared, I could have inserted a hand between the glass and the frame. *How far can it bend before it shatters?* Sheets of rain smashed against the glass, blew sideways, and funneled inside through the inch-wide opening like a hose. Water streamed down the walls around the windows and disappeared below the rug. Drain holes in the tracks of the sliding glass doors funneled pencil-sized streams of water inside, and water blew under the front door in a constant stream. Chaos began reigning inside the house.

"We need to brace the sliders!" And without thinking, seeing the bending glass, we tried to counteract the wind pressure by bracing against the glass doors from the inside. It was a gut reaction, futile and fool-hardy. If the glass shattered, we would have become human pincushions, killed by flying glass shards. By the time we realized we should move away from the doors, it was too late. Now we were afraid to let go, because we thought without our extra support, then they would surely shatter. We stood pressed against the glass, muscles cramping, for almost three hours.

Meanwhile, the kids danced excitedly around the dining room in the candlelight.

"Get back in the inside hallway!" I shouted over the howling wind. "It's safe there. You don't want to be out here if the glass breaks." But they preferred being with us to the dark interior hallway, and kept coming out. Sustained winds now exceeded 185 mph, and gusts continued to exceed 200 mph.

After several hours, the wind speed abruptly dropped as quickly as it began. The glass settled back into the door frames, the rain slowed to a drizzle, and we could see the house below us again.

"We're in the eye! Now is our chance to leave the sliding doors! Get the mattress to brace the doors!" Fleet Weather Central had predicted the typhoon's eye would pass directly over the island, but no one knew exactly where it would hit. Now we realized the rotating twelve-mile eye was passing directly over the house. From space, the typhoon appeared as a rotating swirl of donut-shaped storm clouds surrounding a circle of open sky in the middle, but we didn't venture outside to look.

The comparative calm was our chance to prepare for the second act. Exhausted, we left the sliders, and took advantage of the lull to lug a heavy mattress from the bedroom, press it against the doors, and brace it with our heavy, Philippine hardwood dining table. It supported the doors better than we could, and if the glass broke, the mattress should catch the glass.

"I'll change the windows before the storm returns," Carlos yelled, heading to the other side of the house.

Typhoons cause huge pressure differences as they pass through. Conventional wisdom says to equalize pressure inside and outside the house as the storm approaches by closing windows facing the storm and opening a window on the leeward side of the house. As the eye passes over, reverse the process, closing the open windows, and opening a closed window on the opposite side of the house.

Too late, we remembered the windows in the enclosed carport. A glance into the carport showed the pressure difference had already sucked the glass in the large front windows out of the frames and smashed it on the driveway. We hadn't even heard it go. Too late, I also realized the dishwasher contained dirty dishes. It didn't appear important at the time, but we would regret it later.

The eye's lull lasted less than an hour. As suddenly as the winds had abated, the howling winds and beating rain returned with an abrupt crash, slamming our house at full strength. Now on the back side of the rotating eye, the wind came from the opposite direction. The sound was the worst part. We lit more candles and listened to the storm's fury howling outside in the darkness. The wind sounded almost alive, and angry that it couldn't enter the house.

The change in wind direction was welcome because now the house above sheltered us a bit, and instead of being fully exposed to the brunt of the storm, only two small uphill windows faced the wind. The incoming water slowed, but our problems were just beginning. So much water had entered, yet the wall-to-wall carpet remained dry. *Where was it all going?*

Then the carpet began feeling like a waterbed. Water was trapped underneath the carpet pad. Unable to seep through, it pushed the carpet up, and it began floating. Excited, the kids jumped and rolled around on it like a Bouncy Castle.

Previously we had battled the wind. Now we fought the water. We tried stuffing bath towels next to the sliding doors, but they became saturated in seconds. The wind pressure outside was unrelenting; we couldn't stop the water. Eventually, it found a way around the rubber pad and began seeping up into the carpet. We found ourselves standing in several inches of water. I never imagined a house on a mountain top could flood, but the door frames trapped two or three inches of water that were unable to exit.

We waded around the living room, using towels to soak it up and wringing them into pails until our hands gave out.

"Does the water feel soapy to you?" Carlos asked.

"Yeah, it does, and look at my legs!" After a few hours, our hands, calves, and feet were covered with ugly red welts, and beginning to sting.

"It's got to be a reaction to toxic chemicals and pesticides in the rug."

That made water removal even more imperative but, without the weather stripping, water continued to enter around the windows and under the door. We struggled for several more hours before going to bed exhausted. We lay listening to the howling storm.

For 48 hours, the storm raged on. When the sun returned to bake the soggy landscape, people emerged to stare in stunned disbelief at the remains of the island. The beautiful green landscape was gone. Palm trees, adapted to typhoons, still stood, but the wind had whipped and shredded their fronds into thin, dry, brown strings. Our avocado tree lay split in half, branches splintered, and the remaining leaves stripped bare. Trees and shrubs lay broken and splintered in pieces. Mangled brown tangles of vegetation, piles of house debris, signposts, telephone posts, downed wires, and random pieces of metal littered the ground. The wildlife was decimated; most insects and birds on the island were blown out to sea.

Over 33 inches of rain fell, 24 of them in a 24-hour period. We never knew the exact maximum speed, because a wind gust broke the Naval Air Station anemometer at over 200 mph. A Vietnamese refugee who spent several years collecting hundreds of thousands of aluminum cans from bars all over the island hoping to recycle them, now found his mammoth pile scattered over the entire island and surrounding reefs in a spectacular display of littering. It was hard to go anywhere without finding cans. Months later, while diving in Marbo Cave, I even saw a beer can lodged deep down inside the third small underwater chamber, bizarrely skewered on a stalagmite.

The island infrastructure sustained the biggest beating. When the storm abated, not a street sign remained on the island. Nearly every streetlight and telephone post was flattened. Downed wires littered the streets everywhere.

A massive storm surge had raised the sea level an incredible 27.5 feet[12], flooding the power plant with saltwater. To order, ship, and install new parts from the mainland would require months. It would be nearly a year before the power came back online.

The winds and water damaged eighty percent of the buildings on the island, destroyed 3300 houses, and undermined roads. The entire island looked and felt like a war zone. Overnight, the island retrogressed 100 years in time, as people began washing in the rivers and cooking outside on grills.

Typhoon Pamela was the third most damaging typhoon of the twentieth century, and President Ford declared Guam a disaster area. Estimated civilian and military property damage exceeded $500 million,[13] over $2 billion by 2020 standards. Pamela and other disasters put the Red Cross into debt in 1976. Even basic cleanup and recovery took months. Yet, despite the devastation, the island had only one fatality because people had relocated to the schools.

Nimitz Hill's concrete slab houses fared better than most, and although everyone had water damage and most lost windows and central air conditioners, houses retained their structural integrity. The storm flattened the older, flimsier board and sheet metal houses on the southern coastline in Merizo and Umatac. Luckily, those simple structures could also be rapidly reconstructed. Before the storm, the southern villages were a rainbow of pastel-colored houses, but, after the storm, when people rebuilt, they scrounged whatever material they could find. A few weeks later, the towns had rebuilt, every house now a mixture of various colored boards and tin sheets.

Our house, although habitable, was not without problems. Aside from the carport windows, the heavy central air conditioner, bolted into the concrete slab roof with six thick, eight-inch steel bolts, was ripped out. In all the noise we never heard it go, and never recovered it.

All of our screens were gone, but the mosquito population, initially reduced, rebounded with a vengeance. Without air conditioning, the nighttime heat and humidity were oppressive. We had two poor choices: close the windows and suffocate, or open them and become a mosquito buffet. Scrounging around, we propped a few pieces of someone's screen against the bedroom windows as best we could for a bit of mosquito protection, but the whine of mosquitoes filled the humid nights, and I slept with a sheet over my head.

At least we had more sleep. Nightfall comes around 6:00 in the tropics, and without lights or TV, most of us went to bed hours earlier than normal.

Before the storm hit, panicked people stripped the supermarket shelves clean, and it would take a couple of weeks to replenish them from the mainland. The mainland asked about our three most urgent needs. Guam's reply: "Coke, Pampers, and ice."

Nice to have our priorities straight. I thought bottled water and canned food might have figured more prominently, considering the empty store shelves.

The Philippines had taught us to maintain a stored food supply, and our stove used natural gas, so at least I could cook. With our house essentially intact, we fared better than many people but, without power, the wells couldn't pump. In times like this, the military's manpower, equipment, and expertise were invaluable.

Anderson Air Base used their large generators to bring a few wells online within a day, and announced, "We're filling large water trucks, and stationing them in the downtown areas. Bring your large water containers to the water truck in downtown Piti."

Who keeps a bunch of large empty water containers lying around? Some people, maybe, but not us. At least we had a couple of large pots. I began to appreciate the military and wondered how people in poorer countries managed without similar support systems. We were almost three weeks without water.

Without air conditioning, the stifling concrete house baked in the tropical sun. Within two days, the soggy carpet was stinking, and the house was rapidly becoming uninhabitable.

"It's never going to dry in here. The carpet is going to get moldy."

"We've got to move it outside." Carlos cut the soggy carpet into pieces with a box cutter and we dragged the heavy pieces outside onto our sloping driveway. I rolled them with a rolling pin to remove as much water as possible and we left them to dry in the tropical sun. The light beige carpeting had never looked so clean. Once dried, we rolled up the carpet pieces and stashed them underneath the wrought iron furniture in the enclosed carport, to await the island's carpet installer.

Within two days, the water stored in the bathtub became undrinkable, so I dumped our pile of dirty clothes into the bathtub and stomped up and down on them like grapes in a winepress. Anderson imported more generators and soon brought other wells online. Within three weeks, all the island wells were up and running, and at least we had water, although, without power, washing machines and dishwashers were useless.

But our water was cold. Then I began smelling gas in the carport and discovered that when we lost the carport window, the winds extinguished the pilot light in the water heater. Unthinking, I held a lighted match in the small hole to relight it. The explosion burst out through the small bottom hole with sufficient force to fry the bristles on a nearby plastic broom. It charred my thumb and index finger, and I smelled burned hair. Going to the mirror, I found the blast had singed off my eyebrows and frizzled the front of my hair.

A couple of weeks later, I went into the kitchen at night with a flashlight to make some instant coffee, and encountered an astounding number of giant brown spiny-legged cockroaches and small palmetto bugs swarming over the kitchen. *Ugh! Where did all these come from?* They seemed to be particularly centered around the dishwasher. Without water, we had been using paper plates, so I hadn't missed our dishes. I finally realized the dishwasher still held dirty dishes, and robust colonies of roaches had established inside it and between its double walls.

Cockroach brains contain a chemical that makes them light-averse, so we rarely saw roaches in the daytime. It takes about 45 minutes of darkness for the chemical to break down. Then a swarm of cockroaches began emerging from the dishwasher to forage.

They became our nightly entertainment. We waited for them to appear at night and then descended on them with flashlights, cans of Raid, and flyswatters. It was satisfying but, despite valiant efforts, we never entirely eradicated them.

At typhoon signal 3, everyone struggled back to work. It was surprisingly difficult to navigate without the normal subconscious visual cues we use to drive. Public Works had pushed the downed telephone posts, wires and debris off the streets but, with all the street signs missing and so many buildings destroyed, nothing looked familiar. The first day going back to work I missed the turn-off to the office.

Several months later, Tory invited us over for dinner, and his directions sounded like those in a third world country: "Go to the cross-island road, turn right at the big rock, and continue until you see a Siguenza's Wedding sign, then go 300 yards to the abandoned car and turn right ...." It was over a year before we began getting street signs.

At the office, EPA's windows, built for air conditioning, didn't open, and the hot office rapidly became unbearable. The secretaries had recently upgraded from manual typewriters to new electric memory typewriters, but the new typewriters were useless without electricity. The office came to a standstill.

We stood in the parking lot to brainstorm work we could do without electricity. Someone proposed a typhoon impact assessment. We could survey beaches, reefs, and underwater structures for wave erosion, damage, and sedimentation. We loved the suggestion.

The Guam Police gifted EPA a large rubber Zodiac similar to Jacques Cousteau's boat, with three inflatable air chambers and an outboard motor. They had confiscated it in a drug bust, and sliced long gashes in both side chambers to remove the hidden drugs. Although patched, it still leaked slightly. We used it for our dive survey, and began working our way around the coastline. To ensure we didn't miss something, we towed someone behind the boat on a rope with a mask and snorkel, something that today that seems quite foolhardy. During my turn on the rope, the thought came to me that anyone hanging on the rope made attractive shark bait.

The boat worked well for short trips, but on one exceptionally long day it lost more than the usual amount of air. Most of us were sitting along the sides, which weighed down the midsection of the boat, and as the middle sank, it pushed the remaining air in the chambers toward the ends. Both ends lifted out of the water, and the boat became V-shaped. We looked ridiculous, and with the motor now more in the air than the water, maneuvering and steering became impossible. We found ourselves in a swift current off the northern end of the island, beginning to question whether we could even successfully navigate back to shore.

"Everybody move toward the ends to weigh them down," Tory said. We shifted from the middle, and the heaviest of the group volunteered to flatten the bow, making it easier to navigate. She lay draped inelegantly over the bow, reminding me of a beached, sunburned whale.

Surprisingly, the area of most significant coral damage was inside Apra Harbor. In a testament to the typhoon's power, the winds, waves, and storm surge broke a giant oil tanker loose from its moorings and pushed it shoreward. It bulldozed a wide path through the shallow reef, leaving a massive swath of pulverized coral in its wake. Then waves and storm surge lifted the huge tanker out of the water, stranding it high on the reef flat.

The Navy pumped the oil from the tanker but, even empty, its weight and bulk were too great to move, so the tanker remained perched on the reef flat for several years, releasing an oil slick into the water with every tide change.

The typhoon had generated huge waves and heavy surf, so we also checked the island's main sewage outfall. I thought diving for work would be fun, but the Agaña sewage outfall was an exception. Sixty-five feet deep in Agaña Bay, on the edge of the reef terrace, an estimated six to eight million gallons per day of raw sewage billowed from seven large diffusers at the end of a heavy pipe.

We anchored the Zodiac and descended near the outfall, carefully remaining up-current of the thick brown plume. The outfall location was well-chosen; the currents diluted and dissipated the sewage rapidly. This seemed to vindicate the 60's motto "dilution is the solution to pollution," but the volume was low compared to mainland cities, and sewage contained few of the industrial and household chemicals often found in today's wastewater. The new sewage treatment plant would eliminate much of the solid material.

Except for a few feet surrounding the diffusers, the benthic organism density and diversity of corals and sponges looked little different from elsewhere. Large, curious fish glided in and out of the swirling plume. *This beach needs signage, and from now on I'll pass on eating fish from Agaña Bay.*

The pipe looked undamaged, so we returned to the choppy surface. Two-foot waves above the outfall slapped the Zodiac around like a giant rubber ball, making climbing into the boat wearing forty pounds of gear even more difficult than usual. Struggling, I finally hauled myself over the bouncing side and into the boat.

"We should take surface water samples here above the plume to check for potential beach pollution," someone said.

Nothing on the surface indicated the volume of sewage discharging below… until I removed my mask. The stench was overpowering. Already feeling nauseous from exhaustion, like dominoes, George, Izzy, and I all promptly heaved our lunches over the side, and collapsed in the bottom of the boat. Tory watched the boat with binoculars from shore, wondering why everyone had disappeared.

After almost a year, the power plant came back online. The office returned to normal, and we slowly repaired the house. In retrospect, the year without electricity was comparatively painless; nothing qualified as genuine hardship. Guam's weather is warm, and we realized warmth is more critical for comfort than light. We also adjusted quickly to life without air conditioning, carpet, or TV, and I discovered a new appreciation for the military and Red Cross.

But the typhoon left a legacy of unexpected drama in our carport.

- *Thirty-Five* -
Toads in the Carport

Nimitz Hill 1976-1977

THE POISON TOADS PUSHED ME OVER THE EDGE. MOST animals have more intelligence than we give them credit for; they can plan, recognize the difference between objects, and feel emotions. Some even use tools. No one disputes horses, dogs, and other mammals are intelligent, but toads? The toads looked dumb and often acted dumber, but the toads in our carport showed a degree of reasoning and intelligence that left me in awe.

Giant cane toads are invaders. *Bufo marinus* is a particularly large, ugly, bumpy brown toad. When stressed, poison glands on its back exude bufotenine, a white milky poison responsible for killing many of the island's cats and dogs and even an occasional human ignorant enough to eat them. Mistaking them for bullfrogs, some Korean men ate five for dinner. They became quite sick, and one man died.

Toads lay smashed on Guam roads by the hundreds, but most people saw them only when it rained. Then dozens of toads materialized all over our yard. After the typhoon, most disappeared. However, a few discovered the open door in our enclosed carport and moved in.

The carport door remained open because many feral cats called our enclosed carport home. Our problem started with a beautiful, friendly Siamese cat someone abandoned when they left the Island. Abandonment was far too common, and Guam was so overrun with feral dogs and cats that the government conducted an annual 1080 poisoning program to reduce their populations. Since the cat was friendly, we gave her a home in the carport and left the side door open so she could move in and out at will, removing the need for a litter box.

We assumed she was spayed, but soon she presented us with a litter of five kittens. I managed to find homes for all the kittens with my Academy students, but we made a big mistake not spaying her when we had the opportunity. Soon she became pregnant again. This time, I couldn't find takers for all her kittens, so many remained with us, hanging around the carport. Although we fed them, we never established any relationship with them, and all were feral. Soon the kittens grew up and began having kittens too. The cats clearly didn't care about us, but they loved our cat food. We never saw them all together because they spent very little time in the carport, but one day I realized with shock that we were feeding perhaps thirty feral cats, with more soon to follow.

The population was on an exponential growth curve, and the carport teetered on the cusp of a cat explosion. Suddenly, cats were everywhere. Sometimes, a helpless wave of panic swept over me when I saw them all. I had run out of students to take kittens, and we couldn't afford to have them all spayed. At this point, we didn't want any of them, but it didn't feel right to lock them out, sink-or-swim, to fend for themselves among the hordes of other feral animals.

The toads and cats shared the carport with our wrought-iron porch furniture. It usually sat outside on a small concrete patio facing the ocean but, with Typhoon Pamela imminent, we moved it inside, and never got around to moving it back out. We had jammed a chair, the three-seat sofa, and a second chair tightly together along one wall under the windows, next to a short glass side table in the corner. On the adjacent wall, we placed the third chair next to the glass table, followed by a love seat and the fourth chair. The tall, round, glass-topped dining table sat at the very end. Once the typhoon-soaked carpet on the driveway dried out, we rolled it up and stored it underneath the furniture on the window wall. It protruded about a foot out from below the first chair.

One day, hauling a load of laundry to the carport washer, I nearly tripped over a toad. I knew we had a couple but, looking around, I realized toads seemed to enjoy the carport, and more and more were moving in. We now had perhaps 20 resident toads, but I didn't particularly mind them. Since the toads excrete potent poison when attacked or stressed, I even began harboring a few wistful fantasies. *Perhaps the toads will reduce our cat population?* But the cats co-existed amicably with the toads and seemed more interested in our cat food than tangling with the toads, and neither group was pooping in the carport.

When toads began spending time sitting around the cat-food dish, I realized the carport's attraction. *It's expensive enough to feed 30 cats; I'm not feeding a couple of dozen fat toads too.* I moved the cat food dish off the floor and placed it atop the tall round glass table at the end of the second wall. The cats could reach it this way, but the toads, terrible jumpers, could never jump that high. *Problem solved.*

Two days later, my estimation of the toads rose considerably. I entered the carport to find a fat toad sitting atop the tall table in the cat food dish. Even more impressive, it wasn't eating; it was using its large webbed feet to scatter cat food out of the dish onto the floor below, where three other toads sat gazing upward with longing, patiently waiting for a shower of cat food. This was mind boggling. *The toads below could undoubtedly sense the cat food up above, but why would they expect to be fed? And why would the altruistic table toad kick food to other toads below? And most curious of all, how could it possibly have gotten up there?*

As I surveyed the room, on the far side of the garage under the window wall, I saw a toad sitting atop the rolled carpet extending out from beneath the first chair He was eyeing the chair cushion a few inches above him.

Movement caught my eye. Another toad, already on the chair, was actually climbing up the back. I watched in amazement as he hooked his elongated, webbed toes into the metal mesh, and slowly and laboriously pulled himself up the chair back. He struggled to heft his fat body over the top and then, with some effort, plopped down onto the broad windowsill behind the chair. *I would never have believed they could climb like that.* As he clumsily walked the length of the broad windowsill, I suddenly realized, *He's on a journey to the cat food!*

When he reached the end of the sill, he sat staring at the glass end table in the corner and then jumped a few inches down onto it. From the table, it was a short hop down to the abutting chair and loveseat cushion on the adjacent wall. He hopped across the cushions of the chair, the loveseat, and the last chair, and began climbing the mesh backing to get level with the tall round end table holding the cat food.

The toads had mastered the intricate and elaborate obstacle course I had unwittingly created for them. We had created a toad ladder to the cat food: up the carpet roll, chair cushion, and chair back; across the window sill; down to the corner glass end table; across the chair seat, loveseat, and chair seat; up the chair back and onto the tall glass table and cat food. This pathway worked only because the carpet roll helped them access the first chair; the window sill was wide; and the furniture pieces touched each other.

Think about it. Mastering a route going around two sides of the carport took foresight and analytical ability, even some long-range planning. Even more interesting, there must have been some sort of a rational thought process related to helping each other, because when the first toad reached the food on the tall table, instead of hoarding it for himself, he also ensured his pals waiting down below got some too. *Toads with an instinct for cooperation? And how did the three toads below know to wait for a shower of food? Communication?* The more I thought about it, the more impressive it became. *Agile rats and squirrels can master a maze like that, but toads?* The toads had more intelligence than I had given them credit for. I wish digital cameras were available then! I considered writing this up for a journal. *But who would believe it?*

Fascinating as all this was, the toads pushed me over the edge. I was tired of feeding feral cats and tripping over toads. We needed to regain our sanity and our carport. We gave the friendly Siamese to the vet, threw out all the toads, and slammed the carport door, locking out several generations of feral cats to fend for themselves. Heartless? At least a shock, but natural selection needed to operate. Without cat food, the cats, already feral, immediately dispersed without a trace. We breathed a sigh of relief.

As a species, humans, smug in our superiority, tend to underestimate animals. We often assume only mammals and birds have emotions, feelings, and personalities. Yet the toads showed they could reason, plan, communicate, and even help each other out. How else to explain the tabletop toad showering food down to his fellow toads waiting below?

Today, the internet is full of videos of so-called lower animals having the most extraordinary interactions with humans and other species. Amazing stories abound: an octopus who loved her snorkeler friend and would exit her den and wrap her tentacles lovingly around him; the humpback whale who carried a snorkeler back to her boat to save her from a tiger shark; the elephants who came to a human for help when their baby was in trouble; and many others. They show us that many lower species are not only intelligent, but also have emotions and thought processes that we smugly prefer to consider strictly human.

The toads' intelligence was a reminder that most life forms are probably more intelligent than we give them credit for. We are the Earth's stewards, and all species deserve our respect and care, although I do draw the line at armies of cockroaches and ticks in the kitchen, and hordes of snails in the yard. I only hope that someday we don't learn plants have feelings, because then mowing the lawn would be too horrible to contemplate!

- Thirty-Six -

The Blue Hole

Offshore Orote Point 1977

WHEN CARLOS WENT TO FIJI ON BUSINESS, I BOUGHT a Zodiac and motor for $2,000. Carlos isn't a boat lover, and he's predictably negative when it comes to anything mechanical like motors. However, Zodiacs didn't often come available. I knew if I waited, I'd lose the chance. So, I grabbed it. Sure enough, when Carlos returned, he gave the boat only a disinterested glance and dismissed it with a tinge of annoyance in his voice.

"It's a waste of money. I'm never going to drive it." I expected this response, and was ready.

"You won't have to. And I'll have so many dive buddies I won't have to drive it either." A boat allowed access to some of the offshore wrecks and more isolated areas, and as predicted, I never lacked for dive buddies.

Almost immediately our friend Will noticed the boat. "I've always wanted to dive the Blue Hole," he said.

I'd been there before with George. The Blue Hole lies outside the mouth of Apra Harbor, below the steep cliffs of Orote Point. There, 300-foot cliffs plunge almost straight down into the water, making the site only accessible by boat. Offshore, at a depth of about 65 feet, an elongated, heart-shaped hole in the reef terrace provides entrance to a vertical shaft descending another 230 feet down inside the reef. The shaft gradually widens as it descends, ending on a flat sandy bottom inside the reef, at about 300 feet. Yet it's not dark, because at 125 feet, a slit-like split in the shaft wall opens out onto the wall of a vertical submarine cliff, and continues down another 175 feet, to the bottom of the hole.

The Blue Hole dive is deceptive, because the dive tends to feel it begins when you enter the shaft but, in reality, the entrance is already 65 feet deep, about the depth of an average Guam dive. Guam's exceptional 200-foot visibility and underwater magnification also make depth deceptive; the 300-foot bottom looks closer than expected. Because light enters the slit, the bottom is visible from the moment you enter the shaft.

One man supposedly drowned at the Blue Hole when he dropped his dive knife and went to the bottom of the hole to retrieve it. That wasn't a rational decision. He was either a bit narked, or he forgot the depth, but he lost more than his knife on that dive.

At depth, nitrogen narcosis affects the brain, and skews the thinking. On several occasions, after surfacing, I realized some things I did hadn't made much sense. Once, we planned a 60-foot dive, but I spent the entire dive at 80 feet because my depth gauge was defective. I couldn't understand why everyone stayed so far above me, yet somehow, I never thought to go up to their level to see why they didn't descend. And they didn't think to descend and show me their depth gauges or tell me come up, either.

Impaired thinking at depth became more obvious when I took notes underwater. My notes seemed normal while taking them, but the effect of depth became obvious once I surfaced. The first notes were clear and complete but, the longer I stayed down, the sloppier they became, until the last entries became little more than scrawls, with half the data missing.

On a sparkling sunny morning, Will and I motored the Zodiac out of Apra Harbor and around the massive vertical cliffs of Orote Point to the vicinity of the hole. Although the hole was on the deep end of the dive spectrum, the dive itself was straightforward. Our dive plan was simple: anchor near the top of the hole and slowly descend into the shaft, checking the wall for unusual species of corals, sea fans, sea whips, and other organisms only seen in deeper water. When we reached 125 feet, at the top of the slit, we would exit the shaft onto the cliff face, hang around on the cliff for a few minutes to see what swam by, and then surface, a maximum dive time of perhaps twenty-five minutes.

Outside on the smooth vertical cliff face at about 130 feet, with your back to the cliff, hanging suspended in the empty greenish void, nothing is visible but water fading into nothingness in all directions. With nothing to focus on, it could be somewhat eerie and disorienting. The longer light wavelengths are already absorbed, so the predominant color is greenish. Outside the slit, looking outward and downward, the cliff face continues down hundreds of feet, fading into the green depths and disappearing into the gloom below. Bathymetry maps show a 600-foot contour in the vicinity that may mark the bottom of the cliff.

Having no reference points always felt somewhat unsettling but, if time permitted, I enjoyed hanging out on the cliff face for a few minutes near the top of the slit, watching to see what came swimming by. The excitement was in the unexpected. Often very large fish passed by, and once, I watched in awe as enormous shadowy shapes silently glided by, almost out of sight, and tantalizingly just beyond my ability to identify them. I assumed they were whales.

We dropped anchor near the Blue Hole, swam down 65 feet to the reef flat, and anchored the boat securely near the entrance. Then we started down the shaft inside the reef. Many sea fans growing on the walls aren't found in lighter, shallower depths, so those were my main focus, and I descended slowly.

Suddenly Will grabbed my arm and pointed downward in excitement. Over two hundred feet below us, the largest manta ray I'd ever seen was swimming around and around in lazy circles in the bottom of the shaft. Manta rays, the world's largest ray, have 'wingspans' up to 29 feet and weigh up to 5,300 pounds, yet they are gentle plankton eaters. Watching it glide gracefully and effortlessly through the water was almost mesmerizing.

But we'd seen mantas before, and it swam at 300 feet. *We can't get much closer to it anyhow.* I watched it for a bit, and returned my focus to the rare sea fans on the walls. When I turned around to show Will a particularly unusual sea fan, he was no longer with me. Buddies were supposed to stay together, but often he wasn't very good at that. I looked around, not seeing him. Then I looked down. He was already forty feet below me, dropping like a stone toward the manta, and about to pass the 125-foot slit opening. Apparently intent on the manta, he was heading to the bottom with no thought for the depth or our dive plan.

I rushed down after him, aware of nitrogen narcosis and the bends. *When should I stop? How deep am I willing to go before I stop chasing him and let him go?*

The U.S. Navy considers 130 feet the limit for no-decompression dives[13], and training establishes it as the depth limit for normal recreational diving. Few recreational divers ever go deeper than 125 feet because depth uses up air faster, reduces dive time, and may require decompression.

I decided if I couldn't catch him at 150 feet, I wouldn't go deeper but, at 150 feet I was closing in. He continued dropping, his eyes focused on the manta. *He's forgotten the depth, and heading for the bottom,* I thought. *If I don't stop him soon, this can't end well.* I grabbed the tip of his fin at 170 feet. Startled, he turned, first in alarm, then in surprise, to see me. I pointed to his depth gauge. Even through his mask, I saw his eyes widen in shock.

Without decompression tables, rather than guessing at decompression depths and times, we aborted the dive and surfaced, shortening our dive considerably. On surfacing, he ripped off his mask, still shocked.

"I was going for the bottom…" He was in disbelief.

"I know. And you almost got your wish. I'm not sure how deep I would have gone to catch you." I still wonder about that.

He had forgotten our dive plan, and probably also forgotten that when we entered the hole, we were already at 65 feet. Luckily, I noticed him when I did, because any later, he could have been too far ahead to catch, and if he had reached the manta, I doubt he would have returned. Oxygen toxicity sets in around 220 feet[11]; 300 feet is much too deep for diving on normal air. It would not have ended well.

Unfortunately, we had to skip hanging outside on the cliff in open water. I found that part the most interesting, because there we expected the unexpected. But I expected few surprises inside the dirtier waters of Apra Harbor.

- *Thirty-Seven* -
The Black Hole

Apra Harbor 1978

EVERY TIME I BEGAN A DIVE, I HOPED TO SEE A GIANT
shark, not as a caudal fin disappearing into the distance, but close-up.
Yet after almost 200 dives, it had never happened. Sharks were there, of
course, but most were skittish, saw people first, and disappeared. Other
people often saw small sharks that I missed, because I focused on the
bottom, with its diverse fish and invertebrates, oblivious to things farther
away in the water column. I assumed when I saw a large shark it would be
in open water, maybe along the reef slope with the big fish.

Guam's Apra Harbor is a large deep-water harbor enclosed on one side
by a long artificial rock breakwater. The same characteristics that make
it a good harbor also restrict water movement and reduce water quality.
Industrial facilities line the edges of the Harbor, so stormwater and wash-
water runoff from a power plant, a large military complex, and Guam's
Commercial Port, the busiest port in the Marianas Islands, all contribute
toxics, dirt, and debris. Much of the turbid harbor water is also filled with
bits of floating detritus and filmy whitish material shed by the surviving
stressed corals. Reduced visibility makes many parts feel gloomy.

Apra wasn't typically a pretty dive, but the Harbor's main attrac-
tions weren't marine life. Wrecks from two World Wars and numerous
typhoons littered the bottom. Their ghostly, coral-encrusted outlines
silently emerged from the murky greenish depths, and eerily faded into

the distance, reflecting little of the noise, fire, confusion and death that attended their sinking.

Along the breakwater, near the harbor mouth, lay a huge American water tanker we called the cement barge, because the surface was cement. The top deck lay at about 65 feet, an oasis of solid substrate on the otherwise silty-sand bottom. It provided an attachment for algae, sponges, corals, and other sedentary organisms that attracted fish. We decided to dive it.

I'm somewhat uneasy suspended in the water when I can't see the bottom. I feel vulnerable, like a piece of bait, and I'm relieved when the bottom comes into view, and I become part of the ecosystem.

As we descended through the turbid water, the cement barge began emerging into view. The yellowish light filtering down illuminated the deck and a gigantic, circular black hole that had probably caused its sinking. We touched down on the deck near the hole. From the edge, I peered down into the inky darkness inside.

No one I knew had ever gone down inside, or even swum across the hole, and I could see why. Even looking into the pitch-black hole from the deck always made me uneasy. Blackness shrouded the unknown. Anything could be down there. *You've seen too many monster movies*, I told myself. It brought back memories of the Illinois peat bog dive but, here, the possibility of something unfriendly inside was very real. In some inexplicable way, the hole felt ominous. I often have a sixth sense about danger, and I'd learned to pay attention to it.

I'd been on the barge several times, but now, for the first time I noticed a giant vase sponge growing on the far side of the hole. *Why hadn't I ever noticed it before?* I decided to check it out. My buddy, seemingly ignorant of the buddy concept, was already on the other side of the barge, staring over the edge into the deeper water, oblivious to my location. We should stay closer together but, we could still see each other.

On the bottom, anything in the water column is easily seen from beneath, because it's silhouetted against the brighter surface above. Over the hole I would feel like bait because I knew I would be quite visible to anything down inside, so I never gave it a second thought or debated; I instinctively swam around it.

This time, although it looked as unknown and forbidding as usual, for some odd reason, despite my uneasiness, as I peered down into the inky darkness, I felt oddly urged to swim across it. Yet uncomfortable, I began swimming around it by habit, and had gone perhaps a quarter way around the hole. *This is ridiculous. I should cross it, conquer my fear. What are the chances anything unfriendly is below and looking up at this moment? How long will I be exposed anyhow? A couple of minutes? It only seems scary because it's pitch black.*

Almost feeling propelled, I found myself turning and swimming toward the edge of the hole, perhaps six feet ahead. *What am I doing?* Yet, pushing down my irrational fear, eyes downward on the barge surface, I started across the inky blackness, arms and legs dangling like pieces of bait. But almost immediately, instead of looking down into the blackness, I was above something solid. *Didn't I already start across the hole? I should be looking down at blackness.* Apparently, I hadn't reached the edge. The mask restricted my view to an oval in front of my face, so I raised my head to look forward. The gaping edge of the hole was still several feet ahead, yet the hole extended behind me on both sides. *I should be over the hole.* It was disorienting.

I realized I was above a broad, somewhat rounded blunt object extending several feet out from below the broken deck. Somehow, I'd never noticed it earlier. It was wider than I and about three feet right below me. In the filtered light, the flat, smooth surface appeared similar in color to the silty barge deck. *It's too wide to be a protruding broken cement beam. I don't remember ever seeing anything in the hole before.* But it felt comforting to be above something other than open blackness.

Not wanting to linger there, I continued swimming but wasn't getting any closer to the end of the beam. *What IS this? Why didn't I notice it earlier?* Disoriented, I turned my head sideways to recheck the location of the hole, just in time to see five gigantic gill slits slowly gliding through my field of vision, two or three feet below my right shoulder.

The impact registered with shock: *Gill slits?! I'm right above a truly massive shark!* I'd never seen such gigantic gill slits. They looked over a foot long, and opened far wider than I expected. I could look directly down inside and watch the five white cartilaginous branchial arches and gill rakers moving back and forth in synchronized motion, so close I could almost reach down and touch them. I was surprised to feel only a focused calm. I was wary, but not particularly fearful.

Gill rakers vary by species. Fish with densely spaced, comb-like gill rakers filter tiny prey, but carnivores have more widely spaced gill rakers. The scientist piece of me couldn't help analyzing them. *These. Are. Really. Widely. Spaced. It's a gigantic carnivore, and its slow cruising indicates it's hunting.*

That broke my focus. *The mouth! Where's the mouth?* Raising my head to look forward, now I recognized what I originally thought to be a cement chunk was actually the top of a massive head with a broad, rather blunt snout, so large it filled my entire mask. It seemed oblivious to my presence. I couldn't see the dark, lidless black eyes on the sides of its head. *Good. Then it can't see me either.* Going eyeball to eyeball with its vacant stare was the last thing I wanted; I didn't trust how I would react. Yet somehow, I sensed a presence watching out for me.

The five gray gill covers rhythmically opened and closed in unison as the shark took in water through its mouth and pumped it out through the gills. The surprisingly delicate edge of gray skin on the smooth covers rippled slightly as they closed. I looked down into the highly-vascularized purple interior. *This would look blood red in shallower water.* All five sets of arches moved in precision, like gears in a machine. I was mesmerized. The only branchial arches I had ever seen were in dead fish; seeing them move was like watching a choreographed ballet.

I realized I had been holding my breath, and now my breathing had become oddly synchronized with his. As the gill covers closed, and it took in water through its mouth, I inhaled. As the gill covers opened to expel water, I exhaled. I felt cautious but, oddly, not afraid. I felt almost a oneness with it.

But I couldn't swim with it forever. *How can I separate from it without being noticed?* I didn't know, but, for the moment, being behind the mouth, out of sight of the eyes, and away from the lateral line system all seemed like good things. *I'm in the perfect spot to be invisible,* I thought.

And then, reality hit. *Who am I kidding? Of course, it knows I'm here! I'm right above the head, which has the largest concentration of sensory cells on the body.* The ampullae of Lorenzini, a series of pores on a shark's head, detect tiny electrical impulses from prey, and the lateral line system along the sides is very sensitive to vibrations in the water. These adaptations allow a shark to hunt in darkness and detect hidden prey, which probably explains why it didn't mind swimming inside the pitch-black barge. It knew I was there, but at the top of the food chain, it didn't feel threatened.

I briefly considered stopping to let it go on ahead, but realized I couldn't. Large dorsal and caudal fins were right behind me, and I didn't want to advertise my presence by kicking them. I had no time to turn around and look for them, and I certainly didn't want to alert the lateral line system by dodging to the side and disturbing the water, so I continued swimming along on top of it, trying to figure what to do. In fact, to avoid the fins, I realized I should speed up slightly to keep pace with the moving gill slits. I swam along, schooling with the shark, trying not to make too many vibrations or kick it with my fins.

It was confident, massive. I didn't know why I felt so calm, but I felt thankful for it. Sharks can't smell fear, but they can sense heartbeat and movement, and are sensitive to electrical fields. It's believed they associate fear with weakness, and weakness with opportunity. I was well aware of being opportunity.

I flattened out, instinctively reducing my leg movements to slow, rhythmic straight-legged strokes, and pulling my dangling arms in close to my sides; no point in advertising my presence by trolling. For lack of other options, I kept moving. *What do I do if it decides to exit the hole?* We continued to school together until we reached the cement deck on the other side of the hole. Then it continued on underneath, slowly cruising into the blackness below on the other side. I continued on above-deck.

I wish I had turned to observe the rest of the shark, but suddenly I became intent on putting distance between me and the hole. I swam over to hide behind the giant sponge, watching the hole, half expecting the shark to come out at any moment. When it didn't, I skirted around the hole, and went to find my buddy, so far away that he had missed everything.

Back at the dive shop, I described what little I saw of the shark to Willie, the shop owner, but I was too close to have seen much.

"How big was it?"

All I could estimate, having seen only a piece of it, was to unscientif-ically classify it as 'gigantic.' I could swim with my head and shoulders adjacent to the gill slits without kicking the dorsal fin with my fins. It was much broader than I; looking straight down from three feet above it, the snout filled my entire mask. That's all I knew.

"Do you have any idea what kind it was?"

"Given the size, either a great white, a bull, or a tiger shark," Willie said.

All are large, often very aggressive, and none are particularly friendly, but great whites are rare on Guam, and their snouts are more pointed than this shark. Tigers and bull sharks have broad and somewhat blunt snouts. I never saw the side, where a light stripe-like pattern could definitively confirm a tiger.

Size was a good indicator. Bull sharks average eight to ten feet. The tiger gets much larger, and its dorsal fin is located farther toward the tail than other species, which would allow my feet more room to move without kicking it. Tigers estimated sixteen to eighteen feet long have been doc-umented,[12] and some unverified reports describe individuals up to twen-ty-four feet long. Given those factors, a tiger shark, *Galeocerdo cuvier*, appears most likely.

Tigers are large, solitary, primarily nocturnal species, so it wouldn't mind the dark inside of the barge, and they're known to frequent harbors and river mouths. That fit. They're garbage eaters, and will eat almost any-thing. Inedible items, including oil cans, and incredibly, even tires, have been found in their stomachs. I remembered the tiger shark in Hawaii, with the human pelvis.

Miles, another dive buddy, later said, "Once I saw a gigantic shark swimming alongside the cement barge on the bottom," so maybe it hung out there more than we knew. In later dives on the barge, I kept a sharp eye out, and swam around the hole, but I never saw it again.

The next time we dove there, the beautiful giant sponge had disappeared. I couldn't even find evidence of its attachment on the deck.

Later I thought about the encounter. What amazing timing! The shark was swimming inside the barge, right below the deck, at my exact speed, at the same place and time I was swimming on the deck surface right above it. Timing synchronized to the second, we both arrived at the hole at the same exact place and almost the same time. If I'd started crossing from my original location, instead of starting to swim around the edge, or had been ahead of it, or off to the side, and therefore in his field of vision, I might have looked appetizing. If he had been farther ahead of me, I'd have seen the fin and definitely avoided the hole.

But my unnatural calm was interesting. I had felt cautious but not fearful. The shark would surely have sensed a fearful heartbeat, with unknown results. Although it sounds illogical, I swam with more comfort over the shark's head than over the open unknown of the black hole. Seeing and knowing what I was facing, was preferable to imagining unseen, unknown danger lurking somewhere. But I never would have imagined anything so huge.

God has a great sense of humor, and I suspect sometimes He takes pleasure in giving us experiences, simply to please us. He knew how much I wanted to see a big shark, and I can almost envision Him saying, "You want to see a big shark? OK, I'll show you one! A special glimpse, so you can appreciate how intricately I made it." Of course, perhaps it was merely a random coincidence, but location and timing were perfect, rather like the big wave that saved my class, or my hiring at the Academy. Were they all just amazing coincidences? Maybe. Yet I think often what we call coincidences are simply times where we have an unexpected glimpse of an unseen hand moving behind events, orchestrating part of an as-yet unrevealed plan.

- *Thirty-Eight* -
Open Water

Offshore Guam 1978

HOW IS IT POSSIBLE TO GET LOST IN THE OCEAN IN thirty-five feet of water? A series of underwater reef terraces surrounds much of Guam. The first terrace gradually slopes downward to 60-65 feet deep, and then perhaps a couple hundred feet offshore, it drops steeply down to a lower terrace. The drop-off roughly follows shoreline contours, so it's difficult to get lost underwater, because if you swim perpendicular to the drop-off, you'll reach shore.

My dive buddy Jerry said, "You want to try a dive in Cocos Lagoon?"

"Sure," I said. "I've never been there."

On Guam's southern tip, a large shallow shelf about thirty-five feet deep extends out for several miles, with no abrupt drop-off or depth change near shore for orientation. Cocos Island, a one-hundred-acre sliver of long, flat barrier reef lying in the southwest corner, is the only structure in the lagoon. At that time, Cocos was barren except for the crumbled remains of a former Coast Guard LORAN station and a toxic legacy of PCBs.

"Water entry should be easy. Waves are small, and there aren't any jagged reef edges to cross. This should be an easy dive."

"Let's just head straight out and see what's there."

We headed out straight west, perpendicular to shore, without any predetermined destination in mind, only wanting to see the area. The sun sparkled on the clear, bright water, and depth remained about 35 feet everywhere. At that shallow depth, it felt safe. But the one predictable thing about ocean diving is that it's unpredictable. One moment everything is fine, and then in an instant, everything spins out of control.

The lagoon was disappointing. It was flat, without surge channels or coral outcroppings. We saw few large corals or other sea life of interest. We hardly even saw fish. *This sure is a boring dive,* I thought. *All the low, stubby corals and small algae covering the bottom indicate strong currents prevent larvae from settling.* Yet I felt no current.

However, soon the algae below us began bending in the current, and tiny sand grains began bumping along over the bottom. A surprising, strong current began pushing us, too, making swimming easy. We hardly needed to kick as we moved almost effortlessly across the bottom. We went with the current, hoping to see something better a bit farther out. Unnoticed, the current now carried us southwest, away from the island, as we swam.

After a while, something didn't feel quite right. Jerry pointed upward, signaling to surface. I nodded, wanting to check our position. On the surface, we stared in shock. My stomach lurched. We couldn't see land. Anywhere. *No Guam. Not even Cocos Island.* How could that be? Even from the shore, we could see Cocos. Now we saw nothing but long, rolling waves, in every direction.

"Where's Guam?" My stomach clenched up.

"It's still shallow, so we're still in the lagoon."

"I guess. But which way is shore?"

"You look that way, I'll look this." With a sinking feeling, back-to-back, we turned around scanning the horizon. Nothing but waves. That was disorienting. Near land, waves move toward the shoreline, so you can follow them in, but without land to block them, waves on open water come from several directions. We should be near Cocos Island, but couldn't see that either. *We're adrift at sea, without reference points. And a strong current is carrying us somewhere.* Two small divers, pinpoints in a vast ocean. Small tentacles of fear tickled my brain.

At this point, a bit late, I realized something I had never realized before; we were too low in the water. Something easily seen from a boat riding above the waves is often impossible to see with eyes less than a foot above the water surface. Swells higher than our eyes would obscure anything on the horizon unless it was either close-by and tall, or the waves aligned perfectly, enabling us to look along a wave trough. Guam's highest point was only about 1000 feet high, and Cocos was almost flat. Both could easily be seen from aboard a Zodiac, but not from so low in the water.

Uncomfortable memories of a movie I'd seen of people adrift at sea, encircled by sharks, flashed unbidden into my mind. We suddenly felt achingly alone.

The lagoon extended about four miles offshore. I assumed we were at least a couple of miles out, but we weren't stationary. Every minute the strong current was carrying us farther offshore. Cocos Lagoon lies on Guam's southern tip; we wouldn't be west offshore of the island for long. *The current will sweep us past the island entirely, if it hasn't already done so. But exactly where is the island?* If we couldn't locate it, the next land mass was over 1000 miles away. I pushed back the sliver of fear nibbling at the edge of my brain, needing to focus. Panic wasn't something we could afford. We continued to scan the horizon.

After what seemed like an eternity, the waves lined up perfectly, and Jerry happened to be looking in the right place at the right time. For only a brief second, he caught a glimpse of shoreline, so low on the water he almost missed it.

"I see it! It's over there!" I turned, staring northward at the horizon, but the waves had again obscured it from view.

"Are you sure? I don't see anything."

Then, only for a second, waves aligned. I glimpsed a hazy, thin, purplish sliver of shoreline, so low on the horizon it was almost invisible. I was stunned. "What's it doing there, so small? And so far north?"

"There's nothing else. That's got to be Guam."

We had begun swimming perpendicular to shore, but now we were south of the island, a couple of miles offshore at least. Guam looked so tiny and remote. If I didn't know better, I would have thought it ten miles away.

I don't know which emotion was stronger, relief at locating the island or shock at seeing how far offshore we had come.

We were fortunate to surface when we did; much longer, and we would never have seen Guam at all. Barring an unexpected rescue, we could have been toast. Now that we knew the general direction back, logic kicked in, pushing away fear. We debated on the easiest way to get back.

"It will be confusing to orient on the surface with nothing to look at but moving waves," I said. Although inflated buoyancy compensators could keep us afloat if needed, trying to battle waves and surface currents while swimming in them is difficult. We could conceivably expend a great deal of energy yet make little progress.

"Swimming on the surface is hard work with a 30-pound tank and ten pounds of lead weight dragging us down. It's easier to move underwater."

Then we realized we could probably find our way without seeing land. "If a strong bottom current brought us here, submerging and swimming against it should lead us back." Assuming we had enough air. Swimming back against the current would be exhausting.

We decided to go to the bottom and head in what we hoped to be a straight line toward where we had seen land. *If we run out of air, we can surface and swim for it, if we are close enough to see land by then, and we can even ditch the empty tanks if necessary.* Facing toward where we had glimpsed the island, we submerged, and adrenalin spurred us on.

To swim in a straight line, I mentally lined up three bottom features on the reef that formed a line pointing toward shore. As I reached one point, I added another point to continue the line. (Thank you, Geometry 101.) This reassured me we were weren't going in circles. I just hoped the initial direction was still correct.

Fortunately, we were both calm, and knowing my limits made me confident. I have strong legs, and if I could see it, I knew with fins, I could swim it. On long, sustained swimming or biking, after an initial effort, my legs and breathing tend to fall into an almost automatic cadence. At that point, once I'm 'in the zone,' my legs move as if on auto-pilot, and then I feel as if they can continue moving almost mindlessly forever. I focused on maintaining the direction, and blocked out nagging stray thoughts. *You can do this*, I told myself.

Swimming against the strong current was exhausting. In places, I nearly had to pull myself along the bottom. The current helped us orient; as long as we swam against it, we hoped we were more or less retracing our former route.

After perhaps fifteen minutes of hard swimming, we surfaced to check our position. *I only hope we can see land, and that it's closer now. If not, we're in trouble.* With great relief, we immediately saw Guam, still distant, but no longer a thin purple line, now we could at least distinguish mountains and some color.

"We're on track! There it is!"

"It's still a long way off, but we've made a lot of progress!" Even now, we were still much farther offshore than I had ever been, even in a boat, but at least we were headed in the right direction

Thankfully, a tank of air lasts a long time at 35 feet, and we expended little energy on the way out. Tiring, but now encouraged and grateful for fins, we submerged again, swimming determinedly perhaps another fifteen minutes. The current began dropping off, and corals became more common. Finally, the shelf became shallower, signaling the approach of shore. At last, with a sigh of relief, we staggered onto the beach, dropped our gear, and collapsed on the sand. After a couple of minutes, we lugged our gear back to the car and drove perhaps only a block before I said "Stop the car!" And I heaved up my breakfast from exhaustion.

On reflection, we should have checked currents before going to a new spot. We knew better. A compass would have been helpful too, although I'd never been in a position to need one before. We might also have inquired about conditions inside the Lagoon, and the best places to go. A couple of good patches for diving do exist near Cocos Island, but no one goes there without a boat, and I hadn't bought mine yet.

***

Flash forward fourteen years. Jerry was now president of a large consulting firm, and I was managing the EPA Region 10 Underground Storage Tank Program. My friend Denise and I bumped into him at a Seattle conference.

"We were diving partners; I saved her life once," he announced almost gleefully.

"Yeah, right," I said, laughing. Then, I realized he was probably right. As we treaded water adrift far from land, being swept out into open ocean, by lucky chance he had managed to spot the thin line of Guam on the horizon. If he hadn't caught that split-second glimpse, we might have ended up as fish food.

- *Thirty-Nine* -
Apocalypse

<u>**Guam 1977**</u>

HOW CAN YOU CHANGE SOMEONE'S THINKING? OVER the last ten years, we had begun communicating with Mom and Dad by cassette tapes, rather than letters. Now that he didn't have to write, Dad became involved with the tapes, and in almost every tape, he continued to ask, "When are you coming home?" I think he sensed his years were limited.

Maintaining relationships requires communication, but I felt our communication was one-sided. Although we tried to tell them about our life, they saw everything through a Midwest filter. If we said "We had a great trip to Saipan," I would think they might respond by asking something like "What was it like?" But instead, their response was "That's nice. We have a new gas station on Main Street now." Either they had no interest, or they still couldn't relate to our lives enough to even ask basic questions.

We had returned to Glen Ellyn twice, both times on Citibank money, but my parents never once mentioned they wished they could come see us. This annoyed me. I knew their money was tight, but they were only two, and we were four. We decided to force the issue.

"Let's send them tickets," Carlos said. So unannounced, we sent them two plane tickets to Guam, with a note saying, "If you want to see us, you need to come here."

We didn't hear anything for some time. Then Lynn called me at work. "Dad's liver is failing; he's in the hospital, not expected to live. I thought you might want to come home." That explained their delayed response.

The two tickets had left us no money. I felt conflicted; either we could go home, or they could come over. Not both. *Should we change the tickets to our names, and go home, perhaps to see Dad for the last time? If he recovered, they wouldn't have tickets to come visit. Or should we remain in Guam, leave the tickets with them, and gamble he would recover enough to be able to visit?* I desperately wanted them both to have a chance for their first, and probably only, big trip. Praying for dad's recovery and wisdom on how to proceed, the answer seemed to be, "Stay; wait for his recovery." So, we did. Against all odds, amazing the doctors, he rallied within the week.

Mom and Dad hadn't traveled anywhere in years, and never more than a few hundred miles from home. Dad, formerly the trip initiator, was now unsure about traveling anywhere, but Mom became assertive. "We're going, and stopping a few days in Hawaii too."

Pagsanjan

Back in the Philippines, once the Paco house sold, Victor, Mario and Fe moved to Pagsanjan. Using my friend Lori's Makati house plans, Mario built a modern American-style house in a 10-acre field near Pagsanjan. Mario liked privacy, so he placed the house well back from the street, at the end of a long gravel driveway, and shielded it with bamboo, fruit trees, and coconut palms. The large *sala* and covered back porch were pleasant for entertaining. and the modern kitchen was comfortable to cook in, although a dirty kitchen, where most of the cooking actually happened, soon sprouted up outside. The American style and secluded surroundings were unusual for the area.

When she saw his new house, Solita asked rhetorically, "If my children have nice houses, why shouldn't I?" She demolished the old wooden stilt house, replaced it with a concrete house, and began building a new rural bank, too.

Then an American movie studio arrived to film *Apocalypse Now*, a war movie directed by Francis Ford Coppola, starring Marlon Brando, Martin Sheen, and Robert Duvall. Coppola wanted a place resembling the movie's Cambodian environment, and found it in the jungle-lined gorge along the Pagsanjan River in Dingin, a barrio of Pagsanjan.

The movie crew rented houses during production. Perhaps because of the newer features, relative privacy, and space for entertaining, Coppola's production designer, Dean Tavoularis, liked Mario's house, and offered him P8,000 pesos a month. This was a windfall in 1976. Mario and Fe jumped at his offer, and moved out to a small house on the edge of their property for the year. Once *Apocalypse* filming ended, the movie crew went home, but left their impressive, authentic-looking movie set on the river bank for several months, in case they needed to reshoot a scene or two.

Guam

Dad recovered and finally, ten years after I left, Dad and Mom came to visit. They disembarked from the plane, visibly apprehensive, but they relaxed once we brought them home. For a week, we toured the island and had beach picnics, quite a contrast to the freezing Chicago winter at home. They reacquainted with Lisa and David, now eight and six, experienced the island lifestyle, and saw our home. I told them about diving and my job as safe drinking water section chief. Now I hoped they could at least better visualize the things we talked about.

"I guess you've made your mark," he said, sounding satisfied, as if he had been waiting for that.

One sunny morning, as I packed the kids and a beach picnic into the car, perhaps remembering our family beach trips to Michigan, Dad sighed, and said with a tinge of sadness, "Well, I guess nobody needs me anymore."

"Mom needs you," I said. Yet I couldn't help thinking, *But there were years when we did need you, and you weren't there for us. Now, forced to be sober, would he ever realize what a toll his alcohol had taken on the family?* My own buried bitterness for both his lost years and ours, surprised me.

Pagsanjan

This trip was the only time my parents would have to meet Carlos' parents, see the Philippines, and the other half of our life. With his American passport, now Carlos could finally go home to the Philippines without paying the income tax levied on overseas Filipinos. We decided to all fly to Manila for a week.

We spent a few days in Manila, braving reckless taxi rides, touring Corregidor and the old city of Intramuros, seeing the church where we were married, and our Marcelo house. We stayed in Makati, no longer a thin line of buildings in the middle of rice fields, but now a large modern metropolis of shopping malls, theaters, restaurants, and businesses. We stayed in the InterContinental hotel. They didn't seem to have expected any of this.

Solita invited us to Pagsanjan for the town fiesta. As we drove the sixty miles south to Pagsanjan, and the Makati traffic and crowded urban areas gradually transitioned to the slow life of the province, I realized rural provincial life was obviously more what they had expected: mountains, coconut fields, women washing clothes in the rivers, and water buffalo plowing rice paddies.

Both parents had been so quiet most of the drive, I found their lack of questions puzzling. I wondered, *Are they in culture shock?* We passed through the large historic stone gate marking Pagsanjan's entrance and started down the main street. Now Dad looked around. "What's all this construction?"

"That's Solita's new bank."

"She works in a bank?"

"No, she owns the bank." I watched him absorbing this surprise.

"What's going on over there, next door?"

"She's building a new house, too." He didn't know what to say; he clearly hadn't expected this. Perhaps he expected only poor people living in small huts. It was beginning to dawn on him possibly the Cabrezas had more money than he did.

As we watched, an interesting transformation began. Dad, normally life of the party, almost seemed to shrink in stature. He became quiet, perhaps even a bit apprehensive. We pulled up to the house and introduced the Cabrezas. Solita, outgoing and hospitable, always welcomed visitors, but Victor was unpredictable. When asked to go somewhere or meet someone new, his dry response was often a terse, "It's an ordeal," and he disappeared into his bedroom, so we were unsure what to expect.

Now, to our surprise, he became an expansive host, jovial, welcoming, and outgoing. We watched in astonishment at the two dads in total role reversal. My parents seemed almost tongue-tied. Predictably, Victor said, "I can die now since I've met Joan's parents."

That night, the town fiesta culminated in a very long, solemn religious procession. It seemed nearly the entire town, mostly dressed in white, silently walked along the main street carrying lighted candles. Large, elaborately decorated statues of saints and the Virgin Mary, extracted from the local church, rode transported on motorized trailers for the occasion. I'm not sure my parents knew what to make of the procession.

The following day, we all took the banca ride to the waterfall. They sat uneasily in their small narrow banca, looking a bit apprehensive, as the banqueros paddled us upstream through the jungle-lined gorge, over the seven sets of rapids to Pagsanjan Falls. Our timing was fortunate; the movie set of *Apocalypse Now* still remained intact. Although only wood, canvas and plaster, the impressive complex of ancient Cambodian temple ruins along the river looked convincingly old and authentic. It was good enough to fool the uninitiated, and had been carefully situated around a river bend for maximum visual effect.

Paddling around the bend, the vine-covered 'stone' ruins loomed into sight. Glen Ellyn had nothing exotic like this. Awed, Dad grabbed his Super 8 movie camera to catch them on film. Eventually, we told him it was a movie set but, somehow in his mind, they remained authentic ruins.

It later occurred to me perhaps neither of them had ever been in a dugout canoe before. In fact, I wasn't sure they knew how to swim, so perhaps shooting the small rapids on the return trip was a bit scary. Certainly, this type of experience was totally foreign to both of them. It was quite safe but, probably to them, it felt like a risky adventure. *Good.*

Glen Ellyn

After two weeks, we drove them to the Guam airport to return home. Considering how seldom we saw them, we hoped they would stay for Christmas, but they seemed determined to leave. It had been nice. I realized I had never really known my parents as an adult. It was also the first time in years I had actually talked to Dad without a veil of alcohol between us.

Later, my brother Phil told me that after Mom and Dad returned home, for the remainder of his life, Dad talked about the fantastic trip and the temple ruins in Pagsanjan. Significantly, he also told Phil, "Now I see why she doesn't come home." And he never pestered me about returning again.

That surprised me. *Why did he think I had left?* I even wondered if perhaps all these years he felt guilty, wondering whether his alcoholism was a factor in my leaving. But now, he finally understood I had escaped the Midwest in search of something more. He had learned I could live a good life apart from Glen Ellyn. He saw I was diving and traveling, and having adventures I had always needed, and could never have easily had back home.

For my part, I realized his concern over our long-distance separation had long since eclipsed any initial racist objections he may have had to our marriage.

Chuck Missler, one of my favorite writers, said, "The only barrier to truth is the presumption that you already have it.[15]" Presumption implies a closed mind. Exposure to new views, people, and experiences are the best way to pry open closed minds. The trip did that for my parents. I hoped now they could visualize our lives enough to understand some things we talked about, and maybe even muster enough curiosity to ask a question or two.

During the trip they saw the *Apocalypse* ruins but, ironically, I believe they also had a personal apocalypse. "Apocalypse" derives from a Greek word meaning an unveiling, or revelation, but it can also mean destruction.

I believe the trip was both a destruction and an unveiling for them. The trip destroyed their previous assumptions and stereotyped ideas of Asia, and also unveiled our lives for them, stripping away their unfounded concerns and hopefully replacing them with positive images. Little was as they assumed, and Dad seemed reassured. He had lived ten years with skewed perceptions and unnecessary fears. I was so thankful we had sent them tickets. I only wish we had been done it sooner.

***

We would see Mom again, but not Dad. Now that cirrhosis forced him to stop drinking, our former neighbors, the Carps, dragged him along with them to AA meetings, but it was too little, too late. His liver was non-functional. He died at sixty-two, a year after returning home.

Now, at last they understood my decision to leave Glen Ellyn, and I believe Dad died finally at peace with it.

- *Forty* -

The Being of Light

<u>Guam 1976-1977</u>

WHAT ARE THE ODDS TWO STUDENTS IN TWO DIF-
ferent countries would both give me a book, let alone the same
book, for no apparent reason? In the Philippines, an IS student had given
me a copy of Hal Lindsey's *The Late Great Planet Earth.* I had read it, but
left it behind when we moved. I guess God thought, "She's a slow learner,
so I'll send it to her again." Now three years later, in Guam, another student gave me the very same book. Between EPA and part-time teaching
at the Academy, I had been too busy to do much reading or think much
about Lindsay's book, but I decided to re-read it.

Reading it in bed, a statement caught my attention. Lindsey said something about imagining how God must have felt, watching His son dying
on the cross. The idea of God having a son seemed weird to me anyhow,
but Lindsay's feelings puzzled me. *Why did he feel so deeply about this? The
Romans crucified thousands of people. What made Jesus' crucifixion different?*

I turned out the light, and lay mulling this over. I had researched so
many religions, cults, and isms. Each had contained bits and pieces that
rang true, but I hadn't fully bought into any of them. Terms from various places floated in my head, unconnected: lambs, blood, judgment, sin,
mercy, justice, a cross, a resurrection. Despite growing up in a church, I
didn't understand Christianity, and I understood little when I 'chose God's
side,' in the chokecherry tree at twelve. I'd searched a lot since then, but

had learned relatively little. I had no problem believing in God, yet I didn't understand how this man Jesus fit into everything, although we celebrated a couple of nice holidays connected to Him.

Lindsay maintained Jesus was alive. Of course, I knew the Easter story, but I never grasped why or how that affected me or anyone else. How His dying could save the world wasn't clear. *If His death changed everything, why was the world still in such a mess?* None of the books I read talked about that.

The *Late Great Planet Earth,* had a lot of challenging ideas to absorb on a first-time read. Now, the second time through the book, grappling with all the pieces, suddenly I realized, *This crucifixion would be different from the others only if Jesus were somehow different.* But how? He was somehow a unique man, someone God wanted, even needed, to die. If sin required a substitute death, maybe one man could die for someone else, but certainly not for everyone. Anyone whose death could save the entire world somehow *had* to be more than simply a man.

Lindsay claimed the Bible said Jesus was both God and man, something difficult to comprehend. With a sudden epiphany, I lay there internally processing the extraordinary possibility that perhaps the Bible was right.

It shouldn't have taken me ten years to figure this out, but I had been reading so many kinds of books. They all had different ideas, but often mixed in pieces borrowed from Christian theology. I had become a spiritual fruitcake, ingesting a little fruit here, a lot of nuts there. I'd never understood the whole picture. I realized Lindsay's book was actually the first Christian book I'd read.

Suddenly, I found myself facing a glowing robed figure surrounded by a dark purplish void. He faced me, arms outstretched, radiating a bright light. Jesus needed no introduction. I couldn't see the face, but I knew Who He was. I just didn't know where I was, or what state I was in. I wasn't dreaming, and He wasn't standing in the corner of my room. *Was this a vision in my head or an out-of-body experience?* I still don't know, but, at the time, it was the Who, not the where, that occupied my mind.

What struck me most was the feeling of indescribable love emanating from Him. Although I couldn't see the face, I knew He was male, but I also sensed a definite feminine side. The love emanated from Him so intensely I felt *physically* enveloped in it, somewhat analogous to physically feeling heat or cold. You can know someone loves you or feel love toward someone, but that's emotional; it doesn't physically envelop you that same way, and I perceived it with some sense I don't usually have, or at least don't use.

Clichéd statements like "God is love" float around a lot, but I never comprehended them, because I envisioned God's love being like human love, but the two aren't comparable.

Then I saw a floating pinkish-purplish cerebrum with all of its convolutions, looking somewhat like a transparent hologram. Mine, I assumed. An almost transparent right hand of ethereal purplish fingers was strolling through the convolutions as if leafing through a set of files in a filing cabinet, and I physically felt Him going through my head. It was an odd picture, with no explanation, but I interpreted it to mean, "I see everything about you. Nothing's hidden from me." I wished many things were hidden, but I sensed no feeling of condemnation or judgment, only an overwhelming love and acceptance.

I have no idea where we were or how long the encounter lasted, whether a few seconds or an hour. I had an odd sensation of being outside of time and place, and don't recall being conscious of having a body, either. Was this encounter in my head, or was I outside of myself, somewhere else? I still don't know. I only know He wasn't physically standing there glowing in the bedroom. Location didn't matter. He commanded my attention and I could focus on nothing else. At that moment, I felt I would do anything for Him.

Then, He began slowly receding and dimming. I willed Him not to go, but He left, and the light faded away. I realized I was in bed. Excited, I elbowed sleeping Carlos. "Guess Who I just saw!" He mumbled something, rolled over, and continued his sleep. So much for sharing my experience. Although I didn't have any other instant revelations, over time, I realized that somehow, my God-shaped hole was filled.

I'm surprised I didn't lie awake all night, thinking about it, but I fell asleep almost instantaneously. The next day I woke up with an incredible high, and a compulsion to read the Bible. I dug around to find it, dusted it off, and began reading the New Testament. I read every spare moment, and seemed able do little else. Fortunately, I knew my lectures so well I didn't need to prepare for class.

Students asked, "Have you graded our tests yet?" No, but soon.

Carlos asked, "Have you started dinner yet?" No, not yet.

I was on an amazing high for about three weeks. Interestingly, the Bible now had new depth. I could understand passages I didn't understand before. In Manila, I had covered the margins of my Bible with question marks and challenging semi-sarcastic remarks. I looked at my old comments, marveling how clear the words had suddenly become. Today I know that just as a lamp won't provide light until you plug it in, without the Spirit's guidance, the Bible's words are flat, their meaning hidden. I still didn't understand many things, yet I wasn't left floundering.

A few months later, a quiet voice intruded into my head, holding out a thought. It said almost conversationally, "You should start going to church." A suggestion, not a command. Hmm. I considered this. We hadn't been in a church since our wedding, over a decade earlier. Carlos would think I'd lost it. I'd never seen a Protestant church on the island either, not that I was keen on going anyhow, because Sunday morning was my primary diving time, so I searched for alternatives.

I bargained with the voice in my head. "If I knew where there was a Bible study, I could do that." Perhaps on some subconscious level I felt safe saying that, because I'd never been to a Bible study in my life. Except for the nuns at the Academy, I didn't even know anyone who attended church, let alone a Bible study.

Be prepared when you ask for something. Within a short time, Ann, my assistant scuba instructor called me at EPA. We were barely acquaintances, and we'd never exchanged more than a few words. We'd never connected after I became certified, and I was surprised she even knew where I worked. She invited me to a Bahai meeting. *Well, why not? I've been through everything else.*

When she met me at the dive shop on Friday night, a young guy named Chris was already in the car. We drove to a small house in Dededo to join a somewhat rambling discussion on life after death, astral projection, ghosts, auras, and similar topics. There seemed to be no meeting agenda or doctrine of any kind. Most people seemed as in the dark as I was, in terms of knowledge. Chris didn't contribute anything. We started home, and as Ann dropped him off, he turned to me and said, "If you're interested in joining a Bible study, we meet at my house on Tuesdays at 7:30. Here's my phone number." I pocketed the paper, Ann dropped me off, and I promptly forgot about it.

Four days later, driving home from work about 5:30 on Marine Drive, as I passed Coral Reef Marine, where Ann worked, something like a ticker tape began scrolling across the top of my vision, with the words "Bible study, Chris, 7:30." It was strange, but I didn't question it; I knew Who it came from. It had been a long tiring day. Excuses leapt quickly to mind: *I'm exhausted; I'm not prepared; I have to cook dinner; I have a lot to do.*

Once home, I promptly forgot all about it. Until the following Tuesday. As I passed the dive shop on the way home, the same message appeared. I pulled out the same excuses, went home, and again forgot about it. Oddly, I never remembered the study except on Tuesdays after work.

The third Tuesday, passing the dive shop, the meeting again popped into mind, but before I could even articulate excuses, a clear, authoritative voice in my head said reasonably, "*You* asked for a Bible study. *I* showed you a Bible study. Now, what are you going to do about it?" A question, not a command. It was left up to me, my choice.

Yikes, I thought. *I guess I'm going to go.* I went home, dug up Chris's phone number, and told Carlos I was going to a Bible study after dinner. He looked at me incredulously. I asked if he wanted to come. He didn't. I went alone. Chris was with Youth with a Mission, but he was also a scuba diver, and several divers attended the study. I could continue diving on Sundays, and found some new dive buddies as well.

The group met for a year, until Chris left Guam and the study fell apart. Yet one of his comments stuck with me. "Knowing *about* someone isn't the same as actually *knowing* them. You may know many facts about the President, and believe he exists, but if you've never met him, you can't say you *know* him. Similarly, it's not enough to believe God exists; you need to *know* Him." I suddenly realized despite wandering through everything from the Ouija, spirit writing, the Mormons and Jehovah's Witnesses, to Edgar Cayce, the faith healer, and everything in between, I didn't really know Him.

Guam's one small bookstore was a Christian bookstore, so I bought a couple of books and began reading about God's attributes, to learn who He was. Once I understood the attributes of holiness, love, justice and mercy, for the first time, the whole gospel finally made sense.

I was amazed. *I must be a slow learner. Why had it been so difficult to grasp that we are separated from God because He is holy and we aren't? Or that Jesus was the bridge across the holiness gap, offering a gift of fellowship to the whole world?* Now, I realized that in the chokecherry tree, when I decided I wanted to 'be on God's side,' twenty years earlier, I was accepting the gift of fellowship based on what I knew, which wasn't much. But my heart was in the right place, and that was apparently enough. Perhaps most people start their journey with only fragmented knowledge.

Of course, we have free will; we can accept the gift of fellowship He offers or not. A gift is only a gift when it's accepted. And why would anyone resist an offer of fellowship with the creator of the cosmos, the ultimate designer, who creates things like coral reefs and rain forests?

But I didn't go off the religious deep-end. After Christmas, the Guam Science Teachers Association was sponsoring a trip to Nepal, and we signed on. Nepal's previous contact with the West was limited to hippies and drug-seekers, but it had now recently opened to tourists, despite not being prepared for them. No sweat; after our recent year without electricity, our group of sixteen figured we could easily rough it a bit.

- *Forty-One* -
The Crocodiles Were Well-Fed

<u>Nepal 1978</u>

I T WAS ONLY SLIGHTLY ABOVE FREEZING WHEN OUR plane landed outside Kathmandu. The dreary late December day was overcast with intermittent drizzle. A bone-chilling wind swept unhindered across the wide gray sky and sodden brown fields. From our small mini-bus, the tiny isolated, unlighted houses scattered among the colorless fields of dead rice stubble looked dingy, dark, and uninviting.

Sanjiya, my EWC roommate, came from Kathmandu, but I had lost touch with her. *Had she returned home? If so, could she ever be happy here, after Hawaii?* I found it hard to imagine.

I assumed 4,600 feet altitude in the Himalayas never became hot, but local people were used to it. Driving toward Kathmandu in our heated mini-bus, bundled in down jackets, hats, gloves, and boots, we passed two mothers standing outside their houses pouring basins of water over naked children. I hoped they had at least heated the water. *I'm glad we'll be staying in a warm hotel*, I thought, feeling slightly guilty.

Kathmandu seemed in a time warp, as if we had dropped through a wormhole in time and emerged several hundred years in the past. The streets around Durbar Square thronged with people, bicycles, carts, wandering sacred cows, an occasional elephant, and one car. Fascinating tiered buildings with intricate wood carvings lined the streets, their wood darkened with smoke and time. Everything looked old and in need of repair. *It* looks like everything this culture ever built or accomplished happened several hundred years ago, and they haven't done anything since.

The newly re-opened Yak and Yeti, the single hotel geared to foreigners and now in the last stages of a renovation, seemed to be the exception. As we passed it, I thought, *I'm glad we're not staying there; non-Western hotels have more atmosphere.* We were staying at the Woodlands.

It was raining when we arrived at our small wooden hotel. Nepalese are small people, and the Woodland's front door was correspondingly short and narrow, obviously not built for Westerners. It swung both inside and out. Seeing us coming, the doorman came out and stood in the rain to hold the door open. As I passed him, I said, "You don't need to stand outside here getting wet. Why don't you stand inside?"

With a somewhat tight smile, he nodded toward the three people ahead of me. "Big people. Door opens wider this way." Most Americans probably looked large to the small Nepalese, but three of our Haole group were large even by Guamanian standards. I realized if he stood inside, opening it inward, he might stay dry, but some people might have difficulty fitting through the short, narrow door.

If asked to describe the trip in one word, it would be either Cold or Hungry. Unbelievably, the hotel had no electricity, although the temperature hovered around freezing both inside and out. Despite the cold, our beds lacked blankets, and the showers had a small soap chip but no hot water. At least they provided toilet paper. Actually, it was crepe paper but, all things considered, still something to be thankful for.

Guam had programmed our internal thermostats to tropical, and we were already chilled. The hotel had nowhere to sit and relax, have a coffee, or even get warm. In most third-world markets, street vendors and small shops sell food or hot tea, so we walked toward Durbar Square looking for something hot. Leeks, onions, lettuce, a few carrots, and raw pieces of what I assumed to be lamb or goat, were the only food we saw. No one was selling hot food.

Later, the guide told us Nepal had a national policy: "If we don't manufacture something, we won't import it; we do without it." Nepal manufactured very few things, so everyone did without a lot. By the end of day one, I would have killed for a hot coffee.

The warmest part of the hotel was the staircase, where each step held a lighted candle balanced on a small saucer, to light the way upstairs. I could easily visualize a candle falling over in the middle of the night and burning down the hotel. *Although at least for a short time, we would be warm.*

Given the state of the hotel, requesting blankets seemed pointless. We skipped the icy shower and slept in our clothes, down jackets, hats, gloves, and hiking boots. Despite my usual preference for local hotels, I found myself already yearning for the Yak and Yeti.

Hotel meals were a particular torture. At breakfast, fancy printed menus seemingly copied from the Waldorf or Ritz Carlton listed every breakfast item known to man. Then reality and fiction soon blurred.

A waitress starting at my end of the table asked what I wanted. I said, "I'll have the pancakes." They would be hot and easy.

"We don't have pancakes today."

"OK, I'll have the waffles."

"We're all out of waffles."

"How about an omelet?"

"No omelets."

"French toast?" I could see where this was heading. By now, I knew the answer.

"We don't have any."

"Well, what *do* you have?"

"Cornflakes."

Admitting defeat, I said, "OK, I'll have cornflakes."

She disappeared without taking any other orders. About ten minutes later, a bowl of strange cornflakes arrived. Each cornflake looked very, very thick and somewhat round. They appeared to be dry corn kernels smashed flat with a hammer. They were very chewy, close to inedible, and came with a glass of odd-tasting milk I assumed to be yak milk.

The waitress moved on to Carlos, and asked for his order. After hearing my exchange, he ordered cornflakes too. She disappeared into the kitchen, and emerged ten minutes later with another bowl of cornflakes. *Is it possible they're actually making the cornflakes in the kitchen after each order?* Then she turned to take the third person's order. And on it went. Each order had to be made and served before she took the next.

After eyeing our cornflakes, one couple made the mistake of ordering a fried egg, slowing the process further. *Are they waiting for a hen to lay the eggs first?* It took over two hours for thirteen of us to order. The last three people declined breakfast altogether. Sensing our restlessness, the waitress brought everyone cups of yak butter tea. It tasted rancid but, having no prior yak-butter experience, I had no standard to determine whether that was the normal taste or not. Either way, I wasn't a yak butter fan.

People began fidgeting, painfully aware of fleeting time and our shrinking morning itinerary, but nothing sped the glacial serving progress. By the time we finished breakfast, lunchtime was fast approaching, and it was too late for much of our scheduled walking tour. Two days later, we discovered the hotel could cook only one item at a time, because it operated with only one hotplate. They seemed unaware they could at least streamline the ordering process. Fortunately, we were the hotel's only guests.

Lunch was faster because they provided no choice. They served everyone rice and mutton curry. Its unusual taste was nothing to rave about, and I suspected it contained yak butter, but it tasted better than the cornflakes. At dinner, they served it again. *They must have overestimated the amount of curry to make for lunch. They must not want to waste it, so they're serving the leftovers for dinner.* The next lunch, they served it again. And the next dinner. And lunch and dinner on the third day. I usually enjoy both lamb and curry, but this wasn't even particularly good to begin with. By day four, our stomachs were in rebellion. Unfortunately, the tour had paid all of our Kathmandu meals in advance to this hotel.

When someone discovered a downtown restaurant with a small space heater and less-than-freezing dining room, we abandoned the Woodlands' dinner *en masse*. We still ate in our down jackets, but anything in a slightly warm room without mutton curry seemed too good to pass up, and the restaurant's mutton burgers were a positive change. The manager was excited to have so many customers. Overhearing our complaints about Woodland's meals, he offered to serve us a special celebration dinner if we all returned to eat at his hotel on New Year's Eve. We needed no urging.

He must have expended great effort researching favorite American foods and even greater effort finding the ingredients. When we arrived, he proudly brought out course after course: first, a rubbery agar-based version of raspberry Jell-o, followed by small dishes of shrimp cocktail, a bowl of Mac and Cheese, bread, mutton meatballs, and the finale, tiny pieces of fried chicken. We praised it lavishly. Everything is relative; it was indeed a feast compared to mutton curry. We didn't even mind the salivating rat quietly crouched in the corner, greedily eying our table and waiting for us to leave.

Woodlands had lost face. Realizing their customers were migrating to another restaurant, they wanted a chance to redeem themselves. They promised us some lovely box lunches for the next day's bus trip to Pokhara.

The following morning, we stood on a mountain in freezing pre-dawn darkness, waiting to watch sunrise over Mt. Everest. We huddled in a circle, bundled in scarves, hats, gloves, boots, and down jackets, watching our breath steam in the cold air and stamping our feet, trying to keep circulation going. An icy wind swept down from Mt. Everest, seeping into our clothes. We were accustomed to Guam's heat, and needed more layers than our down jackets provided. My toes were icicles inside my leather Costa Rican jungle boots. Once the sun peeked over Everest, we gave it only a cursory glance and left, wanting to be out of the wind.

After breakfast, we waited outside the hotel for our bus to Pokhara. Small boys swarmed around us, wearing nothing more than shorts and ragged sweaters. Carlos asked one of them, "Aren't you cold?"

Surprisingly, the boy understood us. His answer was both heart-wrenching and straightforward. "Only rich people get cold." Someone offered him a knit wool hat. He snatched it up. The hat disappeared inside his sweater, and a moment later he looked around hopefully for more donations. We piled into the mini bus with Woodland's box lunches and began the scenic drive to Pokhara.

By mid-morning everyone began opening their lunch boxes. Inside we found a mutton burger sandwich. It came with two hardboiled eggs that somehow, even in the shell, managed to taste like yak butter; an orange so sour I would have sworn it was a lemon; and a bland, crumbly biscuit of some kind. Most of us ate the biscuit and part of the mutton burger and passed the remaining food out the windows to the children who swarmed around the bus whenever we stopped. They rewarded us with broad toothy smiles, delighted to get anything we handed out.

The following day we left for the highlight of our trip: a two-night visit to Tiger Tops, a treetop lodge in Chitwan National Park in southcentral Nepal. At least we knew it would be warmer at 300-foot altitude. I just prayed they wouldn't serve mutton curry.

Chitwan contained increasingly sparse populations of the rare one-horned rhinoceros and endangered Bengal tiger, and was fighting to protect the remaining fragment of natural habitat from poachers and wandering sacred cows. Our small STOL (short take-off and landing) prop plane landed on a vacant field adjacent to the park that doubled as a landing strip.

Sacred cows had grazed the vegetation down to the roots, cropping it more closely than a putting green. Barbed wire fence kept cows outside the park, and the skinny, half-starved cows looked longingly at the luxuriant growth inside.

"Our biggest battle is people continually cutting through the wire fence to allow their cattle to graze inside the Park," the park ranger told us. "Only seven rangers patrol and defend the entire 360 mi^2 area against poachers and wire cutters, and they spend most of their time repairing fences."

The situation was dire. *Slaughtering a few cows to reduce the population would benefit the cows, the environment, and the owners.* However, in a Hindu country, of course that wouldn't happen. The cow is Nepal's national animal; killing them is illegal, although apparently allowing their slow death by starvation is permissible. But at the moment, seeing so many starving sacred cows roaming around, all I could visualize were very lean walking hamburgers.

A line of tall African elephants wearing square, open-sided box-like saddles waited on the edge of the landing field. Compared to the smaller Asian elephants seen in most zoos, African elephants were giants. They stood up to 13 feet high and weighed up to 16,500 pounds. A combination of safari and taxi, they provided an exciting introduction to the park. It wasn't a tourist gimmick. Elephants were the safest way to tour the park, and because the park had no roads, they also provided transportation to the treetop lodge, our hotel for two nights.

For several hours, we lumbered slowly through the forest and grasslands, seeing gharial crocodiles, spotted deer, and various birds, and having a close encounter with one of the park's few rhinos. A mammoth rhino walked within five feet of us without a second glance. From atop the elephant, we looked down on him by several feet, and I understood why it might be advantageous to be on an elephant rather than inside a low, open jeep.

We navigated through dense jungle and eight-foot grasses, sometimes following odd linear paths. At first, I didn't realize what they were. Elephants are enormous, so I expected they would leave wide pathways of flattened vegetation, but the elephant track was a single solidly compressed linear mud trail only about a foot wide, exactly the width of an elephant's foot. It looked like a one-wheeled tire track, so precise and flat it looked mechanically made. It seemed impossible elephants would make it until I observed the line of elephants walking in front of ours. They moved like models down a runway, hips slightly swaying as they swung their feet one in front of the other, all four feet landing precisely on the same narrow path. Walking single file, every elephant placed all four feet on the same track. This method restricted the elephants' impact on the environment, but they made up for that by each eating about 600 pounds of vegetation a day. In the wild, elephants are incredibly destructive, pushing over or pulling down large stands of trees with their trunks to reach the leaves. *One elephant's food could feed a lot of sacred cows,* I thought.

We clung tightly to the bamboo bar on the top of our saddle, jerking and swaying side to side as the elephants awkwardly lumbered down a steep bank into a river. As the water deepened, we began submerging. I stared at the water rising up the elephant's sides, wondering how wet we would get. The river was deeper than I expected; the water stopped barely short of submerging our feet. The elephant was totally submerged, with only the saddle and the tip of his trunk poking out of the water. Surprised, I realized he was swimming, and using his trunk as a snorkel.

After several hours, we arrived at a tropical lodge situated high in the leafy tree canopy. It had no door; the elephants walked up to the side of the treehouse and discharged us directly into the tree itself. It provided our most unique, pleasant stay in Nepal. Lanterns cast a warm nighttime glow over comfortable, mosquito-netted beds, and a small solar shower with tepid water allowed us our first shower in four days. With relief, we welcomed meals of vegetables, meat, stews, and fruits, and celebrated the lack of mutton curry. I wondered how they managed to obtain these foods despite the national import restrictions.

The following day we motored upstream in shallow dugout canoes through a broad, silt-filled river. Our canoe had only two or three inches of freeboard and rode so low in the water I feared even leaning a bit to the side would capsize it. A bask of fat, torpid crocodiles sunbathed on the muddy riverbanks, uninterested in our passage. *How easily one could overturn our boat or jump from the water and grab someone.* The guide assured us this never happened. I wondered why crocodile encounters were so uncommon with humans such easy prey.

We motored a few miles upriver and disembarked at a wooden landing. After a short jungle walk, we arrived at a small group of canvas tents equipped with comfortable cots and a friendly, good-looking uniformed park ranger. The blonde divorcee in our group perked up. She asked around and discovered with dismay that the camp had nowhere to plug in a hairdryer. *What could she be thinking? Even our Kathmandu hotel had no electricity, so why on earth would she expect to find a plug in the remote jungle? For that matter, why would anyone even lug a hair dryer on a trip like this?*

While she set her sights on charming the ranger, Carlos and I decided to take a jungle hike. The ranger pointed us to a nearby path that "should be safe enough," despite the fact we were in a tiger reserve on a crocodile-filled river. It felt good to be back in a jungle again. We wandered leisurely along a trail near the river, swatting insects, admiring the lush vegetation, and keeping an eye out for crocodiles. Then, coming around a bend in the path, suddenly I saw it.

On a muddy flat right beside a small pool of water, a human skull stared up at us through empty eye sockets. Its macabre appearance gave me pause; the jawbone was missing, but a few small clumps of black hair and dried skin indicated relative freshness. I was elated, not repulsed. Finding a human skull, one of the original goals on my 1955 goal list, was something I never expected to complete. Yet it sat there waiting, even begging, to be taken. There was no way I could leave it there. (In case you're wondering, no biologist I know would leave it there either.)

I didn't know the park policies about removing things, but I decided to chance it. I wrapped it carefully in my sweatshirt and brought it into camp.

Then I began feeling guilty. The mud-filled skull had a round hole about the size and shape of a bullet hole in the maxilla. *If I cleaned it out, would I find a bullet? Surely, someone might want to know about this?* Desire to smuggle it out warred with the feeling I should tell someone. My Western background provided many possible scenarios. *Maybe it's a murder victim or a missing person. Perhaps he was the missing piece of a crime scene.* I reluctantly sought out the ranger, now chatting animatedly on the front porch of his tent with the divorcee.

"I found a skull."

"Human or animal?" He asked almost rhetorically as if this were a common occurrence.

"Human."

"Why are you telling me?" This apparently happened a lot.

Hope blossomed. *Why indeed? He didn't appear to care.* "Well…. I thought he might be a murder victim. It appears to have a bullet hole in it."

He didn't even ask to see it. "Do you want to keep it?"

"If it's OK. I teach physiology in Guam. I could use this for class." I was thinking more along the lines of my personal collection, but it seemed a little too crass to say so. "You aren't interested in identifying who it is?"

"Bodies float down the river here every day. There's no way to know where they come from; it might be a long way upriver. They used to cremate them, but everything's been so deforested, there's not a lot of extra wood for cremation, so often they cremate a small piece, like a finger, and throw the rest of the body into the river."

Deforested. Another country's jungle had been decimated for production of livestock and firewood. *So that's why the lazy crocodiles on the riverbank weren't interested in people in the dugouts; they were already well-fed.* I took some solace that at least the bodies were being returned to the trophic cycle.

"If you want to keep it, go ahead," the ranger said. I tucked it into my duffle bag.

The purpose of our tent camp stay was to see a Bengal tiger. At night, the Park tied a baby goat or water buffalo to a stake in the jungle as bait, while a watcher sat in a nearby tree with binoculars and a radio. If a tiger made a kill, the watcher radioed the tent camp, and we would walk out to a blind to watch it eat.

It was after dinner, and dark when the call came; the tiger had made his kill.

"Everyone, remove your shoes. We make less noise this way." The ranger carried the only flashlight. Gingerly picking our steps mainly by feel, we set out to watch the Bengal tiger have dinner. Someone had cleaned and leveled the trail, so it had no holes, sharp stones, or roots to trip us, but my bare toes felt vulnerable. I hoped biting things were in their holes for the night.

"Tiptoe quietly and no talking; we don't want to scare it off."

Somewhere in the middle of the walk, the lunacy of our walk hit me. *We're walking barefooted, without lights, through a jungle at night to meet a hungry tiger who just made a kill?*

That prompted me to quietly ask, "Did you bring a gun?"

"No, it's safer for the animals this way." No doubt. Yet I wondered how the unarmed watcher in the tree felt, sitting alone, knowing a hungry tiger prowled about below his tree.

"We've only been surprised once. People made too much noise getting into the viewing blind. When we turned the light on the kill, the tiger was gone. Curious at their noise, the tiger left his kill and wandered over to check out the blind. People heard a noise and turned to find the tiger in the blind with them." I could visualize the pandemonium in the blind, and the ranger didn't elaborate further.

We walked perhaps a half-mile to a large palm-covered blind, enclosed on three sides. Once everyone stepped inside, the ranger flipped on a floodlight, illuminating the tiger and his kill. The tiger's massive head jerked up, and he looked around, startled. His head was immense, nearly twice the size I expected. Seeing no one, he bent down to continue his meal.

We had a perfect view from perhaps 30 feet away. Watching the tiger tear into the goat, I suddenly visualized Romans in the Colosseum, cheering as gladiators died for their vicarious thrills. Suddenly the bait scenario seemed barbaric. *How terrified the baby goat must have been, tied to a stake, sensing the tiger's approach and unable to escape.* It was horrifying to contemplate. I'd like to think they've stopped the practice, but probably not; it's a tourist moneymaker, and with over 100 tigers in the park, maybe the tigers need supplemental prey.

The ranger was right; skulls were common. I wasn't sure how Guam viewed importing skulls, so I wrapped the skull inside a bag of dirty clothes to protect and camouflage it. At immigration, a large officious customs lady plunged her hand in, expertly groping around in the bag of clothes.

"Ah," she said matter-of-factly. "You have a human skull in here." She didn't even remove it from the bag. I thought, *Darn. Now she's going to confiscate it.*

But she smiled. "You must have been in either Samoa or Nepal."

"Nepal."

"We see a lot from there," she said, waving me through without further thought.

Luckily, we took the trip when we did, because although we didn't realize it, drastic change was right around the corner.

***

Years later, while inspecting the skull, a dentist friend remarked, "These are a young person's teeth, probably a male in his mid-thirties." Whether a bullet or a crocodile incisor caused the hole in the maxilla, he likely didn't die of natural causes. I couldn't help wondering how the original owner would feel to learn his skull has gained a certain immortality by sitting on a shelf with my fossil collection.

- *Forty-Two* -

Decision Time

Guam 1978

THE EPA ADMINISTRATOR APPEARED AT MY DESK, looking pained. "The governor is upset. He wants us to stop publishing water contamination notices in the Pacific Daily News."

"We wouldn't have to publish notices if PUAG kept the water chlorinated," I reminded him. "If we stop enforcing, San Francisco could rescind our enforcement authority."

EPA San Francisco had recently delegated their federal enforcement authority to Guam. Whenever drinking water didn't meet national standards, regulations required publishing a Notice of Water Contamination in the local newspaper. San Francisco had been lax about publishing contamination notices, but they were 6,000 miles away and didn't have to drink our water. I wanted to enforce this provision. Once I began posting contaminated water notices in the Pacific Daily News, citizen complaints flooded the governor's office.

Guam's drinking water consistently failed the coliform standard because the well operators didn't keep the chlorinators working. This particularly galled me because one of my responsibilities as safe drinking water section chief was training the water and wastewater treatment plant operators. I knew the operators understood the procedures, but they seemed to minimize the importance of chlorination.

"I guess fiestas are more important to them," the deputy said. Although facetious, that probably contained a kernel of truth.

To my mind, this was PUAG's problem; they operated the water system. Unfortunately, EPA enforcement coincided with the election of a new governor, and the governor viewed me as the problem, thinking that the public notices reflected poorly on his administration. The administrator wanted to appease him, so with backward logic, rather than stopping the pollution, he would stop the notifications. Sewage contamination in the water supply was a secondary concern for both of them.

The obvious solution was for EPA to lean on PUAG's well operators, but it wasn't an option the administrator wanted to pursue. He preferred to avoid confrontations, and we both sensed I would be an obstacle. He was a command-and-control manager, and instead of getting my input and discussing solutions, he walked away to think up his own plan. I knew change was coming, but I expected to have some input.

The following morning, the administrator called the unit chiefs together and unveiled his brilliant idea: we would have an agency reorganization to cross-train everyone. It was a thinly-veiled attempt to stop enforcement by moving me to another job while kindly letting me save face.

Like musical chairs, everyone shifted positions. I became the new pesticides unit manager, the pesticides manager moved to solid waste, the solid waste manager moved to community relations, and so on. He put the person least likely to enforce the standards in charge of safe drinking water. He cavalierly moved us around like pawns without even consulting us about our preferences. The reorganization blindsided everyone, leaving the agency in chaos.

I'm sure the administrator thought it was the perfect solution, but he underestimated people's attachment to their jobs. People were upset and bitterly angry. It also severely impacted the agency's effectiveness because science jobs require years of specific technical training. It didn't seem to occur to him that most unit managers were mainlanders, and we had other options.

The sunny days, unhurried pace, and laid-back lifestyle of the South Pacific tend to produce people who don't measure time by appointment books or happiness by dollars and possessions. This lifestyle often appeals to stressed, overworked mainlanders who come for vacation and end-up staying for a lifetime. However, Carlos and I always knew Guam wasn't our permanent home, and we would leave at some point, but any discussion about leaving always became so complicated that we dropped it. Now, given my job change, it felt time to revisit the issue.

Carlos is a creature of habit, and he seemed to enjoy his job and his water polo. I wondered if he was open to discussing a move. It would mean a significant lifestyle change.

The kids were also getting older, and another issue had also been lingering on the edge of my awareness for months.

"What does a train look like?" Lisa had asked. She was almost ten, but how could she know? Guam had no trains. It lacked many other simple things too. One building had recently installed the island's first escalator. It was such a novelty that people lined up all day to ride the escalator up and down, over and over, like a carnival ride. It became practically an island holiday. The kids needed wider exposure and better schools. We mistakenly tried Lisa in the local school system for third grade, and she was bored to death.

Now the house was quiet, the kids in bed. Carlos and I sat comfortably on the living room couch, flipping TV channels, trying to find something worthwhile watching, but we weren't having much luck. Guam's TV was limited to whatever came over the undersea cable, and wherever the cable originated had few decent programs.

I obliquely broached the topic. "Lisa asked me what a train looked like."

"I guess she's never seen one."

"Our kids are seven and nine, and they've never seen a train. Doesn't it bother you?"

He sat back, considering. "I guess we could expose them to more on our trips."

I persisted. "Guam is so small; what else are they missing by living here? When they attend college in the States, how much disadvantage will they have, dealing with the complex Stateside culture, when they haven't even seen a train, ridden a bus, visited a museum, or whatever? The kids are bright, but they're missing a lot."

He looked surprised. "Do you want to leave?"

I hesitated to put it in words. "Yes…. I think so." It was difficult to admit, knowing what that meant.

Then he surprised me. "I've been ready for a long time. I was just waiting for you to feel ready." I had no idea he felt that way.

That's one thing that made our relationship work. We gave each other space. Thankfully, we weren't joined at the hip, and I never felt pressured into anything. If we disagreed on something, eventually, one of us converted the other to our way of thinking. We're culturally very different, but we share core values, and after seven years, we both knew it was time to leave.

"OK. Let's do it." Without agonizing or further deliberation, we had crossed the first and biggest hurdle: agreeing to leave the island. Once we selected a destination, we could go from there.

I could see Carlos shifting internal gears. "Do you want to return to the Philippines?"

"It seems like a step backward. We came here to earn dollars. I'm not ready to return to IS or De La Salle and a peso salary. Are you?"

Somewhat to my surprise, he said, "No," and as quickly as I had left the States, he jettisoned the Philippines. In one stroke, we had just killed Solita's hopes for Carlos as her future bank president.

We implicitly agreed our next move would be to the mainland, but international moves are never easy without company assistance and pre-arranged jobs. We had so many questions, and from our distant vantage point on Guam, we couldn't know any answers with certainty. Where to go? When to go? What about jobs? What about our Guam and Philippine pensions and social security?

It would have been easier to move with only two of us, but we had two school-age kids to consider. Would it be better to move kids during summer vacation or mid-year? The kids needed a school, so ideally, one of us should arrive with a job, so we could buy a house and begin putting down roots. Yet how would we get a job from Guam?

We would have to sell our house and buy one in an unfamiliar city, but without jobs, how would we know where to buy? What about the dog? And all our belongings? Shipping costs were insane, and we had accumulated a lot in twelve years.

The move was a giant decision tree. The choices were all interconnected, yet all unknowns. Each decision we made removed some options but opened a flood of new questions, possibilities, and decisions. The more we discussed the issues, the more complicated they became.

Carlos, the analyzer, would prefer to examine every possible contingency and nail everything down in advance. This quality made him a good bank examiner but, in something this complicated, we couldn't figure out everything in advance before making decisions. We needed to avoid analysis paralysis.

"This is impossible," I said. "We can't know everything upfront. It has to be one step, one decision at a time. My brain is getting in a knot."

The possibilities were wide open. I felt game for anywhere but the Midwest. I needed ocean and mountains, and the West Coast had both. It was also closest to Asia, and would make trips home to the Philippines easier. All the news from California involved demonstrations, riots, hippies, drugs, and free-love culture. It didn't seem promising for raising young kids. Oregon and Washington were in recession, but many Guam friends loved Seattle, so we decided to look there first.

We each sent out a dozen resumes. Between us, we netted only one non-committal, "If you ever come to Seattle, stop by and talk to us." Sending out resumes from 6,000 miles away, and expecting jobs to materialize without interviews was unrealistic, but we couldn't afford to just move, camp out in a motel somewhere and possibly spend months looking for work with the kids not in school. Although the mainland was in recession, one of us needed a job before moving.

We decided to make a ten-day exploratory job hunt, and if one of us could land a job, the rest of the decisions would fall into place. We could deal with the details as they came along. If nothing panned out, we would return and try again next year. Friends from the Bible study agreed to house-sit the kids while we went job hunting.

Many friends were slightly envious because they wanted to leave too, but staying was too comfortable. The singles said, "It's easier for you; you're married." Those married without kids said, "It's easier for you; you have kids." *Really??* Those married with kids said, "It's easier for you; your kids are already big (or still small)." Everyone justified their own lack of initiative.

God was obviously behind the move, and things moved at lightning speed. We flew to Seattle. At the end of a week, despite the recession, Carlos received not one job offer but two. We went house-hunting with only three days to buy a house in the unfamiliar Seattle area. Carlos' job was in Seattle, and I thought mine might be in Olympia, so the new area of Federal Way seemed like a good midway location.

After Guam's few simple housing choices, Seattle's variety was overwhelming. Everything looked good; we bought the third house we saw. Now we were committed to leaving.

We returned to Guam and listed our house for sale in the Pacific Daily News. With Guam's perennial housing shortage, we expected it to sell fast, but we were surprised at *how* fast. The first morning our ad hit the paper, our telephone worked – somewhat – for the first time in weeks. At 8:15, I happened to be right next to the phone when it produced a single low *burp*, sounding nothing like a ring. Standing anywhere else, I would have missed it. There was a buyer on the other end. Without preliminaries, he said, "I want to buy your house."

"When do you want to see it?"

"No. I'll buy it. When can we sign?" He didn't argue price. Afraid to miss out, he bought it sight unseen, fifteen minutes after the paper arrived. I recognized his desperation, remembering how Carlos had spent three months in the Hilton house-hunting after he arrived. After our conversation, the phone went dead and never worked again for the remainder of our time in Guam.

As we began the daunting process of another international move, we knew neither our island clothes nor furniture would work in Washington. Off-island shipping was prohibitive at $0.82 a pound (1979 dollars), so the best way to reduce moving costs was to revisit the flea market.

We were attached to very little that we owned, and planned to sell almost everything: the furniture, bedding, linens, magazines, records, dishes, most of our clothes, kitchen appliances, wrought iron patio furniture, tools, and both cars. We kept only our teak Filipino dining table, stereo system, books, Asian art, and my shelf of fossils and collectibles.

As sellers, we experienced the flea market from an entirely new perspective. We borrowed a pickup to haul oversized items like the barbecue, and made eight Saturday visits to the flea market. As buyers, we never arrived before 8:00 or 8:30 a.m., but, as sellers, now we went early, hoping to get a good spot in a well-traveled area.

It was still dark when we arrived at 5:00 a.m., but hundreds of people were already walking around with flashlights. The atmosphere pulsed with expectation. As we drove in, people swarmed eagerly around our pickup, grabbing at items in a feeding frenzy, even trying to lift things out of the truck. I got out to fend them off as Carlos slowly navigated through the crowded aisle to our assigned spot. Several people walked alongside the truck, their hands firmly clamped on whatever they were claiming the first right to. Within half an hour of parking the pickup in this madhouse, we sold almost everything with any resale value.

We always knew when we sold too low because the item soon popped up for sale in another stall, or we saw a second owner carrying it down the aisle. On arrival in Guam, we bought Lisa a cheap desk for $15 at the flea market. Over time, somehow, the front got bashed in, but we still re-sold it six years later for $20. Soon I saw it passing by on someone's back and couldn't resist asking what he paid. "Only $30," he said. Later we saw a third person lugging it down the aisle. He had paid $50. We had obviously under-sold.

As hours passed, we found there was a buyer for everything. We sold stacks of old magazines, empty glass Nescafe coffee jars (10 for $2), my heavy, hard-sided 1960 Samsonite suitcase with rusted hinges ($10), broken lawn chairs, rusty barbecue, and similar treasures.

Carlos was selling two pairs of Florsheim shoes, each with a hole in the left sole. In the frantic pre-dawn feeding frenzy, someone bought a pair for $2. He either bought two right shoes by mistake in the mad scramble or he looked only for shoes without holes in the soles. He left us with two black left shoes, one round-toe and one square-toe, both with a hole in the sole. I was sure we'd never be able to sell those, but later in the morning, a Korean construction worker looking for shoes pointed out the remaining two shoes didn't match but then bargained for them anyhow. We sold them at a reduced price of fifty cents. At least both were Florsheim, the same color and size, but they certainly would have been uncomfortable to wear, unless he was the one who bought the original two good shoes, in which case he now cleverly got the second pair almost free.

After a month of flea market trips, the administrator realized I was serious about leaving. He stopped at my desk, smiling. "You can have your old job back."

I looked at him in amazement. "It's too late. We've already sold our house and bought one in Seattle."

"You could buy another one," he said hopefully, but the damage was done. The two air unit chiefs, water division manager, and lab manager were also planning to leave.

The deputy said, "You'll never find a job you like as well as this one," and in many ways, he was right. Yet, within five years he also left.

After eight Saturday flea markets, we were down to a residue of partially used cereal boxes, mustard, ketchup, soap pieces, rusty can openers, remnants of half-used cleansers, furniture wax, lotions, shampoo, and paint cans. Nothing went to the landfill. As I sat with my box of treasures, marked at $6, a Filipina appeared and bargained furiously. When I refused to budge, she became nasty, accusing me of price gouging. She belittled the quality of the products, declared no one would buy them, and said everything derogatory she could think of.

"Then don't buy them." I wouldn't budge. It was a fair price. The slivers of soap and rusty can openers wouldn't win any prizes, but the cleansers and polishes were almost full. New, they would cost perhaps $35. She wouldn't buy at my price, but she wouldn't go away, either. She stood, one hand clamped on the box, appropriating it and fending off everyone else.

A Guamanian woman approached her. "Are you going to buy this box or not? Because I'm going to buy it if you don't."

Challenged but unwilling to let go of her find, the Filipina sullenly forked over $6 and left with the box, muttering to herself. To my surprise, she went only across the aisle and set the box down for resale in her own spot.

The Guamanian woman came over, smiling. "I don't want your old cleansers, but I get so tired of people trying to get things so cheaply from everyone!" I laughed, thanking her. Some bargain hunters made a big scene when a seller asked a dollar for a $30 dress, and I could understand the exasperated seller who would throw it in the garbage or give it away to someone else rather than sell it for ten cents.

We sold every last thing we brought, even the broom with melted nylon bristles from the water heater explosion. We drove home with an empty pickup, happy to be rid of true junk, while numerous buyers around the island celebrated their bargains.

We sold both cars through the newspaper. My ladybug-covered VW sold to the first looker. So did the Mazda, but buy-sell also flourished outside of the flea market. As we turned over the car keys, the buyer paid us, and then right in front of us, turned to a second man, handed him the keys, and accepted a big wad of cash. We obviously undersold. *He could at least have waited until we drove off before reselling it.* Last of all, I sold the Zodiac to my dive buddy, Miles.

Bringing Georgie and a couple of suitcases, we surrendered our remaining belongings to Asia Trans-Pacific for two months and nostalgically said goodbye to Guam. Guam had been good to us. We'd had seven years of good times and exciting experiences, built equity in a house, and established a toe-hold in the American culture. I'd finally found my career path and gained familiarity with new regulatory programs that I hoped would be invaluable on the mainland. Although still ignorant, I'd also filled my God-shaped hole.

Mom finally got her wish. We were finally returning to the States. But it was too late for Dad; he had died the year before. Drinking hadn't cost him his self-estimated two or three years, it cost him three decades.

Our last year on the island we began experiencing an increasing number of power outages. Guam Power blamed them on snakes disrupting circuits on the power poles, but Guam had no endemic snakes, and I'd never seen a single snake, so it sounded like a feeble excuse for poor power management to me. However, as we drove to the airport, leaving for Seattle, I saw my first snake, smashed on the road. It was a portent of things to come.

SEATTLE:
AT HOME AT LAST

(1979-2022)

The heron sunbathing on our dock, 2011

"Travel far enough, and you'll meet yourself"

- David Mitchell

- Forty-Three -

Culture Shock

<u>Seattle, WA 1979-1981</u>

W E HIT TWO SNAGS WITHIN THE FIRST HALF-HOUR of arriving in California. An unexpected domestic airline strike grounded all American planes and canceled all connecting flights for the foreseeable future. Worse, Georgie wasn't on our plane, and no one knew where she was or when to expect her. Welcome to the mainland.

"She's checked through to Seattle, so waiting here is pointless; they'll forward her whenever they can." Worried, but unable to do anything, we rented a car and rushed to Seattle, hoping to find her there when we arrived.

Ten minutes after crossing into Washington, a flashing red light appeared in our rear-view mirror. A traffic cop pulled Carlos over for driving a whopping 84 in a 55-mph zone on I-5. That was probably Carlos' personal speed record; with the Philippines congestion and Guam's single lane roads, I doubt he'd ever driven over 50 mph. The cop examined Carlos' unfamiliar license with interest.

"Wow you made my day! I never caught one from Guam before!" And with glee, he issued a $300 speeding ticket. We pleaded ignorance of the speed limit. Glowing with goodwill, he amended the ticket to show we were driving only 65 mph rather than 84 and reduced our ticket by $200. Welcome to Washington.

The following day, we found Georgie awaiting us in airport shipping. When she heard our voices, her tail pounded the cage so ecstatically I thought it would break. We piled her into the back of the rental car, and she settled in happily on the floor, radiating relief and contentment.

Seattle didn't look or feel like a major West Coast city. Downtown was so small and nondescript, if we hadn't recognized the Space Needle, we would have driven right through it. We navigated the mass of unfamiliar one-way streets to the Travel Lodge, where we would stay until our new Federal Way house closed. Two weeks later, Carlos started work, the kids started school, and all three came home with chickenpox. None of them had been exposed to it in Asia. Welcome to Seattle.

I never expected to experience culture shock in my own country, but, after sixteen years, everything had changed, and I now looked at things with an Asian/Pacific Island-programmed brain. I had also lived my entire adult life abroad, and my adult head wasn't American.

The Philippines and Guam had simple roads without bridges, overpasses, or cloverleafs. Now, with so many lanes, new road markings, and new driving rules, even driving seemed confusing.

Telephones had changed too. Willa, from Balesin camp, had left the Philippines and now lived an hour from us. She invited us to visit. Confused by the highway signs, we got lost and stopped at a gas station to use the phone. The attendant pointed to the wall. *It's on the wall?* I'd never seen a private phone on the wall. I removed the receiver from the hook and stared at the box.

"Where's the dial?" The attendant gave me an odd look, and pointed to the receiver in my hand. Dialing had migrated from the main phone to a hand-held receiver, and push buttons now replaced the rotary dial.

During my absence, the U.S. population had increased by almost 50 million, and area codes had multiplied like mushrooms as the population grew. When I left in 1964, an area code normally indicated a long-distance call. Now, it could be the next town over. I could never figure out when I needed an area code.

We settled into our new house with only our suitcases. Things coming by boat would take another two months, but at least we could buy a phone. The following Saturday, we visited the phone store.

"We need a phone and a new phone number."

The clerk apologized. "Of course, but I'm really sorry; we can't do it today."

"No problem. When do you think it will be available?"

"Do you mind waiting until Monday?" Carlos and I burst out laughing. Her brow furrowed with anxiety. "Is that too long? We might be able to make a special installation tomorrow."

"No, it's fine," we laughed. "In the Philippines and Guam, we waited two years for phones. When we finally got them, they never worked ninety percent of the time. Then we found it didn't matter because most of our friend's phones, if they even owned one, weren't working either, so we couldn't call anyone anyhow." She looked at us as if we were Martians.

Moving to a new culture is always challenging. A step up in quality of life is generally much easier than a step down, but if the transition is too dramatic, it can be overwhelming. Change would have been easier to handle without memories and expectations; I kept looking for what I remembered but saw little of it. It had been easier adapting to the Philippines than moving back here. I felt jolted because nothing felt familiar.

People assumed I had the same general knowledge they did, but I had missed years of tumultuous change that had shaped my generation and profoundly impacted the country. People casually referenced the turbulence and rebellion of the Sixties; the unrest of the Civil Rights Movement; the multiple assassinations of prominent people; the Vietnam War protests; the hippie movement; drug and free-love culture; and the Jesus movement. I couldn't relate to any of it. References to popular rock bands, TV shows, or people meant nothing. When I asked, "What's a Super Bowl?" people gave me the now-familiar incredulous look, but the first Super Bowl happened three years after I left.

Now, in a different life stage, and a new part of the country, I couldn't relate to the culture. Attitudes, vocabulary, and slang had changed.

Initially, shopping was a nightmare. The bewildering variety of choices complicated life immensely until I learned what I wanted. Aside from Cheerios, Wonder Bread, and Jell-O, little on the supermarket shelves looked familiar. There used to be milk. Now, in addition to regular milk, which few people seemed to drink anymore, I found shelves filled with skim milk, two percent, four percent, acidophilus, dairy-free, lactose-free, almond milk, goat milk, and chocolate milk. The bread, cheese, cereal, and coffee choices were equally overwhelming. Without preferences, shopping became time-consuming and surprisingly stressful. My first supermarket trip took four hours. Once I knew the brands I wanted, the second trip was much faster, but new brands appeared on the shelves almost daily.

Everything in this country felt excessive. The newspaper was so thick; who could read it all? Packaging was incredibly wasteful. In Asia, fish came wrapped in a piece of old newspaper or banana leaf, and maybe a plastic bag. Here, meat sat on absorbent pads in Styrofoam trays covered with plastic wrap and butcher paper, all enclosed in a plastic bag. Fruit came in plastic cups, covered with lids, inside a cardboard box, and covered with clear wrap. Packaging inside packaging, all non-recyclable and primarily non-biodegradable. This country generated incredible amounts of waste yet still only paid lip service to recycling.

To complicate things further, although he denies it, Carlos changed too. In the Philippines, he was Mr. Take-Charge. He knew how to do everything, who to call, where, and how to get anything done. Now, the roles reversed. He waited for me to call people, fix problems, suggest solutions, and make things happen, but I knew little more than he did. Overwhelmed, I needed a co-problem solver, not a co-dependent. I had two different husbands, depending on which country we were in.

My friend's husband, a Nepalese Sherpa, expressed similar feelings years later. Now living here, he divided his year between being a Sherpa guide, an influential position in Nepal, and working in the U.S. Post Office.

When I asked him how he was adjusting to U.S. life, he said, "The United States makes me feel very small." I knew what he meant.

As Easter approached, I began feeling the kids needed religious exposure. In Guam, God had wanted me in a church, but I had bargained with Him, and He had sent me to a Bible study. Now, He appeared to be dusting off His request, and my old excuses seemed feeble. I wondered how to bring it up. Carlos would think I had lost my mind; we hadn't been in church since our wedding.

The day before Easter, I sat at the kitchen table with a coffee, watching Carlos fiddle with the microwave, and wondering how to bring it up, when he said, "Do you think maybe we should start going to church?"

I was astonished. I never saw that coming. "I was thinking that too, but I wasn't sure how you'd react." Remembering how a high school friend and I had fruitlessly visited all the Glen Ellyn denominations our senior year in high school, I said, "Let's find something non-denominational."

I opened the phone book. Evergreen Bible Chapel, a small non-denominational family church only a couple of miles from our house, jumped off the page at me right away. I called for service times, still awed that we had a working phone.

The next day, shivering in our tropical clothes, we set out for Evergreen. I wore sandals and a thin tropical dress, Carlos had a lightweight tropical suit, and the kids wore light pants and sandals. Everyone assumed we were visiting missionaries.

The greeters, Dr. and Mrs. Parks, had done mission work in the Philippines, and we developed an instant rapport. After the Easter service, Sunday school was studying the book of Revelation. "We have to stay for this," I said. And when it finished, I thought, *I want to return next week to hear more on Revelation.* By the time the series ended, we were regular attenders.

After several weeks, the Parks asked if they could come to visit.

I said, "Our furniture's still on the boat," but they didn't care and came over anyway. At some point, they asked if I was "saved." *Saved from what?*

That terminology was new. But I told them about my searching and the Being of Light encounter.

Wistful, Pauline said, "Why haven't I ever had an experience like that?"

"You probably didn't need one. I was into the occult and had seen the other side's power. God knew I needed this."

Then they asked Carlos. *This should be interesting.* Whatever being saved meant, I was pretty sure that he wasn't. He apparently didn't know what it meant either, but he seemed confident.

"My grandmother went to mass every day, and Joan went to a Bible study in Guam," he said, as if that settled everything.

Keeping a straight face, Tom informed him he needed a personal relationship with Christ. "You can't get into heaven on someone else's coat-tails," he said. Carlos looked surprised. He thought his grandmother's calloused knees had earned him a spot.

Over time Carlos got saved, and within a year or so, Carlos, David, and I got baptized, and Lisa became a counselor at Lakeside Bible Camp. In hindsight, I believe God catapulted us out of Guam because we needed a church community to grow, and weren't finding it in Guam. GEPA's reorganization was the one factor that would make me leave. Then He smoothed our transition every step of the way, from Carlos' four-day job hunt to our one-day house hunt in Federal Way, to our 15-minute house sale in Guam, and the selection of time and place for an introduction to Evergreen, right down to the final hook: the Revelation Bible study.

One cold April morning, we awoke to a freezing house. The thermostat didn't work. We had no idea how to fix it or who to call. It shocked me to realize I didn't know how to operate common American appliances like furnaces or thermostats. Dad had always dealt with those, and post-Glen Ellyn life in the tropics hadn't included furnaces or thermostats. Carlos had never lived with those things either, and he made no effort to help solve the problem. We huddled around the fireplace at night, freezing for a week.

Today, it seems odd that we didn't try harder to fix it, but an overwhelmed brain in a new culture can reduce its owner to almost a state of paralysis. We'd never had a furnace, and didn't know where to start. The phone book didn't list 'thermostat repair,' and we had no friends or family, no Siri, Google, or Angie's List to ask. Lack of heat was only one of so many things competing for my time: learning to navigate the area; getting the kids situated in school; finding climate-appropriate clothes for everyone; furnishing the entire house with bedding, furniture, kitchen utensils and lawn tools; ordering drapes, buying cars and getting driver's licenses; updating everyone's shots and dental work; putting in a yard; getting Georgie's shots, looking for a job; not to mention the everyday tasks of just cooking and cleaning, laundry and living.

The benefits of a church community became apparent when an acquaintance at church said, "I'm a furnace repairman; I'll come check it out." Roy took one look, said, "It's not the thermostat; it's the furnace," and went to the garage. Within a minute, he returned, grinning. "Come look," he said, leading us to the garage. He reached down, flipped a switch, and the furnace roared to life. *Furnaces have a switch?* It was news to me. I thought that's what thermostats did. For some ridiculous reason, the furnace on-off switch was located a foot off the floor in the garage, next to where Georgie sometimes slept. She had bumped the power switch and turned it off.

After settling in, I began looking for work. Carlos' job transition had a relatively easy learning curve; loan reviews were loan reviews, regardless of the country. The environmental field was quite different, and challenging to break into. We were in a recession, so most agencies had hiring freezes. The competition was stiff, and the few available openings were specialized. Jobs that twenty years earlier would have advertised simply for a biologist, now wanted specific expertise in forestry, fisheries, wetlands, ecology, botany, air and water quality, or other fields. My jungle and tropical marine experience fascinated everyone, but they weren't relevant to the forest and salmon culture of the Pacific Northwest.

The learning curve was steep. The Northwest ecosystem was a different set of biomes, organisms, and landforms than Chicago. Even a casual reference to a vine maple, a common northwest tree, made me feel ignorant.

Is a vine maple a tree like a vine, or a vine like a tree? Should I keep quiet and remain ignorant, or ask and reveal the huge extent of my ignorance?

After the simple village structure on Guam, the complex multi-layered governmental system of feds, states, counties, cities, Indian tribes, local interest groups, advisory committees, and other stakeholders was overwhelming. The local industries, state rules and regulations all differed too. Most important, I lacked both local work history and a contact network.

One of the few things that hadn't changed much over the decades was sex discrimination. I never felt it in Asia or Guam. The Philippines, a matriarchal society, encouraged women to excel at whatever they wanted, and Guam was simply excited to find anyone with education or expertise. Here, it was disconcerting to encounter the not-so-subtle bias against females in science almost immediately.

I interviewed for a temporary air quality job with EPA, and the interviewer said, "Check with your husband first to be sure it's OK, and let me know."

What?? "I don't need to check with him. I'll take it."

After three days of hearing nothing, I called him to follow up. "Oh darn. I didn't hear from you, so I didn't think you wanted it." *Since when did a woman need to check with her husband before accepting a job?*

King County Conservation District offered me a water quality job, but the pay was too low. I reluctantly declined, but the interview helped me realize that program development, environmental planning and government grants, most closely matched my Guam experience.

After three aborted attempts at non-biology jobs, I finally decided to be content at home and wait until God showed me what he wanted me to do, instead of trying to be in control. Maybe He was waiting for that, because the next afternoon the phone rang.

The Washington Department of Ecology offered me a nine-month temporary job over the phone, sight unseen, without even an interview or an application. I was stunned. People would kill for a state job. I'd never even talked to anyone in Ecology, let alone applied for anything there, and

I wasn't on any state registers. A year later, I learned the female manager at King County Conservation District had recommended me to Ecology, giving me a needed toehold in the local network.

Despite the Civil Rights and Women's Liberation movements of the Sixties, twenty years later, white males still dominated everything. Only half a dozen of Ecology's 300 employees were technical women. Taking advantage of my newness, two men on my floor repeatedly subtly tried to sabotage me, encouraging me to do small things they knew would circumvent established procedures and irritate my superiors. It was often an uncomfortable work environment, and I always felt like an outsider, slightly off-balance.

But Ecology was tailor-made to provide exactly the experience I needed, and I couldn't have landed in a better place. They hired me to manage the Statewide Water Quality Advisory Committee and edit the department's Waterline Newsletter. The Committee familiarized me with the layers of state and local bureaucracy, local players, and state environmental regulations, and the newsletter vastly improved my writing skills and educated me on state environmental issues.

When my temporary job ended, I applied for two permanent jobs within Ecology. The first manager said, "You're qualified, but Eastern Washington dairy farmers will never accept a woman." The second said, "You're qualified, but we don't hire women for monitoring jobs because there are no bathrooms for women in the field." I could see why Ecology had so few technical women. But I felt some consolation: Tory had left Guam and moved to Seattle a few months after we did. He got the job, and he needed it more than I.

The skills I learned at Ecology gave me the credibility needed to open doors in environmental consulting, which familiarized me with Northwest fieldwork, grants, and contracts.

It took three years to feel at home in the States and five years before I joined USEPA Region 10, which finally brought my career back where I felt called to be.

Although I initially found the variety of choices here bewildering, it became a blessing. I realized one of the best things about America is the diversity of people, lifestyles, activities, and opportunities. Those things are often small, but small things make up the warp and weft of life. If you want to pick apples or berries, there are u-pick farms. Want to go for a quick hike, go fishing, crabbing, kayaking, sculling, sailing, paddle boarding, long-distance bicycling, skiing, learn Korean cooking, snowboarding, or rock climbing? Hunt fossils? Make quilts or model rockets? Join a bible study? Buy model train parts or collect science fiction books? So many ways and places were available to do all of those here.

And no matter how esoteric or exotic the interest, a group of people existed who shared it. Clubs, fairs, and events were available for everyone from poodle and miniature horse owners, antique collectors, air-stream RV'ers, motorcyclists, kite makers, gardeners, knitters, and jousters, to mushroom pickers, rock climbers, quilters, giant pumpkin growers, and powerlifters. Few of those activities were available anywhere I had lived. I began to appreciate the richness of American life.

I liked sports, but the few sports activities in Asia usually involved difficulty, time, and money. Without public tennis courts or pools, you needed membership in an expensive club. Outdoor activities in the Philippines required several hours to reach a decent location, so they were a planned treat, not an everyday activity. We hadn't even owned bikes, because there was nowhere easy to bicycle. Here, free libraries, parks, tennis courts, and swimming pools were everywhere.

I also began to see that I had slowly shed pieces of myself one by one over the years. In my younger years I collected fossils and stamps, but, overseas, I never saw fossil sites or stamp albums, stores, or shows. Few people seemed to collect or sell either of those, so they slowly dropped off my radar. I had enjoyed reading sci-fi books, but neither Makati nor Guam had libraries or decent bookstores. My sci-fi reading died too. Of course, new experiences replaced these things, but the sum of the losses had narrowed my life.

I discovered the U.S. is the land of opportunity for many things besides economic opportunity. I bought a fat new stamp album, began buying fossils and reading sci-fi books again. I became a Master Gardener, Amphibian Monitor, and Native Plant Steward. For the first time, I planted a vegetable garden, joined a fossil dig, and began hunting fossils. Carlos and I joined a bike club and became powerlifters and serious long-distance bikers. I began reclaiming the lost pieces of my life.

- *Forty-Four* -
A Simple Trip to the Beach

Pagsanjan 1989

A DECADE LATER, ALTHOUGH NOW FULLY ESTABLISHED in the States, Carlos and I still maintained strong connections to the Philippines. We straddled both worlds, and retained our Marcello house and a solid connection to the Philippines. The kids were not yet in school when we left the Philippines. Lisa, now in college, and David, just graduated high school, had grown up American. We felt they took the ease of living in the States for granted, and lacked appreciation for what they had in both cultures. They needed to reconnect with their Filipino roots.

Once we moved to Seattle, Solita, Carlos' mom, began coming to visit. In 1989, she came for cataract surgery and needed someone to accompany her back to the Philippines. David volunteered.

We said, "Great." It could be an eye-opener into the culture, a graduation present. How much trouble could he encounter just taking his grandmother home?

"That's not fair!" Lisa protested. "I didn't get a trip for graduation." She went to Hawaii with her friend's family for a week after graduation, but she thought David was getting a better deal. Lisa could use some cultural appreciation too, so we said, "OK, you go with him." There was safety in numbers. The Filipino culture moves with a very different rhythm, and they would see another side of their grandmother in her own country.

David, always the bargainer, upped the ante. "Since we'll be so close, I'd like to stop in Thailand." He had heard my tales of Thailand and wanted to see the temples. Closeness is relative; it was a 1450-mile detour, but having lived there, I wanted the kids to appreciate Bangkok as I had.

"If he adds Thailand, then I want to go to Hong Kong to go shopping," Lisa said.

This simple trip was becoming complicated, and I envisioned our children running amok in Bangkok and Hong Kong night markets. *Maybe I should go along.* Carlos had used all his vacation time, so I invited my sister, Lynn, and added my own destinations of Kuala Lumpur and Penang, Malaysia. As long as we were in the Philippines, we should also stay long enough to explore something of Pagsanjan, and perhaps visit the former head-hunter region of Baguio and Banaue, too.

In typical Filipino fashion, a simple trip to take Solita back to the Philippines had expanded into a five-person, five-country, month-long junket.

I told everyone, "Only bring what you can carry. We're not checking luggage on this trip. Too many things disappear in Asian baggage areas." But Solita made up for all of us. Her two huge suitcases and two large boxes were filled with weeks of accumulated buying, including a toaster oven, an inhaler, and hard-to-find things in the Philippines like American shampoo, cheap shitake mushrooms, Swiss Miss hot chocolate mix, and American candy bars. Thankfully, she decided to forgo the microwave and oak toilet seat. Now I saw why she needed a traveling companion; there was no way she could manage all those boxes herself in the airports.

Nothing in Asia ever seems easy or straightforward, but usually snafus don't begin until arrival. This trip, things began going awry at SeaTac airport. As we checked in Solita's baggage, by pure luck, I noticed her suitcase was mistakenly ticketed to Singapore, and managed to grab it back just as it began disappearing down the luggage chute.

A malfunctioning engine delayed, then canceled, our flight. The airline shifted us to another airline and routed us through Los Angeles, adding an additional flight and layover, before a grueling twelve-hour flight to Seoul, another layover, and three and a half hours more to Manila. The airline change added eight hours to an already long trip.

Even at midnight, the humid heat in the mostly un-airconditioned Manila airport descended on us like a soggy blanket. We collected Solita's luggage and prepared to battle with Customs. Manila was my personal nomination for the world's worst arrival airport. Collecting baggage and clearing Customs always became a two-hour nightmare because most returning Filipinos lugged home enough large *balikbayan* boxes to fill two or three baggage carts.

Despite her comparatively few pieces of luggage, unsympathetic Customs officials charged Solita's imports 100 percent of their value plus P31.65 in "stamps." Expecting this, of course, she lied about the value and claimed $25 for the oven plus $15 for the inhaler. Knowing she would lie they upped her values to $30 and $25. She proposed new deals. Whatever she ended up paying, she came out ahead because the inhaler alone cost $150.

The hot season was winding down. A few scattered showers signaled the coming rainy season, but the heat was unrelenting, and the sprinkles only increased the humidity. Sometime after midnight, we wrestled the luggage through Customs. Exhausted and saturated with sweat, we emerged from the airport into a blast of hot, humid night air. An army of sampaguita lei sellers, baggage boys, and taxi drivers immediately descended on us despite the late hour. We formed a guard around Solita's pile of luggage, returned the unwanted leis draped over our shoulders, and successfully fended off taxis while waiting for Carlos' brother, Mario, to find us in the milling crush of people.

Mario spotted us in the crowd. We piled into two cars and drove to my friend Nan's house in Magallanes Village, our base for several days while in Makati. Our exhausting thirty-hour, door-to-door trip had ended, but Solita continued on to Pagsanjan, 60 miles south of Manila. It was past

1:00 a.m., and multiple traffic and military checkpoints ensured she would still have a couple of hours drive ahead. We would meet her in a few days

We experienced exciting but convoluted adventures around Manila, Corregidor, and Baguio, by *calesa* or horse carriage, bus, jeepney, tuk-tuk, tricycle, boat, and taxi. We dealt with brownouts, non-working toilets, water shutoffs, facilities closures, lost reservations, overcharging taxis, persistent beggars, and a pick-pocketed wallet in Baguio. I hoped everyone was beginning to appreciate the ease of travel and life back home.

At the end of the week, Mario picked us up from Magallanes and drove us home to Pagsanjan. Although the oppressive humidity and heat still sapped our strength and energy, vegetation in the province provided some relief from the unrelenting heat. Manila had been hectic; now, we looked forward to a restful time. All we wanted was to have a swim and get a tropical tan.

"Go to Pagsanjan Lodge," Solita suggested. There, a cool, natural stream flowed through the property and emptied into the Pagsanjan River. A portion of widened stream channel was cemented to form a long, snakelike pool, and a cemented area alongside the stream, surrounded by coconut palms, contained a few lounge chairs for sunbathing.

It sounded perfect. Grabbing our bathing suits and towels, we walked the few blocks through dusty streets up to the Lodge. There we saw a sign: "Closed for pool painting." Worse yet, they didn't know when it would open. They floated many explanations to us, but it was dry season; obviously the stream was simply awaiting the rains. For us, this was a minor disaster.

Dripping sweat, clothes sticking to our backs, we returned to the house and collapsed in air-conditioned cool for an early siesta. The following two days, realizing we wanted to swim, Solita arranged for a banca ride to Pagsanjan Falls and took us to Hidden Valley, a beautiful jungle resort with multiple natural pools of various water temperatures, surrounded by enormous buttressed jungle trees. It was beautiful, relaxing, and refreshing but, to us, swimming meant sunbathing and tanning, and there was no place for that.

The Philippines has some beautiful ocean beaches, but they require a couple of hours' drive, so I suggested we borrow a family car and driver. "That way we can go without inconveniencing anyone. We can swim and lie on the beach as long as we want, and no one needs to sit around, bored and uncomfortable, waiting for us."

Mario said, "No need for a driver. I'll drive you to Nasugbu." I heard it had excellent scuba diving, so I thought the beach should be nice, and his wife Fe, at least, liked swimming. Although a bit of a squeeze, we could fit the six of us in the car.

Mario, not a swimmer, suggested leaving Pagsanjan about noon, but then we wouldn't arrive until two, missing the best tanning time, so he agreed to pick us up at eight. With any luck, we would arrive at the beach around ten and be back around five.

Then things began going south.

When Solita asked what we wanted to do the next day, we said, "Mario's driving us to the beach."

Filipinos don't like lying on the beach. They value light skin, and avoid tropical heat and sun. Whenever I'd been swimming with her, we'd always gone in the late afternoon or early evening, so we didn't invite her, because I knew she would hate what we had in mind.

That night at dinner, smiling brightly, Solita said, "Good news! We can stop to see Fanny Aldaba at lunch tomorrow in Tagaytay. It's on the way anyhow." *We? Lunch? Tagaytay?* Solita liked swimming, but I couldn't imagine she would enjoy sitting on the beach. She would put a serious crimp in our style, so we tried to dissuade her.

"We plan to lie out on the beach, Mom. You'll hate it." I knew if she came along, we would feel guilty and cut short our stay. "It's going to be hot. Why don't we drop you off at Fanny's and pick you up on the way back?" But she dug in, determined to come. I had a sinking feeling.

She was being a good hostess and meant well, but she had just hijacked our trip; we had never intended to stop in Tagaytay. Mario and I groaned, exchanging glances. If she came, we knew what this would do to our trip because there was no way she would sit for hours on a hot beach. We needed to kill her plan before it got well-hatched.

Since Tagaytay lies halfway between Pagsanjan and Nasugbu beach, logistically, we needed to be at Fanny's by 9:30 at the latest to take advantage of the beach. With food, it became more complicated because meals are always a lengthy affair when Filipinos are involved. If we stayed for lunch, we were trapped. The earliest we could diplomatically leave Fanny's would be 3:00, reaching Nasugbu by 4:00, the time we originally planned to be done swimming and on our way home.

Solita somehow always managed to get her way, and we knew if she were determined to come, we couldn't avoid a stop at Fanny's. Filipino hospitality would require eating, but we hoped to minimize the damage. Mario argued for a mid-morning *merienda* instead of lunch. Since no one in the Philippines visits without bringing food, we could bring merienda food: pan de sal, bibingka, and fruit. He suggested an early start and an early merienda. If we left Fanny's by 10:00, we could be in Nasugbu by 11:00, buy lunch there, and eat at the beach. I expected opposition to his suggestion but heard none. This seemed far too easy.

The following day became a crescendo of catastrophe. In true Filipino style, overnight, the entourage expanded. Solita had invited her friend Alice. With eight people, now we needed a second car. And a second driver.

At 8:00 a.m. Mario called. "We're going to be a bit late. The car has a fan belt problem, but Paquito took it to the garage. We should be there soon." No problem, because we were waiting for Alice, expected to be over an hour late. Solita wasn't ready either. We were now running on Filipino time.

Meanwhile, Mom was packing a merienda, which looked suspiciously like lunch: a massive pile of Tupperware containing rice, shrimp, gabi, pancit, and other things quite hard to eat on the sand or in a boat, and she packed no silverware or plates.

At 9:30, Mario and Fe finally arrived, bringing their daughter Kuling and Mario's friend Paquito. As we waited for Alice to arrive, Paquito had an inspiration; he would invite his niece, Dina. That made eleven, plus two drivers. The trip had now morphed from five to 13 people and three cars. Alice arrived. Dina finally arrived, having first stopped at the market to buy a large basket of *balut,* boiled duck embryos, to contribute to the 'picnic,' as it was now being called. We left Pagsanjan at 11:00, already three hours behind schedule.

Traffic was terrible. We arrived in Tagaytay and pulled up to Fanny's house, conveniently arriving about lunchtime. The fan belt had broken again, so Paquito stopped to take the car to a garage. Mario told him to meet us at Fanny's.

Tagaytay's claim to fame is the Taal volcano, a massive crater with a sparkling blue lake in the center. Fanny had a fantastic view of Taal from her living room because her house sat right on the edge of the giant caldera. We could look down into Taal Lake and see Volcano Island in the middle. It's one of the Philippines' most iconic scenes, a million-dollar view.

We could also see a wonderful lunch displayed on a big table under the picture window. Fanny had gone to a great deal of trouble. There was no way to avoid it: we were staying for lunch. Mom was already unpacking her big bag of food.

The fan belt required longer than expected to fix. Finally, Mario said, "We might as well go ahead and eat lunch. If Paquito doesn't arrive by 12:30, we'll leave Mom and her entourage at Fanny's and go on ahead." At this point, a fatalistic resignation had replaced our growing frustration. We all sat down to eat. Solita beamed. Mario muttered under his breath, "She won again."

Paquito and Dina arrived at 12:25. Dina brought along her giant basket of balut. Although we had finished lunch, almost everyone greeted this present with enthusiasm. Of course, we had to wait for them to eat lunch, and they were in no hurry. Lunch stretched leisurely out until 1:30, as Mom peeled and ate her grapes one at a time.

I was doggedly determined to salvage even a piece of the afternoon. I whispered to the kids, "Go change into your swimming suits, and we'll tell Grandma we have to leave."

Meanwhile, Mom, her face serene, leaned back and suggested, "It's so restful. Why don't we all spend the rest of the day here?" I could almost feel everyone's heart plunge, and I could have strangled her. This was a catch-22. If we agreed, we would forgo the beach. If we disagreed, we would insult Fanny. Everyone remained silent.

As if on cue, the kids appeared in their bathing suits, signaling they were ready to go. This clinched it. I said to Fanny, "We'd love to stay, Fanny, but the kids are set on going to the beach today. Mom, why don't you stay and visit? We'll pick you up on the way back." But a good hostess, Solita still insisted on coming along.

With effusive thanks and protracted goodbyes to Fanny, we piled into the cars and departed at 2:30, with still at least another hour's drive. But not done yet, Solita insisted we detour to see a property she had bought in Tagaytay and intended to gift to us, probably a bribe to lure us back to the Philippines. Yet no matter how beautiful or perfect, we didn't want more long-distance property to manage.

Being an overseas property owner invites problems with squatters and taxes, and property is extremely difficult to sell unless you live in the country because things usually sell by word of mouth. However, it would be ungrateful not to at least pass by and mumble appropriate expressions of thanks, so we detoured to see the lot. A half-hour later, at long last, we departed for Nasugbu. *At least the kids are experiencing a new side of Filipino culture.*

Traffic jammed the narrow provincial roads. We arrived at Nasugbu after 4:00 p.m., now over six hours behind schedule. The beach community, a closely packed group of tin-roofed shanties walled with nipa fronds, sat conveniently along the high tide line. Perhaps somewhere had beautiful beaches, but not here. Trash, mainly plastic, lay everywhere. Much of it had probably washed in with the tide from Manila's Smoky Mountain seaside garbage dump, and no one bothered to clean it up.

Everything imaginable littered the once-beautiful white sand, from garbage, cans, plastic bags, food containers, old fishing nets, stray flip-flops and broken nipa fronds, to dog poop. People living in small huts along the beach also seemed to pitch their garbage out the door without regard for health or aesthetics, and made no attempt to even pile it up. There was no way we would lie on that beach, and I assumed underwater looked little different, not to mention the addition of the raw sewage from the huts along the shore.

Mario wasn't dismayed. "There are beautiful islands nearby good for swimming. We can take a boat," and he gestured to many large bancas with bamboo outriggers and outboard motors moored offshore. Bancas stretched for a quarter mile down the beach, proof the offshore islands sometimes attracted hordes of tourists.

By now, we were resigned to not swimming. "Never mind. It's OK," we said.

Fe said, "I'll be right back. I'm going to make a quick stop at the Philippine Constabulary (PC) to check something out with them."

At long last, Mario and Paquito suddenly developed a sense of urgency and began frantically scanning the beach for a banca driver. Independently, each rushed off, bargained, and struck a deal for a banca. But we only needed one. Business was slow, so this precipitated a minor crisis and dispute between the two banqueros that took some time to sort out and negotiate. After settling the argument, we agreed on one, waded out to his banca, and climbed aboard. Paquito refused to take off his shoes, so the tiny banquero had to piggyback him through the ocean to his banca.

We waited while the banquero attempted to start the motor. Fifteen minutes and many tries later, it sputtered but still wouldn't start. The second banquero stood on the shore, watching all of this with interest. We waved him over and transferred to his banca. With some coaxing and cussing, his motor coughed to life. Underway at last! But a few hundred yards out, he began making a U-turn back to the beach.

He looked sheepish. "We forgot the anchor." We all agreed we needed an anchor, so back we went, to wait while he waded ashore to hunt up an anchor. Delays were now beyond comical; they had reached the absurd. A couple of us began spontaneously laughing a bit hysterically.

The banquero returned with an anchor. Now, almost 5:00, we were truly underway. Mario and Mom were relieved; everything was under control. At this point, the four of us had given up any hope of swimming, and we had lost all desire anyhow. It was no longer sunny, and way too late for getting a tan. In fact, as I looked up, the previously blue sky seemed to have sprouted quite a few dark clouds. We were resigned to not swimming, but a boat ride to see the offshore islands could still be pleasant.

A discussion began; exactly which beautiful island were we going to? "Well, it's over that way," Fe said, motioning vaguely to the right. *It?*

Mario had an inspiration. "Let's stop and see if The Dead is still there."

It sounded morbidly fascinating. Long past feeling urgency, we agreed. And in fact, The Dead had quite a story. Mario and Fe were considering purchasing a small nearby island, and three weeks earlier, they had come to see it. There, above the high tide line, they discovered the body of a young woman. She had been shot through the head and dumped on the island. They returned to Nasugbu, sought out the PC, reported the body, and returned home, unsure whether the PC had bothered to follow up on the report. Today Fe had stopped to ask the PC how they had handled her report.

"We didn't bother to check it out because no one was reported missing," they told her. They apparently felt this absolved them from further responsibility. I suddenly flashed-back to the murder in San Juanillo, Costa Rica. This murder seemed backward too. The woman was missing from somewhere. Advertising her discovery might have allowed an identification. Yet they had done nothing, so perhaps she still lay on the shore.

We slowed down as we approached The Dead's island. We saw no body, but something vaguely resembling a mass of black hair lay on the beach where she had been. Either someone had retrieved the body, or more likely, crabs, seabirds, and three weeks in the tropical sun had taken care of disposal, reducing her to a fragmented skeleton, her bones blending in with the large chunks of bleached coral on the beach. Beaching the banca was difficult, so we didn't go ashore to investigate further.

The blue sky had now turned leaden and overcast but, undeterred, we continued to the swimming beach. Five minutes later, the sky opened, and a sheet of driving rain slammed our open boat with a blast of ferocious force. Mist covered the water, and visibility dropped to almost nothing. We were all thoroughly soaked within seconds. Tropical rain never feels cold, but the wind was cool, and we hunched over in the banca, shivering, our hair plastered down and dripping over our faces.

Alice huddled under a towel, looking like a gnome. Mom pulled the top of her neon pink bathrobe, originally intended as a sunscreen, over her head like a hood, and closed the top, leaving only a pair of dark eyes staring miserably out into the rain. A picture of ET floated across my mind. Both of them wanted desperately to go back.

But Paquito had bought one of the offshore islands sight-unseen, and now he wanted to see it. Dina opened her basket of balut, and offered it to everyone. Once Alice realized we were going to continue, even when soaked and uncomfortable, she decided to eat. She sat serenely in the downpour, opening one balut after the other, slurping down the contents, and tossing the eggshells, embryo heads, and feet overboard. She ate almost the entire basket.

I had tried balut a few years earlier and rather liked it. It tasted like chicken soup, but boiling the embryos seems very cruel, and balut are not pretty. They have heads and feet, and depending on the age of the embryo, sometimes the chick even has rudimentary feathers, which are quite off-putting. When I bit into my balut, the head fell out and rolled on the table, as the large embryonic eyes stared accusingly up at me. That was my last balut.

I glanced at Lynn. She looked slightly green. She sat huddled, squinting against the rain, not feeling too well, and eyeing Alice with fascination as she ate boiled embryos one after the other, dribbling duck juice all over the boat. Lisa and David hunched over, heads bowed against the rain. The absurdity of the delays struck us as irrationally comical, and again, the four of us began to giggle.

The boat passed several small coral islands with fringing coral reefs, a few mangroves, and white sandy coves. After perhaps 30 minutes of torrential downpour, the rain abated as quickly as it began. The last shafts of a glowing sunset parted the clouds just as we pulled up to a beautiful sandy beach.

Mom came out from under her bathrobe, beaming. "There. Look at the nice beach! Now you can go swimming." This, of course, was her preferred swimming time, but our desire had long evaporated. We declined. It was after 6:00 p.m., eight hours past our planned swimming time, and almost dark. We were all soaked and cold, but she was determined we would have our swimming experience.

"Go, go, get in and swim!" Solita urged, shooing us with her hands. And everyone sat there expectantly waiting for the four of us to swim. We were already soaked, and they weren't budging, so finally, we went in. The ocean felt warm compared to the cool breeze. Fe and Kuling joined us too. Now Mom was happy. We had attained the goal and had our swim, even if only five minutes.

"Isn't this better? She gushed. We don't have to worry about getting sunburned this late in the day."

A small thatch-roofed bar sat on the deserted beach. Now shivering, everyone waded ashore to order hot instant Nescafe, the only thing available that time of day.

The cars already waited for us behind the bar. We piled in, still soaking wet. The group split up, two cars returning to Pagsanjan and the other taking the four of us to Nan's house in Magallanes. After a silence, David said incredulously, "What was *that* all about?' And we all started laughing again.

As we discussed the frustrating day, we laughed at the cultural differences. Lynn decided Mom had a 'cultural, mental block.' There was no other way to understand her polite stubbornness. She couldn't comprehend what going to the beach meant to us because it meant something so different to her. Why would anyone want to get dark anyhow? The sun was something to be avoided. Time wasn't important to her, but the social aspect was. Now she felt satisfied; we had met Fanny and seen Taal, and we still went swimming, if only briefly.

The Philippines' first McDonald's had recently opened, and upon reaching Makati, we asked our driver to stop there. We all ordered Big Macs, a real treat for the driver. No one had ever bought him a McDonald's before because its Stateside prices were quite expensive by Philippine standards. He ate only half, carefully wrapping up the rest to take home. He had to be hungry; I asked him why he didn't eat it all. He said he would keep it for later. His wife had never eaten a McDonald's either, and he thoughtfully wanted to save it for her. We insisted he eat the whole thing and bought him another one to bring home.

The next day we left the Philippines for Malaysia, and the first thing we did in Penang was head to the beach. And we stayed there all day, enjoying our sunburns.

***

A week after returning home the Seattle Times ran a front-page story about a freak airline accident in the Philippines. It showed a picture of a Philippine Airlines jet sitting on the superhighway, surrounded by several cars, obliterated beyond recognition. I recognized the highway near our Marcello house but saw no personal connection.

That night we received a shocking phone call from Mom. Emotionless, without preamble, she said, "Fe's dead,"

"Dead? We just saw her!" It was difficult to comprehend.

"There was an airline accident on the superhighway."

"We saw a picture of it on the front page of the Seattle Times. But Fe….?"

In a bizarre and tragic accident, a Philippine Airlines jet had overshot the airport runway during a rainstorm and plowed down the superhighway, colliding with several cars and killing eight people. One car was Mario's. Mario's wife Fe, the driver, and our friend Radhi were all decapitated and killed instantly.

This was so unexpected it was hard to process. I was so glad we had made the trip and had a last chance to see Fe. The family weren't picture takers, so they had few photos of Fe. Certainly nothing recent. Fortunately, I had just taken a few pictures, which we sent to Mario, and once people learned of the photographs, many of her friends began asking me for copies.

The accident was a grim reminder that none of us know how long we have on earth or what the next day may bring. Each morning we wake assuming today will be similar to yesterday, that life will continue as it always has, and family and friends will be alive and well. Yet, in only a moment, a split second, everything can change.

The accident was a reminder to live life to the fullest and make the most of every opportunity. Perhaps most of all, it was a reminder to leave every encounter with no unresolved conflicts or regrets, because it may be the last chance to make amends or make a memory. I can still see Fe sitting in the rain, in the banca.

- Forty-Five -

Rescue on the STP

<u>**Oregon 1990**</u>

I N OLD TESTAMENT TIMES, COVENANTS WERE BINDING
agreements in which two people assumed responsibility for each other's
welfare as if it were their own. In other words, both parties in the covenant
'had each other's backs.' The New Testament says believers are in a new covenant relationship with God. If you think about it, God having a believer's
back is a rather mind-blowing concept. How might He accomplish that?

The Bible leaves the concept of guardian angels open to conjecture.
I'd been skeptical about them, but a somewhat enigmatic experience in
Oregon made me think perhaps guardian angels are one method God
uses to ensure He has our backs and keeps His part of the new covenant.

Some people ride the 200-plus mile Seattle to Portland bicycle ride
(STP) in one day, but, like most people, we always rode it in two. Organizers
provided no route maps, but maps weren't needed because the 13,000 registered and unregistered riders quickly sorted out by speed, stringing out
along the road for miles, and providing a line of people ahead to follow.

The sheer number of riders precluded the organizers from providing
sag wagons or rescue vehicles. You couldn't count on help from friends,
either, because everyone has their own comfortable riding pace, and groups
starting together tend to become separated over time. In the pre-cell phone
days, we rode without communication. The bottom line: you had to be able

to change a tire and make your own minor repairs, because you couldn't count on having help in a crisis.

The Puyallup hill and Longview Bridge were the most challenging parts. The Puyallup hill was a steep one-mile uphill with a seven percent grade. Local kids made it even more difficult by sprinkling thousands of carpet tacks on the road, just for the enjoyment of watching hundreds of people stop to change flat tires.

Our friend Johan joined us on the ride, but his younger and faster legs soon left us behind. We had barely started up the Puyallup hill when we found him standing by his bike, staring dejectedly down at a flat tire. It was Johan's first STP, and he was unprepared; he didn't bring a tire patch kit, pump, extra innertube, or even bother to learn how to change a tire. Carlos and I stopped and fixed his flat. Then he sped off, leaving us in the dust.

A bit farther on, a flapping plup, plup, plup, of rubber on the asphalt told me I had a flat. Since Carlos usually rides a couple of miles an hour slower than I, he decided to ride on ahead. I patched my tire and rode on, figuring I'd eventually catch up with him at a food stop.

But a mile later, I found Johan again standing along the road, staring morosely at a second flat. *Tire changing is getting old.* Once again, I patched his tire and watched him jump on his bike and speed off. These three stops caused at least an hour delay.

Many two-day riders break the ride at the approximate halfway point in Centralia, but we prefer to ride longer on the first day, to have a shorter ride on the second. We spent the night in Winlock, "Home of the World's Largest Egg," about 130 miles from Seattle. With all the flat tires and the longer ride, the first day was a bit stressful. I looked forward to an easy, short second day, only about 75-miles.

The only stress I anticipated was the dangerous Longview Bridge. A very long uphill approach lifts the highway steadily up above the wide Colombia River floodplain, arches over the broad Columbia, and slopes down the approach on the other side.

The difficulty wasn't the long uphill grade; the problems were traffic and slow speed, because at that time, the bridge remained open to traffic during the STP. Thousands of riders approaching the bridge condensed into single-file and began ascending the bridge on-ramp at a pace barely fast enough to stay upright on a bicycle. Crossing the traffic-filled bridge was always tense, because it had no bike lane. Riders rode on the very narrow shoulder in single file without passing, forcing the entire line to move at the speed of the slowest rider.

Once starting over the bridge, it was imperative to keep moving, because a long line of bumper-to-bumper cyclists, biking at a snail's pace, followed close behind you. Riding up the incline at a slow speed was difficult, but stopping would cause a domino of crashes, and spill a lengthy line of cyclists into the narrow traffic lanes, and the heavy traffic had no options to avoid them. After the bridge, I breathed a small sigh of relief. *The rest should be easy. Only perhaps 45-50 miles to go.*

After a few miles of a long, sustained bike ride, once my legs warmed up, I fell into the automatic cadence that happened when diving: a pedaling and breathing rhythm of body and bike. Once I was 'in the zone,' with my legs on auto-pilot, I felt I could mindlessly pedal forever. Sometimes the brain became lulled into auto-pilot mode too.

In the early hours of a golden afternoon, now on the Oregon side of the Columbia River, I was pedaling almost robotically, when I noticed perhaps a dozen porta-potties lining the roadside. A row of concrete Jersey barriers in front of them separated the toilets from the passing riders. The barriers began ten feet before the first potty, and the width between barriers and potties progressively funneled down to about three feet, before abruptly ending at the last potty.

As I approached, pondering a stop, I unwittingly pedaled into the narrow lane between the barriers and the potties. Although my eyes registered the approaching end, my legs continued pedaling with a life of their own. I crashed into the cement barrier at the end, at full speed of 15 mph, wedging myself between the last potty and the concrete barrier. My left ankle smashed painfully into the concrete and my bike and I crashed to the ground in a tangle. The impact was so violent it knocked the bike chain off the sprockets.

I untangled myself from the bike with difficulty, and examined the chain. It was unbroken, but now bent. I straightened it as much as possible, but one link had a kink I couldn't remove. I reattached the chain and begin riding.

My bleeding ankle was already swelling and too painful to put much weight on. I found I could only pedal with my right foot. *I can't expect a rescue. I'm on my own, with no option but to continue riding.* I pedaled mechanically, with one foot, trying to ignore the pain. Every slow turn of the pedal hit the kink in the chain with a loud metallic click, click, click. After several hours and perhaps fifteen or twenty miles of slow, noisy, one-footed pedaling, I found myself in a quiet, densely-treed residential suburb somewhere west of Portland.

Without maps, I usually followed the line of bikers by sight, but now I saw few people anymore. *Where did everybody go? Am I that late?* I followed another biker for a while, but when he turned up a driveway and went into the house, I realized I had been following someone who wasn't even on the STP. It slowly dawned on me; *I'm off the route. I'm lost, with no idea where to go next.*

I stopped and searched both ways on the empty street. It was as quiet and deserted as a ghost town. Not even a car or lawnmower broke the silence. *Could a nearby house direct me to the finish line?* I dismissed it as unlikely. Shadows were lengthening, and I estimated I still had perhaps ten miles to go, so I continued my awkward one-footed pedal, not knowing where to go, but hoping to somehow reconnect with other cyclists somewhere on the route.

As I approached an empty crosswalk, the pedal hit the kink one last time. The chain finally had enough. With a loud metallic clank, it snapped in two and slithered down onto the ground in a heap. *That's great. Now I can't even ride or coast. And I'm lost. Even if I knew where to go, I couldn't possibly walk the rest of the way.*

I stopped and dismounted to pick up the broken chain. A voice asked, "What happened?"

I looked up, and directly ahead, on what a second earlier had been an empty crosswalk, now a short, freckled Irish-looking guy stood beside a bike. He was not so close or so big as to feel intimidating, but easily close enough to talk to. He dressed in a spiffy, brand-new turquoise, purple, and black shirt with matching bike shorts, and he stood next to what looked like a new turquoise and black bike.

"My chain broke," I said, holding up the dangling remains of my greasy chain. "Are you riding in the STP?" I hoped he could give me some directions.

"No." He just stood there, doing nothing.

"Where are you headed?" He shrugged, mumbling something about just watching. *What was there for him to watch? An empty street?*

He motioned to my bike. "Get on. I'll push you." I looked at him. He was small, maybe even slightly shorter than I, but he looked wiry and muscled. I appreciated the offer, but I didn't see how he could possibly push me, not only because he was small but because our bikes would need to ride so close together, I felt our wheels would certainly collide at some point, and we would crash in a tangle.

I don't recall him even asking where I was headed. "Get on," he said again, this time with authority. So, I did.

He got on his bike, and put his right hand on my lower back. Although I expected some initial wobbling and effort at first, we began smoothly moving forward from a dead standstill. He pushed me, pedaling for both of us. He did all of the steering and braking with his left hand, which must have been tricky. We flew down the street, speeding smoothly uphill and down, zipping around corners, seemingly without effort. I don't recall even having to really steer. Our bikes moved as if locked together, responding and turning together as one.

He had to be incredibly strong to push me uphill with one hand, yet he never slowed his pace, stood up to pedal, changed a gear, got out of breath, or worked up a sweat. Surprisingly, even going uphill, when he would have needed to push me strongly, I barely sensed the pressure of his hand on my back. Our bikes almost seemed to have an external power source.

Since he seemed to have so much energy and wasn't even breathing hard, I ventured to ask him a couple of things about himself, but all his answers were vague. He offered me only an unusual first name that somehow, I couldn't quite catch, and when I asked what he did, he said, "Oh, a little of this and a little of that."

He "didn't exactly" live in Portland; he lived "here and there." His answers were so vague and non-informational that I learned nothing about him at all. He didn't ask me anything about myself or the STP either, which I found curious. He was not into talking. I gave up on conversation and let him pedal.

Amazingly, for someone not in the STP, he seemed to know the route to the finish line without riders or signs to follow. At some point, we began seeing other riders, and with surprise, I realized we were now back on the route. We moved so fast we even passed a paceline. We reached the finish line in perhaps fifteen minutes.

Abruptly, we were in a crush of people. Thousands milled around the finish line, cheering the heavy stream of incoming arrivals. He gave me a big shove so I could coast across the finish line on my own and followed me to get out of the path of the incoming riders.

I carried one dollar for a drink. Wanting to thank him, I offered to buy him a lemonade for his effort. He looked surprised, but said, "OK." I left him holding my bike and painfully hobbled and pushed my way through the crowd to a nearby lemonade stand. I returned with his lemonade, took back my bike, and glanced briefly around to see if, by chance, I could catch sight of Carlos in the thousands of milling people and bikes. Impossible.

I turned back to thank him. In those few seconds, the guy, the lemonade, and his bike had all vanished! He couldn't possibly have turned his bike around, let alone gotten so far away that I couldn't see his bright outfit, especially with the difficulty of navigating through the crowd while one-handedly pushing a bike and holding a lemonade. I checked the ground; there was no lemonade cup. He had taken it. He vanished as quickly and mysteriously as he had come. I never had a chance to thank him properly and never saw him again.

I'll leave it to you to decide whether he was an angel. If so, maybe someday I'll see him again, and next time I'll be sure to get his name. But whether he was or not, I know God is a Covenant God, and that day, once again, He had my back.

And it wouldn't be the last time.

- Forty-Six -
Learning to Listen

Seattle, WA 1992

AFTER THIRTEEN YEARS IN FEDERAL WAY, WITH THE kids now both in college, we built our dream house, and were moving north to rural Redmond, a five-acre wooded property with two streams, a half-acre pond, and a wetland. I had always wanted rural living, surrounded by nature, and I felt I was finally coming home.

This move should be easy. Student Movers would load and unload the van, but they wouldn't drive it. No problem. Carlos would drive the van, and the movers would follow us to Redmond in their car and unload it. Three hours before the movers' arrival, I dropped Carlos off at the Port of Tacoma to pick up a moving van.

Once I returned home, I rushed around, stuffing remaining last-minute items into moving boxes. Tacoma was only a few miles from our house, but Carlos was taking forever to return. Around 11:00 a.m., a gigantic white moving van pulled up in front of the house. Carlos came in, looking pale and unnerved. Shakily, he got a cup of coffee, sat down at the kitchen table, and said with finality, "I'm not driving that van to Redmond."

"But the movers are coming in less than an hour!"

He was adamant. "I don't care. Driving here was terrible. I nearly had several accidents coming here with an empty van. I won't drive it loaded down I-5."

In addition to being gigantic, its stick shift had fifteen or sixteen gears. *What had he been thinking?* He'd never driven anything with more than five gears. *Did he drive the entire distance in first gear?* Angry horn blasts and numerous near-miss accidents had punctuated his hilly five-mile drive back to the house. It had been a nightmare for him.

I agreed. Driving a heavily-loaded van forty miles to Redmond in heavy stop and go traffic could be a disaster, but movers were coming within the hour; the timing was critical.

While Carlos nursed his coffee in the kitchen, decompressing and obsessing over his trauma, I went downstairs to empty the dryer and fold the remaining laundry while trying to think through our few unpromising options. Nobody we knew could drive a big rig like that. It was Thursday, before the start of the 4th of July weekend, so many people had left town. The movers could fill the van, but there seemed no way to get it to Redmond. I sent up a quick "lightening prayer," the way people do when stuck in a tight situation, more out of desperation than expectation.

The phone rang almost immediately. It was Don, an old friend from Evergreen Chapel, now living in Auburn. We hadn't seen or heard from him in well over a year.

"I suddenly felt I needed to call you guys. How are you doing?"

"Not well at the moment. Carlos is in the kitchen upstairs having a meltdown. We're moving to Redmond today, and we have a huge moving van. The movers will be here in less than an hour to load it, but Carlos says there's no way he can drive the van to Redmond."

I explained the gear problem. "Oh. I used to drive those giant rigs all the time when I lived in Alaska. I'm off today. I'll be right over!"

What were the chances? Few people can drive those rigs, and the response to my prayer for help was almost instantaneous. He arrived ten minutes before the movers. They whisked all the furniture into the van, and Don drove the ponderous van to Redmond, right on schedule. The movers unloaded the van, and Don returned the van to Tacoma. We drove to Auburn, picked up his wife Beth, and took them out to dinner. Within a couple of months, they took to the highways in a gigantic RV and we haven't seen them since.

Without Don's help, I don't know what we would have done. Once again, God had our backs. But He's not pushy. I've found He often waits for us to turn to Him for help before jumping in to assist. And He often uses others to answer our needs. In our case, He used Don. But, to be used we must be tuned in to His quiet voice, and thankfully, Don was tuned in to his "God channel," so when he received a nudge to call us, he responded immediately. He could have said, "Sometime I should give those guys a call," and missed the opportunity. Being attuned to the nudge, or the voice, is important but, often, timing is everything. I soon learned that a bit later myself.

Camano Island 2006

Within a few years, we had settled into our new house, put in a yard, completed a wetland mitigation for the county, planted a big organic garden, and begun raising chickens. We loved the area, and realized we would probably never move again.

We also owned beautiful waterfront property on Camano Island in North Puget Sound. At one point we thought we might build on it, but now we realized we would never live there, and owning it had become a headache.

"Perhaps we should clean it up and sell it." Carlos was always into simplification.

"Probably. It's a never-ending workload."

Two-thirds of the property sat some thirty feet above the water, atop a steep bluff. Large maple trees anchored the cliff, and winter storms regularly littered the property with broken branches. The remaining third of the property lay along the beach below. Accessing it required battling horsetails and sprawling branches of gigantic blackberry bushes that threatened to obliterate the steep board stairway notched into the sandy bluff.

Homeowner's covenants required us to control a population of fast-growing wild cherry trees. They appeared to spontaneously generate every year, and grew as if on steroids. The source, a large wild cherry tree just over the lot line on the neighbor's property, produced a never-ending abundance of fruit. Local birds loved the cherries and dropped the seeds on our property. We were resigned to making yearly trips to cut the seedlings and clean up fallen maple tree branches.

In the fall we made our annual cherry-cutting pilgrimage to Camano to attack the dozens of new three-foot cherry saplings. We stacked them in a large pile, along with fallen maple branches, planning to burn the pile that day, but, at day's end, exhausted, we only wanted to go home.

"It's OK, Carlos said, "We can burn next spring."

Relieved, I agreed. "The branches will be drier and easier to burn then, anyhow."

Next summer, in early July, we heaved the heavy lawnmower into our ancient pickup and drove to Camano to burn the pile. We also hired a couple of local boys with brush cutters to help Carlos cut grass while I burned the pile.

We pulled up to the lot to find a field of two-foot grass parched into straw and interspersed with dozens of new cherry saplings. At 10:00 a.m., the blinding sun already seared our skin, and the oppressive heat came in waves without a wisp of wind to alleviate it. I stared at the big pile of branches in the sea of tall grass, visualizing the work.

We had left home hastily, and I discovered although I had brought rubber gardening shoes, I had forgotten to bring socks. Without socks, my feet would sweat and stick inside the rubber shoes. Teva sandals, my primary summer footwear, would be much more comfortable. As I opened the truck door, the familiar, almost audible voice, which I recognized wasn't mine, intruded into my head before my foot even hit the ground. *"Put on your garden shoes."*

My impulse was to protest; the rubber shoes would be uncomfortably sticky without socks, but the voice had carried a note of caution that over time, I had learned to trust. I pulled on my rubber shoes, envisioning my sweaty feet melting into the rubber.

The large size of the pile gave me pause. I didn't remember it being over six feet high. The county no doubt had a burn ban too, although we hadn't checked. We had made dozens of fires over the years, and arrogantly felt on top of this.

The pile sat on a large area of bare ground hardened by previous burns. Carlos close-mowed an additional four-foot swath around the bare dirt as a precaution, and then left to begin mowing the front of the lot. The two brush cutters fired up their noisy machines and started whacking down grass and cherry saplings. The racket from the mower and the brush cutters made even talking difficult. I worried we might disturb the neighbors, but the neighborhood looked deserted.

I usually needed a waxed fire log to start a fire, but not this time. With only a squirt of charcoal starter and one match, it caught immediately, blazing with such ferocity it took me aback. We'd made dozens of brush fires, but this one felt different. I watched it with apprehension. It blazed with a fury unlike any fire I'd ever seen. The term "demonic" actually sprang to mind. Then I remembered; these were thin, dry stems of cherry and maple, and those woods burned much hotter than the dozens of alder trees we had burned over the years.

Without leaves, the pile burned hot and clean, emitting neither sparks nor smoke. I backed away from the searing heat and waited for the pile to burn down. In a surprisingly short time, the pile collapsed into a three-foot heap of scorching, glowing embers. *Without sparks or wind, at least it's not going anywhere.* My unease disappeared. It seemed safe. *It should be OK to leave it for just a moment while I check the area below the cliff.*

Pruners in hand, I turned and started carefully down the trail of aging board planks in the hillside, prepared to battle my way through the overgrown blackberry canes to the beach. Scarcely six or seven steps down the cliff, the small voice in my head returned. *"Don't leave the fire."*

I didn't expect it to go anywhere, but Don had taught me that immediate obedience to these prompts is important, so I reconsidered. *It is awfully hot. It won't hurt to let it burn down a bit more first.* I turned back and ascended the steps, just in time to see a small fire ignite on the edge of the mowed area, perhaps five feet from the fire. The fierce heat was so intense it had spontaneously ignited a small clump of grass stubble. I ran toward the fire, and the heat hit me like a blast furnace. Shielding my face with my arm, I darted in sideways, stamped out the small fire with my rubber shoe, and backed up quickly, my legs stinging. I heard a crackle and smelled singed hair.

A few seconds later, another fire spontaneously ignited on the opposite side of the pile. Throwing my arm over my face, I darted in again, stamped that one out too, and quickly jumped back. Even five or six feet from the fire, I could stand it only for an instant. My jeans were scorching to the touch, and I thought they were ablaze, but looking down, they appeared normal. Whenever I moved and they touched my skin, it felt like touching a hot iron. It was excruciating.

I assumed the heat would be hotter on the outside of my jeans but, if anything, it seemed hotter inside. I backed off to let my jeans cool down. My legs felt like roasted hot dogs. *How can this be when my jeans aren't even singed?*

Then, in rapid succession several other small fires began springing up all around the central fire. The left leg now felt so painful I switched to stamping with my right foot. Adrenalin pumping, I circled the fire like a crazy woman, running from one side to the other, darting in to stamp one fire out, backing off, and darting back in to put out the next. I had no choice but to stamp them out, but I couldn't keep up with them.

I yelled, "I need some help over here!" as loud as I could, but the two brush cutters couldn't hear me. The roar of their machines masked my voice. Carlos, intent on running the noisy mower, and deaf even without the noise, never even looked up. Small fires were igniting faster than I could put them out, but I didn't dare leave the fire long enough to grab someone.

Finally seeing me running madly around the fire, one of the brush cutters yelled out, "Do you need some help?"

"Yes!" I yelled. "I can't keep on top of this!"

He ran over, stomped out one small fire, and backed out quickly. "Man, that's hot," he gasped. And he wouldn't go back again.

But it helped enough to get me on top of the small fires. I stomped out two more, and then, everything that could combust had done so. A circle of charred grass stubble ringed the dirt around the fire, and the fires stopped. The cutter returned to his brush whacking, and I kept vigil, watching the pile burn down. The coals were only about two feet high now, but the heat from the pile of glowing red embers raged unabated. Thank goodness I had responded quickly and hadn't waited or debated returning to the fire. The fire would have spread like lightning through the tall grass.

Once my jeans cooled down, the pain stopped, but soon my legs began feeling strange. I looked down at my jeans. They felt tight and looked oddly bumpy, as if I had bubble-wrapped my legs. Something wasn't right. Ducking into some bushes in the corner, I pulled down my jeans and stared at my legs in disbelief. Giant brown, three-inch blisters covered the outside of both legs from ankle to hip. Each held several tablespoons of fluid.

I'd never seen brown-skinned blisters before, but they didn't seem like a big deal, despite the size. I worried more about the loss of fluid than the blisters. I was all for popping the blisters with a pin to let the fluid out, like a regular blister. Perhaps I was in shock. I called Carlos over to show him. He recoiled, gasping in disbelief. "Get your things; we're going to the hospital now."

My Girl Scout training kicked in. "We can't leave the fire burning like this." So, we waited for it to burn down a bit more, found a stick, and did what we could to scatter and extinguish the coals. I couldn't believe we had come so unprepared. Not only had I forgotten my socks, but we had forgotten to take our usual precautions and bring rakes, water, or other means to control and extinguish the fire. Familiarity breeds complacency, and we had become careless.

Overlake Hospital took one look at my legs and said, "We can't deal with this: you need to go to the Regional Burn Center at Harborview," and called an ambulance. We protested we could drive ourselves, but they refused, insisting "An ambulance will speed things up on the other end."

Doctors estimate the extent of burn damage by palm size. Each area the size of your hand represents about one percent of your body's surface area. My hair had been singed to a frizzle in the front, but my legs took the brunt of the fire. The doctors estimated my legs had ten palms of damage, primarily third-degree burns. The third-degree, or full-thickness burn, destroys two entire layers of skin. This type of burn destroyed the nerve endings, which possibly explains why, once my pants cooled, I didn't immediately feel much pain. Or perhaps I was just in shock.

My brother, Steve, said the Army taught soldiers and helicopter pilots to wear their pants stuffed inside their boots to prevent creating a "stove-pipe effect," where heated air rises and gets trapped inside the pants. That explained how I could have such burns while my pants escaped unscathed. Rising heat, trapped in the jeans, had steamed my legs.

Harborview stuffed me full of pain killers, popped the blisters, lathered me up with some silver antibiotic compound, and wrapped me up in material looking like a neoprene wetsuit. After two nights in the hospital, they sent me home for a week. *If they don't want to see me for a week, it can't be so bad.* I even thought maybe I could skip a pain pill or two because I worried about getting addicted to Hydrocodone. Big mistake. The first time I skipped a pill, it took only a few minutes before the pain roared back with a vengeance, and I had an excruciating twenty minutes waiting for the new pill to kick in. I never skipped another one.

After a week, as the doctors lifted off the neoprene wrap, big chunks of flesh fell off with it. *Like pieces of over-cooked chicken from a bone.* Watching my legs deconstruct seemed like a sci-fi movie. I could observe them dispassionately, without emotion, perhaps because what remained didn't look anything like legs. Huge, angry purple craters, uneven, bumpy, and raw looking, covered both legs. Once again, I felt the same odd detachment as in the Chinese operating room and again above the tiger shark. *I'll get through this. It will be OK.* Carlos looked about to be sick.

"Don't you dare throw up! You have to help me; I can't manage this on my own."

Every day I sat on the edge of the bathtub, washing and debriding charred skin with my microfiber camping washcloth, the only fabric my skin could tolerate. Thankfully the hospital allowed me to do it myself rather than having someone else do it, so I could gauge the pain and leave tough spots for the following day if it became too painful. The excruciating debridement took about an hour, and then Carlos changed the bandages.

I spent the rest of July and August drugged and almost immobile, legs encased in bandages from hips to ankles, continually oozing fluids. The bandages kept slipping, so I generally remained sedentary except for washing and bandaging the open wounds.

After eight weeks, the deepest burns on the right leg and hip were still large open wounds, raw and oozing. The doctors said skin grafts could cut eight weeks off the remaining open wound time. Since my pen pal Akemi and her husband were arriving soon to tour the Southwest with us, I agreed.

A Chinese doctor, looking like he had recently graduated high school, checked the burns and assured me he had done hundreds of graft procedures before.

"Hmm," ... he mused. "Where can we get enough skin?" They needed a large piece. "Maybe from the inside of your legs?"

"Oh, please," I said. "The legs have had enough trauma already; surely you can find another place."

As he looked at my flabby stomach, his eyes lit up. "I think we have more than enough here," he said with a straight face. That was an understatement. "Would you mind if we take it from here?"

"Help yourself. Take all you want." He removed a transverse, eighteen by four-inch strip of skin and ran it through a machine to perforate it with hundreds of tiny holes and make it stretchable. Then he cut it into pieces and fastened them into my leg with dozens of wire staples.

When I came out of the anesthesia, he said, "I'm sorry, I hope you don't mind, but we had to remove a wedge-shaped piece of stomach fat underneath to pull the sides of the skin back together." I couldn't read his impassive face.

"Mind? Are you serious? I'm not possessive about my fat!" Gleeful, I thought, *I got a free tummy tuck!* My jeans fit better, but between my appendectomy, two cesareans, and the graft donation site, the scars made my stomach look like a road map. I told Carlos, "I think I just doomed my chances of winning the Miss America pageant."

Fortunately, we planted our vegetable garden before the accident. During the long summer, I had ample time to visualize the weeds spreading and the pests eating and multiplying unopposed. I had plenty of time to rethink the accident, too.

I knew although God doesn't generally *cause* bad things to happen, he may *allow* them to teach us something. Since He allowed this painful accident, no doubt He had a reason for it. I wondered what I was supposed to learn from this experience, because I've found those who don't learn from a trial are usually doomed to repeat it in one form or another.

Pondering it, I began to recognize God's mercy through all of this. The burns could have been so much worse. If the small voice hadn't told me to change out of my sandals into my rubber garden shoes, I would have been stomping out the fire in my sandals, a sure disaster for my toes. Joints are the most difficult parts to heal after a burn, and charring my toes could have affected my long-term mobility. Thankfully, I had heeded the voice.

If the small voice hadn't returned me to the fire when it did, the fire would have rapidly spun out of control, raced through the field of tall, dry grass, engulfed Carlos and the brush cutters, and likely burned down our neighbor's fence, possibly even his attached house. If it spread over the cliff, it would have been almost impossible to stop and probably would have burned its way around a chunk of the island. The cost would have been horrendous.

I also realized with surprise that most emails, cards, food, and visits I received came not from family or close associates but from others. Mere acquaintances from church and neighborhood brought meals and lotions, and word spread. I heard from some old sixth-grade classmates I hadn't spoken with in over fifty years.

This brought an Aha Moment, an epiphany. *I hadn't been very good about helping others in the past, especially those I didn't know well, because I always assumed or rationalized that people had family or closer friends than I to help them deal with their situations. Yet what if they didn't? Or maybe their family would have appreciated a hiatus from the oppression of caregiving.* With a shock, I realized I was expected to learn compassion and caring. On reflection, I was even more surprised to realize that if it required the burns to make me learn this, I felt OK with that.

Now I make more effort to reach out to people I think might need help, even when I don't know them well. And it's probably brought more blessing to me than to the recipients.

This incident also reminded me how essential it is to pay attention to the quiet voice in my head. God often guides or communicates, but He whispers, He doesn't shout or write flaming messages on the wall. Hearing takes practice and obedience to the voice, but the more you learn to listen and respond, the clearer it becomes.

- Forty-Seven -

Full Circle

"Home is not where you're born.
Home is where all your attempts to escape cease."
- Omar Taher

Redmond, WA 2022

L IFE HAS COME FULL CIRCLE. I LEFT THE STATES
searching for adventure and a place that resonated with me, where
I felt truly at home. I found my niche in Washington state. People here
appreciate jeans and flannel shirts, outdoor life, and environmental protection. I feel at home in the Northwest in a way I never did growing
up. Overseas, I found the adventures I was searching for, and gained a
new appreciation for this country and the diversity of opportunities and
activities it provides. Along the way, I discovered myself, my life's work,
and my faith.

I was too young to fight for the Glen Ellyn fields, but I've since spent
over forty years working in environmental protection, and I'd like to
think I've helped save a bit of the planet for a while, anyhow. Although not
on as grand a scale as my mentors, Carl Welty and Les Holdridge, who
both established preservation areas, we are a WDFW Urban Wildlife
Sanctuary, and much of our five acres here are in conservancy. We garden
organically to attract wildlife and occasionally participate in local garden
shows, where our theme generally centers on environmental restoration
and sustainability. We live less than fifteen miles from downtown Seattle,

but cougars, bobcats, bears, deer, river otters, and of course, the great blue heron, all visit and seem quite at home here.

My journey changed me. Unless your mind is slammed shut, the value of exposure to cultural differences is that it forces you to confront, candidly evaluate, and then either reinforce or readjust your own beliefs, values, and priorities. My head and heart will always reside partially in the Asia-Pacific region, and now I subconsciously tend to evaluate things from a multicultural viewpoint.

The East-West Center and my years away opened my world and changed my perspectives. The planet now feels a much smaller and more interconnected place on the human level, just as it is on the biological level. I now view the world through a more holistic lens, having spent decades living in, and with, different cultures.

Hawaii's East-West Center was transformative. With good friends and experiences in so many cultures, I find the nightly news feels personal, and I cringe when I hear bad news because I often know people in the countries being affected. In the Sixties, the Vietnam War, only a distant Asian war far from our shores, became personal for me after meeting Mai Phuong's family in Saigon and Pheng and Sengphet's families in Vientiane.

Now, half a century later, in another war, I recently watched the Afghanistan evacuation unfolding, and found myself wondering about the EWC Afghanis. The last time I saw some of them in person, they were dancing in a circle at the 2010 EWC reunion, waving their arms in happy abandon to an almost ear-splitting rendition of the disco song, *YMCA*. Now I wondered if they were among those fighting for their lives beyond the airport barricades.

Today, our country is in dangerous and gut-wrenching turmoil, but looking through the filter of the tumultuous struggles and centuries of unrest in the Philippines and Southeast Asia helps put America's chaotic, sometimes horrific, events in perspective; it reminds me no nation is exempt from trials. And I've come to lean on the fact that God is always in control and He has an ultimate plan in mind, for both nations and individuals. I may not always understand why He allows something to happen, and sometimes trials are a difficult road, but I'm confident His plan has a good, carefully thought-out ending. Although often we don't sense His immediate involvement in something, in retrospect, we can often see His fingerprints all over it. I can see that now, in my own life.

Costa Rica taught me to follow my heart, even when the path is unclear and the end is not yet in view. If I had avoided Costa Rica simply because the program seemed mysteriously vague, rather than following my gut and jumping in, I would have missed unique and unforgettable experiences. Likewise, if I had opted for the security and prestige of a good position at De La Salle University, and remained in the Philippines rather than ditching that opportunity for Guam's unlikely and unknown possibilities, it would have derailed my life's real passion.

These days, work is such a major part of our lives, we should fight to follow our heart and do what we love. American poet Maya Angelou said, "I've learned that making 'a living' is not the same as making a life."[14] I didn't want to just settle for making a living. I wanted an interesting life, and you can't make a life; you have to experience it.

The Philippines taught me to cope with adverse situations by appreciating and focusing on the moment and absorbing the experience, rather than comparing it to more pleasant or comfortable times or places. It not only made difficult situations easier to bear, but I invariably found I learned something from each difficulty. And learning to look for the lesson in each situation, helped me understand and accept disasters such as my terrible bonfire burns.

Guam's island-living taught me not to sweat the small stuff. We in the States are so privileged and have so much, yet few are at peace. Newspaper advice columns and internet blogs are full of people ranting, raging, and wrapped around the axle over an unkind remark, a middle finger salute, a perceived slight, being cut-off on the freeway, or obsessing because a stranger has dropped a nicely bagged doggie 'present' into their curb-side garbage can. Isn't that what garbage cans are for? In the big picture, these things are such small stuff; way too small to let them combust your inner peace.

Guam also taught me the somewhat related corollary: in the larger picture, everything's small stuff. The man who said, "Don't worry, it's only the bumper," and drove off after I mangled his rear bumper on Guam's Marine Drive understood this. He didn't fret about insurance and liability. His ego wasn't wrapped up in his car. He knew his bumper was, well, only a bumper. Small stuff.

Five years ago, a new driver rear-ended my relatively new CRV. It did little to her car, but it pushed my rear panel out of alignment. The accident happened in her first month of driving, and she was distraught. I decided to pay my Guam accident forward.

"No problem. It's only the rear panel," I said. "Don't start your driving record with an accident. Don't report it. I'm not going to." And I drove off, leaving her melted in relief. We never bothered to fix the panel. A good thing, because just last week another young driver hit the same panel again. We screwed it back on, but we're not fixing the dent and paint job this time, either.

I've learned that things I thought rather insignificant at the time have produced amazing long-term payoffs, so I feel it's important to be open to trying many small things that interest me, because I never know where they might lead.

The small act of establishing a goal list in 1955 spurred me to numerous adventures that I might never have otherwise experienced. It focused my life, reminding me of things I wanted to do, and helping prepare the groundwork so that I was ready to take advantage of unexpected opportunities when they arose. Its impact would be difficult to quantify, but I won't die with a long list of unfulfilled dreams.

In a similar vein, neither I nor my Japanese friend, Akemi, could ever have imagined how the seemingly insignificant act of becoming pen pals in 1958 would enrich our lives. We have continued corresponding throughout our lives, sharing our jobs, marriages, parent's deaths, births of our children and grandchildren, retirements, and now impacts of covid.

Perhaps equally important, along the way, our friendship has pulled in four generations of parents, siblings and spouses, children, and now grandchildren. We've exchanged ten home visits and traveled extensively in each other's countries. The visits have mended war memories, built bridges, and changed cultural preconceptions in both cultures. We never imagined our correspondence would span over six decades.

My spiritual searching was certainly convoluted and protracted, but the simple declaration in the chokecherry tree that "I want to be on your side" was apparently enough of a start to allow God to plant his hooks into me. I didn't need great knowledge or have to recite some formalized speech first. I just needed to want him to hook me in.

I've come to believe God is weaving us all into His giant tapestry of life. Occasionally circumstances converge, and we are lucky enough to get a behind-the-scenes glance of His loom in operation and understand the bigger picture when something happens. Yet often, we don't glimpse that, and when an experience is a trial, we question "Why me?" and maybe even get angry at God for allowing it to happen. Yet "Why *not* me?" might be a better question.

I believe that when he allows something bad to happen, there's always an underlying reason, a teaching moment, although we may not understand it at the time. That was certainly true of my horrible burns. Now, when facing a difficult time, it's comforting for me to remember that while we can only see a portion of our small piece of the tapestry right now, at some point, I suspect we'll have a more panoramic view that answers many of our "why" questions.

Someone once said, "You can't always see where He's going, but you can almost always see where He's been." Looking backward, I can see so many incidents where God had my stubborn back: arranging my job at the Academy, saving my students and me with the rogue wave; rescuing me on the STP; helping me at the fire; calming me on top of the giant tiger shark; and on other occasions, too numerous to count. In hindsight, it's clear that everything I have, material and otherwise, I ultimately obtained more because of His assists along the way than through my own efforts. It reminds me to hold material things lightly.

I hope these stories will inspire readers and seekers to search their own lives for traces of God's fingerprints.

As the church librarian, I notice that the 'Heaven, Hell and Afterlife' section is quite popular these days. In many books on near-death experiences, people claim to have met Jesus, who asked, "What did you learn on Earth?" or "What did you do with your life?" before they were sent back here. Good question. Before too long, I may have to answer this question myself. How will I answer it if I am asked? How would you answer it? At this stage in my life, it seems something worth pondering.

Belatedly, I've discovered that getting to know God is an adventure that competes well with all the experiences this world offers. I suspect learning to know and love Him and to love others are likely to be the main currency that matters in eternity. At least that's how I'll answer His question if asked. And I suspect that's what He hopes we will all discover.

Recently, covid curtailed our travel and relegated us to semi-isolation much of the time. It would be easy, even tempting, to join the old heron on our pond, enjoy the quiet life, and fade slowly into the sunset. And yet.... Carlos, now 80, has come from the house, waving a travel pamphlet. "We need to re-schedule our canceled trip down the Nile."

It's been quite a ride, but I still have a few unfulfilled goals on my list, so I guess the journey hasn't ended quite yet...

Epilogue

WHEN I WAS BORN IN THE 1940S, EARTH'S ECOSYStems were still relatively intact, but teetering on the cusp of tremendous and transformational worldwide change. Today, it saddens me how much of the natural world I was privileged to experience in the 1950s through 1970s has vanished, *just within my lifetime*. Earth's ecosystems have gone from relatively intact to widespread global degeneration. Ecosystems are weakened to the point where they are beginning to crumble and lose their balance. Yet there is a slim hope.

British naturalist David Attenborough, filmmaker of the BBC Planet Earth series, makes the case that restoring and rewilding our habitats is the only way to maintain and promote species diversity, stabilize climate, and save our planet. I agree.

Costa Rica is a success story, and provides an encouraging example that change is possible. As I feared in 1964-1965, the rainforest logging and deforestation I witnessed continued. By 1987, Costa Rica had lost *two-thirds* of its jungles, and the percentage of forested land area declined to a low of twenty-one percent. Yet today, forested land covers an astounding seventy-five percent of the land area, thanks to changes in government policies and spending, the establishment of private conservation incentives and reserves, and the creation of nearly thirty national parks.[15] And this is *despite* a four-fold population increase from less than 1.3 million in 1960 to approximately 5 million today. Costa Rica has shown it is possible to rewild its land, and gives me hope that it's still possible to turn things around elsewhere, if there is political and personal willpower.

Today, <u>Dr. Holdridge</u> is generally considered the pioneer of private forest conservation in Costa Rica. In 1964, <u>La Selva</u> was simply Holdridge's modest cabin. Since then, it has morphed into the modern La Selva Biological Station, one of the world's premier tropical rainforest research sites. Holdridge was already buying rainforest while I was there, and he apparently bought a great deal. La Selva now protects 3,794 acres, approximately six square miles, of jungle. His foresight made La Selva one of the first private forest reserves and spurred the development of what is now an extensive network of private reserves. Fortunately, I believe Holdridge saw his dream of forest conservation beginning to come to fruition before his death in 1999.

<u>OTS (Organization for Tropical Studies)</u> has also mushroomed from somewhat humble beginnings into a large consortium of universities and research institutions encompassing the U.S., Costa Rica, and Puerto Rico. And now, it controls La Selva.

<u>San Juanillo, Marbella, and Villa Neily</u> are no longer squatter communities and disreputable spots, but now tourist destinations, with hotels and beautiful natural surroundings.

Like Holdridge, <u>Dr. Welty</u> also left a conservation legacy. He retired a year after I left Costa Rica. His book firmly established him as a foremost ornithologist, and before his death in 1986, he established the Welty Environmental Center and Wildlife Refuge in Beloit, Wisconsin.

<u>The Philippines.</u> After twenty years of rule, President Marcos was finally ousted as head of state in February 1986. He left an infamous and egregious human rights record. Amnesty International charged him with 3,257 known extrajudicial killings, 35,000 documented tortures, 77 disappearances, and 70,000 incarcerations.[17]

Problems in the southern Philippines continued to worsen over time. In 2001, the Abu Sayyaf, a Muslim extremist group, kidnapped missionaries Martin and Gracia Burnham and eighteen others from a Mindanao resort. They beheaded ten victims, and after "marrying" several of the young women, the eight others were eventually released. Perhaps because the Burnhams were Americans, the terrorists kept them continually marching them around the jungle for over a year, hoping for a ransom. The Philippine Army eventually intervened, but Martin died in the rescue attempt.[18]

Guam. Twenty-seven years after we left, we returned to visit in 2006. A large shopping mall with high-end stores catering mainly to Japanese tourists had been constructed near Tumon Bay, providing restaurants and amenities that also benefited the locals. To its credit, Guam managed to confine its commercial development mainly to the Tumon Bay area.

A Chinese ship had collected scrap metal, including about 6,000 rusting cars and metal appliances accumulated in yards around the island. The oil tanker that Typhoon Pamela stranded on the Apra Harbor reef had also been cut up and recycled. Perhaps junk removal stimulated a pride of ownership, because the whole island looked spruced up, with newer, typhoon-proof houses and well-kept yards. Overall, Guam weathered development well.

Time had erased the scars WWII left on the landscape, and native vegetation had finally regained a foothold, but invasive species were on the rise. Cadena de Amor, a pretty but invasive climbing vine I had never noticed in the Seventies, suddenly seemed to be springing up all over, poised to overgrow the island.

The hill behind our house that gifted us with grenades, giant snails, ticks, and poison toads, now harbored a final gift: the large Australian brown tree snake, *Boiga irregularis*, one of the world's worst invasive species. In the 1940s or 1950s, the snake quietly arrived from the Solomon Islands, hitchhiking rides in airplane wheel-wells. The population was still small in 1979, and we saw our first and only snake, smashed on the road, the day we left the island. But within a few short years, the population exploded, and densities of 30,000 snakes per square mile of jungle (47 per acre!) made it one of the highest snake densities ever reported anywhere.[16]

Our Nimitz Hill house now maintained a snake trap in the backyard, and everyone had a snake story: snakes found hanging on the tie rack in Mark's department store, a man bitten while sitting in an outhouse (ouch), and babies attacked in cribs. By 1994, the hospital had treated over 200 snake bites. *Boiga* had disrupted the forest ecosystem in several ways and extirpated at least two endemic bird species, two of Guam's three bat species, and two species of seabirds.

African land snails that once overran our yard were almost impossible to find in 2006. Guam had introduced a parasitic flatworm that exterminated practically all of them. Unfortunately, it has nearly extirpated most endemic mollusks as well. Gun Beach's beautiful foraminiferan sand was gone, too, a sobering indication of some shift in the ocean ecosystem. The feral dog and cat populations however, had if anything, increased in number. Over half of all species found on Hawaii are non-native, and sadly, Guam appears to be headed down the same path.

Glen Ellyn friends have scattered to the winds. Brenda moved to Utah, where she makes pottery, collects arrowheads, and provides water for the wild horses. Jenny moved to Arizona and seems focused on past lives and similar topics. Nancy also lives in Arizona, and works with educational programs.

Mom and Dad are long gone. My sister Lynn is retired in New Mexico, where she is a museum docent, hiker, and prolific reader. My brother Steve lives in Florida. My brother Phil, the only one of the four of us to remain in the Glen Ellyn area, died in 2018. Dad's WWII rubber invasion maps are now in Seattle's Boeing Museum of Flight awaiting completion of an exhibit.

Lisa graduated from the University of California and works as an underwriter for a health insurance company. She lives nearby with her husband, two children, a dog and a large sailboat. David graduated from Cornell University and the London Business School. He and his Scottish husband were the first gay couple to marry in the UK, an occasion London celebrated with great fanfare in 2014. They have two children.

Solita, Victor, Mario and Fe are all deceased. The family sold Solita's Rural bank to Seabank, a digital banking firm from Singapore, in 2020.

Laura, Ed, Mai Phuong and Sengphet still live in Hawaii, where they each have made significant contributions in the business and political arenas. We all remain good friends, and have accompanied Mai Phuong and Sengphet back to Laos and Vietnam on several occasions.

On a more sober note, today, little of <u>the Earth</u> remains unexplored, unknown, or unexploited. Once seemingly unlimited, the prairies and rainforests are gone or fast disappearing. Climate change is accelerating, and glaciers and ice caps are disappearing. Coral reefs are dying in many locations. Whole continents are being affected; 72,000 square miles of Australia burned down in 2019-2020, killing an estimated three billion animals. Much of the Arctic is melting.

A mass extinction of species is underway, and each species lost weakens the web slightly. That's trite, but still true. The land affects the atmosphere, ocean temperature, currents, and weather. It's all connected, just as all peoples of the earth are connected.

Population growth is the major aggravating factor affecting ecologic decline and habitat destruction. In 1940, the planet supported approximately two and a quarter billion people. In 2021, we were approaching eight billion and climbing. Our numbers have unfortunately made man the ultimate invasive species. We are too many people. It is not sustainable. We must make some significant changes to our policies and way of life to stabilize, and preferably reduce, our population. But that's a topic for another book.

It's imperative to stop the ecologic decline, and although it's very late, we still have a tiny window of time to act, provided both governments and individuals have the willpower to do so. Forests are a critical stabilizing component, and Costa Rica has shown rewilding is possible. The future is up to us.

Notes

1. Jobs, Steve. 2005. Stanford Commencement Address, June 12, 2005. http://www.stanford.edu. Accessed July 8, 2022.

2. Baer, Randall N. 1989. *Inside the New Age Nightmare*. Louisiana: Huntington House Inc. pg. 117.

3. Carroll, Louis. *Alice's Adventures in Wonderland*, Lewis Carroll quotes, in www. Kidadl.com. Accessed July 8, 2022.

4. Babcock, Maltbie Davenport.1901. *This is My Father's World*, hymn published posthumously.

5. Washington Post, March 7, 2006. Paul Slud Obituary. Accessed August 8, 2022.

6. Bob Dylan, 1963. *The Times They Are a-Changin'*. Song written by John Denver.

7. *Chuck Missler Quotes*. Goodreads.com. Accessed August 10, 2022.

8. Martial Law Under Ferdinand Marcos. en.m.Wikipedia.com. Accessed May, 2022.

9. News.com.au. "The Mind-Bending Saga of the Stone Age Tasaday Tribe of the Philippines." December 2, 2018. Accessed May 2022.

10. Washington Post. September 4.1986. "Guam Governor indicted in kickback scheme."

11. Sawatzky, DR. K. David. 2008. "Oxygen toxicity- how does it occur?" Originally published in *Diver Magazine*, Dec. 2008-January 2009 issue. Republished in Diverite.com. Accessed August 4, 2011.

12. AZ Animals. 2021. Discover the largest tiger shark ever recorded. The tiger shark: setting world records. Published August 29, 2021. A-Z-animals.com/blog/discover-the-largest-shark- ever-recorded. Accessed August 28, 2022.

13. Chuck Missler Quotes. Quotefancy.com. Accessed August 10, 2022.

14. Maya Angelou Quotes. Goodreads.com. tf8=making+a+life%2c+-maya+Angelou&coment=searchquotes/search. Accessed August 10, 2022.

15. Javaker, Hamoon. June 23, 2019. "Costa Rica's rainforest: how the country managed to restore it." State of the Nation report 2017, Updated March 18, 2022. SpecialPlacesOfCostaRica.com. Accessed August 10, 2022.

16. U.S. Department of State. Archive 2001-2009. *Case study: brown tree snake.* State.gov. Accessed March 15, 2022.

17. *Philippine Daily Express.* September 24, 1972. "Human rights abuses of the Marcos dictatorship." Based on documentation by Amnesty International, Accessed March 15, 2022.

18. Burnham, Gracia. 2003. *In the presence of my enemies.* Illinois: Tyndale House Publishers, Inc.

CPSIA information can be obtained
at www.ICGtesting.com
Printed in the USA
BVHW082125280223
659395BV00002B/222